FoxPro® 2 Programming Guide

The Lance A. Leventhal Microtrend Series

FoxPro® 2 Programming Guide

Michael P. Antonovich

Library of Congress Card Catalog Number: 91-53064

Library of Congress Cataloging-in-Publication Data
Antonovich, Michael P.
    FoxPro 2 programming guide / Michael Antonovich.
        p.   cm. — (Lance A. Leventhal Microtrend series)
    Includes index.
    ISBN 0-915391-48-1 (pbk.)
    1. Data base management. 2. FoxPro 2 (Computer program) I. Title.
  II. Series.
  QA76.9.D3A645   1991
  005.75'65—dc2091-53064
    CIP

Printed in the United States
10 9 8 7 6 5 4 3 2 1

Microtrend™ Books
Slawson Communications, Inc.
165 Vallecitos de Oro
San Marcos, CA 92069

Edited by Lance A. Leventhal, Ph.D., San Marcos, CA
Front cover design by John Odam Design Associates
Produced by Anne Olson, Casa Cold Type, Inc.

Table of Contents

1   Introduction

2   Command Highlights

List of Tables

List of Programs

List of Figures

About the Author

Michael P. Antonovich is a consultant specializing in database applications. His latest projects done for the retail industry involve advertisement tracking, trade promotion analysis, and account review profitability analysis. He has also developed applications for general business and government agencies, including information systems, point of sale systems, custom data collection and reporting systems, and loan tracking systems. He has extensive programming experience in database languages, C, BASIC, and FORTRAN. Mr. Antonovich also teaches programming and computer science classes for several colleges, including both regular and extension courses. He received his Bachelor's degree in chemical engineering and his MBA from Lehigh University.

About the Series Editor

Lance A. Leventhal is the author of 25 books, including *80386 Programming Guide, 68000 Assembly Language Programming, Turbo C Quickstart,* and *Microcomputer Experimentation with the IBM PC.* His books have sold over 1,000,000 copies and have been translated into many foreign languages. He has also helped develop microprocessor-based systems and has been a consultant for Disney, Intel, NASA, NCR, and Rockwell.

Dr. Leventhal served as Series Editor on Personal Computing for Prentice-Hall and as Technical Editor for the Society for Computer Simulation. He has lectured on microprocessors throughout the United States for IEEE, IEEE Computer Society, and other groups.

Dr. Leventhal's background includes affiliations with Linkabit Corporation, Intelcom Rad Tech, Naval Electronics Laboratory Center, and Harry Diamond Laboratories. He received a B.A. degree from Washington University (St. Louis, Missouri) and M.S. and Ph.D. degrees from the University of California, San Diego. He is a member of AAAI, ACM, ASEE, IEEE, IEEE Computer Society, and SCS.

Acknowledgments

This book has taken all my spare time for the past year. It is difficult to complete a book in the fast-paced computer world in a timely manner while working at a full-time job. I know that I stretched the patience of my wife Susan and daughter Natasha, and probably also editor Lance Leventhal and assistant to the publisher Ron Tucker. But it's over now.

Thanks to Lance Leventhal who had to read my wordy phrases and shorten them to keep the book in a single volume.

Thanks to Ron Tucker for keeping production on schedule and for providing encouragement when I doubted that I would ever see the end.

Thanks to Gloria Pfeif, and other technical staff at Fox Software, who got answers to my questions. Gloria was especially helpful in keeping me posted on FoxPro 2.0 developments. And, of course, thanks to everyone at Fox Software for creating such a powerful and useful product.

Dedication

This book is dedicated to my daughter Natasha. I know you would prefer a picture book, but then you are only two. I hope you enjoy books as you grow older just as much as you do now.

Preface

Why Program in FoxPro?

FoxPro is one of the most widely used databases on personal computers. Many reviews have praised its interactive environment, user orientation, and speed. Features that contribute to its popularity include:

- Uses only 280K of memory (the extended version utilizes all available extended memory for data)
- Menu-driven windowed user interface
- Complete application windowing environment
- Powerful screen and menu builders
- Indexes and windows limited only by memory
- Memory variable string length limited only by memory
- The Rushmore™ technology for very fast access to large databases (500,000 records or more)
- RQBE (Relational Query By Example) facility to help visually create complex single- and multi-table queries for programs and reports
- Project manager to track all files required by an application
- API (Application Program Interface) to integrate assembly language and C routines
- Compact and compound indexes with optional filtering
- Segment loader that virtually eliminates overlay contention, thus speeding execution
- Powerful label and report generator
- Fully automated program documenter
- Genuinely useful memo fields for notes and long text
- Modern interface features such as pulldown menus and popup windows
- Powerful debug and trace capabilities
- And, of course, the fastest executing code available

This book deals with programming in FoxPro. It assumes readers have a basic knowledge of both FoxPro (or another dBASE-compatible package) and programming, so it can focus on advanced techniques for application development. It emphasizes intuitive user interfaces, carefully validated data entry screens, and high overall performance. FoxPro helps you achieve these goals through an object oriented windowing environment with integrated mouse support. Practical examples in each chapter illustrate the techniques.

Who Should Read This Book?

This book will appeal to both novice FoxPro programmers and veteran database application developers. It will especially interest database programmers using other software who are searching for a faster, more powerful package. Those working in dBASE III PLUS and dBASE IV will find FoxPro particularly attractive because it provides both extensive compatibility and higher performance.

For programmers just starting with database applications, the book reviews basic concepts. It discusses arrays, memo fields, data input techniques, and searching. For the more advanced programmer, it examines ways to improve an application's interface using windows and to convert systems to network operation. It also discusses FoxPro file structures and presents C routines that manipulate them.

This book shows practical ways to include advanced FoxPro features in everyday coding. It describes them in a series of topically organized chapters. Each contains many complete programs, procedures, and short routines. Most examples come from actual applications. Each chapter stands alone, so you can cover topics in any order or concentrate on ones you find particularly interesting or significant.

Chapter Organization

FoxPro is a large, complex program with many powerful features. Few have mastered all its intricacies. Most FoxPro programmers have areas where they lack skills or need a deeper understanding. The following brief descriptions of the chapters should help you decide where to focus.

Chapter 1 introduces the basic concepts of FoxPro. Unlike other dBASE related products, it has an integrated windowing environment, an object oriented interface, and full mouse support. In fact, the entire interface consists of objects, including windows, menus, and dialog boxes. The chapter also briefly describes utilities and tools provided with FoxPro to aid programmers.

Chapter 2 extends the reader's basic knowledge by discussing FoxPro's special command groups and unique features. It covers screen and window manipulation, database and field functions, low-level file access, structured programming commands, scopes of variables, compact and compound indexes, RQBE, and the Project Manager.

One indication of a superior program is strong data validation. Chapter 3 covers techniques to insure accurate data entry and validation within fields, between fields, and against files. This chapter also shows how to implement context-sensitive help.

Chapter 4 describes the use of procedures and UDFs to build applications. It shows ways to create a library of generalized modules. Using the library with all your programs provides consistency and reduces development time. The chapter also shows how to use UDFs to insert code where FoxPro expects only variables, such as in label or report definitions.

Chapter 5 discusses macro variables and keyboard macros. Macro variables help generalize routines or build commands such as filters with variable contents. Keyboard macros help create demonstration systems or provide the extra keystrokes needed to set up windows.

Chapter 6 covers arrays. We use them to store database information or collect data for reports. For example, we could use an array to hold numeric values from a database field. The values may then serve as a lookup table.

Many database programmers avoid memo fields, thinking they are awkward or difficult to use. Chapter 7 shows how to use them effectively to store long text strings. FoxPro has improved the handling of memo fields. In many ways, it processes them just like strings.

Windowing is a major feature of FoxPro. Chapter 8 covers how to define and manage windows. We may use them to display information or prompt for it. They are also a key part of most menu systems. The chapter includes sections on managing multiple windows and using FoxPro's Screen Builder.

Menus have become a commonplace feature of user interfaces. Chapter 9 provides a short tutorial in interface design with various types of menus. It covers pick lists, popups, horizontal bars, arrays, pulldowns, and component menus. It includes a section on using the Menu Builder.

Sometimes we must import or export data. Chapter 10 describes techniques for exchanging data with other programs. It covers how to read and write delimited ASCII files and how to use low-level functions to perform more complex translations.

In some applications, you may have to access FoxPro files directly to achieve the required speed or precision. This requires detailed knowledge of FoxPro file structures. Chapter 11 provides the necessary descriptions of major file types.

Chapter 12 discusses the implementation of the structures defined in Chapter 11. The examples show how to read and write several important file types with C programs.

Chapter 13 describes the use of externally compiled programs with FoxPro to provide additional functions or processing. We can execute them from a shell or load them into memory to be executed with a CALL statement. The chapter contains examples of both methods.

Chapter 14 discusses changes required for single-user applications to run on a network. Most applications run in single-user mode with few changes. On the other hand, multiuser operation can cause lost updates, inconsistent analysis, and other problems. Manual setting of record and file locks helps maintain data integrity. This chapter shows how to use locks with minimal impact on other network users.

Error trapping and debugging are a major part of any application development. Some sources estimate that as much as 30% of software development time is dedicated to them. Chapter 15 examines error trapping and debugging tools available to FoxPro developers. FoxPro has a powerful debug and trace system to help isolate and solve problems.

Appendixes A and B summarize FoxPro commands and error messages. Appendix C provides a reference list of books about the C language. The bibliography lists further references for the advanced programmer. The book also includes both a glossary and an acronym list.

Getting the Most from This Book

The book contains many examples illustrating major topics. Some are complete programs and can be run independently. Others are procedures intended to be called from larger applications. We have tested all examples thoroughly. For your convenience, the publisher has made available a disk version of them. Ordering information is in the back of the book. We highly recommend the disk because it will save you many hours of typing and avoid the inevitable errors. Besides, you want to spend your time learning new FoxPro programming techniques, not improving your typing skills.

This book will help you write better programs. It will also help you create the modern user interfaces that everyone expects. Note that the appearance of a program and its use of menus, windows, and other visual cues are just part of the overall design. Applications must protect the user from invalid data entries, provide default values and step-by-step guidance, display context sensitive help, and recover from errors gracefully. Furthermore, an attractive, powerful interface means nothing if the program runs slowly. This book addresses all these issues, but it does not stop there. It also helps you prepare applications to run on a network, and it shows you how to use FoxPro's debugging features to simplify maintenance.

FoxPro is a dynamic, powerful language that can handle almost any database application. A skilled FoxPro programmer can solve a wide range of problems in business, finance, administration, science, engineering, government, and other areas. This book will help you gain the skills required to meet such challenges quickly and effectively.

Nomenclature

The following table shows the syntax we have adopted to describe commands and examples.

Syntax Conventions

[]	Indicates optional arguments
<>	Indicates a required argument
()	Delimits function arguments (the parentheses must appear in the actual code)
''	Delimits a string containing double quotation marks or brackets
""	Delimits a string containing single quotation marks or brackets
[]	Delimits a string containing single or double quotation marks
{}	Used to enclose a date constant as in

duedate = {10/31/90}

<command>	FoxPro command
<condition>	Logical expression
<coord>	Screen coordinates with row, then column
<ExpC>	Character expression
<ExpD>	Date expression
<ExpL>	Logical expression
<ExpN>	Numeric expression

The last four expressions may also take the form <ExpXn>, where n is an integer. We use it when a command contains several expressions of the same type.

<text>	Used in program examples to represent a block of commands not supplied as in

<Program branches to report procedure here>

Y|N	Indicates a choice of Y (yes) or N (no)

Program listings adhere to the following conventions:

- FoxPro keywords appear in uppercase.
- Each level of a loop or selection structure is indented two spaces.
- Variables and file names are in lowercase.
- Comments follow normal capitalization rules.

Unlike C, FoxPro is not case sensitive. We can freely mix cases in all areas except string comparisons. We have chosen case conventions for listings to promote readability.

Overview of Major Examples

This section provides a brief overview of the major examples used in the book. Of course, program features vary to illustrate specific points.

Case 1 – Point-Of-Sale/Inventory System

A local distributor has small retail operations at its larger client's facilities. Each location has a small inventory in a room manned by a salesperson. When a worker wants to buy something, he or she places an order.

The salesperson enters the order directly into a computer. The program first verifies the worker's identity via an employee number. The salesperson then enters the items ordered by their product identification numbers or selects them from a list. He or she also enters the quantities desired. The system automatically retrieves each item's description, unit quantity, price, and tax code. It displays the information for visual verification. After all items are entered, the program calculates the total cost of the order and prints an invoice. It also makes an electronic copy of the transaction that it later sends to headquarters.

The system's major benefits are immediate verification of identities, fewer pricing and arithmetic errors, and electronic recording and transmission of invoices. The system also provides for analyzing sales at each location by product group.

Case 2 – Client Loan Tracking

The system tracks credits and debits for client loans for a company in the secondary loan market. (The market provides first and second mortgages, plus financing, for current and prospective homeowners.) It determines interest rate as a function of the contract rate and the amount of prepayment. It can generate a variety of reports, including end of year summaries and payment delinquencies.

The system's major benefit is less time required to record client transactions and report on them. It also reduces errors in calculating interest and produces additional billings for delinquent payments.

Case 3 – Consultant Billing

The system collects hours charged by each employee against each project in a consulting firm. It generates billings and invoices clients directly. It also provides reports on workload by employee and progress on projects.

The major benefits include improved tracking of billable time and automatic generation of invoices.

Case 4 – Job Application Information System

The system helps an employment and training agency collect and maintain data on applicants. Previously, the data was spread across several forms and was entered into a centralized system that provided little feedback. The local agency needed control of it to match employer needs to applicant skills.

The system's major benefit is rapid access to information about the skills and training needs of the agency's applicants. It also provides immediate matching of employer requests.

Case 5 – Telephone Logger

The telephone logging system captures information provided by some PBX systems. It identifies the source extensions of all outgoing calls. It uses this information to track telephone usage and produce reports.

The system's major benefit is that it provides a way to assign telephone costs to clients, employees, and departments. Another benefit is that it identifies abuses such as calls to the local soap opera, sports information, or horoscope hotline.

Case 6 – Newspaper Advertisement Tracker

The advertisement tracker stores information about advertisements appearing for selected manufacturers' brands in cities across the country. It then processes the data, generating reports on coverage by region and comparisons to competitive products.

1

Introduction

FoxPro is a powerful relational database management system that extends and enhances previous products. What makes it so popular?

Perhaps most important, it is fast. Much faster than its competitors according to many tests. Its integrated development environment allows programmers to code, test, and debug without switching packages. The modern windowing interface is also useful in applications. It allows developers to easily include menus, popups, and pulldowns in their programs. We can even adapt FoxPro's help system to provide context sensitive help. FoxPro's rich library of commands and functions simplifies any programming task. The LAN version adds full support of network file sharing. Finally, mouse support is built-in.

In the chapters that follow, we examine all these features. But first, let's quickly review basic concepts needed to understand and use FoxPro.

FoxPro Programming Language

FoxPro is a full-featured programming language. It is both an interpreter and a true compiler. (The compiler is separate in the Developer's Edition.) As an interpreted language, it translates each command into computer instructions as it is executed. The translation takes time, most noticeably during loops. The interpreter must translate each command not just the first time it is executed, but during every iteration.

A compiler improves performance by translating commands to machine instructions just once. It replaces commands such as PRINT or LIST with blocks of machine code. It then stores the machine instructions and executes them directly, saving translation time. Thus compiled programs run faster than interpreted ones. Programs compiled to an EXE are usually smaller and faster than those that require the runtime. The compiler can also directly link routines written in 80x86 assembly language and Watcom C.

For users of the standard edition, FoxPro can compile source statements to an intermediate level. It does not merge code blocks to create a single executable module. Rather, it references them from either FoxPro itself or a separate file called a runtime module. This approach gives FoxPro most of the advantages of a full compiler. At the same time, it keeps programs small by referencing code blocks stored in the runtime. Also, since only the intermediate compiled modules are required, we need not distribute source files.

Relational Database Management Systems

First let us briefly review what a relational database management system is. Although several database models exist, only the relational one is important in the personal computer world.

What is a database? It is a collection of related information. It could be a check register, accounting ledger, payroll, client list, or inventory. Or it could be any of thousands of applications in business, education, engineering, finance, management, the professions, the sciences, and other fields.

In general, a database consists of units called *records*. In a telephone book, a record consists of a name and the corresponding address and telephone number. Each item in it is a *field*. The telephone book has three fields: name, address, and telephone number. Figure 1-1 illustrates the terms.

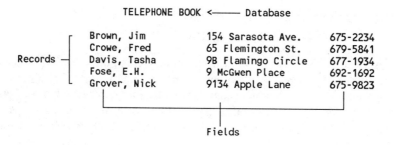

Figure 1-1. Structure of a telephone book database.

Databases often are related. For example, a payroll database contains the number of hours worked by each person on each project. Employees and projects have unique identification numbers. A second database contains each project's budget and expenditures organized by project number. A third database contains employee information, including employee number, name, salary, location, telephone number, and home address. Note that the payroll database contains only the employee number. We can use it to get his or her name from the employee database. Storing most information just once saves disk space, simplifies updates, and reduces the likelihood of annoying inconsistencies. Imagine the increase in data entry requirements if we had to store all the employee's personal data in each payroll record.

The payroll system is therefore a relational database. It uses the employee number to relate the payroll and employee databases. Similarly, it uses the project number to relate the payroll and project databases. Figure 1-2 shows the relations.

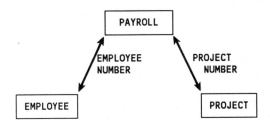

Figure 1-2. Relations in a simple payroll system.

In a relational model, we can access information in either direction. If we know the employee's name, we can retrieve his or her number from the employee database. The program can then use it to search the payroll database, calculating weekly salary from hours worked. Alternately, we could start from the payroll database to print checks. Now we use the employee number to search the employee database for the name.

DBMS Functions

After we define the data in terms of records, fields, and their relationships, we must manipulate it to create and store information. A database management system includes commands to do this. It also has commands to maintain, sort, retrieve, and update data.

Another vital DBMS function is the ability to create reports and view data. We may want to print each employee's hours by project. Or we may just want to view a summary of project charges. FoxPro has many other information management features. For example, it has basic computational abilities that use database fields to create new information. Payroll records track the number of hours worked. To calculate salary based on it, we multiply it by an hourly pay rate.

FoxPro supports arithmetic functions such as addition, subtraction, multiplication, and division. It also provides many special mathematical and financial functions.

Using FoxPro's Object-Oriented Interface

What is an object-oriented interface? First, what is an object? It is any box, control, field, line, menu, popup, text, or window displayed on the screen. Some objects are simple like text, others are complex like windows. Most have attributes that determine how they look and how they work. The programmer or user can control some attributes, but not others. For example, a window has attributes that determine its border type, color, position, and size. By changing them, we control its appearance and other characteristics. If one object, such as a window, contains others, such as fields or text, they come along when we move it. These objects obviously are associated.

Another feature of objects is that we can use them and their attributes without writing code explicitly. For example, when we tell FoxPro to open a browse window, it automatically includes controls such as a close box, zoom box, grow box, and scroll bars. It also provides mouse support and functions that allow us to move the window. We need not write code to implement any of this. Could we create a window from simple @...SAY commands? Of course, but why bother when we can use the browse object directly?

By using objects as building blocks, we can create screens and reports. Furthermore, by applying traditional database commands such as EDIT, SEEK, and USE to objects, we can build complete systems.

To use the programming language effectively, we must quickly review FoxPro's interface and programming tools. We can employ many of its interface objects in custom programs. For example, we can use predefined dialog boxes to load and save files. We can also add specially designed windows to applications, complete with mouse support. We can design menus, queries, and screens interactively and let FoxPro generate their code. First, let's examine how FoxPro uses menus, popups, and mouse support, beginning with its opening screen (Figure 1-3). In later chapters, we will see how to utilize many of these features in our own programs. The main screen combines a menu bar across the top line with a command prompt environment based on the Command window.

FoxPro opens the Command window at the beginning of each session. Commands entered into it execute immediately. Its main advantage is that we retain access to menu selections. Thus, we can switch easily between using the menus and entering commands directly.

FoxPro's interface is non-procedural and event-driven. That is, we control the sequence of actions (events) by selecting desired operations in any order (non-procedural). We do this through the menus, windows, and dialogs or directly via the Command window.

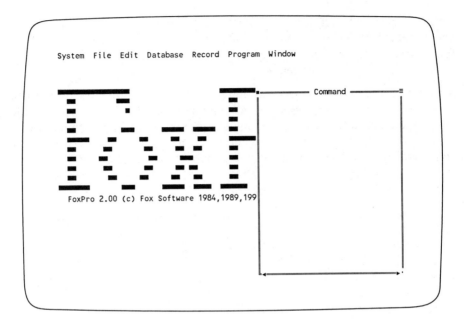

System File Edit Database Record Program Window

Command

FoxPro 2.00 (c) Fox Software 1984,1989,199

Figure 1-3. FoxPro's main screen.

Menu options have two basic looks. Active ones are highlighted and may emphasize one letter in a different color; inactive ones are dim. For example, the Record option in the main menu bar remains dim until we open a database file.

Each main menu option has an associated pulldown menu. Table 1-1 lists three ways to open pulldown menus and select from them.

Table 1-1. Opening a Pulldown Menu

METHOD 1
1. Press F10 to highlight the first menu option (System).
2. Use the left and right arrow keys to select an option.
3. Press Enter to open it.
4. Use the up and down arrow keys to select an option in the pulldown.
5. Press Enter to execute it.

METHOD 2
1. Press the Alt key along with the highlighted letter from the menu option.
2. Press the highlighted letter of the option in the pulldown to execute it.

METHOD 3
1. Point the mouse to the main menu option.
2. Click the left mouse button.
3. Point to the option in the pulldown menu.
4. Click the left button again to execute it.

Options followed by ellipses (...) have more levels or ask for more information before executing. The characters to the right of the pulldown menu indicate a fourth way to execute some options. They are shortcut keys that let you select directly without using the menus.

As we select commands from pulldown menus, FoxPro echoes them in the Command window. This both helps programmers learn the syntax and provides a history. We can scroll through the history to select and reexecute old commands. We can thus easily correct minor errors or issue a series of similar commands. Figure 1-4 summarizes the pulldown menu system.

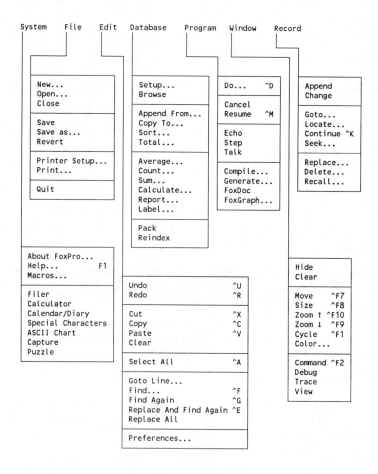

Figure 1-4. FoxPro's pulldown menus.

Control Objects

The main menu and pulldown menus form only part of the object-oriented interface. Although some commands execute without further input, others (indicated by an ellipsis after them) cannot. FoxPro gets more information for them through dialog windows by using the control objects listed in Table 1-2.

Table 1-2. Types of Control Objects

- **Check Boxes**

Check boxes let users select multiple options from a set. Square brackets precede the option text. When we select a box, an X appears between the brackets. Selecting it repeatedly toggles the X on and off.

- **Popup Controls**

These objects open popup windows with more selections. A typical function is to let the user change the default subdirectory or disk drive. Other popup controls might display file types, file names, commands, or functions.

- **Pushbuttons**

Pushbuttons provide control options that complete many dialog windows. They appear between angle brackets. One option may have double angle brackets. It is the default selection if the user presses Ctrl-Enter. A typical set of options is:

<<SAVE>>　　　<OK>　　　<CANCEL>

- **Radio Buttons**

Radio buttons allow users to select one option from a set. Each option is preceded by a pair of empty parentheses. A dot appears between the parentheses of selected buttons. Selecting one button from a set turns all others off.

- **Scrolling Lists**

They are useful where there are more items to choose from than room to display them. To see more of the list, press the up and down arrow keys or click the mouse on the vertical scroll bar.

- **Text Boxes**

Sometimes we cannot predefine choices. For example, only the user can supply the name of a new file. Text boxes allow users to enter freeform information into fields that cannot be predefined.

Figure 1-5 shows the Sort dialog window. It contains all the objects discussed in this section. We will describe them further in Chapter 3.

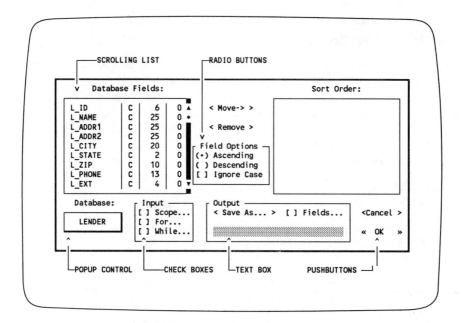

Figure 1-5. Sort dialog window.

Using a Mouse With FoxPro

The object-oriented nature of FoxPro's user interface makes mouse-based selection fast, easy, and natural. Usually you just point to the object with the mouse and click a button.

To use a mouse, we must begin each session by loading its driver. FoxPro provides several drivers in the GOODIES directory. The mouse cursor is a solid box in contrasting colors to the background. A mouse may have up to three buttons; however, FoxPro supports only the left one. Table 1-3 contains special terms used in describing mouse operations.

Table 1-3. Mouse Usage Terminology

CLICK	Press and immediately release the left button.
DOUBLE CLICK	Press the left button twice in quick succession. This usually selects and executes a command or option.
DRAG	Press and hold the left button. While holding it, move the mouse.
POINT	Move the mouse until the cursor appears over the desired screen object.

To open pulldown menus with the mouse, move its cursor over an option and click the left button. To select an option in the menu, highlight it with the mouse and click again. To illustrate the advantages of the mouse over the keyboard, let's examine typical window operations using both.

We begin with the control features of the Command window shown in Figure 1-6.

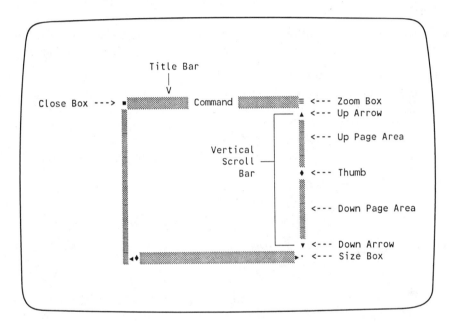

Figure 1-6. *Basic window control and sizing features.*

Moving a Window

We can move and expand or shrink FoxPro windows. For example, we may want to move the Command, Help, or Label Layout window to view text beneath it.

To move a window with a mouse:

    1. Put the mouse cursor anywhere on the title bar.

    2. Press and hold the left mouse button.

    3. Move the window by dragging it with the mouse.

    4. Release the button to fix the window's position.

To move a window from the keyboard:

1. Open the Window pulldown menu.
2. Select the Move option.
3. Use the arrow keys to move the window.
4. Press Enter to fix its position.

Window Zoom

The character on the right side of the title bar with three horizontal lines is the zoom control. It toggles the window between its current size and full screen.

To zoom the active window with a mouse:

1. Put the mouse cursor on the upper right corner.
2. Click the mouse.

To zoom the active window from the keyboard:

1. Press Ctrl-F10 to toggle it between its maximum and normal sizes.

To zoom the active window from the menu:

1. Open the Window pulldown menu.
2. Select the Zoom option to toggle the window between its maximum and normal sizes.

Minimize a Window

We can minimize a window so all that remains is the title bar. This feature allows the user to keep windows active while covering as little text as possible.

To minimize the active window with a mouse:

1. Put the mouse cursor anywhere on the top border (except the two corners).
2. Double click to toggle the window between its minimum and normal sizes.

To minimize the active window from the keyboard:

1. Press Ctrl-F9 to toggle it between its minimum and normal sizes.

To minimize the active window from the menu:

1. Open the Window pulldown menu.
2. Press the letter O or select the Zoom option to toggle the window between its minimum and normal sizes.

Resize a Window

The small dot in the lower right corner of the window is the size box. It lets us change the dimensions.

To resize the window with a mouse:

    1. Put the mouse cursor on the bottom right corner.

    2. Drag the corner.

    3. Release the button when the size is correct.

To resize the window from the keyboard:

    1. Open the Window pulldown menu.

    2. Select the Size option.

    3. Use the arrow keys to resize the window.

    4. Press Enter to fix the new size.

Close Box

The square character at the left end of the title bar is the close box. It closes the window, removing it from the screen.

To close the window with a mouse:

    1. Place the mouse cursor over the upper left corner.

    2. Click the button.

To close the window from the keyboard, just press Esc.

Vertical Scroll Bar

FoxPro adds a vertical scroll bar when there is more data than fits in the window. In such cases, only part of it appears. We must scroll to view the rest. The scroll bar has three active elements:

> Top marker
> Vertical thumb
> Bottom marker

The up arrow or triangle appears at the top of the bar. It represents the top of the data. If more data exists above the window, we can use it to move up a line at a time.

To move up a line in a file with the mouse, click it on the up arrow in the scroll bar. To do the same from the keyboard, press the up arrow key.

Likewise, the down arrow or triangle appears at the bottom of the scroll bar. It represents the bottom of the data. If more data exists below the window, we can use it to move down a line at a time.

To move down a line in a file with the mouse, click it on the down arrow in the scroll bar. To do the same from the keyboard, press the down arrow key.

The small diamond between the two triangles is the vertical thumb. We use it to make quick jumps in the file. Since the triangles represent the file's top and bottom, the diamond represents the relative position of the window.

To move to a new file position with the mouse:
1. Put the cursor on the diamond.
2. Drag it to a new position and release it.

You cannot move to a new file position from the keyboard.

Finally, we can move through the file one screen page at a time.

To move up or down one screen page with the mouse:
1. Put the cursor between the diamond and either the top or bottom triangle.
2. Click the mouse.

To move up or down one screen page from the keyboard, press the PgUp or PgDn key.

Horizontal Scroll Bar

FoxPro displays a horizontal scroll bar when the data is wider than the window. Like the vertical bar, it provides several motion controls. It also has the same three major elements. Figure 1-7 shows the Browse window which implements both vertical and horizontal scroll bars.

Window Splitter

The window splitter character is a special feature of the Browse window. It divides the window vertically, allowing us to see two views of the same file. We control the size of the windows by where we place the splitter character along the horizontal bar. Note that each window has its own horizontal scroll bar. However, they scroll together vertically, allowing us to view widely separated columns. We can also view different groups of records by selecting the Unlink Partitions option from the Browse menu.

To split the window with the mouse, move the cursor over the splitter character and drag it horizontally.

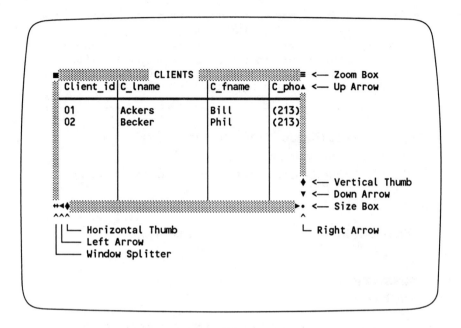

Figure 1-7. Browse window scroll bars.

To split the window from the keyboard:
1. Open the Browse pulldown menu.
2. Select the Resize Partition option.
3. Use the left and right arrow keys to set the partition sizes.
4. Press Enter.

To switch partitions with the mouse, put the cursor in the new partition and click the mouse.

To switch partitions from the keyboard:
1. Open the Browse pulldown menu.
2. Select the Change Partition option.

Cycle

When we open a series of windows, some may overlap. We may want to bring one to the top of the pile to activate it. To do this with the mouse, point anywhere on the window and click.

> **HINT**
> When moving a window left or up, move the top left corner
> first by dragging the title bar. Then resize the window. When
> moving a window right or down, resize it first. This way you
> will not lose its bottom or right edge while moving it.

To bring a window to the top of the pile with the keyboard:
1. Open the Window pulldown menu.
2. Keep selecting the Cycle option until the desired window is on
   top.

or

1. Press Ctrl-F1 until the desired window is on top.

On-Line Help

FoxPro has extensive on-line help for all programming commands. It is available by pressing F1 or by typing HELP at the dot prompt in the Command
window. Help opens a window (Figure 1-8), displaying available topics.

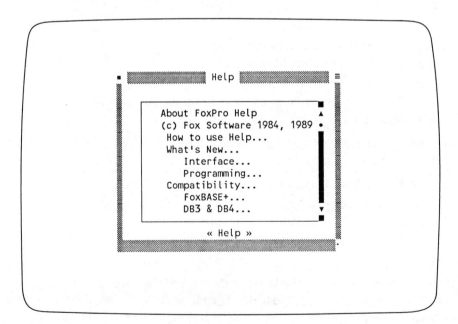

Figure 1-8. Help topics menu.

This window is scrollable (note the vertical scroll bar) to find any help topic. However, a faster way to locate a command is to enter its first few letters. FoxPro jumps to the first match. Use the arrow keys if necessary to locate what you want. With the topic highlighted, press Enter to display the help text. Figure 1-9 shows a typical example.

```
┌─────────────────────────────┐
│            DATE             │
└─────────────────────────────┘
Returns the current system date

┌─────────────────────────────┐
│           Format            │
└─────────────────────────────┘
DATE()

┌─────────────────────────────┐
│         Description         │
└─────────────────────────────┘
The DATE() function returns the current system date.  (The
operating system controls the system date.  There are no
FoxPro commands or functions that can directly change it.)

We can modify the format of DATE() by using the SET CENTURY,
SET DATE and SET MARK commands.

┌─────────────────────────────┐
│          Examples           │
└─────────────────────────────┘

? DATE()

SET CENTURY ON
? MDY(DATE())

USE Invoice
SCAN FOR BETWEEN(inv_date+30,DATE(),DATE()+30)

     ? 'Send notice of payment due for ' + company
ENDSCAN
─────────────────────────────────

In the second example, the INVOICE database is SCANned for all
records for which payment is due (based on today's date), but
not more than 30 days overdue.
─────────────────────────────────

See also:  SET CENTURY, SET DATE, SET MARK, SYS()
─────────────────────────────────
```

Figure 1-9. Help text for DATE().

The Help window displays the following four text buttons and one popup control along the left side of the screen.

<Topics>   Returns the user to the list of help topics.

<Next>   Displays the help text for the next command alphabetically in the topics list.

<Previous> Displays the help text for the previous command alphabetically in the topics list.

<Look Up> Allows the user to branch directly to any command mentioned in the current help topic. Just select it (highlight it with the Shift-arrow keys or drag the mouse through it) and press L or click the Look Up text button.

| See Also | Displays a list of related commands. Use the arrow keys or mouse to select one and view its help text. If you branched to the current command with the Look Up or See Also option, the original one appears at the top of the list, separated from the others by a horizontal line.

HINT

While editing a program, we can view the help text for any command by highlighting it and pressing F1.

The help system is itself a standard FoxPro database with an associated memo file. Thus, we can add or change topics. This fact also plays a key role in creating context sensitive help.

FoxPro Utilities

FoxPro provides several handy utilities, called desk accessories, under its main menu. They are available from the System pulldown. They include:

ASCII Chart   Capture Desk
Calculator   Filer
Calendar/Diary   Special Characters

Figure 1-10 shows a composite screen of the utilities.

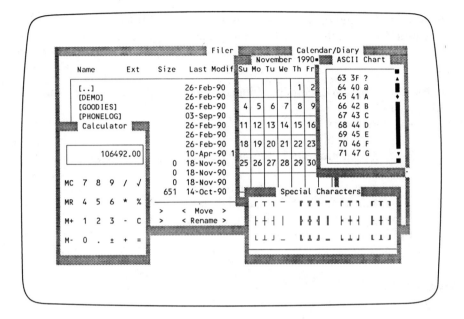

Figure 1-10. Composite of FoxPro utilities.

FoxPro Tools

FoxPro provides six major tools to help programmers develop applications. They are:

RQBE (Relational Query By Example) helps us build an SQL SELECT command for single- or multi-table queries. The resulting command can then be incorporated into programs to help create reports.

The *Screen Builder* allows us to design screens interactively and then generate the code necessary to reproduce them in a program. The screens can include graphics (lines and boxes), input/output fields, controls (buttons, boxes, popups, lists, etc.), and text objects.

The *Menu Builder* allows us to design bar and popup menus interactively and to generate code for them.

The *Report and Label Generator* helps us design output. It generates a form file rather than FoxPro code that we can call from within an application.

The *Project Manager* organizes all files for a specific project and builds a single application file from them. It also insures that the application file contains the latest design information for menus and screens, and the most recent program updates.

The *FoxDoc* program documenter maps the flow of FoxPro systems, automatically generating:

- Data dictionary
- Tree diagram of all modules
- Reformatted program listing with proper capitalization and indenting
- Cross-reference list of all variables
- Set of mockups for reports and labels
- Header for each routine, listing which programs call it and which procedures it calls

Summary

This chapter introduced the basic concepts and terms of DBMSes and FoxPro. We then proceeded to examine FoxPro's object-oriented interface. Next we discussed how the mouse offers an alternative to keyboard control. We also briefly described FoxPro's other utilities and tools. With this introduction complete, we are now ready to delve into the details of using FoxPro to develop applications.

2

Command Highlights

FoxPro has many special commands and functions not found or less developed in other PC database packages. They include features to enhance the user interface and data handling. The specific subjects covered here are:

- screen manipulation
- window manipulation
- database file functions
- low-level file access
- structured programming commands
- public, private, and regional variables

This chapter also discusses the use of compact and compound indexes to make applications run faster. Furthermore, we will build SQL SELECT statements using the Relational Query By Example (RQBE) facility. Finally, we will learn how to organize project files using the Project Manager.

Screen Manipulation Commands

FoxPro enhances basic screen layouts through user defined windows. They create a program's visual environment. They help organize its activities much as procedures organize its logic. Menus appear in them. Dialog boxes are special windows often used to solicit inputs such as file names during tasks. Even help appears in a window.

This section covers basic screen commands and functions (Table 2-1). Some of them also apply to windows.

Table 2-1. Screen and Window Commands and Functions

Command/Function	Definition
@...CLEAR TO	Clears part of the screen
@...FILL	Changes colors in part of the screen
ACTIVATE SCREEN	Redirects output to the screen
CLEAR	Clears the entire screen
COL( )	Returns the cursor's column position
MCOL( )	Returns the mouse's column position
MROW( )	Returns the mouse's row position
RESTORE SCREEN	Rewrites the screen from the buffer
ROW( )	Returns the cursor's row position
SAVE SCREEN	Copies the screen to a buffer
SCROLL	Moves part of the screen up or down
SET CLEAR	Determines when to clear the screen

Clearing the Screen

There are several ways to clear all or part of the screen.

@...CLEAR TO

To clear part of it, use @...CLEAR TO. For example, to clear an area between rows 5 and 10 and columns 20 and 40, use

```
@ 5,20 CLEAR TO 10,40
```

@...FILL

You can change the foreground and background colors of text with @...FILL. The next program creates an error box. The border is white stars on a blue background. An error message appears in the center. The @...FILL statement switches the interior between red on a white background and yellow on a red background. It does this every second until we press a key. Thus FILL lets us change colors without rewriting the text or issuing SET COLOR statements.

```
SET COLOR TO W+/N
CLEAR
SET COLOR TO W+/B

* Create a box for OUT OF STOCK error
  FOR i = 10 TO 14
```

```
      @ i,35 SAY REPLICATE("*",16)
      IF BETWEEN(i,11,13)
        @ i,36 SAY REPLICATE(" ",14)
      ENDIF
   ENDFOR
   @ 12,37 SAY "OUT OF STOCK"
   DO WHILE .T.

   * Change colors to red text on white
     start_time = SYS(2) && Get current time in seconds
     @ 11,36 FILL TO 13,49 COLOR R/W
     DO WHILE start_time = SYS(2)
       keypress = INKEY()
       IF keypress > 0
         EXIT
       ENDIF
     ENDDO

   * Change colors to yellow text on red
     start_time = SYS(2)
     @ 11,36 FILL TO 13,49 COLOR GR+/R
     DO WHILE start_time = SYS(2)
       keypress = INKEY()
       IF keypress > 0
         EXIT
       ENDIF
     ENDDO

   * Key press causes exit
     IF keypress > 0
       EXIT
     ENDIF

   ENDDO
```

CLEAR

CLEAR erases the screen or active window. It also releases pending GET statements. Always clear a new output screen; never assume that old text will be overwritten. Use SET COLOR to change the screen color during a CLEAR.

SET CLEAR ON/OFF

SET CLEAR determines whether the program clears the screen before executing SET FORMAT TO or QUIT. If SET CLEAR is OFF, SET FORMAT TO superimposes new screens on top of old ones. Thus a program can build a complex screen through overlays, as in the following sequence:

```
SET CLEAR OFF
SET FORMAT TO TICKET
SET FORMAT TO CUSTOMER
SET FORMAT TO ITEMS
SET FORMAT TO TOTALS
```

By executing SET CLEAR OFF just before ending, a program leaves the final screen image.

Determining Screen Position

Some programs must know where the cursor is. FoxPro has four functions that provide this information.

COL(), ROW()

COL() and ROW() return the cursor's vertical and horizontal position. They let you place text and data relative to other screen objects rather than absolutely.

MCOL(), MROW()

MCOL() and MROW() are the mouse equivalents of COL() and ROW(). If your program uses a mouse, they determine its position.

Program 2-1 uses MCOL() and MROW() to follow mouse movements and button selections. As you move the mouse, a box character moves on the screen. Pressing the button displays its current position. To stop the program, move the cursor into the 'QUIT' box and click the mouse.

```
* Read mouse position and button
SET TALK OFF
CLEAR
* Initialize position variables
newrow = 0
newcol = 0
oldrow = 0
oldcol = 0
* Define box coordinates
tl = 10
lc = 35
bl = 14
rc = 45
message = 'Q U I T'

DO WHILE .T.
  DO BOX
   * Determine new mouse position
   newrow = MROW()
```

```
      newcol = MCOL()
      * Draw new mouse cursor
      @ newrow,newcol SAY '▮'

      * Erase old mouse cursor if mouse moved
      IF oldrow <> newrow .OR. oldcol <> newcol
        @ oldrow,oldcol SAY ' '
      ENDIF

      * Display position at bottom of screen
      * if mouse button is pressed
      IF MDOWN()
        @ 23, 0 SAY "ROW: " + STR(newrow,2)
        @ 23,20 SAY "COLUMN: " + STR(newcol,2)

        * Exit if mouse button pressed in QUIT box
        IF BETWEEN(newrow,tl,bl)
        IF BETWEEN(newcol,lc,rc)
          CLEAR
          EXIT
        ENDIF
      ENDIF
      ENDIF

      * Update old mouse position
      oldrow = newrow
      oldcol = newcol
      ENDDO
      RETURN


      PROCEDURE BOX
      * Draw QUIT box
        @ tl,lc TO bl,rc
        @ INT((tl+bl)/2),INT((rc-lc-LEN(message))/2+0.5+lc) ;
          SAY 'Q U I T'
        @ 22, 5 SAY 'Press left mouse button to show position.'
        @ oldrow,oldcol SAY '▮'
      RETURN

      * End of program
```

Program 2-1. Read Mouse Position

If the mouse is in an active window, MCOL() and MROW() return values relative to it. If the mouse is outside the window, they return -1. Checking their values is an easier way to determine whether the mouse is in a box than using the BETWEEN function, as shown in Program 2-1. However, we can use BETWEEN to select from several boxes, not just one.

Activating and Saving the Entire Screen

Overlaid windows can make the background screen difficult to access. Commands to activate and save it are useful in a windowed environment.

ACTIVATE SCREEN

It is easy to bury the background screen when using windows. If we must write to it, we could first deactivate each of them. However, ACTIVATE SCREEN redirects I/O to it without removing anything. Text written to hidden screen areas reappears when the obscuring windows are removed.

SAVE SCREEN and RESTORE SCREEN

If no windows are currently in use, SAVE SCREEN saves the entire screen with all color attributes in a buffer or memory variable. RESTORE SCREEN restores it. Each screen requires 4K of memory.

For example, we could use SAVE SCREEN and RESTORE SCREEN during data entry. Suppose the operator needs help. If the program simply overwrites the screen, reconstructing it later may be difficult. However, SAVE SCREEN can first save the image. Then the help message can overwrite it safely. After the user finishes reading the help screen, RESTORE SCREEN restores the original as shown in the following sequence:

> <Display data entry screen>
> SAVE SCREEN
> <Display help screen on top of data entry screen>
> RESTORE SCREEN
> <Continue with data entry>

Scrolling

Scrolling allows access to more information than fixed size windows can hold.

SCROLL<Row1,Col1>,<Row2,Col2>,<ExpN1>,<ExpN2>

SCROLL moves a rectangular area of the screen vertically by <ExpN1> lines and horizontally by <ExpN2> columns. Data is lost if it scrolls outside the area unless we first save it in memory variables. Note the following:

- Text scrolls up if <ExpN1> is positive, down if it is negative.
- If <ExpN1> is zero and <ExpN2> is not supplied, the area is cleared.
- Text scrolls right if <ExpN2> is positive, left if it is negative.

Program 2-2 uses vertical scrolling to view identification numbers and names from a lender file. Only ten names appear in the window at a time. However, pressing the up or down arrow key scrolls through the rest of them.

```
* Scrolling through a list - Program 2-2
*
* Scroll the lender file to help the user
* locate a bank by its ID or NAME field

* Set environment
SET TALK OFF
CLEAR

* Open lender file
SELECT A
USE lender INDEX lender
GOTO TOP
* Determine number of records
numrec = RECCOUNT()
DIMENSION lend(numrec,2)
* Load lender ID and names into array
COPY TO ARRAY lend FIELDS l_id,l_name

* Define and activate window
DEFINE WINDOW bankfind from 2,1 to 13,75 ;
   TITLE 'BANK LIST' DOUBLE CLOSE FLOAT GROW SHADOW
ACTIVATE WINDOW bankfind

* Initialize variables and text for window
i = 1
nrows = WROWS() - 3
? '      BANK ID      BANK NAME'
FOR j = 1 TO nrows
   ? SPACE(7) + lend(i+j-1,1) + SPACE(6) + lend(i+j-1,2)
ENDFOR
@ 9,5 SAY 'Press Up, Down, or Esc'
* Begin scrolling loop
DO WHILE .T.
   * Check for a keystroke
   @ 0,2 SAY SPACE(10)
   rk = INKEY()

   * Case structure to branch to option
   DO CASE

      * Up arrow key pressed
      * Scroll text down
      CASE rk = 5
```

```
      i = i - 1
      IF i < 1
        i = 1
        @ 0,2 SAY "AT TOP" + CHR(7)
      ELSE
        SCROLL 2,0,8,50,-1
        @ 2,0 SAY SPACE(7) + lend(i,1) + SPACE(6) + ;
                  lend(i,2)
      ENDIF

  * Down arrow key pressed
  * Scroll text up
    CASE rk = 24
      i = i + 1
      IF i + nrows > numrec
        i = numrec - nrows
        @ 0,2 SAY "AT BOTTOM" + CHR(7)
      ELSE
        SCROLL 2,0,8,50,1
        @ nrows+1,0 SAY SPACE(7) + lend(i+nrows-1,1) + ;
                        SPACE(6) + lend(i+nrows-1,2)
      ENDIF

  * Esc key pressed
    CASE rk = 27
      EXIT

  ENDCASE
ENDDO

* Deactivate window
DEACTIVATE WINDOW bankfind

RETURN

* End of program
```

Program 2-2. Using SCROLL to View a File

Window Manipulation Commands

Windows are rectangular screen areas used to view data or other information. They also display menus, program options, and help. FoxPro has many commands and functions for creating and using them (see Table 2-2).

Table 2-2. Window Commands and Functions

Command/Function	Purpose
ACTIVATE WINDOW	Displays a defined window
CLEAR WINDOWS	Removes window from screen and memory
DEACTIVATE WINDOW	Removes window from screen
DEFINE WINDOW	Creates a window and sets its attributes
HIDE WINDOW	Removes window from screen, but accepts output to it
MOVE WINDOW	Moves window
RELEASE WINDOWS	Removes window definition from memory
RESTORE WINDOW	Retrieves window definition from disk
SAVE WINDOW	Writes window definition to disk
SET BORDER	Defines border type
SET SHADOWS	Adds shadows behind windows
SHOW WINDOW	Places windows that are defined but not activated on the screen
WCHILD()	Returns the number and names of child windows
WCOLS()	Returns the number of columns in the window
WEXIST()	Returns .T. if window is defined
WLCOL()	Returns column position of upper left window corner
WLROW()	Returns row position of upper left window corner
WONTOP()	Returns .T. if window is on top
WOUTPUT()	Returns .T. if output goes to this window
WPARENT()	Returns the name of the parent window
WROWS()	Returns the number of rows in the window
WVISIBLE()	Returns .T. if window is ACTIVE
ZOOM WINDOW	Changes a window's size and location

ACTIVATE WINDOW

Window definitions stay in memory until activated with ACTIVATE WINDOW. FoxPro automatically directs all screen output to the most recently activated window. A window remains on the screen until we deactivate or hide it.

DEACTIVATE WINDOW

DEACTIVATE WINDOW removes the window, redisplaying the underlying information. The definition remains in memory. A program cannot direct output to a deactivated window.

DEFINE WINDOW

DEFINE WINDOW must precede all other windowing commands. It establishes the window's size, position, appearance, and name. Defining a window does not display it. In fact, we can define all windows at the beginning of a program as long as each has a unique name.

HIDE WINDOW

HIDE WINDOW erases the window without deactivating it. Thus, we can still direct output to it.

MOVE WINDOW

MOVE WINDOW moves a window to an absolute or relative position. It can move either activated or deactivated windows.

SAVE WINDOW/RESTORE WINDOW

SAVE WINDOW saves a window in a file with the extension WIN. A file can hold several window definitions. FoxPro stores the window's status (activated, deactivated, hidden, or shown) along with its contents.

RESTORE WINDOW reads a window definition from a WIN file. The saved status becomes the default status.

SET BORDER

SET BORDER sets border characters for menus, boxes, popups, and windows. FoxPro predefines four styles: SINGLE, DOUBLE, PANEL, and NONE. NONE means no border. SINGLE and DOUBLE create line borders. PANEL draws a solid box border. We also can define a custom border. The following command creates one with double horizontal lines and single vertical lines.

```
SET BORDER TO '=','=','|','|','┌','┐','└','┘'
```

creates the following window:

The order of the characters in the definition is:

> top
> bottom
> left side
> right side
> top left corner
> top right corner
> bottom left corner
> bottom right corner

If we specify just one character, the entire border uses it. For example,

```
SET BORDER TO ' * '
```

```
            ***********
creates     *         *
            *         *
            *         *
            ***********
```

SET SHADOWS ON/OFF

Adding a shadow to a window produces a three-dimensional effect. The shadow can either hide underlying text or change its colors. Use the color option in the WINDOW pulldown menu to set the shadow attribute. Figure 2-1 shows the effect.

SHOW WINDOW

SHOW WINDOW displays windows that are defined but not activated. It also can change the back-to-front order. However, it does not activate windows.

WCHILD (<window name>, <ExpN>)

When we place a new window inside an existing one using the IN or IN WINDOW clause, we say it is the child of the one in which it is placed.

With no arguments, WCHILD() returns the number of child windows in the active window. We can also specify another window.

The numeric expression <ExpN> returns the name of the child window in either the active or named window. A value of 0 refers to the bottom child window. Higher values refer to ones closer to the top. WCHILD() returns a null if <ExpN> exceeds the number of child windows.

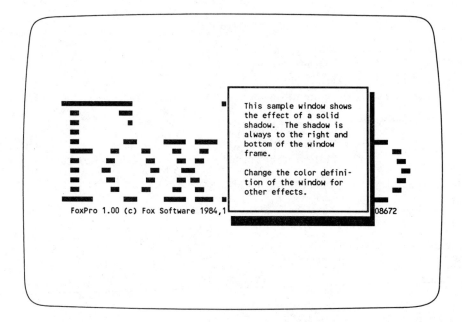

Figure 2-1. Shadow effect for a window.

WCOLS(<ExpC>) and WROWS(<ExpC>)

WCOLS and WROWS return the number of columns and rows in a window. They are useful for positioning text.

Centering text on the full screen requires a simple calculation. The starting column of a centered string is 80 minus its length divided by two. A typical command to center a string is

```
@ row,(80-LEN(string))/2 SAY string
```

To center a string in a window, we must know its width. WCOLS() generalizes the previous command to center a string in a window of any size.

```
@ row,(WCOLS()-LEN(string))/2 SAY string
```

Of course, we could replace the above expression with one using the PADC() function if the output string is the only text on the line.

```
@ row,1 SAY PADC(string,WCOLS())
```

PADC centers the characters of variable *string* within WCOLS() columns of spaces.

WEXIST(<ExpC>)

WEXIST returns .T. for a defined window. It need not be activated or displayed.

WLCOL(<ExpC>) and WLROW(<ExpC>)

WLCOL and WLROW return the screen column and row position of the upper left corner of the window.

WONTOP(<ExpC>)

WONTOP (not to be confused with a Chinese appetizer) without a parameter returns the name of the topmost window. With one, it returns .T. if the window is topmost.

WOUTPUT(<ExpC>)

WOUTPUT without a parameter returns the name of the window to which the program is directing output. With one, it returns .T. if the program is directing output to the window.

WPARENT(window name)

When we place one window inside another using the IN or IN WINDOW clause, the outer one is the parent.

With no arguments, WPARENT() returns the name of the active window's parent if one exists or a null string otherwise. If a window name is supplied, WPARENT returns the name of its parent.

WVISIBLE(<ExpC>)

WVISIBLE returns .T. for activated windows.

ZOOM WINDOW <window name> MIN/MAX/NORM [AT <row1,col1> | FROM <row1,col1> [SIZE <row2,col2> | TO <row2,col2>]]

ZOOM WINDOW allows the user to change the size and location of system or user-defined windows. MIN reduces the named window to just the title bar. MAX expands it to the entire screen. NORM returns it to its original defined size. The AT and FROM clauses define a new position for the window's upper left corner. Similarly, the SIZE and TO clauses stretch its lower right corner.

Database File Functions

FoxPro has two sets of file handling functions. This section deals with the one that handles databases and related files. The USE command opens a database with an optional index file. INDEX creates new index files. There are also commands to APPEND, COPY, DELETE, and CLOSE files. In addition, Table 2-3 lists five special file functions that we now describe briefly.

Table 2-3. Special File Handling Functions

Function	Purpose
FCOUNT()	Returns the number of fields in a database
FIELD()	Returns the name of a specific field
FLUSH()	Writes the buffer contents to disk
GETFILE()	Opens FoxPro's Open File dialog window
PUTFILE()	Opens FoxPro's Save File dialog window

FCOUNT(<ExpN>)

FCOUNT returns the number of fields in an open database. By itself, it applies to the current one. If no database is open, it returns zero. The optional parameter <ExpN> selects a work area.

FIELD(<ExpN1>[, <ExpN2>])

The FIELD function returns the name of the field designated by <ExpN1> in the current database. For example, if <ExpN1> is 5, FIELD() returns the name of the fifth field. It returns a null string if the field does not exist. (Use FCOUNT() to determine how many fields there are.) <ExpN2> selects a work area.

Program 2-3 uses FCOUNT() and FIELD(). It prompts for the name of a database to be sorted, then displays the available sort fields in a menu. After a field is selected, it creates a new sorted database TEMP.DBF. Further enhancements could sort on multiple fields, and offer a choice of ordering methods (ascending, descending, or case-insensitive).

```
* Sort on any field in any database
*    The steps are:
*        Prompt for the database's name.
*        Open the database and store the field names in
*            an array.
*        Use the array to create a menu to select the
*            sort field
*        Use SORT to create a new database TEMP.DBF in the
*            selected order

* Establish environment
  SET STATUS OFF
```

```
SET ECHO OFF
SET TALK OFF
SET BELL OFF

* Clear screen
CLEAR

* Prompt for a database file and open it
filein = SPACE(20)
@ 1,5 SAY  Enter the name of a database file:  ;
     GET filein PICTURE '@!20'
READ
SELECT 1
USE &filein

* Determine number of fields
nfields = FCOUNT()
DIMENSION fd(nfields)

* Read field names
i = 1
DO WHILE i <= nfields
   fd(i) = FIELD(i)
   i = i + 1
ENDDO

* Create menu so user can choose a sort field
STORE 0 TO sortid
@ 5,10 MENU fd,nfields TITLE  Choose a sort field
READ MENU TO sortid

* Create sorted file TEMP.DBF
sfield = fd(sortid)
SORT TO temp.dbf ON &sfield

* End of program
```

Program 2-3. Database Sort Using FCOUNT() and FIELD()

FCOUNT() and FIELD() do not return other field information such as type or size. To obtain it, use the COPY TO STRUCTURE EXTENDED command.

FLUSH()

Most programs write data to a buffer rather than directly to a file. Buffering speeds data transfer because file access is much slower than program processing. Therefore, it makes sense to hold data in a buffer until a large block can be transferred. Only when a buffer fills does the operating system transfer its contents. The normal termination of a program or the explicit closing of the file also empties the buffer.

In FoxPro applications, buffers control data transfers. At any time, they may contain information not yet written into the files. Thus, data can be lost irretrievably if the computer loses power or has to be restarted before it has transferred the buffer. Closing and reopening all databases empties the buffers, but the process is slow and awkward.

Issuing FLUSH after major updates reduces the risk of data loss due to power problems or lockups.

GETFILE(<ExpC1>,<ExpC2>)

GETFILE() uses FoxPro's Open File dialog window (Figure 2-2) to select a file to retrieve. It returns the file name as its value. GETFILE() has two optional character parameters. The first is an extension to use in displaying the directory. The second is a prompt string displayed at the top of the dialog box.

PUTFILE(<ExpC1>,<ExpC2>,<ExpC3>)

PUTFILE() uses FoxPro's Save File dialog window (Figure 2-3) to name a file to save. It returns the name as its value. It has three optional character parameters. The first is a prompt string displayed at the top of the dialog box, the second is a default file name, and the third is a default file extension. Program 2-4 shows how GETFILE() and PUTFILE() work together.

```
* Use open and save file dialog windows
* to get file names from user
*
*     GETFILE is used to select a database.
*     PUTFILE writes the extended structure to a data file.

* Initialize screen
  CLEAR
  SET TALK OFF
* Prompt for database file name
  get_file = GETFILE("DBF","Select Customer Database:")
  IF EMPTY(get_file)
    ? 'No file selected. End program.'
    CANCEL
  ELSE
    USE &get_file
  ENDIF

* Prompt for index file (display all IDX and CDX files)
  get_index = GETFILE("IDX;CDX","Select Index:")
  IF .NOT. EMPTY(get_index)
    SET INDEX TO &get_index
```

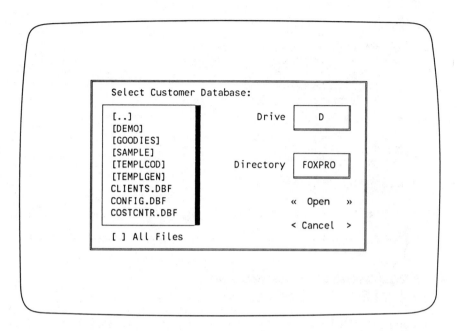

Figure 2-2. *Open File dialog window.*

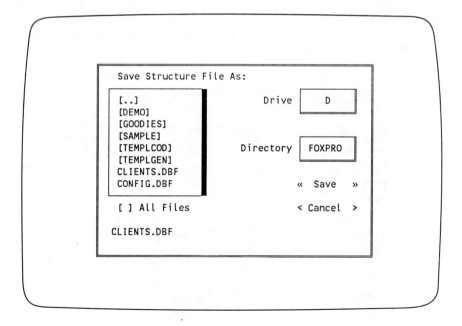

Figure 2-3. *Save File dialog window.*

```
     ENDIF

 *  Prompt for file to hold structure
    org_file = 'COPYEXTD.DBF'
    save_file = PUTFILE("Structure File:",org_file,"DAT")
    IF .NOT. EMPTY(save_file)
      COPY STRUCTURE EXTENDED TO &save_file
    ENDIF

 *  End program
    CLOSE ALL
    RETURN

 *  End of program
```

Program 2-4. Access and Create Files Using GETFILE() and PUTFILE()

Low-Level File Access Functions

The second set of file related functions (Table 2-4) provides low-level (or byte-level) access. They resemble C's file handling commands.

Low-level functions operate on any type of file. FoxPro provides separate functions to create and open a file. It has two functions to read low-level files and two to write them. One pair recognizes carriage returns and line feeds, the other ignores them. Another function moves the file pointer. Special functions test for end-of-file, flush the buffer, and report error codes.

Table 2-4. Low-Level File Access Functions

Function	Purpose
FCLOSE()	Closes the file and flushes the buffer
FCREATE()	Creates and opens a new file
FEOF()	Signals the end of a file
FERROR()	Returns an error number
FFLUSH()	Flushes the low-level file buffer
FGETS()	Reads a string from a file
FOPEN()	Opens a file
FPUTS()	Writes a string to a file
FREAD()	Reads bytes from a file
FSEEK()	Moves the file pointer
FWRITE()	Writes bytes to a file

FCLOSE(<ExpN>)

FCLOSE closes a low-level file. The parameter <ExpN> is the file handle. The function returns .T. if it succeeds.

FCREATE(<ExpC>[, <ExpN>])

FCREATE opens a new file with the name <ExpC>. It overwrites existing files. It returns a handle (a number) that other low-level functions can use to identify the file. A return of -1 indicates an error such as a write protect tab that prevents creation. The second parameter specifies the file's creation attributes as listed in Table 2-5.

Table 2-5. File Creation Attribute Codes

Code	Definition
0	Read/Write (default)
1	Read-Only
2	Hidden
3	Read-Only/Hidden
4	System
5	Read-Only/System
6	System/Hidden
7	Read-Only/Hidden/System

FEOF(<ExpN>)

FEOF() resembles the EOF() function for a DBF file. It returns .T. when the record pointer reaches the end of file. <ExpN> is the file's handle.

FERROR()

When called immediately after any other low-level function, FERROR() returns 0 if it executed correctly. If it failed, FERROR returns a numeric code indicating the cause. Table 2-6 summarizes possible error messages.

HINT

Since most low-level functions return 0 or -1 if they fail, a program should test for those values before calling FERROR() to determine the specific error.

Table 2-6. Low-Level File Access Error Codes

Code	Definition
2	File not found
4	Too many files open
5	Access denied
6	Invalid file handle
8	Out of memory
25	Seek error
29	Disk full
31	Error opening file or general failure

FFLUSH(<ExpN>)

FFLUSH() flushes the buffer identified by the handle <ExpN>. If a file must remain open for a long time, flushing the buffer reduces the chance of data loss. Use FFLUSH() on files opened with buffered low-level functions. FLUSH() does not work on them. This command is especially important when using the extended memory version of FoxPro.

FGETS(<ExpN1>[,<ExpN2>])

FGETS reads data from the file identified by the handle <ExpN1>. It can either read a fixed number of bytes <ExpN2>, or it can continue until it finds a carriage return. The default limit is 254 bytes. FGETS returns the data as a string variable.

FOPEN(<ExpC>[, <ExpN>])

FOPEN is a low-level function that opens any type of file. If the one specified by <ExpC> does not exist, it returns -1. The value returned when a file exists is the handle. Other low-level functions can use it to identify a file.

The second parameter is optional and determines the program's access rights to the file. Note that they augment the creation attributes (Table 2-5). As long as we create the file with read and write access, we can open it in one of the six modes listed in Table 2-7.

Table 2-7. File Open Attribute Codes

Code	Definition
0	Read-only buffered
1	Write-only buffered
2	Read/write buffered
10	Read-only unbuffered
11	Write-only unbuffered
12	Read/write unbuffered

FPUTS(<ExpN1>,<ExpC>[,<ExpN2>])

FPUTS writes the character string <ExpC> into the file identified by handle <ExpN1>. It automatically terminates the string with a carriage return and a line feed. <ExpN2> limits the number of characters to write. The value returned is the actual number written. If it is 0, the write failed.

FREAD(<ExpN1>,<ExpN2>)

FREAD reads data from the file identified by handle <ExpN1>. It can read a fixed number of bytes specified by <ExpN2>. It returns the data as a string variable. In the standard version, FREAD can read up to 64K bytes into a single string variable. The extended version increases this limit to 2 gigabytes.

FSEEK(<ExpN1>,<ExpN2>[,<ExpN3>])

FSEEK() moves the pointer for the file identified by handle <ExpN1>. <ExpN2> is the number of bytes to move forward (positive) or backward (negative). By default, the pointer moves relative to the beginning of the file. However, the optional third parameter can define the starting point (see Table 2-8 for possible values). FSEEK returns the current byte number.

Table 2-8. Relative Starting Positions for Pointer Moves

Value	Meaning
0	Relative to the beginning of the file (default)
1	Relative to the current position in the file
2	Relative to the end of the file

FWRITE(<ExpN1>,<ExpC>[,<ExpN2>])

FWRITE writes the character string <ExpC> into the file identified by handle <ExpN1>. <ExpN2> specifies the number of characters to write. The value returned is the actual number of bytes written. If it is 0, the write failed.

Program 2-5 uses low-level functions to read names from a file and capitalize them properly.

```
* Read a file of names and capitalize them properly
* before writing them to a new file.

* Clear screen and set environment
  CLEAR
  SET TALK OFF

* Define text file names
  filein  = 'NAMES.TXT'
  fileout = 'NAMESOUT.TXT'

* Open input file. Branch to error routine if open fails.
  file_in = FOPEN(filein)
  IF file_in < 0
    fil_error = FERROR()
    DO LOWERR
  ENDIF

* Create output file.
* Branch to error routine if create fails.
  file_out = FCREATE(fileout)
  IF file_out < 0
    fil_error = FERROR()
    DO LOWERR
  ENDIF

* Read file name, convert it to proper case,
* and write it to new file
  DO WHILE .NOT. FEOF(file_in)
    name = FGETS(file_in)
    name = PROPER(name)
    bytes_sent = FPUTS(file_out,name)
  ENDDO

* Close files
  = FCLOSE(file_in)
  = FCLOSE(file_out)
RETURN

****************************
PROCEDURE LOWERR
```

```
* Identify error type
DO CASE
  CASE fil_error = 2
    ? 'File not found'
  CASE fil_error = 4
    ? 'Too many files open'
  CASE fil_error = 5
    ? 'Access denied'
  CASE fil_error = 6
    ? 'Invalid file handle'
  CASE fil_error = 8
    ? 'Out of memory'
  CASE fil_error = 25
    ? 'Seek error'
  CASE fil_error = 29
    ? 'Disk full'
  CASE fil_error = 31
    ? 'Error opening file or general failure'
  OTHERWISE
    ? 'Error unknown'
ENDCASE
WAIT
CANCEL
RETURN

* End of program
```

Program 2-5. Creating and Using Files with Low-Level Functions

---

TIP
A careful program either checks the return value from each low-level file function or follows it with FERROR() to ensure that it succeeded.

Structured Programming Commands

Any programming language supports three basic structures, namely:
- sequence
- selection
- loop (iteration)

Sequence

The sequence structure is the simplest. In it, the computer does one operation after another with no branches or loops. Sequential commands are the most common structure in any language. All FoxPro commands not listed in this section are sequential.

Selection

A selection structure chooses a branch depending on the value of a variable or expression. The most common example is the IF test.

IF...ENDIF

The IF structure evaluates a condition. If it is true, the program executes the statements immediately after IF and before ENDIF. They form the IF condition block. If the condition is false, the program skips the block.

Figure 2-4 shows the IF...ENDIF structure.

IF...ELSE...ENDIF

IF...ELSE...ENDIF also evaluates a condition and executes the block of statements immediately after IF and before ELSE if it is true. However, if the condition is false, the program executes the block following ELSE and before ENDIF. Hence, the IF...ELSE...ENDIF structure (Figure 2-5) selects one of two blocks for execution.

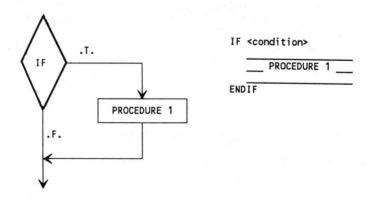

Figure 2-4. IF... ENDIF structure.

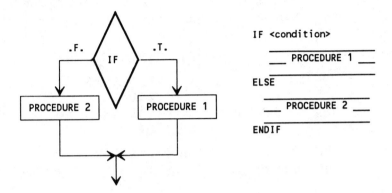

Figure 2-5. IF...ELSE...ENDIF structure.

IIF(<ExpL>,<Expr1>,<Expr2>)

IIF is the functional form of an IF...ELSE...ENDIF structure. It has three parameters. The first defines the logical condition, the second is the expression returned if the condition is true, and the third is the one returned if it is false.

The following program sums and prints the daily sales total for a store. If an item is taxable, it first subtracts the tax to obtain the true income.

```
USE sales INDEX sales
salesdate = date
SCAN
  DO WHILE salesdate = date
    * Sum sales (minus tax if applicable) for each date
    dailytotal = dailytotal + IIF(taxable, ;
      total/(1+taxrate), total)
  ENDDO
  * Print total sales for each date
  ? DTOS(salesdate) + TRANSFORM(dailytotal,'$###,###.##')
  IF .NOT. EOF()
    salesdate = date
  ENDIF
ENDSCAN
```

IIF is shorter and more compact than IF...ELSE...ENDIF. It provides an ideal way to assign a variable one of two alternate values. It can also appear in report and label definitions.

CASE...ENDCASE

The CASE statement selects among blocks of commands, depending on the value of an expression. A common use is in creating menus. Suppose a program has the following menu:

ITEM NUMBER	DESCRIPTION	PROCEDURE
1	Ticket Entry	TICKET.PRG
2	Print Ticket	PRINTTKT.PRG
3	Sales Report	SALESRPT.PRG
4	Archive Data	ARCDATA.PRG

We can implement it naturally with a CASE structure as shown in Figure 2-6. It is clearer and much easier to revise or extend than a series of IF statements.

Iteration

A loop structure repeats a block of statements. A program that reads database records and sums a field is a typical example. FoxPro provides three loop commands:

DO WHILE...ENDDO
SCAN...ENDSCAN
FOR...ENDFOR

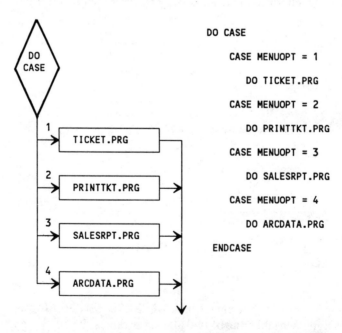

```
DO CASE

    CASE MENUOPT = 1

        DO TICKET.PRG

    CASE MENUOPT = 2

        DO PRINTTKT.PRG

    CASE MENUOPT = 3

        DO SALESRPT.PRG

    CASE MENUOPT = 4

        DO ARCDATA.PRG

ENDCASE
```

Figure 2-6. Implementing a menu with the CASE...ENDCASE structure.

DO WHILE...ENDDO

The DO WHILE statement begins much like an IF statement. It also uses a condition to determine whether to execute a block. After reaching ENDDO, it returns to the top of the loop and evaluates the condition again. If the condition is still true, it repeats the block. This process continues until the condition becomes false.

When the condition becomes false, the program skips everything between the DO WHILE and the ENDDO statements. Execution then continues with the command immediately after ENDDO. Thus, the controlled block will not execute at all if the condition is false initially.

Another way to exit a DO WHILE loop is via the EXIT command. It causes the program to jump to the command immediately after the innermost ENDDO. Use EXIT cautiously, as it produces a loop with two exits rather than just one. Loops with multiple exits are difficult to analyze and debug. Furthermore, they violate a basic tenet of structured programming, the idea that a structure should have a single entry and a single exit.

SCAN...ENDSCAN

A SCAN loop acts like a DO WHILE loop. It reads a database file sequentially. The primary difference is that SCAN advances the record pointer automatically after each iteration. It supports both FOR and WHILE options to operate on a range of records.

FOR <MEMVAR> = <ExpN1> TO <ExpN2> STEP <ExpN3>...ENDFOR

FOR is a loop structure that executes a block of statements a fixed number of times. It increments a memory variable from <ExpN1> to <ExpN2>, stepping by <ExpN3>. If <ExpN3> is omitted, the default is 1. The loop terminates when the memory variable counter goes outside the range.

HINT
Use FOR...ENDFOR in loops when you know the number of iterations. Otherwise, use DO WHILE or SCAN.

Endless Loops

Improper loop logic is a common cause of programming errors. For example, since the condition never changes, the following loop is endless:

```
a = 0
DO WHILE a = 0
   <statements> && Variable a does not appear anywhere
                && in these statements
ENDDO
```

Another problem is failing to increment the record pointer, such as with a SKIP statement. The SCAN...ENDSCAN loop solves this problem, as it does the increment automatically.

A third common practice that leads to endless loops is to use the statement

```
DO WHILE .T.
```

The loop continues until it reaches an EXIT command. If it never finds one, it repeats forever.

Evaluating the Conditional Clause

One way to speed up programs is to remove redundant calculations from inside loop structures. This includes the loop condition, as it is tested at the beginning of each iteration. If you find an expression that never changes, move it outside the loop.

Even expressions that look simple can be time consuming. Program 2-6a sums department sales from the ticket file. The loop continues while memory variable COUNT is less than function RECCOUNT() and the department is '09'.

```
* Sums sales by department and company
* Open database file SALES
  USE sales INDEX deptment
  sumdept = 0
  co_total = 0

* Find first record for department 9
* (Assumes index by department number)
  SEEK dept_id = '09'

* Sum department and company sales
  DO WHILE count <= RECCOUNT() .AND. dept_id = '09'
    sumdept = sumdept + total_due
    co_total = co_total + total_due
    count = count + 1
    SKIP
  ENDDO

* End of program
```

Program 2-6a. DO WHILE Loop before Optimization

We can make two major improvements to Program 2-6a, as shown in Program 2-6b.

First, the DO WHILE condition is complex and time consuming. Every time the program executes RECCOUNT(), it must read the file to get the number of records. As the loop neither adds nor deletes records, the count never changes. We can speed up the loop by saving it in a memory variable and then using the variable in the condition.

The second change is to move the company total calculation outside the loop. Program 2-6a adds the ticket sales from each record to both the department total and the company total. Logically, the department total is a subtotal of the company total. Therefore, we should sum it after the loop. This minor change saves the time required to update the company total with each record.

```
* Sums sales by department
* Calculates company sales by summing department totals

* Open database file SALES
  USE sales INDEX deptment
  count = 1
  sumdept = 0
  totalrecs = RECCOUNT()

* Find first record for department 9
* (Assumes index by department number)
  SEEK dept_id = '09'
* Sum department sales
  DO WHILE count <= totalrecs .AND. dept_id = '09'
    sumdept = sumdept + total_due
    count = count + 1
    SKIP
  ENDDO

* Add department sales to company total
  co_total = co_total + sumdept

* End of program
```

Program 2-6b. DO WHILE Loop after Optimization

SEEK vs. FILTER

Often a procedure needs only part of a database, such as just customers located in Pennsylvania. The programmer must then devise a way to find not only the first record of the subset, but also each subsequent one. Suppose a database contains a company's sales transactions. For a report, you need the records of Pennsylvania customers. How can you find them?

The simplest way is to read each record, starting from the beginning of the file. Then compare the state code to 'PA'. If they match, transfer the data from the record to the report. Otherwise, do nothing. Program 2-7a illustrates the basic procedure.

```
* Search every record from the beginning of the
* database to find all Pennsylvania clients

* Open sales history file
  USE clients
  state = 'PA'

* Loop through every record in database
* Compare CLIENT_ST to STATE
* If it matches, go to report procedure
* Move record pointer to next record
  DO WHILE .NOT. EOF()
     IF client_st = state
       DO REPORT
     ENDIF
     SKIP
  ENDDO

* End of program
```

Program 2-7a. Locating Pennsylvania Records by Sequential Reading

Program 2-7a reads every record. It could take hours for a large database.

A better method (Program 2-7b) locates all Pennsylvania records by setting a filter on the CLIENT_ST field. Once we establish the filter, a simple loop reads each record, capturing the desired transactions. However, setting a filter takes a long time, especially for a large file. The reason is that FoxPro still reads every record in the database and tests it against the filter. Once the filter is set, the rest of the program proceeds quickly.

```
* Set a filter for Pennsylvania, then search
* every record in the filter

* Open sales history file
  USE clients
  state = 'PA'

* Set a filter for CLIENT_ST = STATE
* Loop through every record in filter
* Go to report procedure
* Move record pointer to next record
  SET FILTER TO client_st = state
  GOTO TOP
  DO WHILE .NOT. EOF()
    DO REPORT
    SKIP
  ENDDO
  SET FILTER TO
  GOTO TOP

* End of program
```

Program 2-7b. Locating Pennsylvania Records Using a Filter

There is a time savings here only if the filter is already set or can be used elsewhere.

> **HINT**
> The command GOTO TOP must immediately follow SET FILTER TO to move the pointer to the first record within the filter. Otherwise, it may be outside the filter subset.

If we index the database SALEHIST by CLIENT_ST, there is a fast way to find all records for a specific state. The key here is that, in a database indexed by CLIENT_ST, those records are sequential. Therefore, what we must do is locate the first one with a SEEK command. Then a simple loop finds all records until the state changes. Program 2-7c shows the technique.

```
* Relies on the fact that the database is indexed on
* CLIENT_ST. Seeks the first record for Pennsylvania
* and then reads sequentially until the state changes.
```

```
* Open sales history file

  USE clients INDEX clients
  state = 'PA'

* Use SEEK to locate the first record with CLIENT_ST = STATE
* Loop through database records until CLIENT_ST changes.
* While looping, send each record to the report procedure.
* Remember to move the record pointer.

  SEEK client_st = state
  DO WHILE client_st = state
    DO REPORT
    SKIP
  ENDDO

* End of program
```

Program 2-7c. Locating Pennsylvania Records Using an Index

Program 2-7c is faster than either Program 2-7a or 2-7b. In addition, if there are no Pennsylvania records, the DO WHILE statement fails immediately.

TIP
Generating a report with the SEEK command on an indexed file is much faster than any other method. Therefore, system designers should carefully consider creating indexes to meet report requirements. Of course, you may not want a separate index for every possibility. However, you should index frequently used reports. (Refer to compound indexes for a way to create multiple indexes for a database.)

WHILE vs. FOR

Several commands allow WHILE and FOR options to define a subset of records. The two are not interchangeable. In fact, they serve different needs. We use the DELETE ALL command to illustrate the differences since it allows both. Suppose we want to delete all records in the database for a certain state. Which option should we use? The answer lies in the database's structure.

If a database is sorted by state or is indexed on it, LOCATE or SEEK finds the first matching record. Then the WHILE option marks each subsequent one for deletion until the field value changes. If you do not move the record pointer first, DELETE ALL might stop immediately.

```
state = 'PA'
SEEK client_st = state
DELETE ALL WHILE client_st = state
```

Suppose that the database is not sorted or indexed by the field of interest. DELETE ALL can still mark records that have a specific value. In this case, use the FOR option. Like WHILE, it begins at the current record and tests each one it processes. However, even if a test fails, DELETE ALL FOR continues with subsequent records until it reaches the end of the file.

```
findclient = '34'
DELETE ALL FOR client_id = findclient
```

Use the same logic to choose between FOR and WHILE as applied to FILTER vs. SEEK previously. The WHILE option is faster, but requires a previously sorted database or one indexed on the field of interest. The FOR option works with any database, but is much slower since it must read every record.

TIP
For highest performance, read as few records as possible. The best way to do this is with an index.

Scopes of Variables

A variable's scope specifies how it makes its value known to other procedures and functions. There are four ways to define it in FoxPro. The first and most common method is by default. However, you can also declare a variable as PRIVATE, PUBLIC, or REGIONAL.

Default Scope

The default scope of a variable satisfies most programming needs. Once defined, we can access it in any line of the procedure or of any subsequently called procedure. We cannot access it in a higher level procedure. Thus some applications start by assigning initial values to a list of variables just to define them and make them available everywhere. In such cases, the scope of variables is of no further concern. However, there is a danger in using the default scope. It occurs when we accidentally redefine variables in a lower level procedure.

Public Scope

In some applications, however, the programmer may not want to initialize or use all variables in the main program. Yet some that can be defined only in a lower level procedure are needed in a higher level procedure or in another branch.

A typical example uses the variable OUTPDEST to select the output destination of a report. The report calls a procedure that contains the destination options. However, a higher level procedure must know what was selected to determine formatting parameters such as lines per page and margins.

So the question is how to return OUTPDEST to a higher level. One way is to initialize it in the caller. Another defines it as a PUBLIC variable at the beginning of the first procedure that uses it.

The command PUBLIC <memory variable list> can appear anywhere. It can be in the main program, in the caller, or even in a menu. However, it must appear before the first line that uses the variable. Once we declare a variable as PUBLIC, we can access it from any lower or higher level procedure or anywhere further on in the main program. In our menu procedure, we could declare OUTPDEST as a PUBLIC variable in the procedure that contains the destination options. After a PUBLIC variable is defined but before it is initialized, its default value is FALSE.

Private Scope

We can also declare a variable as PRIVATE. The usual reason for doing so is because it is already defined in a higher level procedure. The two procedures use the same name for different purposes. An easy way to protect variables is to declare them PRIVATE in low-level procedures. When we do this with a variable, FoxPro stores it separately from the same named variable in the higher level procedure. Thus it is truly different.

TIP
Declare variables in utility procedures and functions as PRIVATE to prevent conflict with similarly named ones at a higher level.

Regional Scope

We can declare memory variables and arrays as REGIONAL. In many ways, REGIONAL scope is similar to PRIVATE. Both allow a variable or array to have the same name as a prior variable without destroying its value. However, if the new variable is declared PRIVATE, we can no longer access the original one until we exit the routine. REGIONAL scope lets us select which variable we want to use by changing the region with the #REGION directive.

Indexes and the Rushmore Technology

FoxPro still supports the index structure used in its initial release. Indexes formed this way are called *standard indexes*. However, Version 2 adds two new types of indexes.

The first is a single-key index using a compact structure that takes as little as one-sixth the space of a standard index. Creating a compact single-key index is simple; just include the COMPACT keyword when defining it.

```
USE products
INDEX ON prod_id TO prod2 COMPACT
```

If an index already exists, we can convert it to the compact form by reindexing.

```
USE products INDEX products
REINDEX COMPACT
```

A single-key compact index still uses the file extension IDX. However, as it is smaller, it is much faster when used with commands such as FIND or SEEK. A further advantage is that FoxPro optimized its SQL commands for compact indexes, although it can use standard ones.

The second new type of index is a multiple key version called a *compound index*. Its advantage is that it stores as many indexes as needed for a database in a single file. A common problem with multiple single-key indexes is that they can easily become obsolete if they are inactive when records are added, deleted, or modified. This cannot happen with a compound index.

Compound indexes store multiple keys using the compact form just discussed. Each is stored with a name, called a *tag*. Tags follow the same naming rules as variables. The only limit to the number allowed per index is memory and disk space. Thus it is now easier to define and maintain multiple indexes for specific needs, such as reports.

To define a compound index, we use the INDEX command along with a few extra clauses.

The TAG clause assigns a name to a specific index key. After all, a name is more meaningful than an arbitrary order number when selecting which index to open. It consists of up to 10 characters, which may be letters, numbers, or underscores. We do not need the COMPACT keyword because compound indexes are compact by default. We can, however, include either ASCENDING or DESCENDING clauses to define the sort order. We can even mix orders, so some tags can be ascending while others are descending. Although ascending order is the default, it is a good practice to include the ASCENDING keyword in compound indexes with mixed sort orders.

Compound indexes still support both the FOR and UNIQUE options used by standard indexes. The only difference is in the length restrictions on the index and FOR expressions. IDX files limit them to 220 characters each. Compound (CDX) indexes limit their total to 512 characters. Thus, if there is no FOR expression, the index expression could be 512 characters long.

Using Compound Indexes

A logical question at this point is, "If the compound index contains multiple keys, which one is used when I open the index?" Just as with multiple indexes, we use the SET ORDER TO command to define the master index.

SET ORDER TO is based on numbers. If we have only single-key indexes, they are numbered in the order in which they are opened. If we also have compound indexes, the single-key ones are numbered first. Consider the following line that opens several index files.

```
USE products INDEX prodcode.idx, proddesc.cdx, prodname.idx
```

Here PRODCODE.IDX is the first index and hence the master. The second index is PRODNAME.IDX. If the compound index PRODUCTS.CDX exists, it is used next automatically, even though it is not listed specifically. Its tags get numbers beginning with 3. Finally, the indexes from PRODDESC.CDX are numbered. One way to check the order is to open the database and indexes and then enter the DISPLAY STATUS command. It lists the indexes in numerical order.

TIP

FoxPro always automatically opens a compound index with the same name as the database. We refer to it as a *structural index,* and to other compound indexes as *independent indexes.*

Note that you can name the tag and its CDX file directly with the command

```
SET ORDER TO TAG prodmanufr OF proddesc.cdx
```

With compound indexes, we can also include the ASCENDING or DESCENDING keyword in the SET ORDER TO command. We can thus determine the read order, regardless of how the index was created. For example, we may store an index in ascending order, but in the program read it in descending order.

```
* List products in order of sales volume beginning with
*    the highest
  SET ORDER TO TAG prod_sales DESCENDING
```

This feature allows us to read an index in either direction rather than having to store two separate ones.

What Is Rushmore Technology?

Rushmore Technology is a technique developed by Fox Software that permits fast, efficient access to sets of records. It is particularly effective at reducing access times in files with over 500,000 records. Perhaps its best feature is that the programmer need do nothing special to use it. Rushmore works with all three index structures, although it works best with compact indexes. Because it is designed for large databases, it has large memory requirements and works best with FoxPro's Extended Version. The Extended Version is a true 32-bit product that uses all available extended memory.

In addition, SQL utilizes Rushmore techniques to optimize multi-database queries.

Relational Query by Example (RQBE)

FoxPro provides the Relational Query By Example (RQBE) feature to generate SQL SELECT commands. For more information about SQL (Structured Query Language), see S. Vang, *SQL and Relational Databases* (San Marcos, CA: Microtrend Books, 1990).

Opening a Query

To open a query, select Query from the file list displayed by selecting New... from the File menu, or type

```
CREATE QUERY
```

If no databases are open, FoxPro prompts for one. The RQBE window, like the one shown in Figure 2-7, helps build the query or modify existing queries.

Selecting Databases

The box in the upper left corner shows the currently selected databases. By selecting Add, we can pick others from the Open File dialog. They can come from any directory on any drive. When we select one, we must specify a join condition with an existing database. It relates fields using one of the comparison clauses listed in Table 2-9.

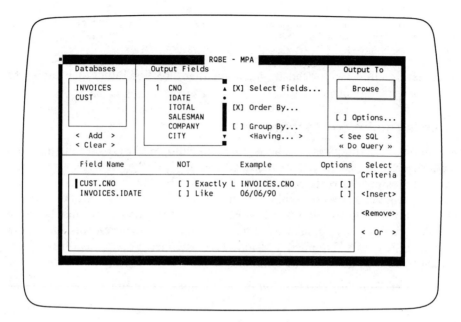

Figure 2-7. RQBE build window.

Table 2-9. Join Comparison Clauses	
LIKE	NOT LIKE
EXACTLY LIKE	NOT EXACTLY LIKE
MORE THAN	NOT MORE THAN
LESS THAN	NOT LESS THAN

When we finish defining the relation, it appears in the lower half of the RQBE window. If we decide to change it later, we can place the cursor anywhere on the line defining it and press Enter.

After opening the databases and defining relations between them, we are ready to select fields for the query output. A query need not use all fields from all databases. If fact, it seldom does. However, we must select each field we want to appear in the result.

Selecting Fields and Sort Order

The box in the top center of the RQBE window lists the fields available for the query. It does not automatically include ones from a selected database. In fact, when we add a new database, we must first select the fields we want to use. To modify the list, press the Select Fields check box. This opens a window shown in Figure 2-8 that allows us to move new fields (highlighted) from the database list on the left to the query output fields on the right.

After selecting the output fields, we may also define a sort order. Choose the Order By check box to display a list of fields on which to sort the query. The dialog box shown in Figure 2-9 has two lists. The one on the left contains all output fields. They are the only ones we can use in a sort. The one on the right contains the order criteria. We can select any number of fields to build the sort order. In addition, each can be in ascending or descending sequence. The initial setting is ascending. However, if we select the Descending radio button before selecting a field, we can display it in reverse order. In fact, we can alternate between ascending and descending with each field. The order in which we select fields defines the sort levels. For example, the first field selected becomes the highest level sort. If there are multiple records with the same value at this level, we can select a second level sort. Suppose we want to build a sales query. The primary level sort might be date. The second level might be invoice number, followed by invoice line item as the third level.

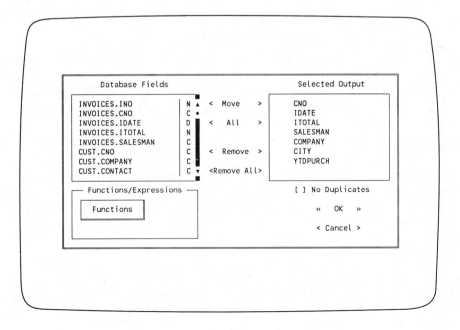

Figure 2-8. Select output fields dialog.

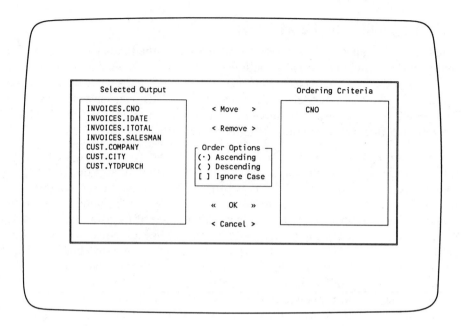

Figure 2-9. Sort criteria dialog.

Selecting Output Type and Destination

Now that we have selected our database and fields, we must define where to send the output and how to format it. Note that the result of a query is a temporary database containing records that match the selection criteria and fields defined by the previous two steps. There are four possible destinations: BROWSE, CURSOR, REPORT/LABEL, and TABLE/DBF.

BROWSE

BROWSE simply opens the Browse window and displays the result when the query finishes. We can use all the browse features to view parts of the data. It remains in the temporary file only as long as a new query is not started and we do not exit FoxPro.

CURSOR

CURSOR creates the temporary database, but does not immediately open the Browse window to display it. Rather, we must select the area labeled 'query' from the View list in the Windows popup. Like BROWSE, CURSOR does not save the temporary database.

REPORT/LABEL

Selecting REPORT/LABEL activates the Options check box. Selecting it displays the dialog in Figure 2-10.

The dialog contains two sets of options, formatting and output. The top three formatting options are radio buttons that indicate overall choices.

The top button formats the output for screen display. Actually, we can send it to the screen, the printer, or a file. This option is really the same as using LIST with a database. The selected fields appear in columns beneath their names. There are no special options except the ability to omit the headings.

The second button formats the output as a report. It can define a Quick Report in which the selected fields appear in a column or form layout. A few more options are active now, including a report heading, page eject controls, and summary controls. However, it does not provide direct control over field placement or formatting. The alternative is to define a form name for the report. We can then edit it later using FoxPro's Report Generator with

```
MODIFY REPORT <reportname>
```

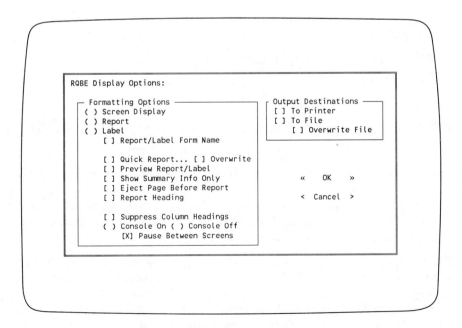

Figure 2-10. REPORT/LABEL output dialog.

The third button formats the output as a label. Like the report option, it can generate a Quick Label with limited features. By defining a form name, however, we can edit it with the command

```
MODIFY LABEL <labelname>
```

Before leaving this dialog, we must select an output destination or accept the screen as a default.

TABLE/DBF

TABLE/DBF prompts for a name that it uses for the temporary database created by the query. With the results saved in a permanent file, we can return to it later for additional processing or reporting.

Viewing the SQL Command

The top pushbutton in the box immediately below the Output section of the RQBE window (Figure 2-7) opens a window to display the SQL commands generated by the query. We can view the query there at any time, but we cannot modify it directly. By choosing Select All from the Edit pulldown menu, we can copy the SELECT command to a separate file or insert it into another application.

Performing the Query

The button immediately below See SQL performs the query. You can thus test it before adding it to an application.

Filtering the Query

So far, we have shown how to define a query using all records in the selected databases. However, we may want only a subset of them.

Returning to the store example, we may want only sales records for a specific day. To add this criterion, we must define it in the lower half of the RQBE window. First move to a new line in the field name column. Press the space bar to display a list of fields. Note that we are not limited to the output fields when defining a filter. Rather, we can use any field from any open database.

In this example, select the field that contains the invoice date. Next, tab to the column that displays the condition Like. To print invoices for a specific day, press the space bar to open the popup and select Exactly Like. Then press Tab again to enter the date. Be sure to enter it in the MM/DD/YY form without delimiters. If we click the NOT check box, the query prints invoices for all dates except the one entered.

We can have any number of selection criteria. However, we should try the query after each addition to ensure that we have not overspecified it. For example, we might request invoices after a certain date for Florida customers who bought snow shovels. Of course, we may not recognize how silly that is if we specify STATE_ID = '15' and PROD_CODE = 5923.

When you have defined the query completely and tested it, save it using the Save option in the File pulldown menu. You may be surprised to learn that FoxPro saves the query as a sequence of commands centered around the SELECT command. We can now merge them into another application. For example, the query in Figure 2-7 generates the following program lines.

```
PRIVATE workarea
workarea = SELECT(0)
SELECT INVOICES.CNO, INVOICES.IDATE, INVOICES.ITOTAL, ;
  INVOICES.SALESMAN, CUST.COMPANY, CUST.CITY, CUST.YTDPURCH;
 FROM INVOICES, CUST;
 WHERE CUST.CNO == INVOICES.CNO;
   AND INVOICES.IDATE = {06/06/90};
 ORDER BY INVOICES.CNO;
 INTO CURSOR MPA_A
BROWSE NOMODIFY
USE
SELECT(workarea)
```

Compiling and Executing Procedures

Regardless of whether we create a program manually or via a generator, we must compile it. FoxPro only runs programs compiled to FXP or APP modules. Compiling programs not only makes them run faster, but it also checks for syntax errors. If any exist, FoxPro writes them to a text file if SET LOG-ERRORS is ON. The file has the same name as the program with the extension ERR.

There are several ways to compile programs. In the first place, FoxPro compiles them automatically the first time they execute. Therefore, we often do not think of compilation as a separate step. When we say

```
DO filename
```

at the dot prompt, FoxPro first compiles the program, creating an object (FXP) file. It is not a standard ASCII file that we can edit directly. We must make all changes to the PRG file. However, even after we make changes, FoxPro may still use old FXP files if SET DEVELOPMENT is OFF. Since FoxPro looks for FXP files before PRG files, our changes may not get implemented.

This problem leads to the second way to compile programs automatically under FoxPro. If SET DEVELOPMENT is OFF, FoxPro compiles a program only if no FXP file exists. If it is ON, FoxPro checks for a compiled version (FXP file) of the module. If none exists, FoxPro compiles the module automatically. However, if one exists, FoxPro compares its creation date to the PRG date. If the PRG is later, FoxPro recompiles the module before executing it. This feature resembles the MAKE utility included with most C compilers.

The third approach is to compile programs manually by issuing the COMPILE command. It accepts wildcard characters, so the command

```
COMPILE *.PRG
```

compiles all PRG files in a subdirectory. Issuing COMPILE from the dot prompt is the same as using it from the pulldown menu system.

COMPILE has two major options. ENCRYPT provides more protection to the object files. It should be used when distributing files with the FoxPro Runtime.

NODEBUG produces a smaller object file by deleting two bytes from each compiled source line that references the original line number. There is no performance gain from this. In addition, you cannot use the Trace window during execution of object files compiled with the NODEBUG option. Figure 2-11 shows the Compile dialog window that appears when the Compile option is selected from the Program pulldown with no source file open.

Defining Projects

The Project Manager tracks all files that are part of an application, including databases, formats, indexes, labels, libraries, menus, queries, programs, reports, and screens. It also tracks dependencies and connections.

Creating a Project Definition

You can create a project definition at any time. However, the best time to do so is when you create the first file. To start one, open the File pulldown and select the New option. From the list of file types, select Project. Figure 2-12 shows the dialog that appears.

Initially, the project definition is empty. Thus the only option available is to add a file. Select Add to open the File dialog window. Now select the first file you want to add. Use the file type popup in the lower left corner of the dialog to select types (the default is programs). When you select a file, its name appears in the Name column. Continue until you have included all files needed for a specific project.

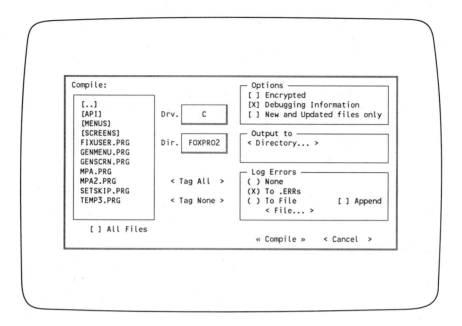

Figure 2-11. Compile dialog box.

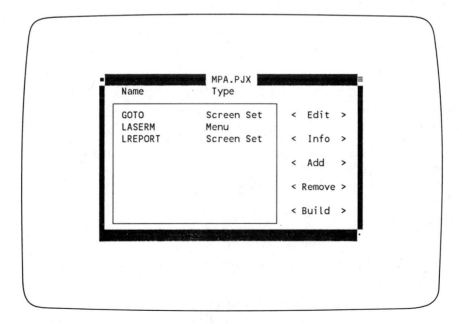

Figure 2-12. Project dialog.

Modifying a Project Definition

To modify a file, just open the project dialog window with

```
MODIFY PROJECT <projectname>
```

and highlight it. When you select the Edit button, FoxPro opens the file properly. If it is a program file, it uses MODIFY COMMAND. It opens databases with BROWSE. Reports and labels open the report and label layout dialogs, respectively. In effect, the project dialog becomes the master control center for further work.

Monitoring Project Information

Besides editing any file defined in the project, we can monitor other information by choosing the Info button. It lists the time and date of the current version, the version last built, and the date of the last build. After we build an application, the list box in this window displays a cross-reference to all procedures and files called in it. If any are undefined, we can identify them without running the program.

Building Projects and Applications

The Build button helps build projects and applications using the options shown in Figure 2-13.

The first option rebuilds a project. Effectively, we can let FoxPro build the project by just adding the name of the main program file, then selecting this option. As FoxPro reads the main program, it locates references to other programs, menus, screens, formats, etc. It adds them to the project. It automatically generates code for referenced menus and screens if it does not exist or if its file date precedes the date of the definition files. If we first check the Rebuild All check box, FoxPro regenerates code for all menus, screens, etc., regardless of their dates.

After defining everything completely, we can build the application. Build Application compiles all the files into a single object module with the extension APP. We can then run it from FoxPro with the command

```
DO <filename>.APP
```

No longer must we manage many individual object files for programs, reports, labels, screens, etc. All object files are combined neatly. This reduces the chance of forgetting or losing one when transferring the program between systems.

If you have the Developers Edition with the EXE compiler, Build Executable compiles the application all the way to an EXE rather than just an APP.

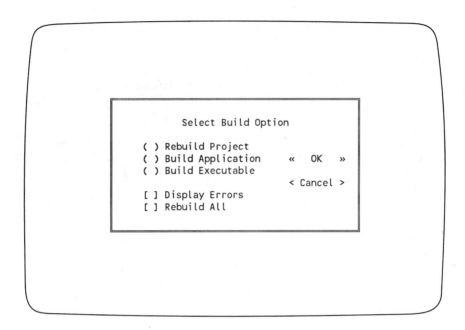

Figure 2-13. Build dialog.

Displaying Errors

The Display Errors option opens a window to display errors encountered during the building of a project, application, or executable.

Summary

FoxPro has an extensive set of commands. This chapter highlights special ones used for screen and window management. High-level database and field functions improve access to database files and their structures. Low-level file functions allow FoxPro to access any type of file.

FoxPro also has commands to support structured programming techniques. IF or CASE statements select from several blocks of statements. A variety of loops, including DO-WHILE, SCAN, and FOR, perform iterations over blocks. Carefully defining the scope of variables helps manage memory usage and prevents conflicts by limiting access to specific procedures.

We saw that FoxPro supports three types of indexes. However, for best performance, you should use one of the two compact types.

Compound indexes allow us to define as many indexes as necessary for an application and save them in a single file. This insures that they are all updated when we add, delete, or edit records.

We also saw how to use the Relational Query By Example (RQBE) facility to build queries interactively. We can then execute them directly or save them as FoxPro commands using the SQL SELECT command.

Compiling procedures produces modules that execute quickly. SET DEVELOPMENT offers a way to force compilation of updated source modules. We can compile modules automatically, manually, or through the Project Manager.

3

Data Entry

Data entry is a vital part of every application. Accurate results require accurate inputs. Checking them takes both development and execution time.

This chapter examines several ways to validate data entries. We begin with the GET statement. It has optional clauses that provide defaults, restrict input formats, and perform range checks. GET can even call user-written procedures for complex validations.

However, validation is pointless unless the user knows what to enter. Help screens are one way to provide assistance. Context sensitive help offers information specifically related to the current input field.

Other key issues are effective use of color and grouping of data. An extensive discussion of data entry methods and help systems appears in J. Powell, *Designing User Interfaces* (San Marcos, CA: Microtrend Books, 1990).

Providing Data Defaults

You have already written programs with defaults, though perhaps unwittingly. FoxPro forces us to define variables before using them in GET statements and calculations. We may initialize numeric values to zero, strings to nulls, and logicals to .F.. Could we assign more useful values, such as the most likely one? We now examine several types of defaults. The idea is to reduce the amount of typing and avoid disastrous errors.

Defaults for Prompt Variables

A prompt in a menu and a choice from a list are ideal candidates for defaults. One style selects the most common option. Another selects the safest. Often the latter is the one that leaves things unchanged. In either case, the program executes the default selection if the user simply presses the Enter key.

For example, the default for the prompt 'Do you want to delete this record?' should be NO. Note the conflict. If users often press the Enter key inadvertently, you want NO as the default. On the other hand, careful users would seldom start a delete process they did not want, making YES a more appropriate choice. You must decide where your application's users fit.

Programs 3-1 and 3-2 show typical uses of defaults.

```
* Program 3-1
* Uses the most likely value (printer) as a default value
* for a memory variable (output destination) in a
* prompt
SET TALK OFF
CLEAR

* Wait for user to enter F, P, or S as output destination
outpdest = ' '
DO WHILE .NOT. outpdest $ 'FPS'

   * Default destination is printer (P)
   outpdest = 'P'
   @ 23,0 SAY 'Output to (F)ile, (P)rinter, or (S)creen';
         GET outpdest PICTURE '!'
   READ
ENDDO

* End of program
```

Program 3-1. Prompt for Output Destination

```
* Program 3-2
* Uses a safe default (NO) for a memory variable in a
* prompt about whether to delete a record
SET TALK OFF
CLEAR

* Ask about deletion, making default NO
delrec = 'N'

* Prompt for deletion
@ 23,0 SAY 'Delete this record? [Y|N]' GET delrec;
      PICTURE 'Y'
READ
```

```
* Delete record if response is YES
IF delrec = 'Y'
  DELETE
ENDIF

* End of program
```

Program 3-2. Prompt for Record Deletion

In Program 3-1, the DO WHILE loop asks for an output destination. Simply pressing Enter selects P, the most likely choice.

> **TIP**
> When a prompt requires a single character response, always convert it to uppercase using the PICTURE clause. Both data entry and validation are easier when tests are case-insensitive.

Program 3-2 prompts for a YES or NO response when deleting a record. Here the default provides safety. An accidental acceptance does not cause a deletion. This method slows down the careful user, as he or she must note the default and change it most of the time. You must decide how far to go in providing safeguards. As John McCarthy (the AI pioneer) pointed out, "No potato in the tailpipe" is a requisite for starting a car, but hardly something you should require a driver to check every time.

> **HINT**
> Consider other ways to protect the user. For example, deleting records is a two step process. First, a user marks a record for deletion. Then he or she must pack the database to remove it physically. Therefore, you may want to provide an option to recall marked records.

Defaults when Appending Records

Most applications have a routine to append individual records via a formatted entry screen. Typically, the screen displays the fields as blanks. However, we can assign default values by putting an assignment statement ahead of each GET.

A more structured approach groups the assignment statements before the first
GET, perhaps even in a separate procedure. Program 3-3 shows this technique.

```
* Program 3-3
* Initializing a record via a procedure
SET TALK OFF
CLEAR

* Open database LENDER containing bank addresses
USE lender

* Initialize memory variables for a new record
DO INITFIELD

* Get new data values
@ 4, 2 TO 9,78 DOUBLE
@ 2,35 SAY "LENDER FILE"
@ 5, 4 SAY "Banker ID:      " GET m->l_id PICTURE '!!!'
@ 6, 4 SAY "Banker Name:    " GET m->l_name PICTURE '@X25'
@ 7, 4 SAY "Bank Address:   " GET m->l_addr1 PICTURE '@X25'
@ 8, 4 SAY "      City:     " GET m->l_city PICTURE '@X20'
@ 8,50 SAY "State: "          GET m->l_state PICTURE '!!'
@ 8,65 SAY "Zip: "            GET m->l_zip PICTURE '#####'
READ

* Add/Ignore the record
addrec = 'Y'
@ 23,0 SAY 'Add this record? [Y|N]' GET addrec PICTURE 'Y'
READ
IF addrec = 'Y'
  APPEND BLANK
  REPLACE l_id    WITH m->l_id
  REPLACE l_name  WITH m->l_name
  REPLACE l_addr1 WITH m->l_addr1
  REPLACE l_city  WITH m->l_city
  REPLACE l_state WITH m->l_state
  REPLACE l_zip   WITH m->l_zip
ENDIF
RETURN

PROCEDURE INITFIELD
* Provides default values for variables in database
* Must declare variables public to pass them back to
* the main routine
PUBLIC l_id, l_name, l_addr1, l_city, l_state, l_zip
* Initialize variables
l_id = SPACE(3)
l_name = SPACE(25)
l_addr1 = SPACE(25)
l_city  = 'Reading          '
```

```
l_state = 'PA'
l_zip    = '19603'
RETURN

* End of program
```

Program 3-3. Initializing a Record via a Procedure

We can also define a default value in the GET statement itself. For example, we can use the DEFAULT clause to simplify the report destination prompt as follows:

```
DO WHILE .NOT. outpdest $ 'FPS'
   @ 23,0 SAY 'Output to (F)ile, (P)rinter, or (S)creen' ;
        GET outpdest PICTURE '!' DEFAULT 'P'
   READ
ENDDO
```

This method also works with GET statements used to enter data into new records. However, if SET CARRY is ON, the fields default to the values from the previous record, not the ones in the DEFAULT clauses. But, of course, carryover is just another type of default.

Using a separate procedure to initialize variables simplifies the maintenance of defaults by making them easier to find. But whenever defaults are part of the program, compiling it fixes their values. Changing them requires access to the source and recompilation. A better design separates defaults from the program.

Defaults as Part of the Database

One way to supply default values is through a special record in the database itself. It contains values for each field, and can be either the first or last record. The only restriction is that the program must be able to find it quickly.

To use a default record, move the pointer to it. Then copy the values to memory variables with the SCATTER command. Next edit the fields using the variables in the data entry form. Then write them to a blank record in the database. Program 3-4 shows the steps, using the first record of LENDER for the defaults.

```
* Program 3-4
* Appending records using a database record for defaults
SET TALK OFF
CLEAR

* Open database LENDER containing bank addresses
USE lender
```

```
* Load first record (defaults) into memory variables
GOTO TOP
SCATTER MEMVAR

* Edit default values
@ 4, 2 TO 9,78 DOUBLE
@ 2,35 SAY "LENDER FILE"
@ 5, 4 SAY "Banker ID:     " GET m->l_id PICTURE '!!!'
@ 6, 4 SAY "Banker Name:   " GET m->l_name PICTURE '@X25'
@ 7, 4 SAY "Bank Address:  " GET m->l_addr1 PICTURE '@X25'
@ 8, 4 SAY "       City:   " GET m->l_city PICTURE '@X20'
@ 8,50 SAY "State: "         GET m->l_state PICTURE '!!'
@ 8,65 SAY "Zip: "           GET m->l_zip PICTURE '#####'
READ

* Add/Ignore this record
addrec = 'Y'
@ 23,0 SAY 'Add this record? [Y|N]' GET addrec PICTURE 'Y'
READ
IF addrec = 'Y'
   APPEND BLANK
   GATHER MEMVAR
ENDIF

* End of program
```

Program 3-4. Appending Records Using a Database Record for Defaults

---

The record with the default values is simply part of the database. We can access and modify it. But because it is special, we must force reports to skip it. If the database has an index, we can compel the default record to be either first or last. But remember that GOTO 2 jumps to a physical record, which may be anywhere if the database is indexed. Instead, you must use:

```
GOTO TOP
SKIP

<Do report here>
```

Storing defaults in a database record lets us change them without recompiling the source. Thus, if you distribute compiled applications without source code, your clients can still change the defaults. One variation maintains a separate database of default values. This eliminates the need to skip the default record in the main file. However, you may have to increase FILES or BUFFERS in CONFIG.SYS to handle the extra open file.

Another variation stores default values in a MEM file. We can load them into memory with

```
RESTORE FROM file ADDITIVE
```

HINT

Store default values you want users to control in a database record or memory variable file they can edit. Place ones you want to protect in the source code.

Input Field Size

When using a GET statement, the size of the variable usually sets the size of the edit field. For character variables, it defaults to the field's current length even if a PICTURE clause specifies a larger format. In fact, if the field is a null string, READ ignores the GET because the length is zero.

On the other hand, GET wraps long edit fields onto multiple lines. However, it stretches them to the rightmost character of the screen or window, overwriting any text that is there. One solution uses the S FUNCTION option to restrict the edit field. If it is longer than the edit area, the arrow keys scroll it.

You can also define the edit area with the SIZE option. It defines the area as a specific number of rows and columns within the screen or active window. Thus we limit its width. We can now place the edit field on the left side of the screen and display other information on the right without overwriting it.

When we edit a character field in a region defined with SIZE, the field's size is the controlling factor. Only the MODIFY STRUCTURE command can increase it. However, a memory variable can use the entire region since we can expand it. Furthermore, if it is larger than the edit area, the text scrolls within it.

WARNING

If you use a PICTURE clause with the SIZE clause, editing is limited to the length of PICTURE.

Program 3-5 uses SIZE to edit long strings.

```
* Program 3-5
* Uses SIZE to edit long strings
SET TALK OFF
CLEAR
@  0, 0,21,79 BOX
@  2, 1 TO  2,78
@  3,40 TO 20,40
```

```
@ 10, 1 TO 10,39
@ 14, 1 TO 14,39

a_hint = 'Use the SIZE option with GET statements that '+;
         'edit long character strings if input must fit '+;
         'in a formatted screen.'

instruct = 'To edit the window on the left, use the left '+;
           'and right arrow keys to move through the '+;
           'text.  DO NOT USE the up and down arrow keys '+;
           'or FoxPro will assume that you are done '+;
           'editing.  Press Enter to accept the edited '+;
           'changes and Esc to abort any changes.'

@  4, 41 GET instruct SIZE 10,37 DISABLE
@  1,  1 SAY PADC('Example SIZE Option in a Form',78)
@ 11,  2 GET a_hint SIZE 3,37
READ
CLEAR
? a_hint

* End of program
```

Program 3-5. Using the SIZE Option

As shown here, we can also use the SIZE option to display text using a disabled GET command.

HINT

When using a disabled GET command to display long text strings, include the COLOR option to set the disabled color to the enabled color. Otherwise, the disabled text stands out.

Input Validation

Data entry procedures involve tradeoffs between speed and accuracy. Validation takes time, but it is faster to correct errors during entry than to track them down later. We must use all of FoxPro's tools to insure accurate, fast data entry. There are five major types of validation: format, range, list, existence, and calculated. We now discuss each of them.

Format Validation

Several simple prompts in earlier examples used format validation or PICTURE clauses. They limit the characters passed to the input variable.

PICTURE Clause

The PICTURE clause restricts entry to specific characters. It validates formats, not values. Table 3-1 lists its options.

Table 3-1. PICTURE Clause Codes

Code	Meaning
A	Letters
L	Logical data including F, f, N, n, T, t, Y, and y. Cannot be mixed with other codes.
N	Letters and digits
X	Any character
Y	Y, y, N, or n, converting them to uppercase
9	Digits only with character data, digits and signs with numerical data
#	Digits, blanks, and signs
!	Converts lowercase letters to uppercase
$	Displays the currency symbol
*	Left fills numeric values such as check amounts
.	Specifies the period position
,	Separates every three digits left of the decimal

We can combine PICTURE codes. For example, to enter a character field that must begin with a letter and has three digits, we use

```
PICTURE 'A999'
```

FUNCTION Clause

The main difference between a PICTURE clause and a FUNCTION clause is scope. A PICTURE clause applies a specific format to a specific character position. FUNCTION codes apply to the entire field. For example, a FUNCTION code may center information in a field, whereas a PICTURE clause limits the type of characters at each position as well as overall size.

PICTURE clauses occur often with GET statements to control the types of characters entered. For example, '999' allows only three digits and signs, ignoring all other keys. FUNCTION clauses occur often with SAY statements to help format output.

Table 3-2 lists the FUNCTION codes.

Code	Meaning
	Table 3-2. FUNCTION Clause Codes
A	Allows letters only
B	Left justifies numeric data during output
C	Displays CR with positive numbers during output
D	Uses the SET DATE format for editing dates
E	Uses European date format for editing dates
I	Centers output in field
J	Right justifies output in field
K	Selects the entire field when the cursor moves to it
L	Displays leading zeros rather than spaces in numeric output
M<list>	Limits input to items within a preset list
R	Displays template characters that are not stored
S<n>	Limits display width to n characters. The field will scroll horizontally to display all characters if necessary
T	Trims leading and trailing blanks during output
X	Displays DB with negative numbers during output
Z	Displays blanks instead of zeros
(	Encloses negative numbers in parentheses
!	Converts lowercase to uppercase
^	Displays numeric data in scientific notation
$	Displays data in currency format

Most codes are obvious, but we will note briefly the features and uses of K and M. With M, we can create a list of possible entries for a field. It works with character, numeric, or date fields. The following commands prompt for race in a personnel system. Note that the first item becomes the default for the GET variable if it is not set otherwise.

```
RACE = SPACE(6)
@ 5,5 SAY 'Enter Race' GET race FUNCTION ;
     'MWHITE,ASIAN,BLACK,INDIAN,OTHER'
READ
```

The K function saves time when a value is either accepted as is or replaced completely. Normally, when the cursor enters an edit field, it is edited as normal text. That is, typed characters either overwrite the existing text or are inserted into it. To replace the default value, we must first select and then delete it, or delete each character individually. When the cursor enters a field defined with the K function, it immediately selects the entire area. Pressing any key (except Enter or Esc) deletes the old value and begins a new one.

The following example has two GET statements. The first one edits the manufacturer's name. In this case, if the name differs, we replace it completely. Thus the K function is appropriate. To accept the current name, press Enter. To replace it, just start typing and it will vanish.

The second GET displays items made by the manufacturer. A company is likely to make several similar items in different sizes. Thus we may want to edit the current size information. Therefore, we do not specify the K function here.

```
* Program 3-6
* Using the K function in a GET
SET TALK OFF
CLEAR

manufact = 'DENTIFRICE CO.   '
product  = 'ULTRA RITE - FAMILY   '

@ 2,5 SAY 'MANUFACTURER: ' GET m->manufact FUNCTION 'K'
@ 3,5 SAY 'PRODUCT:      ' GET m->product
READ
```

Program 3-6. Using the K Function in a GET

FUNCTION codes can also appear in the PICTURE clause. The @ symbol must precede them, and a space must separate them from PICTURE codes.

Range Validation

The RANGE clause limits the values entered in a field to an inclusive range. It works with character, date, and numeric fields. When an improper value is entered, an alert box appears, displaying the correct range. Suppose a payroll system must insure that the number of hours worked is between 0 and 80. The GET statement is

```
@ 5,50 SAY "Hours: " GET wk_hours RANGE 0,80
```

If we specify only one bound, the other becomes the largest or smallest value for the variable type. For example, the following statement limits the registration date to today or earlier.

```
@ 12,5 SAY "Registration Date: " GET regdate RANGE ,DATE()
```

Note that a blank entry is acceptable since FoxPro treats it as a small value.

A drawback to RANGE is that pressing Enter after the alert box appears accepts the current value without verifying it again. Thus, invalid data could still enter the system.

VALID Clause

The VALID clause extends RANGE's capabilities. It uses logical expressions to test input values. The user cannot proceed to the next GET statement until the current VALID is TRUE. Even the Esc key has no effect if SET ESCAPE is OFF. Also, unlike RANGE, VALID does not accept an invalid entry if the user presses Enter again.

The following command uses VALID rather than RANGE to test a registration date.

```
@ 12,5 SAY "Registration Date: " GET regdate;
   VALID regdate <= DATE()
```

The program stays in the REGDATE field until the user enters a date of today or earlier. Pressing Enter again merely rechecks the entry.

Likewise, we can replace the RANGE test for hours worked with two VALID tests using AND. If either fails, the prompt stays in the GET field.

```
@ 5,50 SAY "Hours: " GET wk_hours;
   VALID wk_hours >= 0 .AND. wk_hours <= 80
```

Unlike RANGE, VALID does not display an alert box. The GET statement does, however, support an ERROR clause that prints a message in the upper right corner of the screen. It resembles an alert box, but we must define its contents manually as a string. It can contain any combination of text and variables. A typical example is:

```
maxhours = '80'
@ 5,50 SAY "Hours: " GET wk_hours;
   VALID wk_hours >= 0 .AND. wk_hours <= maxhours;
   ERROR 'Hours entered are outside the range 0 to'+;
      'maxhours+'.'
```

The valid values for input fields may not be obvious. We can reduce confusion over what to enter by adding a MESSAGE clause to the GET statement. It appears on the bottom screen line when the cursor is in the GET field and SET STATUS is ON. An example of its use for hours worked is:

```
maxhours = '80'
@ 5,50 SAY  "Hours: " GET wk_hours;
   VALID wk_hours >= 0 .AND. wk_hours <= maxhours;
   ERROR 'Hours entered are outside the range 0 to'+;
         maxhours+'.';
   MESSAGE 'HOURS WORKED MUST BE BETWEEN 0-'+maxhours
```

```
                         TIP
For consistency, if you use a MESSAGE or ERROR clause in
one field, use it in all of them.
```

VALID can also check discrete values. For example, we can use it to verify that
the report destination is F, P, or S. A RANGE check is obviously inappropriate
here.

```
@ 23,0 SAY 'Output to (F)ile, (P)rinter or (S)creen';
       GET outpdest PICTURE '!' DEFAULT 'P';
       VALID outpdest $ 'FPS'
READ
```

We can also use lists of strings. The following statements test for selected state
abbreviations. Note the use of single quotation marks around individual values
and double quotation marks around the entire list.

```
@ 12,5 SAY 'Enter State: ' GET state PICTURE '!!';
       DEFAULT 'PA' VALID STATE $ "'PA''NY''NJ''DE''MD'"
READ
```

```
                         TIP
Use VALID when the acceptable values are not sequential or
when you must guarantee correct input. Use RANGE for se-
quential values and when exceptions are allowed.
```

VALID can also compare input fields against memory variables and database
fields. An application that uses constants in VALID expressions risks obsoles-
cence if they change. A better programming practice is to store them in a
database or memory variable file.

The arguments for storing validation values in files are similar to those for
default values. In fact, you could use the same file. The following command
sequence uses memory variable file DEFAULTS.MEM to hold constants for
the report destination prompt. It stores the default value for OUTPDEST as
OUTPDEFLT. It also stores the validation check value as DESTINATNS.

```
* Storing validation constants in memory files
* Retrieve memory variables
  RESTORE FROM defaults ADDITIVE
* Prompt for report output destination
  @ 23,0 SAY 'Output to (F)ile, (P)rinter or (S)creen' ;
         GET outpdest PICTURE '!' DEFAULT outpdeflt ;
         VALID outpdest $ destinatns
  READ
  ENDDO
```

TIP

Unless a validation constant will never change, store it in a way that allows updates. Memory variable files are a good repository.

We may also validate fields against others in the same database. Suppose a program collects personal information from job applicants. Common sense suggests that the date they left their last employer must be later than their birthdate. However, the computer has no inherent common sense. We can provide some explicitly by using logic like the following:

```
* Validating against other fields
*     Prompts for three dates.
*     Uses a VALID clause to force the second
*     date to follow the first one.

* Define defaults for all dates as empty fields
birthdate = {}
lastemplr = {}
today     = {}

* Clear screen and prompt for dates
CLEAR
@ 5,10 SAY 'Enter birth date            ' GET birthdate ;
       PICTURE '@D' ;
       VALID m->birthdate <= DATE()
@ 7,10 SAY 'Enter last employment date ' GET lastemplr ;
       PICTURE '@D' VALID m->birthdate <= m->lastemplr .AND. ;
       m->lastemplr <= DATE()
@ 9,10 SAY 'Enter current date          ' GET today ;
       PICTURE '@D' VALID m->today <= DATE()
READ
```

Unfortunately, this program could fail. The reason is that all three GET statements fall under the same READ, and users can move between input fields before completing it. Thus they can change BIRTHDATE after entering LASTEMPLR. If they then press PgDn to exit the READ before the cursor moves into the LASTEMPLR field, the program would not detect an error. We must be aware of the many ways to exit a READ if we want to validate data thoroughly.

An alternate solution provides a separate READ for each GET or group of GETs. We can emphasize the grouping by dividing the entry screen into areas. The GET statements in each area would fall under a single READ. GETs in an area can then safely use entries from previous ones without any concern about changes.

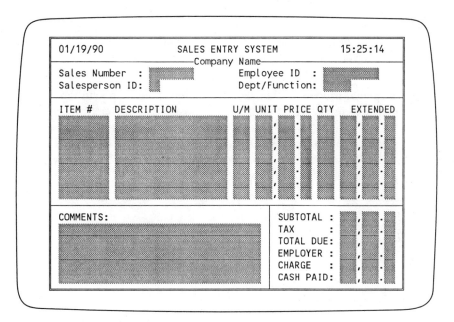

Figure 3-1. Sales entry screen.

Figure 3-1 shows a sales system that divides inputs into five READ groups. Lines separate them visually.

HINT
Try to group input fields logically even if it is not required for validation.

The user must complete one section before proceeding to the next. Thus he or she cannot return to the middle block to change order information after reaching the one asking for the payment method.

Validating fields in the first area of Figure 3-1 could involve checking inputs against other files. For example, we may have a file of salespeople indexed by ID number. Similarly, we might have files of employees and departments. We can use such support files to validate entries in the main file. For example, the program should reject nonexistent salesperson IDs or department numbers.

We verify an employee ID by performing a LOCATE, SEEK, or FIND in the support file. However, we cannot reduce the search to a simple logical test. Fortunately, we can extend the VALID clause with a User Defined Function (UDF).

A UDF is a special procedure that returns a value. Thus, it resembles FoxPro's built-in functions. For VALID clauses, we must create a function that returns TRUE or FALSE. Suppose we write a UDF to search the supporting database. If it finds the value, it returns TRUE. Otherwise, it returns FALSE. We can now call it from the VALID clause. Program 3-7 uses the first block of the point of sale screen to demonstrate this approach.

```
* Program 3-7
* Uses User Defined Functions (UDFs) to validate
* entries in first block of point of sale screen
*
SET TALK OFF
CLEAR
found = .F.

* Define database areas
SELECT 1
USE sales INDEX sales
SELECT 2
USE salesper INDEX salesper
SELECT 3
USE employee INDEX employee
SELECT 4
USE depart INDEX depart
SELECT 5
USE costcntr INDEX costcntr

* Create entry screen
CLEAR
@  1, 0 TO 23,78 DOUBLE
@  3, 1 TO  3,77
@  6, 1 TO  6,77
@ 16, 1 TO 16,77
@ 20, 1 TO 20,77
@ 17,40 TO 19,40
@  2, 3 SAY DATE()
@  2,30 SAY "SALES ENTRY SYSTEM"
@  2,70 SAY TIME()
@  4, 3 SAY "Ticket Number:"
@  5, 3 SAY "Salesperson   :"
@  4,40 SAY "Employee ID   :"
@  5,40 SAY "Dept/Function:"
@  7, 3 SAY "ITEM #      DESCRIPTION        U/M PRICE"+;
            "  QTY EXTENDED  &&U/M is Unit of Measure
```

```
@ 16,42 SAY "SUBTOTAL :"
@ 17,42 SAY "TAX      :"
@ 18,42 SAY "TOTAL DUE:"
@ 19,42 SAY "EMPLOYER :"
@ 20,42 SAY "CHARGE   :"
@ 21,42 SAY "CASH PAID:"
@ 16,42 SAY "COMMENTS:"

* Ask for a record number to edit
SELECT 1
recn = 1
@ 24,5 SAY "Enter a record number between 1 and " + ;
      LTRIM(STR(RECCOUNT(),5)) ;
      GET recn RANGE 1,RECCOUNT()
READ
@ 24,0

* Load memory variables from selected record
GOTO recn
SCATTER MEMVAR

* Print ticket number
@ 4,19 SAY m->ticket

* Define GET statements for first block
@ 5,19 GET m->sale_id VALID SALECK() ;
      ERROR "Invalid Salesperson"
@ 4,50 GET m->empl_id VALID EMPLCK() ;
      ERROR "Invalid Employee"
@ 5,50 GET m->dept_no VALID DEPTCK() ;
      ERROR "Invalid Department"
READ

* Has this record been updated?
IF UPDATED()

  * Update/Ignore this record
  modrec = 'Y'
  @ 24,0 SAY "Update this record? [Y|N]" GET modrec ;
        PICTURE 'Y'
  READ
  IF modrec = 'Y'
    GATHER MEMVAR
  ENDIF
ENDIF

RETURN

FUNCTION SALECK
* Checks salesperson file for valid ID
  SELECT 2
  SEEK m->sale_id
```

```
* FOUND is .T. if salesperson record found
  found = .NOT. EOF()
  SELECT 1
RETURN found

FUNCTION EMPLCK
* Checks employee file for valid ID
  SELECT 3
  SEEK m->empl_id
* FOUND is .T. if employee record found
  found = .NOT. EOF()
  SELECT 1
RETURN found

FUNCTION DEPTCK
* Checks department file for valid number
  SELECT 4
  SEEK m->dept_no
* FOUND is .T. if department record found
  found = .NOT. EOF()
  SELECT 1
RETURN found

* End of program
```

Program 3-7. Using UDFs in VALID Expressions

> **EXERCISE**
> All the functions in Program 3-7 are similar. By adding a few
> parameters, you can replace them with one general function.
> Write it.

VALID clauses can also help prevent duplicate keys. Every record in a database should have a unique key. In fact, it provides the only way to retrieve a record. A key can consist of one field or a group of fields. For example, Social Security number might provide a unique key for tracking people. However, last name by itself is insufficient (since there are usually many Smiths, Joneses, and Browns).

Program 3-8 is a simple database that uses two indexes to help a hospital receptionist locate patients. The first keys on Social Security number (SSN) to prevent duplicate entries. The second uses the patient's name to provide easier searching.

```
* Program 3-8
* Uses VALID to prevent duplicate records

CLEAR
SET TALK OFF
SET EXACT OFF

* Initialize memory variables
validrec = .F.
recn = 0
mode = 'E'

* Define database and indexes in area 1
SELECT 1
USE patient INDEX pat_ssn,pat_name
* Overall loop
  DO WHILE mode # 'Q'
  GOTO TOP

  * Display entry screen
    DO DOSCREEN

  * Edit or append record or quit
    @ 24,5 SAY "Edit or Append Record or Quit [E|A|Q] " ;
          GET mode PICTURE '!' VALID mode $ "AEQ"
    READ
    @ 24,0

  * Quit program
    IF mode = 'Q'
      CLEAR
      EXIT
    ENDIF

  * Edit mode
    IF mode = 'E'

    * Cannot edit if database is empty
      IF RECCOUNT() = 0
        @ 24,0
        @ 23,79
        WAIT "There are no records in this database.  "+;
            "Press any key to continue."
        EXIT
      ENDIF

    * Prompt for Social Security number (SSN) or last name
      search = SPACE(15)
      @ 24,0
      @ 24,5 SAY "Enter SSN (XXX-XX-XXXX) or Last Name" ;
            GET search PICTURE  "@15!"
```

```
      READ
      @ 24,0

*  Test if SSN or last name entered. If the fourth
*  character is a hyphen and the first three are
*  numeric, entry was an SSN, not a name.
      IF SUBSTR(search,4,1) = '-' .AND. ;
         VAL(SUBSTR(search,1,3)) > 0

   *  SSN entered, search for corresponding record
         SET INDEX TO pat_ssn
         SEEK TRIM(m->search)

   *  If SSN found, load data from record into memory
   *  variables and edit it. Otherwise, display NOT
   *  FOUND message.
         IF FOUND()
            SCATTER MEMVAR
            validrec = .T.
            DO REC_EDIT
         ELSE
            DO NOTFOUND
            validrec = .F.
         ENDIF
      ELSE

   *  Last name entered
   *  Search for corresponding record
         SET INDEX TO pat_name
         SEEK TRIM(m->search)

   *  If last name found, load data from record into
   *  memory variables and edit it.
   *  Otherwise, display NOT FOUND message.
         IF FOUND()
            SCATTER MEMVAR
            validrec = .T.
            DO REC_EDIT
         ELSE
            DO NOTFOUND
            validrec = .F.
         ENDIF
      ENDIF

   ELSE
   *  Append mode
   *  Initialize memory variables
   *  Perform record edit
      DO INIT_VAR
      validrec = .T.
      DO REC_EDIT
   ENDIF
```

```
       * Has this record been updated?
       IF UPDATED() .AND. validrec
       * Update/Ignore this record
         modrec = 'Y'
         @ 24,0
         IF MODE = 'E'
           @ 24,0 SAY "Update this record? [Y|N]" GET modrec;
                  PICTURE 'Y'
         ELSE
           @ 24,0 SAY "Add this record? [Y|N]" GET modrec;
                  PICTURE 'Y'
         ENDIF
         READ

       * Save record modifications in database
         IF modrec = 'Y'
           IF mode = 'A'
             APPEND BLANK
           ENDIF
           GATHER MEMVAR
         ENDIF
       ENDIF

     * End of main loop
     ENDDO

 * End of program
 RETURN

 PROCEDURE DOSCREEN
 * Draws data entry screen
 CLEAR
 @  1, 0 TO 12,78 DOUBLE
 @  3, 1 TO  3,77
 @  2, 3 SAY DATE()
 @  2,27 SAY "HOSPITAL PATIENT REGISTER"
 @  2,70 SAY TIME()
 @  4, 3 SAY "Social Security Number:"
 @  6, 3 SAY "Patient Name:         :"
 @  8, 3 SAY "Wing:"
 @  8,15 SAY "Floor:"
 @  8,30 SAY "Room:"
 @  8,45 SAY "Visitors Allowed:"
 @ 10, 3 SAY "Admitted on:"
 @ 10,40 SAY "Discharged on:"
 RETURN

 PROCEDURE INIT_VAR
 * Initializes variables for PATIENT. Make them
 * PUBLIC since they are initialized in a lower
 * level routine.
 PUBLIC admit,discharge,floor,fname,lname,room,ssn,;
        visitors,wing
```

```
      admit     = CTOD("  /  /  ")
      discharge = CTOD("  /  /  ")
      floor     = "  "
      fname     = SPACE(10)
      lname     = SPACE(15)
      room      = "   "
      ssn       = "   -  -    "
      visitors  = .F.
      wing      = " "
RETURN

PROCEDURE NOTFOUND
* Reports that the requested record was not found
   @ 24,0
   @ 23,79
   WAIT 'Patient '+search+' was not found. Press any key.'
RETURN

PROCEDURE REC_EDIT
* Edit current memory variables.
* Load the record into memory variables first,
* then copy them back to the database when done
   @  4,27 GET m->ssn        PICTURE '999-99-9999';
           VALID CHECKSSN();
           ERROR 'There is already a patient with this SSN.'
   @  6,27 GET m->fname      PICTURE '@!10'
   @  6,40 GET m->lname      PICTURE '@!15'
   @  8, 9 GET m->wing       PICTURE 'A';
           FUNCTION '!' RANGE 'A','E';
           MESSAGE 'Wing is a letter from A-E'
   @  8,22 GET m->floor      PICTURE 'A9' FUNCTION '!';
           MESSAGE 'Floor is a <letter><number> combination'
   @  8,36 GET m->room       PICTURE 'A99' FUNCTION '!';
           MESSAGE ;
              'Room is a <letter><number><number> combination'
   @  8,63 GET m->visitors   PICTURE 'L'
   @ 10,16 GET m->admit      PICTURE '@D';
           VALID m->admit <= DATE();
           ERROR 'Admission date cannot be a future date.'
   @ 10,55 GET m->discharge PICTURE '@D';
           VALID m->discharge <= DATE();
           ERROR 'Discharge date cannot be a future date.'
   READ
RETURN

FUNCTION CHECKSSN
* Checks whether the entered SSN already exists in the
* database. It saves the current record number in a memory
* variable so the pointer can be reset afterward.
* Then it performs a SEEK on the entered SSN. If the SSN
* is found (except for the edited record during edit mode),
* the function has detected a duplicate and returns
* FALSE to the VALID function. This forces the user
```

```
* to enter a new SSN.
  recn = RECNO()
  GOTO TOP
  SEEK m->ssn
  found = EOF()
  IF mode = 'E' .AND. m->ssn = ssn
    found = .T.
  ENDIF
  GOTO recn
RETURN found


* End of program
```

Program 3-8. Check for Duplicate Records

EXERCISE

A problem with Program 3-8 is that, when searching by last name, it shows only the first match. Modify it to display all matching records.

Calculated Fields

Database fields may be derivative rather than user-entered. Programs may calculate values internally or retrieve information from other files. For example, consider a simplified point of sale system for a video store.

It prompts the salesperson for the number of tapes in each rental category (1, 2, or 3 day). For overdue rentals, it also prompts for the number of days they are late. Using fixed charges, it then calculates the total cost as:

```
TOTAL = RENT1 * RENT1FEE +
        RENT2 * RENT2FEE +
        RENT3 * RENT3FEE +
        RENTLATE * LATEDAYS * LATEFEE
```

Calculating TOTAL each time we need it would slow system performance. Therefore, a calculated field makes sense.

In Program 3-9, the VALID clause for each GET calls function TOTAL. It performs calculations and displays information using fields in the READ group. Note that TOTAL does not validate the input. Instead, a RANGE clause restricts it to 0 through 6 for each rental period. TOTAL just does a running calculation of total rental cost. Note also that it always returns TRUE to satisfy VALID's requirement for a logical value.

```
* Program 3-9
* Video rental calculations using calculated fields

* Set environment
  SET TALK OFF
  SET STATUS OFF
  SET ESCAPE OFF
  CLEAR

* Default values
* All fees are total rental costs except for late fee
* which is a daily cost
  rent1fee = 1.50
  rent2fee = 2.25
  rent3fee = 2.50
  latefee  = 5.00
  mode     = 'E'
  total    = 0
  totaldue = 0

* Open database
  USE video INDEX video

* Draw screen
  DO DOSCREEN

* Main loop
  DO WHILE mode <> 'Q'

    * Edit or add record
    @ 24,0
    @ 24,5 SAY 'Edit or Add Record or Quit [E|A|Q]';
           GET mode PICTURE '!' VALID mode $ 'AEQ'
    READ
    @ 24,0

    * Exit loop if Q pressed
    IF mode = 'Q'
      EXIT
    ENDIF

    * If edit, prompt for customer name
    IF mode = 'E'
      IF RECCOUNT() = 0
        @ 24,0
        @ 23,79
        WAIT 'No records in this database. '+;
```

```
                      'Press any key to continue.'
            CANCEL
          ENDIF
          cust = '      '
          @ 24,0
          @ 24,5 SAY 'Enter Customer ID: ' GET cust;
                  PICTURE '!!!!!'
          READ
          @ 24,0

        * Search for customer
          SEEK TRIM(cust)
          IF FOUND()
            SCATTER MEMVAR
            validrec = .T.
            @ 14,30 SAY m->totaldue
            DO MOD_DATA
          ELSE
            DO NOTFOUND
            validrec = .F.
          ENDIF
        ELSE
          DO INIT_VAR
          validrec = .T.
          DO MOD_DATA
        ENDIF

      * Has this record been updated?
        IF UPDATED() .AND. validrec

        * Update/Ignore this record
          modrec = 'Y'
          @ 24,0
          IF mode = 'E'
            @ 24,0 SAY 'Update this record? [Y|N]';
                    GET modrec PICTURE 'Y'
          ELSE
            @ 24,0 SAY 'Add this record? [Y|N]';
                    GET modrec PICTURE 'Y'
          ENDIF
          READ
          IF modrec = 'Y'
            IF mode = 'A'
              APPEND BLANK
            ENDIF
            GATHER MEMVAR
          ENDIF
        ENDIF

    * End main loop
    ENDDO

* End program
```

```
RETURN

PROCEDURE DOSCREEN
* Creates data entry screen
  @  1, 2 TO 16,79
  @  2, 4 SAY DATE()
  @  2,30 SAY 'Your Video Store'
  @  2,70 SAY TIME()
  @  3, 3 TO 3,77
  @  4, 5 SAY 'Enter Video Rental Quantities'
  @  6,10 SAY 'Customer ID:    '
  @  7,10 SAY 'Date:    '
  @  9, 5 SAY 'Number of 1 Day Rentals: '
  @ 10, 5 SAY 'Number of 2 Day Rentals: '
  @ 11, 5 SAY 'Number of 3 Day Rentals: '
  @ 12, 5 SAY 'Number of Late Rentals:  '
  @ 12,45 SAY 'Days Late: '
  @ 14,15 SAY 'TOTAL COST:    '
  @ 19,30 SAY 'Press Esc when done'
RETURN

PROCEDURE INIT_VAR
* Initializes fields
  PUBLIC custid,latedays,rent1,rent2,rent3
  PUBLIC rentlate,renttotal,saledate
  custid    = SPACE(5)
  latedays  = 0
  rent1     = 0
  rent2     = 0
  rent3     = 0
  rentlate  = 0
  renttotal = 0
  saledate  = DATE()
RETURN

PROCEDURE MOD_DATA
* Modifies video record
  @  6,30 GET m->custid   PICTURE '@6!'
  @  7,30 GET m->saledate PICTURE '@D';
          VALID m->saledate <= DATE()
  @  9,35 GET m->rent1    RANGE 0,6 VALID TOTAL()
  @ 10,35 GET m->rent2    RANGE 0,6 VALID TOTAL()
  @ 11,35 GET m->rent3    RANGE 0,6 VALID TOTAL()
  @ 12,35 GET m->rentlate RANGE 0,6 VALID TOTAL()
  @ 12,55 GET m->latedays RANGE 0,99 VALID TOTAL()
  READ
RETURN

PROCEDURE NOTFOUND
* Reports requested record not found
  @ 24,0
  @ 23,79
  WAIT 'Customer '+custid+' was not found. '+;
```

```
      'Press any key.'
RETURN

FUNCTION TOTAL
* Even though this function is called from a VALID clause,
* it does not validate the input. Rather, it maintains
* a running total of all rentals while in the GET.
total    = m->rent1 * rent1fee
total    = m->total + m->rent2 * rent2fee
total    = m->total + m->rent3 * rent3fee
totaldue = m->total + m->rentlate * m->latedays * latefee
@ 14,30 SAY m->totaldue
RETURN .T.


* End of program
```

Program 3-9. Video Store Sales Using Calculated Fields

Program 3-9 sets ESCAPE to OFF. When a VALID clause fails, FoxPro blocks all characters except the Esc key. The program could look for it using the READKEY function and act on it. An alternative is to block it with SET ESCAPE OFF.

A more robust version displays the video's name. If the salesperson enters it, inconsistency is likely. (Is the title 'A Night at the Opera', 'Night at the Opera', or 'A Knight at the Opera'?) A better method is to assign an inventory number to each tape. Then, when the user enters the number, the program can find the name in a database. Program 3-10 uses a VALID statement to perform this step during the ID GET.

```
* Program 3-10
* Shows the use of calculated fields for both
* simple calculations and cross-referencing
* other files

* Set environment
  SET TALK OFF
  SET STATUS OFF
  SET ESCAPE OFF
  CLEAR

* Default values
  rent1fee = 1.50
  rent2fee = 2.25
  rent3fee = 2.50
  latefee  = 3.00
  mode     = 'E'
```

```
total   = 0
totaldue = 0
DECLARE MOVIEID(6),RENTDAYS(6),MOVIENAME(6),MOVIECOST(6)

* Open database
SELECT 1
USE video2 INDEX video2
SELECT 2
USE movies INDEX movies
SELECT 1

* Main loop
DO WHILE mode <> 'Q'

  * Draw screen
  CLEAR
  DO DOSCREEN

  * Edit or append record
    @ 24,0
    @ 24,5 SAY 'Edit or Append Record or Quit [E|A|Q]';
         GET mode PICTURE '!' VALID mode $ 'AEQ'
    READ
    @ 24,0

  * Exit loop if Q pressed
    IF mode = 'Q'
      EXIT
    ENDIF

  * If edit, prompt for customer name
    IF mode = 'E'
    * Edit record
      IF RECCOUNT() = 0
        @ 24,0
        @ 23,79
        WAIT 'No records in this database. '+;
             'Press any key to continue.'
        CANCEL
      ENDIF
      cust = '      '
      @ 24,0
      @ 24,5 SAY 'Enter Customer ID: ' GET cust;
           PICTURE '!!!!!'
      READ
      @ 24,0

    * Search for customer
      SEEK TRIM(cust)
      IF FOUND()
      * Customer found. Load rental data.
        SCATTER MEMVAR
        SCATTER FIELDS rent1,rent2,rent3,rent4,rent5,rent6;
```

```
        TO movieid
   SCATTER FIELDS days1,days2,days3,days4,days5,days6;
        TO rentdays
   SCATTER FIELDS cost1,cost2,cost3,cost4,cost5,cost6;
        TO moviecost
   SCATTER FIELDS name1,name2,name3,name4,name5,name6;
        TO moviename
   validrec = .T.
   @ 17,30 SAY m->totaldue PICTURE '$999.99'
   DO MOD_DATA
 ELSE
 * Customer not found.
 * Set variables to blanks or zeros.
   DO NOTFOUND
   FOR count = 1 TO 6
     movieid(count)  = SPACE(10)
     rentdays(count) = 0
   ENDFOR
   validrec = .F.
 ENDIF
ELSE
* Append record
 DO INIT_VAR
 validrec = .T.
 DO MOD_DATA
ENDIF

* Has this record been updated?
 IF UPDATED() .AND. validrec

   * Update/Ignore this record
   modrec = 'Y'
   @ 24,0
   IF mode = 'E'
     @ 24,0 SAY 'Update this record? [Y|N]';
            GET modrec PICTURE 'Y'
   ELSE
     @ 24,0 SAY 'Add this record? [Y|N]';
            GET modrec PICTURE 'Y'
   ENDIF
   READ
   IF modrec = 'Y'
   * Write customer information to existing record,
   * or a blank record for a new customer
     IF mode = 'A'
       APPEND BLANK
     ENDIF
     GATHER MEMVAR
     GATHER FROM movieid;
         FIELDS rent1,rent2,rent3,rent4,rent5,rent6
     GATHER FROM rentdays;
         FIELDS days1,days2,days3,days4,days5,days6
     GATHER FROM moviecost;
```

```
            FIELDS cost1,cost2,cost3,cost4,cost5,cost6
        GATHER FROM moviename;
            FIELDS name1,name2,name3,name4,name5,name6
      ENDIF
    ENDIF
  * End main loop
  ENDDO

* End program
RETURN

PROCEDURE DOSCREEN
* Creates data entry screen
  @  1, 2 TO 16,79
  @  2, 4 SAY DATE()
  @  2,30 SAY 'Your Video Store'
  @  2,70 SAY TIME()
  @  3, 3 TO 3,77
  @  4, 5 SAY 'Enter Video Rental Quantities'
  @  6,10 SAY 'Customer ID:   '
  @  7,10 SAY 'Date:         '
  @  9,10 SAY 'MOVIE ID        # DAYS       Cost       Name'
  @ 10, 8 SAY '1'
  @ 11, 8 SAY '2'
  @ 12, 8 SAY '3'
  @ 13, 8 SAY '4'
  @ 14, 8 SAY '5'
  @ 15, 8 SAY '6'
  @ 17,15 SAY 'TOTAL COST:    '
  @ 19,30 SAY 'Press Esc when done'
RETURN

PROCEDURE INIT_VAR
* Initializes fields
  PUBLIC custid,latedays,rent1,rent2,rent3
  PUBLIC rentlate,renttotal,saledate
  custid = SPACE(5)
  saledate = DATE()
  FOR count = 1 TO 6
    movieid(count) = SPACE(10)
    rentdays(count) = 0
  ENDFOR
  renttotal = 0
RETURN

PROCEDURE MOD_DATA
* Modifies video record
  @  6,30 GET m->custid   PICTURE '@6!'
  @  7,30 GET m->saledate PICTURE '@D';
          VALID m->saledate <= DATE()
  FOR count = 1 TO 6
    @ 9+count,10 GET movieid(count)  PICTURE '9999999999';
                 VALID movie()
```

```
       @ 9+count,25 GET rentdays(count) PICTURE '99' ;
                VALID total()
      IF mode = 'E'
        @ 9+count,38 SAY moviecost(count) PICTURE '$999.99'
        @ 9+count,48 SAY moviename(count) PICTURE '@S28'
      ENDIF
   ENDFOR
   READ
RETURN

PROCEDURE NOTFOUND
* Prints a message if customer is not found
   @ 24,0
   @ 23,79
   WAIT 'Customer '+custid+' was not found. '+;
        'Press any key.'
RETURN

FUNCTION MOVIE
* Locates movie name
   rrow = ROW()
   SELECT 2
   SEEK movieid(rrow - 9)
   IF FOUND()
     @ rrow,48 SAY LEFT(moviename,28)
     moviename(rrow-9) = moviename
   ENDIF
   SELECT 1
RETURN .T.

FUNCTION TOTAL
* Even though this function is called from a VALID
* clause, it does not validate the input. Rather
* it just recalculates the total cost of the rentals.
totaldue = 0
FOR count = 1 TO 6
   DO CASE
     CASE rentdays(count) = 1
       rent = rent1fee
     CASE rentdays(count) = 2
       rent = rent2fee
     CASE rentdays(count) = 3
       rent = rent3fee
     OTHERWISE
       rent = latefee * rentdays(count)
   ENDCASE
   IF count = ROW() - 9
     @ ROW(),38 SAY rent PICTURE '$999.99'
     moviecost(ROW()-9) = rent
   ENDIF
   totaldue = m->totaldue + m->rent
ENDFOR
@ 17,30 SAY m->totaldue PICTURE '$999.99'
```

```
RETURN .T.

* End of program
```

Program 3-10. Using Calculated Fields for Computations
and Cross-References

We could further extend the system to include routines to log out videos and maintain inventory. Other fields could contain information on actors, type of movie, year released, director, or awards. You could even provide customers with access to this database to help them select videos.

```
┌─────────────────────────────────────────────────────────┐
│                          TIP                            │
│  Note how easy it would be to integrate a bar code       │
│  system into an application that already uses a unique   │
│  identifier such as the movie ID in this example.        │
└─────────────────────────────────────────────────────────┘
```

Control Objects

FoxPro has the following special object types (or *control objects*):
- check boxes
- invisible buttons
- lists
- popups
- pushbuttons
- radio buttons
- text editing regions

Before discussing each separately, we consider their common features.

Normally, moving the cursor into a GET field during a READ enables its control object. However, we can display objects without letting the user change them by including the DISABLE clause. For example, the following line displays a check box for sales tax, but disables access to it.

```
@ 11, 3 GET sales_tax FUNCTION '*C \<SALES TAX' DISABLE
```

```
┌─────────────────────────────────────────────────────────┐
│                         HINT                            │
│  The DISABLE option lets the programmer control which    │
│  fields a user can modify based on prior selections      │
│  without reformatting the input screen or changing the   │
│  options displayed.                                      │
└─────────────────────────────────────────────────────────┘
```

As with standard GET statements, we can include a message that appears centered on the bottom screen line. (The SET MESSAGE TO command can change the position.) The following command displays a message when the cursor reaches the sales tax check box.

```
@ 11, 3 GET sales_tax FUNCTION '*C \<SALES TAX' ;
    MESSAGE ' Select this box if sales tax is due'
```

Although we can use a VALID clause with control objects, one is seldom needed for validation since the selections are already limited. Rather, a VALID clause usually calls a UDF to process the selection further. It could even perform a complex validation of other data.

The WHEN clause tests a logical expression to decide whether to activate a control. It is often used to determine which ones are appropriate, based on previous user input. The following line displays the sales tax check box for Pennsylvania customers only.

```
@ 11, 3 GET sales_tax FUNCTION '*C \<SALES TAX' ;
    WHEN m->state = 'PA'
```

Finally, the COLOR and COLOR SCHEME options temporarily override the default colors used by @...GET. COLOR SCHEMEs are predefined sets of 10 color pairs (foreground and background). Alternately, we can use the COLOR clause to custom define a scheme. A particular object uses only certain pairs (see Table 3-3).

Table 3-3. Color Pairs Used by @...GET Control Objects

Pair	Check Box	Invisible Button	List	Popup	Push-button	Radio Button	Text Edit Region
1	N/A	N/A	N/A	N/A	N/A	N/A	N/A
2	N/A	N/A	N/A	N/A	N/A	N/A	N/A
3	N/A	N/A	N/A	N/A	N/A	N/A	N/A
4	N/A	N/A	N/A	N/A	N/A	N/A	N/A
5	Message	N/A	Message	Message	Message	Message	Message
6	Selected	N/A	Selected	Selected	Selected	Selected	Selected
7	Hot Key	N/A	N/A	Hot Key	Hot Key	Hot Key	N/A
8	N/A	N/A	N/A	N/A	N/A	N/A	N/A
9	Enabled	Enabled	Enabled	Enabled	Enabled	Enabled	Enabled
10	Disabled	Disabled	Disabled	Disabled	Disabled	Disabled	Disabled

Check Boxes

Check boxes appear as options each preceded by a pair of square brackets. They are useful for logical (true/false) conditions or other binary states. The GET field is set to 1 if the check box is selected (.T.) and 0 if not (.F.). A window can contain any number of check boxes, and the user can select one or all of them.

We define check boxes with the FUNCTION '*C' clause or the PICTURE '@*C' clause. A space and the box's label must follow. Each GET statement defines a single box.

Invisible Buttons

The oddly-named invisible button is not the latest fad in high-technology sewing or the key to mending the Invisible Man's clothes. Rather it simply defines an area on the screen or in a window. We can place text over it; selecting it highlights the text. We define an invisible button with the FUNCTION '*I' clause or the PICTURE '@*I' clause.

Popups

We can create a popup menu from a list of options or an array (using a FROM clause). This control does not open the popup immediately. Rather, it displays the current or default element in a box with single line top and left borders and double line bottom and right borders. Only when we select the box does the popup expand.

We define a popup by starting the FUNCTION clause with '^' or the PICTURE clause with '@^'. A space and the list of option prompts (separated by semicolons) must follow. It cannot reference an array or an existing popup. For example, the following command creates a popup with five options.

```
@5,5 GET car FUNCTION '^ HONDA;TAURUS;SATURN;ACURA;CIERA'
```

Lists

Although M in a FUNCTION clause of a standard @...GET lets the user select from a list, only one option appears at a time. We can use the list control to display multiple options in a scrollable window. There are two approaches: referencing the values in an array and using a previously defined popup window. Lists do not generally require a special FUNCTION or PICTURE clause, but you must use the FUNCTION '&' or PICTURE '@&' to terminate the READ upon selection.

Lists use a FROM clause to identify an array or POPUP to reference a popup. With a one-dimensional array, each row corresponds to an option. With a two-dimensional array, options are loaded by element number (read across the columns one row at a time). If we use a popup, it defines the list's contents.

Pushbuttons

Pushbuttons initiate actions. For example, they can provide alternate ways to exit a window such as OK, CANCEL, or SAVE. The text appears inside angle brackets. We define a pushbutton by starting a FUNCTION clause with '*' or a PICTURE clause with '@*'. A space and the button's text follow.

Radio Buttons

Radio buttons come into play when users must select one and only one option from a group. Furthermore, they should be able to change their selection easily. The buttons work like the ones traditionally used in car radios. Selecting one releases any prior selection immediately. A pair of parentheses appears ahead of each prompt. A bullet inside them indicates the selected button.

We define a radio button by starting a FUNCTION clause with '*R' or a PICTURE clause with '@*R'. A space and the button's text follow.

Special Features of Buttons, Boxes, and Lists

The control objects just described support many special features (see Table 3-4 for a summary). Definitions can include them singly or in combinations.

Table 3-4. Special Features of Control Objects

		— Individual Object Features —					
Control	Hot Key	Disable	Default	Escape	Range	Size	Default
Check box	X	X				X	X
Invisible button		X				X	X
List					X	X	X
Popup	X	X			X	X	X
Pushbutton	X	X	X	X		X	X
Radio button	X	X				X	X
Text edit region						X	X

Terminate or Non-Terminate

Except for pushbuttons, controls do not terminate a READ when a selection is made (see Table 3-5). However, by adding the T (terminate) option to a FUNCTION definition, we can force this to occur. For example, we can insure that the user selects only one option from a popup by putting T after ^ as in:

```
@ 5,5 GET car FUNCTION '^T HONDA;TAURUS,SATURN;ACURA;CIERA'
```

In contrast, adding the N (non-terminate) option insures that selecting any button or box will not terminate the READ.

Table 3-5. Control Object Syntax

Control	Function Code	Additional Function Options
Check box	*C	N - Non-terminating (default) T - Terminating
Invisible button	*I	N - Non-terminating (default) T - Terminating H - Horizontal V - Vertical (default)
List		N - Non-terminating (default) T - Terminating
Popup	^	N - Non-terminating (default) T - Terminating
Pushbutton	*	N - Non-terminating T - Terminating (default) H - Horizontal V - Vertical (default)
Radio button	*R	N - Non-terminating (default) T - Terminating H - Horizontal V - Vertical (default)
Text edit region	N/A	I - Centered J - Right justified

Hot Keys

Most buttons and boxes support hot keys. To define one, precede it with the characters ' \<'. Hot keys are inactive when the cursor is not in a control object field. However, once an object that supports them is active in a READ group, all hot keys are active. Therefore, we must select characters carefully to avoid duplication. For example, we can define hot keys for a popup with:

```
@ 5,5 GET car FUNCTION;
      '^T \<HONDA;\<TAURUS;\<SATURN;\<ACURA;\<CIERA'
```

The first letters of each option (H, T, S, A, and C) are the hot keys.

Disabling Buttons

All controls that support hot keys also support the disabling of individual buttons. To disable one, precede it with a double slash, as in:

```
@ 5,5 GET car FUNCTION;
        '^T \<HONDA;\<TAURUS;\\SATURN;\<ACURA;\<CIERA'
```

Here SATURN is disabled (examine the list carefully!), as it has \\ in front of it, not \<. We can thus preserve the screen's appearance and structure when some options are unavailable.

Note that we can also disable the entire GET for any control type with the DISABLE clause, as in:

```
@ 5,5 GET car FUNCTION;
        '^T \<HONDA;\<TAURUS;\\SATURN;\<ACURA;\<CIERA' ;
        DISABLE
```

Default and Escape Buttons

The pushbutton control supports default and escape buttons. If we precede a button with \!, the user can select it by simply pressing Ctrl-Enter. Similarly, he or she can select one preceded with \? by pressing the Esc key.

Defining Multiple Buttons

Some controls allow multiple instances within a single GET. Just put a semicolon between them. One by itself produces a blank control. For example, the clause '*I ;;;' generates four invisible buttons. When multiple controls occur, the default is to arrange them vertically. However, an H immediately after the specifier (as in '*IH ;;;' for invisible buttons) makes FoxPro arrange them horizontally.

Ranges in Arrays

When an array is involved, as with lists and popups, we need not use all of it. The RANGE clause defines a subset using two parameters, the first element and the number of elements. It selects elements by number.

Sizing Controls

All controls use the SIZE clause to define their appearance (Table 3-6). It may take up to three parameters. Each control uses them somewhat differently, but the general rules are:

- The first parameter is the control's height. Most controls default to one row. However, the invisible button (reasonably enough, given its strange name) defaults to zero (a truly invisible "invisible button"). With lists, the value includes the two lines occupied by the top and bottom borders. Popups ignore it.

- The second parameter is the control's width. The default is the widest button if the width is not set or is too small. With lists, the value includes the two columns occupied by the left and right borders. Popups use it only for the initial value box. The actual popup window is sized automatically according to its contents' widths.

- The third parameter is a separation factor. For vertical buttons, it is the number of rows to skip between them. For horizontal ones, it is the number of columns to skip. However, the text edit region uses this parameter for the number of characters that can be edited.

Table 3-6. Use of SIZE by Control Objects

SIZE <ExpN1>,<ExpN2>,<ExpN3>

Control Object	ExpN1	ExpN2	ExpN3
Check box	Height (always 1)*	Width (width of prompt)	
Invisible button	Height (0)	Width (0)	
List	Length in rows	Width in columns (longest option)	
Popup	Height (always 1)	Width in columns (longest option)	
Pushbutton	Height (always 1)	Width in columns	Space between options Rows if vertical, columns if horizontal
Radio button	Height	Width in columns (longest option)	Space between options Rows if vertical, columns if horizontal
Text edit region	Height	Width in columns	Number of characters to edit

*Values inside parentheses are defaults.

Defaults for Controls

We can initialize the GET field before executing READ. That value then becomes the default. An alternative is to use the DEFAULT clause to both define and initialize the default. READ ignores DEFAULT if the GET variable already exists.

Examples of Control Objects

Program 3-11 uses check boxes to prompt for payment method in order processing. Note the use of the T option to terminate the READ when a check box is selected. The sales tax box has a separate READ so the user cannot skip it before selecting a payment method.

We may provide a default for a check box by predefining the GET field; a zero value indicates 'not selected'. We can also define the FIELD in the GET statement with the DEFAULT clause as in:

```
CLEAR MEMORY
@ 1,3 GET sales_tax FUNCTION '*C \SALES TAX' DEFAULT .T.
READ
? m->sales_tax
```

All GET fields used with check boxes return 1 if they are selected, and 0 if not.

```
* Program 3-11
* Use of check boxes
  SET TALK OFF
  CLEAR

  @  0, 0,21,79 BOX
  @  2, 1 TO  2,78
  @  3,40 TO 20,40
  @ 10, 1 TO 10,39
  @ 12, 1 TO 12,39

  instruct = 'Use the Tab key to select a check box and '+;
             'highlight it. The space bar toggles the '+;
             'box on and off. The Enter key also toggles '+;
             'the box, but then exits the read. The '+;
             'Payment method section will not exit '+;
             'until one check box is toggled on.'
  @  3, 1 GET instruct SIZE 7,37 DISABLE
  @ 11, 3 GET sales_tax FUNCTION '*C \<SALES TAX' DEFAULT .T.
  READ

  @ 13, 1 SAY 'PAYMENT METHOD:'
  co_paid = 0
  cash    = 0
  check   = 0
  charge  = 0
  DO WHILE co_paid + cash + check + charge = 0
     @ 14, 3 GET co_paid FUNCTION '*CT Company Reimbursed'
     @ 15, 3 GET cash    FUNCTION '*CT Cash'
     @ 16, 3 GET check   FUNCTION '*CT Check'
     @ 17, 3 GET charge  FUNCTION '*CT MC/VISA'
```

```
      READ
   ENDDO
   ? 'Company Paid: '+IIF(co_paid=1,'YES','NO')
   ? '        Cash: '+IIF(cash=1,'YES','NO')
   ? '       Check: '+IIF(check=1,'YES','NO')
   ? '      Charge: '+IIF(charge=1,'YES','NO')

   * End of program
```

Program 3-11. Use of Check Boxes

Program 3-12 uses invisible buttons to select a payment method. The user picks one by clicking on it with the mouse or by highlighting it with the Tab key and pressing Enter. The program initializes the GET field to 0. Any other value activates the corresponding button when the READ begins.

```
   * Program 3-12
   * Use of invisible buttons
   SET TALK OFF
   CLEAR

   @  0, 0,21,79 BOX
   @  2, 1 TO  2,78
   @  3,40 TO 20,40
   @ 10, 1 TO 10,39
   @ 12, 1 TO 12,39

   instruct = 'Use the Tab key to select a check box and '+;
              'highlight it. The space bar and Enter key '+;
              'also toggle the box, but then exit the '+;
              'READ. The Method of Payment section will '+;
              'not exit until one check box is toggled on.'
   @  3, 1 GET instruct SIZE 7,37 DISABLE
   READ

   @ 13, 1 SAY 'METHOD OF PAYMENT:'
   meth_pay = 0
   DO WHILE meth_pay = 0
     @ 14, 3 SAY 'Company Reimbursed'
     @ 15, 3 SAY 'Cash'
     @ 16, 3 SAY 'Check'
     @ 17, 3 SAY 'MC/VISA'
     @ 14, 3 GET meth_pay FUNCTION '*IT ;;;' SIZE 1,20,0
     READ
   ENDDO

   DO CASE
```

```
      CASE meth_pay = 1
         ? 'Company Reimbursed'
      CASE meth_pay = 2
         ? 'Cash'
      CASE meth_pay = 3
         ? 'Check'
      CASE meth_pay = 4
         ? 'Charge'
   ENDCASE

   * End of program
```

Program 3-12. Use of Invisible Buttons

Program 3-13 creates a list from the array DATABASE. The user can press the Tab key to highlight the desired name, then Enter to select it.

```
   * Program 3-13
   * Select a database package from a list
     SET TALK OFF
     CLEAR

     DIMENSION database[10]
     database[1]  = 'FoxPro'
     database[2]  = 'Clipper'
     database[3]  = 'Quicksilver'
     database[4]  = 'dBASE'
     database[5]  = 'Focus'
     database[6]  = 'Oracle'
     database[7]  = 'Paradox'
     database[8]  = 'R:base'
     database[9]  = 'Alpha 4'
     database[10] = 'Reflex'

     =ASORT(database)

     @ 2,32 GET db FROM database SIZE 7,15 DEFAULT 1
     READ

     ? 'Selected database: ' + database[db]

   * End of program
```

Program 3-13. Select a Database Package from a List

Program 3-14 shows a popup list of disk types defined in an array mediatype. GET displays a box of the default size with double lines for the right and bottom borders. When it is selected, a popup appears displaying the options. The user presses the arrow keys to highlight and select a disk type.

```
* Program 3-14
* Using a popup to select a disk type
SET TALK OFF
CLEAR

DIMENSION mediatype[4]
mediatype[1]   = '360K  5.25"'
mediatype[2]   = '720K  3.5"'
mediatype[3]   = '1.2M  5.25"'
mediatype[4]   = '1.44M 3.5"'

@ 2,32 GET media FROM mediatype FUNCTION '^ ' DEFAULT 3
READ

? 'Selected media: ' + mediatype[media]

* End of program
```

Program 3-14. Using a Popup to Select a Disk Type

Program 3-15 uses pushbuttons to select among ways to exit a program.

```
* Program 3-15
* Using pushbuttons to exit a program
SET TALK OFF
CLEAR

* The first button is disabled
* The default button is 3
* Pressing Ctrl-Enter also selects 3
* Pressing Esc selects 5

@ 2,32 GET pushbutton DEFAULT 3 SIZE 1,1,0 FUNCTION   ;
    '* \\Save Files;\<Begin Timer;\!\<Do Program;' + ;
    '\<End Timer;\?\<Quit'
READ

? 'Selected pushbutton: ' + str(pushbutton,1)

* End of program
```

Program 3-15. Using Pushbuttons to Exit a Program

Program 3-16 uses radio buttons to choose the extension when listing files in the GETFILE command.

```
* Program 3-16
* Using radio buttons to make a selection
SET TALK OFF
CLEAR

DIMENSION ext[4]
ext[1] = 'DBF'
ext[2] = 'PRG'
ext[3] = 'MEM'
ext[4] = 'TXT'

@ 2,32 GET radiobuton DEFAULT 1 SIZE 1,1,0 FUNCTION ;
  '*RT DBF;PRG;MEM;TXT'
READ

filenm = GETFILE(ext[radiobuton],'Select a file')
IF EMPTY(filenm)
  ? 'No file selected.'
ELSE
  ? 'File Selected: ' + filenm
ENDIF

* End of program
```

Program 3-16. Using Radio Buttons to Make a Selection

Text Edit Region

The text edit region is a rectangle used to display and edit a memory variable, array element, database field, or memo field. It is actually an extension of the normal edit field, defined by using the @...EDIT command rather than @...GET. The only restriction is that the field must be of type character. All editing features (such as those found in the MODIFY COMMAND window) are available. Text is automatically word-wrapped and scrolls vertically if it overruns the available space.

The FUNCTION clause supports just two options. I centers text in the region, and J right-justifies it. The default is left-justified.

The NOMODIFY clause displays text from the EDIT variable in the defined region, but prohibits editing.

Tab and Ctrl-Tab normally save changes made to text, whereas Esc exits without saving them. However, the NOTAB option lets us use tabs in the edit region; Ctrl-Tab still exits the field.

The SCROLL clause makes FoxPro include scroll bars if the text field overruns the editing region. The arrow keys, PgUp, PgDn, Home, and End alone and with the Ctrl key still move the cursor, as does dragging the mouse.

The SIZE clause takes three numeric parameters. The first two define the region's height in rows and width in columns, respectively. The third one limits the total number of characters edited, beginning with the first character in the edit field.

Program 3-17 edits the memo field in the first record of database LENDER using a text edit region.

```
* Program 3-17
* Using a text edit region to edit memo fields
SET TALK OFF
CLEAR
CLOSE DATABASES
USE lender

@ 0,2 SAY 'Memo field editing using a text edit region.'
@ 2,5 SAY 'Use Ctrl-W to close memo'
@ 5,5 EDIT l_notes SIZE 5,40
READ

CLEAR
? 'The modified memo now reads:'
?
? l_notes

* End of program
```

Program 3-17. Using a Text Edit Region to Edit Memo Fields

READ Options

Most programmers think of READ as just the activator of a set of @...GET commands. However, it also has many powerful options.

First, a READ can span several windows. That is, it can activate @...GET commands in them. The GETs are still activated in the order in which the program defines them. READ, however, jumps from window to window during processing. If a GET is in a hidden window, READ activates it and brings it to the top. If it is in a released window, READ stops, ignoring subsequent GETs.

FoxPro has two clauses that execute when READ changes windows, namely DEACTIVATE and ACTIVATE. Before READ exits the current window, it checks for a DEACTIVATE. This clause includes a logical expression that must return .T. before READ can proceed. Often it calls a UDF to validate the fields in the current window. If the validation fails, the UDF returns .F..

ACTIVATE applies to activating a new window. The logical expression following it must return .T. before READ activates the window and proceeds with the next GET. For example, we may use ACTIVATE to check if a database is open before reading a field that might use it to validate input. If the database is not open, the ACTIVATE procedure could open it. As with DEACTIVATE, the logical expression could be a UDF as long as it returns a logical value.

We can nest READs up to four levels deep. One place where nesting is necessary is in a UDF called by the VALID clause of a READ. It may open a window to prompt the user for more information to validate the original field. In the window, a second READ activates more GET commands. That READ is nested within the first because it is still open.

Normally, a READ terminates when we try to move beyond the last GET or ahead of the first one. The CYCLE option makes FoxPro move instead from the last GET to the first one or vice versa. It usually appears with a terminating button (the T option). Ctrl-W or a TIMEOUT clause can also terminate the READ.

The TIMEOUT clause specifies how many seconds can elapse without user input before READ terminates. For example, to READ a group of GETs with a 60 second timeout, we use the command

```
READ CYCLE TIMEOUT 60
```

We can detect if the READ times out by checking the value returned by READKEY(). It returns 20 when a READ reaches the TIMEOUT setting.

READ supports both VALID and WHEN clauses. They work just like similar options in @...GET commands. However, when used with READ, they affect all pending GETs.

Normally a READ begins with the first GET defined. However, an OBJECT clause can tell FoxPro to begin with any pending GET. Just put its relative number (based on the order in which the program defines GETs) afterward. For example, to begin with the third GET, we would use the command

```
READ OBJECT 3 CYCLE TIMEOUT 60
```

> **HINT**
> If you use OBJECT to select a starting GET, use CYCLE to ensure that the ones before it are not ignored. Of course, Shift-Tab can return to the earlier GETs. But the user is more likely to press Enter upon completing each field, thus terminating the READ at the last GET.

Context Sensitive Help

A major recent addition to user interfaces is context sensitive help. It provides immediate, specific assistance on how to fill the current input field. Some implementations just describe the field. Others display values the user can choose. Context sensitive help may appear automatically when the cursor enters the field. Or it may require the user to press a key. This section reviews several ways to implement it.

Message Help

The easiest type of help to add uses the MESSAGE clause available in several commands. It prints a string on the line specified by SET MESSAGE TO when the cursor enters the input field. We can also specify the horizontal justification. By default, messages appear centered on the bottom row of the screen or window. The following commands show other options.

    SET MESSAGE TO 24 assigns line 24 for the message
    SET MESSAGE TO 20 LEFT assigns line 20 and specifies left alignment
    SET MESSAGE TO 22 RIGHT assigns line 22 and specifies right alignment

The message itself is a text string. However, it can include variables, as long as we represent them as strings. As with default values, we can store them in special records or a separate database file. Then we can edit them without changing the source code.

We discussed the MESSAGE clause earlier when describing GET statements. However, other menu-related commands (Table 3-7) also support it. The message should briefly describe the function of the highlighted option or menu choice.

Table 3-7. Commands That Support MESSAGE

Command	Purpose
@...GET	Enter a single value
@...PROMPT	Create a menu bar
DEFINE BAR	Define an option on a menu popup
DEFINE MENU	Define a menu bar
DEFINE PAD	Define a pad on a menu bar
DEFINE POPUP	Create a popup menu

TIP

If you use MESSAGE, use it for all input fields. Similarly, if some menus use MESSAGE, add it to all of them. The goal here is consistency. On the other hand, just because you use MES-SAGE with menus does not mean that you must use it with other inputs.

Help Windows

Another way to provide help uses FoxPro's ability to create and save windows. The first part of Program 3-18 creates two windows and saves them in file HELP.WIN. The second part simulates an input screen for an inventory system. The input fields use the windows stored in HELP.WIN for help information.

```
* Program 3-18
* Create and use a help window file
*
* First create two windows, one for PRODUCT ID and one
* for size

  CLEAR
  SET TALK OFF
* Define both windows
  DEFINE WINDOW prodid FROM 9,10 TO 18,49 ;
     TITLE 'PRODUCT ID';
     CLOSE FLOAT GROW SHADOW ZOOM
  DEFINE WINDOW size FROM 8,30 to 16,71 TITLE 'SIZE';
     CLOSE FLOAT GROW SHADOW ZOOM
```

```
* Define help text for product ID
  ACTIVATE WINDOW prodid
  @ 1,1 SAY 'The product ID is a 13 digit number.'
  @ 2,1 SAY 'It is located immediately below the'
  @ 3,1 SAY 'bar code label on each package.'
  @ 4,1 SAY 'Enter the full number. No letters,'
  @ 5,1 SAY 'spaces, or special characters are'
  @ 6,1 SAY 'allowed.'

* Define help text for size
  ACTIVATE WINDOW size
  @ 1,1 SAY 'This product comes in the following'
  @ 2,1 SAY 'sizes. No other entries are accepted.'
  @ 4,1 SAY '       6-S   7-S   8-S   9-S   10-S'
  @ 5,1 SAY '5-M   6-M   7-M   8-M   9-M   10-M'
  @ 6,1 SAY '       6-L   7-L   8-L   9-L   10-L'

* Check if window file already exists. If so, erase it
  IF FILE('help.win')
    ERASE help.win
  ENDIF

* Save window definitions
  SAVE WINDOW ALL TO help
  DEACTIVATE WINDOW ALL
  CLEAR WINDOWS

* Begin second part of program. It simulates a data entry
* screen using the two help windows.
  CLEAR
  prod_id = SPACE(13)
  size    = SPACE(4)

* Draw data entry screen
  @ 0, 0 TO 23,79
  @ 1,32 SAY 'INVENTORY ENTRY'
  @ 3, 5 SAY 'Product ID:'
  @ 5, 5 SAY 'Size:'

* Get product ID
  RESTORE WINDOW prodid FROM help
  ACTIVATE SCREEN
  @ 3,17 GET prod_id PICTURE '9999999999999'
  READ
  CLEAR WINDOWS

* Get product size
  RESTORE WINDOW size FROM help
  ACTIVATE SCREEN
  @ 5,17 GET size FUNCTION '!' PICTURE '#9-A';
```

```
         VALID VAL(LEFT(size,2)) > 4 .AND.;
               VAL(LEFT(size,2)) < 11 .AND.;
               RIGHT(size,1) $ 'SML'
      READ
      CLEAR WINDOWS

   * Other inputs would continue from here
     @ 7,5 SAY 'Other inputs would continue from here.'

   * End of program
```

Program 3-18. Saving and Using Help Windows

In Program 3-18, the help window appears as soon as the cursor moves into the input field. It stays open as long as the cursor remains there. Therefore, we do not need a special clause with the GET statements. A disadvantage of this method is that we must open each help window separately before a GET-READ statement pair. We cannot group all GETs under a single READ. So once we exit a field, we cannot easily return to edit it.

Invoking Context Sensitive Help with a Function Key

We may not always want help windows to appear automatically when the cursor enters input fields. Instead, we may want a special trigger key. ON KEY does the job. The command

```
      ON KEY = <ExpN> <command>
```

sets a trap for a specific key (ExpN is its ASCII value) during a READ operation. When the user presses that key, the command executes. Controls, punctuation marks, digits, letters, and other typewriter symbols form the first 256 ASCII values. They appear on the ASCII Chart in the System menu. Table 3-8 shows the values of nonprinting keys and key combinations. (This set is also called (IBM PC) *Extended ASCII.*)

The command to call procedure PROGHELP when the user presses the F1 key (a common assignment) is

```
      ON KEY = 315 DO PROGHELP
```

A drawback to using extended ASCII values is that they make programs difficult to read. For example, who except a fanatic would know that 315 is the F1 key? An alternative uses key labels (Table 3-9) for nonprinting keys. The form is

```
      ON KEY LABEL <key label> <command>
```

Table 3-8. Extended ASCII Values for Nonprinting Keys

ASCII Value	Corresponding Keys
272 - 281	Alt Q, W, E, R, T, Y, U, I, O, P
286 - 294	Alt A, S, D, F, G, H, J, K, L
300 - 306	Alt Z, X, C, V, B, N, M
315 - 324	F1 to F10 (function keys)
327	Home
328	Up
329	PgUp
331	Left
333	Right
335	End
336	Down
337	PgDn
338	Ins
339	Del
340 - 349	Shift-F1 to Shift-F10
350 - 359	Ctrl-F1 to Ctrl-F10
360 - 369	Alt-F1 to Alt-F10
370	Ctrl-PrtSc
371	Ctrl-Left
372	Ctrl-Right
373	Ctrl-End
374	Ctrl-PgDn
375	Ctrl-Home
376 - 387	Alt 1, 2, 3, 4, 5, 6, 7, 8, 9, 0, -, =
388	Ctrl-PgUp

Table 3-9. Key Labels for Nonprinting Keys

Key	Label
Alt-0 to Alt-9	Alt-0, Alt-1, Alt-2, ..., Alt-9
Alt-A to Alt-Z	Alt-A, Alt-B, ..., Alt-Z
Alt-F1 to Alt-F10	Alt-F1, Alt-F2, ..., Alt-F10
Backspace	Backspace
Ctrl-A to Ctrl-Z	Ctrl-A, Ctrl-B, ..., Ctrl-Z
Ctrl-End	Ctrl-end
Ctrl-F1 to Ctrl-F10	Ctrl-F1, Ctrl-F2, ..., Ctrl-F10
Ctrl-Home	Ctrl-home
Ctrl-Left	Ctrl-leftarrow
Ctrl-PgDn	Ctrl-pgdn
Ctrl-PgUp	Ctrl-pgup
Ctrl-Right	Ctrl-rightarrow
Del	Del
Down	Dnarrow
End	End
Enter	Enter
F1 to F10	F1, F2, ..., F10
Home	Home
Ins	Ins
Left	Leftarrow
PgDn	PgDn
PgUp	PgUp
Right	Rightarrow
Shift Tab	Backtab
Shift-F1 to Shift-F10	Shift-F1, Shift-F2, ..., Shift-F10
Tab	Tab
Up	Uparrow

The command to call procedure PROGHELP when the user presses the F1 key is now

```
ON KEY LABEL F1 DO PROGHELP
```

This version is more readable than the one based on an Extended ASCII value. Program 3-19 uses ON KEY LABEL to invoke PROGHELP. It opens a window to display a help message. Then it waits for a key press using WAIT before closing the help window and returning to the input prompt.

```
* Program 3-19
* Context sensitive help using a function key
*
* Shows the use of a function key to display a
* context sensitive help window

* Set environment
SET TALK OFF

* Redefine F1 as the help key
ON KEY LABEL F1 DO proghelp

* Define help windows
DEFINE WINDOW prodid FROM 9,10 TO 19,49 TITLE 'PRODUCT ID'
DEFINE WINDOW size FROM 8,30 to 18,71 TITLE 'SIZE'

* Initialize screen and input variables
CLEAR
prod_id = SPACE(13)
size    = SPACE(4)

* Draw data entry screen
@  0, 0 TO 20,79
@  1,32 SAY 'INVENTORY ENTRY'
@  3, 5 SAY 'Product ID:'
@  5, 5 SAY 'Size:'
@ 19,31 SAY 'Press F1 for help'

* Get product ID and size
@ 3,17 GET prod_id PICTURE '9999999999999'
@ 5,17 GET size FUNCTION '!' PICTURE '#9-A';
    VALID VAL(LEFT(size,2)) > 4 .AND.;
          VAL(LEFT(size,2)) < 11 .AND.;
          RIGHT(size,1) $ 'SML'
READ

* Other inputs would continue from here
@ 7,5 SAY 'Other inputs would continue from here.'

@ 21,79
```

```
WAIT
RETURN

PROCEDURE PROGHELP
DO CASE
  CASE VARREAD() = 'PROD_ID'
  * Define help text for product ID
    ACTIVATE WINDOW prodid
    @ 1,1 SAY 'The product ID is a 13 digit number.'
    @ 2,1 SAY 'It is located immediately below the'
    @ 3,1 SAY 'bar code label on each package.'
    @ 4,1 SAY 'Enter the full number. No letters,'
    @ 5,1 SAY 'spaces, or special characters are'
    @ 6,1 SAY 'allowed.'
    ?
    WAIT
    DEACTIVATE WINDOW prodid

  CASE VARREAD() = 'SIZE'
  * Define help text for size
    ACTIVATE WINDOW size
    @ 1,1 SAY 'This product comes in the following'
    @ 2,1 SAY 'sizes. No other entries are accepted.'
    @ 4,1 SAY '5-S    6-S    7-S    8-S    9-S    10-S'
    @ 5,1 SAY '5-M    6-M    7-M    8-M    9-M    10-M'
    @ 6,1 SAY '5-L    6-L    7-L    8-L    9-L    10-L'
    ?
    WAIT
    DEACTIVATE WINDOW size

  ENDCASE
RETURN

* End of program
```

Program 3-19. Using a Function Key to Display Help

> **EXERCISE**
> Combine the ON KEY features of Program 3-19 with the ability
> to save help windows in a WIN file shown in Program 3-18.

Using FoxPro's Built-In Context Sensitive Help Facility

FoxPro has a built-in help facility accessed by pressing the F1 key or by typing
HELP in the command window. When we invoke it, we actually tell FoxPro to

read a database file along with its corresponding memo file. The database has three fields. The first, TOPIC, is a character field containing the topic name (commands, functions, general information, interface topics, and system memory variables). The second, DETAILS, is a memo field containing the help text on the selected topic. The third field, CLASS, defines the help topic class and includes: Command, Function, General, Interface, and System Memory Variable. Table 3-10 lists the class codes used by FoxPro.

Table 3-10. Help File Class Codes

Abbreviation	Category
General	**General**
cf	Configuration
cm	Compatibility
em	Error Messages
wn	What's New
Command	**Command**
db	Database
eh	Event Handlers
en	Environment
er	Errors and Debugging
fm	File Management
in	Interface
km	Keyboard and Mouse
mp	Menus and Popups
mu	Muitiuser
mv	Memory Variables and Arrays
pe	Program Execution
pr	Printing
sp	Structured Programming
sq	SQL
tm	Text Merge
wi	Windows
Function	**Functions**
ch	Character
db	Database
dc	Data Conversion
dt	Date and Time
en	Environment
fm	File Management
km	Keyboard and Mouse
ll	Low-Level
lo	Logical
mp	Menus and Popups
mu	Multiuser

Table 3-10. Help File Class Codes (cont'd.)

Abbreviation	Category
mv	Memory Variables and Arrays
nu	Numeric
pr	Printing
wi	Windows
Sysmemvar	**System Memory Variables**
da	Desk Accessories
in	Interface
pr	Printing
sn	System Menu Names
tm	Text Merge
Interface	**Interface**
di	Dialogs
ge	General
me	Menus
wi	Windows

We can use any field (including class codes) to search for or limit information in the help window. The SET HELPFILTER command can filter topics in many ways. Once the filter is set, pressing F1 or selecting HELP from the SYSTEM pulldown menu displays topics that satisfy it. The most restrictive filter limits help to a specific topic, class category, or class code, as in:

```
SET HELPFILTER TO topic = 'DEFINE WINDOW'
SET HELPFILTER TO 'Sysmemvar' $ class
SET HELPFILTER TO 'db' $ class
```

The first example limits help to a single command, the second displays only topics related to system memory variables, and the third includes topics related to databases.

A less restrictive filter searches for a keyword. Suppose we want all topics related to windows. We can use the filter

```
SET HELPFILTER TO 'WINDOWS' $ topic
```

It restricts help to topics containing the word WINDOWS. Of course, some commands related to windows may not contain the word in the topic field. A more inclusive approach uses the class code wi.

```
SET HELPFILTER TO 'wi' $ class
```

We can even search the help text for specific words or phrases. A thorough search for all topics related to windows might use the filter

```
SET HELPFILTER TO 'WINDOWS' $ details
```

When a help filter is no longer needed, we can restore the full list by issuing the command

```
SET HELPFILTER TO
```

or by including the keyword AUTOMATIC in the original filter.

```
SET HELPFILTER AUTOMATIC TO 'wi' $ class
```

HINT

In an application with a custom help file, we may want to restrict topics to those related to currently visible fields. An easy way to do this is to assign a class code to variables from each screen. Then when we define the help topics, we assign each a class code. When the program executes, it can change SET HELPFILTER to the new code before starting a new screen.

Still another FoxPro object is the SEE ALSO popup list. FoxPro automatically determines whether to activate it and what commands and functions to include in it by examining the memo field DETAILS.

If the memo field begins a new line with the text string

```
SEE ALSO:
```

FoxPro assumes that the subsequent text lists other topics in the help file. It parses the list using commas as separators between topics. For example, in a financial application, we may have a help topic NPV (Net Present Value). The SEE ALSO: line might refer to related topics such as

```
SEE ALSO: FV, BALANCE, INTEREST, PERIODS
```

The format of this line has the following restrictions:
- SEE ALSO: must begin it.
- All text is case insensitive.
- The colon after ALSO is mandatory.
- Commas must separate topics.

Now that we understand the structure of the help database, we can use the built-in facility to read our own files. First we must create a database containing at least two fields. The first must be a character field called TOPICS containing the help topic names (perhaps the names of the database fields). The second must be a memo field called DETAILS. The third field is optional. When included, it must be called CLASS and contains codes we define to help filter the topics. We can define other fields for purposes such as default values or messages.

```
                    ┌─────────────────────────────────────────────┐
                    │                    HINT                     │
                    │ The help file is a good place to store default or validation values │
                    │ if it has one record per field.             │
                    └─────────────────────────────────────────────┘
```

After creating the database, enter one record per entry field. Use the memo field for help text. Unlike our previous help windows, it is unlimited in size since we can scroll it.

Add the following command near the beginning of the program. It redefines the file used by FoxPro's help facility as INVHELP.DBF.

```
SET HELP TO invhelp
```

Next put an ON KEY statement before the first GET statement to trap the F1 key. The following statement executes the procedure DISPHELP when the user presses F1.

```
ON KEY = 315 DO DISPHELP
```

Within DISPHELP, we must determine where the cursor is before calling HELP. The SYS(18) function returns the name of the current input field during a READ. We can set the help topic to it with the statement

```
SET TOPIC TO SYS(18)
```

Now a simple call to HELP displays the appropriate text from memo file INVHELP.FPT. Before the program ends, remember to restore FoxPro's standard help file. Also turn off the SET TOPIC TO prompt. Program 3-20 uses the help facility in an inventory example.

```
* Program 3-20
* Context sensitive help using FoxPro's help facility
*
* Shows the use of function key F1 to display a context
* sensitive help window based on the built-in help
* facility

* Set environment
SET TALK OFF
```

```
* Redefine help file invoked with F1 key
  SET HELP TO invhelp

* Initialize screen and input variables
  CLEAR
  prod_id = SPACE(13)
  size    = SPACE(4)

* Draw data entry screen
  @  0, 0 TO 20,79
  @  1,32 SAY 'INVENTORY ENTRY'
  @  3, 5 SAY 'Product ID:'
  @  5, 5 SAY 'Size:'
  @ 19,31 SAY 'Press F1 for help'

* Get product ID and size
* Use ON KEY to call procedure DISPHELP when F1 is pressed
  ON KEY = 315 DO DISPHELP
  @ 3,17 GET prod_id PICTURE '9999999999999'
  @ 5,17 GET size FUNCTION '!' PICTURE '#9-A';
      VALID VAL(LEFT(size,2)) > 4 .AND.;
            VAL(LEFT(size,2)) < 11 .AND.;
            RIGHT(size,1) $ 'SML'
  READ

* Other inputs would continue from here
  @ 7,5 SAY 'Other inputs would continue from here.'

  @ 21,79
  WAIT

* Restore normal FoxPro help
  SET HELP TO foxhelp
  SET TOPIC TO

RETURN

PROCEDURE DISPHELP
* First set help topic to input field name
  SET TOPIC TO SYS(18)
* Now invoke HELP
  HELP
RETURN

* End of program
```

Program 3-20. Using FoxPro's Built-In Context Sensitive Help Facility

Using Context Sensitive Help to Select Values from a File

A variation on context sensitive help goes beyond static windows. It displays a scrollable list of possible values from a database. The user can then select from the list. Program 3-21 displays a scrollable list of bank IDs and names from file LENDER. It then places the selected values in the corresponding input fields.

```
* Program 3-21
* Context sensitive help with a scrollable list
*
* Shows context sensitive help featuring a scrollable list
* from which the user can select input values

* Set environment
  SET TALK OFF
  CLEAR

* Open lender database
  SELECT A
  USE lender INDEX lender
  GOTO TOP

* Determine number of records and dimension
* ID and NAME to hold all data
  numrec = RECCOUNT()
  DIMENSION lend(numrec,2)

* Load data into array
  COPY TO ARRAY lend FIELDS l_id,l_name

* Display data entry screen
  CLEAR
  @ 0,0 to 20,78
  @ 1,30 SAY 'BANK LOAN ENTRY FORM'
  @ 3, 5 SAY 'Bank ID:'
  @ 4, 5 SAY 'Bank Name:'

* Get bank id and name by displaying a list
* Define HELP window and activate it
  DEFINE WINDOW bankfind FROM 7,10 TO 18,70;
     TITLE 'BANK LIST' DOUBLE FLOAT SHADOW
  ACTIVATE WINDOW bankfind

* Initialize variables and text for window
  i = 1
  nrows = WROWS() - 3
  @ 9,2 SAY '<UP> or <DOWN> selects, <ENTER> picks,'+;
             '<ESC> escapes'
```

```
@ 1,0 SAY '      BANK ID        BANK NAME'
* Display first set of banks
  FOR j = 1 TO nrows
  * Highlight first item in list
    IF j = 1
      SET COLOR TO B/W
    ELSE
      SET COLOR TO W/B
    ENDIF
    ? SPACE(7) + lend(i+j-1,1) + SPACE(6) + lend(i+j-1,2)
  ENDFOR
  atrow = 1

* Begin scrolling loop
  DO WHILE .T.
  * Blank message at top of window
    @ 0,2 SAY SPACE(10)
  * Check for a keystroke
    rk = INKEY()

    DO CASE

    * Up arrow key pressed
    * Scroll text down
      CASE rk = 5
      * First check if highlight can move up
        IF atrow > 1
          @ atrow+1,0 SAY SPACE(7) + lend(i+atrow-1,1);
              + SPACE(6) + lend(i+atrow-1,2)
          atrow = atrow - 1
          SET COLOR TO B/W
          @ atrow+1,0 SAY SPACE(7) + lend(i+atrow-1,1);
              + SPACE(6) + lend(i+atrow-1,2)
          SET COLOR TO W/B
        ELSE
        * Highlight is already at top of window
        * Try to scroll list down
          i = i - 1
          IF i < 1
          * Already at top of list
            i = 1
            @ 0,2 SAY "AT TOP" + CHR(7)
          ELSE
          * Scroll list down, display new item at
          * top of window
            @ 2,0 SAY SPACE(7) + lend(i+1,1) + SPACE(6);
                + lend(i+1,2)
            SCROLL 2,0,8,50,-1
            SET COLOR TO B/W
            @ 2,0 SAY SPACE(7) + lend(i,1) + SPACE(6);
                + lend(i,2)
            SET COLOR TO W/B
          ENDIF
```

```
            ENDIF

* Down arrow key was pressed
* Scroll text up
  CASE rk = 24
    * First check if highlight can move down
      IF atrow < 7
        @ atrow+1,0 SAY SPACE(7) + lend(i+atrow-1,1);
            + SPACE(6) + lend(i+atrow-1,2)
        atrow = atrow + 1
        SET COLOR TO B/W
        @ atrow+1,0 SAY SPACE(7) + lend(i+atrow-1,1);
            + SPACE(6) + lend(i+atrow-1,2)
        SET COLOR TO W/B
      ELSE
        * Already at bottom of window
        * Try to scroll list up
        i = i + 1
        IF i + nrows > numrec
          * Already at bottom of list
          i = numrec - nrows
          @ 0,2 SAY  "AT BOTTOM" + CHR(7)
        ELSE
          * Scroll list up, display next item
          * at bottom of window
          @ nrows+1,0 SAY SPACE(7) + lend(i+nrows-2,1);
              + SPACE(6) + lend(i+nrows-2,2)
          SCROLL 2,0,8,50,1
          SET COLOR TO B/W
          @ nrows+1,0 SAY SPACE(7) + lend(i+nrows-1,1);
              + SPACE(6) + lend(i+nrows-1,2)
          SET COLOR TO W/B
        ENDIF
      ENDIF
* Enter key pressed
  CASE rk = 13
    * Fill input fields with selected item
    bankid = lend(i+atrow-1,1)
    bankname = lend(i+atrow-1,2)
    * Close window and exit
    DEACTIVATE WINDOW bankfind
    EXIT

* Esc key pressed
  CASE rk = 27
    * Fill fields with blanks, close windows,
    * and exit
    DEACTIVATE WINDOW bankfind
    bankid = SPACE(6)
    bankname = SPACE(25)
    EXIT

ENDCASE
```

```
    ENDDO

* Display id and name of bank
  @ 3,16 SAY bankid
  @ 4,16 SAY bankname

* Rest of input form would follow here
  @ 15,20 SAY '<<< Rest of form would continue here. >>>'
  @ 20,79
  WAIT 'Press any key to exit program.'

RETURN

* End of program
```

Program 3-21. Selecting Values from a Scrollable Window

Screen Design

What makes a screen design good? Important techniques include using color effectively, grouping variables, supplying defaults, performing validation, and providing help. They make screens clear, attractive, readable, and easy to use.

Screen Colors and Color Schemes

Unless your application runs solely on monochrome monitors, color selection is important. You should use contrasting foreground and background colors such as white or yellow characters on black, blue, or red. Reversing the contrast also works, such as black letters on white, yellow, green, or cyan. Table 3-11 rates all standard color combinations.

Another consideration in color choices is ensuring that the program works on monochrome monitors. Even ones that can display shades lose many color distinctions. Use high contrast between foreground and background within an object. High intensity foreground characters permit brighter backgrounds. If you are not sure how to combine colors for a monochrome monitor, try one of the predefined monochrome color sets provided with FoxPro.

A common error with color is overuse. Just because a monitor supports 16 colors does not mean that you have to use them all. Your aim is to maximize productivity, not create a patchwork quilt.

Table 3-11. Color Combination Ratings

FORE-GROUND	BACKGROUND							
	Black	Blue	Green	Cyan	Red	Purple	Brown	White
Black	AVOID	AVOID	BEST	BEST	BEST	BEST	BEST	BEST
Blue	AVOID	AVOID	BEST	BEST	GOOD	GOOD	GOOD	BEST
Green	GOOD	FAIR	AVOID	AVOID	FAIR	FAIR	FAIR	POOR
Cyan	GOOD	FAIR	AVOID	AVOID	FAIR	FAIR	FAIR	FAIR
Red	GOOD	FAIR	GOOD	GOOD	AVOID	AVOID	AVOID	FAIR
Purple	GOOD	FAIR	FAIR	GOOD	AVOID	AVOID	AVOID	FAIR
Brown	GOOD	FAIR	FAIR	GOOD	AVOID	AVOID	AVOID	GOOD
White	GOOD	GOOD	POOR	POOR	GOOD	FAIR	FAIR	AVOID
Gray	AVOID	AVOID	GOOD	GOOD	GOOD	GOOD	GOOD	GOOD
Light Blue	FAIR	POOR	FAIR	GOOD	POOR	POOR	POOR	GOOD
Light Green	BEST	GOOD	GOOD	GOOD	GOOD	GOOD	GOOD	FAIR
Light Cyan	BEST	BEST	GOOD	GOOD	GOOD	GOOD	GOOD	FAIR
Light Red	BEST	BEST	POOR	POOR	FAIR	FAIR	FAIR	FAIR
Light Purple	BEST	GOOD	POOR	POOR	FAIR	FAIR	FAIR	POOR
Yellow	BEST	BEST	BEST	BEST	BEST	BEST	BEST	GOOD
Bright White	BEST	BEST	BEST	BEST	BEST	BEST	BEST	GOOD

Using Color Schemes

A good way to define colors in an application is to use predefined sets. Each includes 24 schemes. FoxPro defines the first 11 as listed in Table 3-12 automatically.

Table 3-12. Predefined Scheme Objects

Number	Scheme
1	User Windows
2	User Menus
3	Menu Bar
4	Menu Pops
5	Dialogs
6	Dialog Pops
7	Alert Boxes
8	Windows
9	Window Pops
10	Browse
11	Reports

Some FoxPro objects (see Table 3-13) allow redefinition of their colors by specifying a new scheme number.

Table 3-13. Commands That Reassign Color Schemes to Objects

Command
@...FILL TO
@...SAY/GET
@...TO...
BROWSE
CHANGE
DEFINE POPUP
DEFINE WINDOW
EDIT

The main reason to use predefined color sets is to get consistency throughout an application and across installations.

Grouping Data

Grouping data for display or editing can be difficult. However, the following guidelines should help:

- If the user enters data from a form, lay out the screen fields in the same order as on the printed material.
- Grouping may depend on your data validation techniques. A field used in validating another must precede it.
- Limit the number of fields displayed at one time to avoid crowding. Do not make more room by using abbreviations or eliminating labels. Leave space around each field and its label to clarify which ones go together.

Data Defaults and Validation

Evaluate every field in an application to see if it needs a default or a validation check. Examine the consequences of invalid data or the acceptance of a default value in making the decisions.

Context Sensitive Help

Context sensitive help lets the user obtain more information about the current field with a single key. Although it does not eliminate the need for a manual, it provides the first line of assistance.

Summary

This chapter examined factors that contribute to efficient data entry. The first one it covered was ways to provide default values for variables. Not all cases require them, but they are useful to preload fields with the most common entries. They can also provide safe choices for decisions such as whether to overwrite files or delete data.

Next we looked at several ways to validate data. We can validate formats as well as actual values. Methods vary from simple range checks to complex cross-references using support files. As with defaults, not every field requires validation. Many text fields use freeform entry.

We also discussed ways to provide users with help during data entry. They should not have to hunt for the program manual to determine how to enter a field. Regardless of whether it appears automatically or at the touch of a key, context sensitive help simplifies data entry. It can even take advantage of FoxPro's built-in help facility.

Finally, we looked at screen design considerations and provided a few general rules for color use and grouping of data.

4

Procedures and User Defined Functions

Most programs perform many individual tasks. A task might involve loading data, saving it, editing a record, or displaying one. To organize distinct tasks, most programmers implement them in separate modules. Dividing programs into tasks is a basic tenet of modular programming.

Procedures and User Defined Functions (UDFs) are two major components of program structures. Both help organize code by task. This chapter describes when and how to create them. It also shows how developing libraries of them increases programmer productivity.

Procedures

What Is a Procedure?

A procedure is a set of commands that performs a specific task. As programs become larger, the number of individual tasks increases. Even the simplest database maintenance program involves many tasks.

Procedures have several advantages. As we add tasks to a program, its flow becomes increasingly difficult to follow. Procedures modularize programs by task, much as subroutines do in other languages. They allow us to divide a large program into small units that are easy to understand.

A second advantage is that we can execute common code from many places. We may also be able to reuse code in different programs. This saves development time. After all, the code has already been tested, debugged, and documented. Furthermore, it provides consistency among applications.

As we write procedures to perform tasks, we can code, test, document, and save them individually. We then use them as building blocks, linking them via calls from the main program to form the final application.

Let's examine the procedures required to create a maintenance and reporting program for the file LENDER.DBF. First, list the tasks involved. They include displaying, adding, modifying, and deleting records. Still others involve printing labels and generating reports. The following list summarizes the major tasks:

- Select actions from a main menu
- Display a screen form
- Find or retrieve a record
- Display current record
- Edit current record
- Create a blank record
- Add a new record
- Return record in memory to database
- Delete a record
- Create label or report forms for records

Writing one program to do all this sounds like a major undertaking. However, procedures help us focus on individual tasks, making the job manageable.

Looking at the tasks, we see that some are interdependent. For example, to display or edit a record, we must first find it and display its fields.

We can further divide the task of displaying the current record's fields into several steps. The first displays the screen form. The next displays the fields. A third adds GET statements that prompt the user for changes. Finally, a fourth step saves the data.

Figure 4-1 displays the system flowchart for the lender maintenance system generated by FoxDoc. It looks more like an enormous "spreading chestnut tree" than a simple drawing (and this is only a small part of a real application!). It consists of the major procedures described briefly in Table 4-1. Most of them call lower level tasks or subprocedures. In addition, the diagram shows that several tasks call common routines. For example, GETKEY appears in procedures that append, browse, edit, pack, and create labels and reports. We store such common routines in one file, LEN_APPS.PRG.

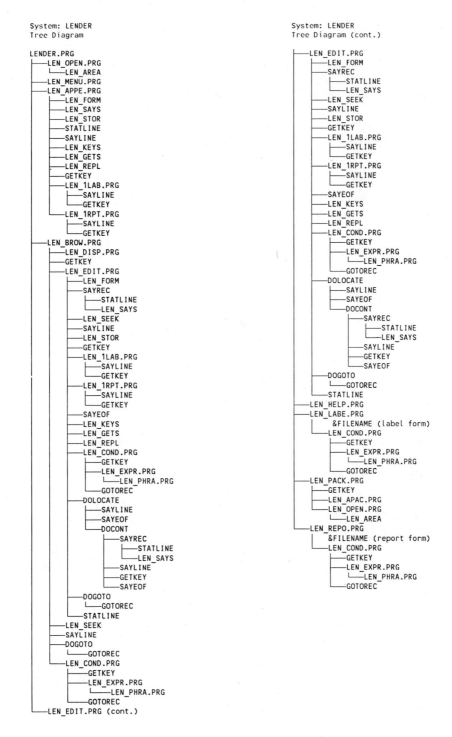

Figure 4-1. System flowchart for lender file maintenance.

Table 4-1. Major Procedures in Lender File Maintenance

Name	Purpose
LENDER.PRG	Main driver program that controls the selection of main menu options
LEN_APAC.PRG	Packs memo fields
LEN_APPE.PRG	Appends a new record to the database
LEN_BROW.PRG	Enters a browse mode to view data
LEN_COND.PRG	Builds and maintains filter conditions
LEN_DISP.PRG	Displays data in a simple list format
LEN_EDIT.PRG	Edits current database record
LEN_EXPR.PRG	Driver for logical phrase builder
LEN_HELP.PRG	Displays a program flowchart
LEN_LABE.PRG	Creates and runs custom labels
LEN_MENU.PRG	Displays the main menu
LEN_OPEN.PRG	Opens database and index files
LEN_PACK.PRG	Pack driver for the database
LEN_PHRA.PRG	Builds a logical phrase
LEN_PROC.PRG	Contains general procedures
LEN_REPO.PRG	Creates and runs custom reports
LEN_1LAB.PRG	Prints labels
LEN_1RPT.PRG	Prints a simple report

Creating a Procedure

A procedure is distinguished by its first and last lines. The first usually contains a PROCEDURE statement that names it. This is unnecessary for a procedure stored in a file by itself as the file name identifies it. However, it is required for identification when you combine procedures in a single file. Procedures can have any valid FoxPro name, but we obviously try to select ones that are meaningful and descriptive.

The last line must be a RETURN statement. It indicates the end of the procedure and returns control to the caller. Although a procedure can have several RETURNs, good coding avoids multiple exit points.

If a procedure does not depend on data from other procedures, we can test it independently. This reduces debugging time later. Procedures that require data from others can be tested only by writing a 'driver' program or by combining them with previously tested procedures.

> **TIP**
> Test all procedures before including them in a main program.
> You then need test only the linkages between them.

The disk for this book contains the entire LENDER program. It shows how vital procedures are in modularizing practical applications.

When saving a procedure separately during development, you should assign its name to the file to help FoxPro find it. Large applications usually consist of many files.

A way to avoid the proliferation of files is to group procedures in a module. When storing them, use the SET PROCEDURE TO command to tell FoxPro where to put them. We can even store them in the same file as the main program by placing them at the end. In fact, we can store up to 1,170 procedures and functions there.

Calling a Procedure

Use DO to call a procedure. The form is

```
DO   <procedure name>
```

When FoxPro encounters DO, it must find the procedure and transfer control to it. It follows a few simple rules when searching for procedures. The result is that their locations affect a program's overall performance. FoxPro first looks in the current program file. Next, it looks in a separate procedure file or library if one is open. Finally, it looks in the current directory for a file with the procedure's name. If all searches fail, an error message appears.

Table 4-2. Search Order for Procedures

Search level	Where FoxPro searches for a procedure
1	Current program file
2	Separate procedure file defined by SET PROCEDURE TO
3	Current directory for a file with the same name as the called procedure

After FoxPro transfers control to the procedure, execution continues in it until a RETURN statement is reached. FoxPro then exits and returns to the caller. Execution resumes at the line immediately after the DO.

Figure 4-2 illustrates the flow of control when a program calls a procedure.

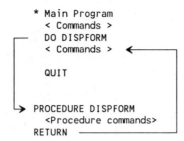

```
* Main Program
  < Commands >
  DO DISPFORM
  < Commands >

  QUIT


PROCEDURE DISPFORM
  <Procedure commands>
RETURN
```

Figure 4-2. Program flow through a procedure.

We can call procedures from other procedures. FoxPro allows up to 32 levels of nesting. The order in which procedures are called affects the availability of variables. Remember, the default scope of a variable is to have its value known to the procedure that creates it and any that it calls subsequently. Thus a variable defined in the main program of Figure 4-2 is known in procedure DISPFORM. However, variables defined in DISPFORM are unknown in the main program unless we declare them PUBLIC.

Upon exiting a procedure, FoxPro erases from memory all variables defined in it with a default or PRIVATE scope. Even if control returns to it later, we cannot access the old values.

Using Parameters in Procedures

The PARAMETER statement lets us pass variables between procedures. If ones defined in the main program are available automatically in called procedures, why is such a statement necessary? Given the default scope of variables, it seems redundant.

By examining how parameters are passed to procedures, we can answer the question. First, we must add a WITH clause to the DO statement. It specifies the variables to be passed. They can be of any type, even constants. The following DO statements show several ways to pass values in the WITH clause.

```
DO PROFIT WITH sales,costs
DO SALES WITH 50000,20000,region
DO BIRTHDAY WITH 'Natasha',{08/04/88}
```

The called procedure must have a PARAMETER statement that immediately follows the PROCEDURE statement and defines local variables to receive the values. Each variable in the WITH clause must match one in the PARAMETER clause. A variable defined by the PARAMETER clause assumes both the value and the type of the passed variable.

Consider a simple example. Suppose we want to verify the existence of a database before using it. The procedure CHECKDBF in Program 4-1 tests whether a file exists.

```
* Program 4-1
* Calls procedure CHECKDBF to see whether the database file
* exists before trying to open it.
* Use this procedure at the beginning of applications to
* verify that all essential files exist.

* Set environment
  SET TALK OFF
  SET STATUS OFF
  SET SCOREBOARD OFF
  CLEAR

* Set initial errors to zero
  dbferr = 0

* Check whether database and index file exist
  dbfname = "LENDER"
  idxname = "LENDER"
  DO CHECKDBF WITH dbfname,idxname

* Program continues from here if there are no errors.
* Otherwise, exit
  IF dbferr > 0
    CANCEL
  ELSE
    ? "Continue with rest of program, database exists."
  ENDIF

RETURN

* Begin program-specific procedures and functions

* CHECKDBF checks whether a database or index file exists
*
PROCEDURE CHECKDBF
PARAMETER dbfname,idxname
  line_cnt = 4

* Set up display screen
  SET COLOR TO BG+/N
  CLEAR
  @ 0, 0 TO 22,79 DOUBLE
  SET COLOR TO GR+
```

```
@ 1,20 SAY '<< DATABASE AND INDEX FILE CHECK >>'
SET COLOR TO W+
@ 2,20 SAY 'Filename         Database        Index'
@ 3,20 SAY '_____         _____        _____'
SET COLOR TO BG
IF EMPTY(dbfname)
   IF .NOT. EMPTY(idxname)
      @ line_cnt,20 SAY idxname
   ENDIF
ELSE
   @ line_cnt,20 SAY dbfname
ENDIF

* Report whether database was found
IF EMPTY(dbfname)
   SET COLOR TO BR+
   @ line_cnt,35 SAY 'N/A'
ELSE
   IF FILE(dbfname + '.dbf')
      SET COLOR TO G+
      @ line_cnt,35 SAY 'FOUND'
   ELSE
      SET COLOR TO R+
      @ line_cnt,35 SAY 'NOT FOUND'
      dbferr = dbferr + 1
   ENDIF
ENDIF

* Report whether index was found
IF EMPTY(idxname)
   SET COLOR TO BR+
   @ line_cnt,50 SAY 'N/A'
ELSE
   IF FILE(idxname + '.idx')
      SET COLOR TO G+
      @ line_cnt,50 SAY 'FOUND'
   ELSE
      SET COLOR TO R+
      @ line_cnt,50 SAY 'NOT FOUND'
      dbferr = dbferr + 1
   ENDIF
ENDIF

* Display error count
@ 22,79
IF dbferr > 0
   WAIT STR(dbferr,2)+;
      ' DBF error(s) found. (Missing Files)'
ELSE
   WAIT 'Database and index files are present.'
ENDIF
CLEAR
```

```
RETURN

* End of program
```

Program 4-1. File Existence Check

Here the variables that define the database and index files have the same names in the main program and the procedure. The default scope of the main program's variables mean that, once defined, they exist in all subsequently called procedures. We could thus achieve the same result without the PARAMETER statement.

> **EXERCISE**
> Remove the WITH clause from the DO statement and the PARAMETER statement from procedure CHECKDBF to verify the scope of the main program's variables.

However, usually we must check several database and index files. Of course, we could assign the same memory variables to the database and index names before calling CHECKDBF. But that is not always practical. Do we need new procedures to handle different names? Of course not. All we need is the PARAMETER statement.

Program 4-2 executes CHECKDBF twice with different parameters in each call. The names defined in it thus act as temporary aliases for the passed variables.

Note one other change in Program 4-2. We have defined all variables in the procedure except DBFERR as PRIVATE. This precaution avoids overwriting variables with the same names in the caller or other higher level procedures. However, we must return DBFERR to the caller, as it indicates the number of missing files. Therefore, we initialize it in the main program to give it a default scope.

> **TIP**
> Declare local variables in procedures and functions as PRIVATE to avoid overwriting ones with the same names in higher level procedures.

```
* Program 4-2
* Checks whether a database exists before opening it
* Uses PARAMETER for flexibility

* Set environment
  SET TALK OFF
  SET STATUS OFF
  SET SCOREBOARD OFF
  CLEAR

* Set initial errors to zero
  dbferr = 0

* Call CHECKDBF for first database and index file
  dbfname1 = "LENDER"
  idxname1 = "LENDER"
  DO CHECKDBF WITH dbfname1,idxname1

* Call CHECKDBF for second database and index file
  dbfname2 = "SALES"
  idxname2 = "SALES"
  DO CHECKDBF WITH dbfname2,idxname2

* Program continues from here if there are no errors.
* Otherwise, exit.
  IF dbferr > 0
    CANCEL
  ELSE
    ? "Continue program, files exist."
  ENDIF

RETURN

* Begin program-specific procedures and functions

* CHECKDBF checks whether a database or index file exists
*
PROCEDURE CHECKDBF
PARAMETER dbfname,idxname
PRIVATE dbfname,idxname,line_cnt
  line_cnt = 4

* Set up display screen
  SET COLOR TO BG+/N
  CLEAR
  @ 0, 0 TO 22,79 DOUBLE
  SET COLOR TO GR+
  @ 1,20 SAY '<< DATABASE AND INDEX FILE CHECK >>'
  SET COLOR TO W+
  @ 2,20 SAY 'File Name      Database      Index'
  @ 3,20 SAY '_____      _____      _____'
  SET COLOR TO BG
  IF EMPTY(dbfname)
```

```
        IF .NOT.EMPTY(idxname)
           @ line_cnt,20 SAY idxname
        ENDIF
     ELSE
        @ line_cnt,20 SAY dbfname
     ENDIF
* Report whether database was found
     IF EMPTY(dbfname)
        SET COLOR TO BR+
        @ line_cnt,35 SAY 'N/A'
     ELSE
        IF FILE(dbfname + '.dbf')
           SET COLOR TO G+
           @ line_cnt,35 SAY 'FOUND'
        ELSE
           SET COLOR TO R+
           @ line_cnt,35 SAY 'NOT FOUND'
           dbferr = dbferr + 1
        ENDIF
     ENDIF

* Report whether index was found
     IF EMPTY(idxname)
        SET COLOR TO BR+
        @ line_cnt,50 SAY 'N/A'
     ELSE
        IF FILE(idxname + '.idx')
           SET COLOR TO G+
           @ line_cnt,50 SAY 'FOUND'
        ELSE
           SET COLOR TO R+
           @ line_cnt,50 SAY 'NOT FOUND'
           dbferr = dbferr + 1
        ENDIF
     ENDIF

* Display number of errors
     @ 22,79
     IF dbferr > 0
        WAIT STR(dbferr,2)+' error(s) found. (Missing Files)'
     ELSE
        WAIT 'Database and index files are present.'
     ENDIF
     CLEAR

RETURN

* End of program
```

Program 4-2. Check Existence of Two Databases

> **NOTE**
> The main purpose of using parameters in procedures is to allow calls with different variables.

Passing Different Types of Variables

Procedures often perform calculations using passed parameters. Suppose we have one that adds two values passed to it. Its variables are independent of the original names or types. They could have numeric values in one call, dates in the next, and strings in another. How can we define a variable as numeric sometimes and a date or a string at other times? Simply because FoxPro recreates the parameter variables with each call. It does not retain the previous type definitions or values, thus allowing us to pass different ones each time.

Changing Parameter Values

When we change a parameter's value, FoxPro returns the change to the corresponding variable in the caller. Not even making procedure variables PRIVATE can prevent this. The parameter names are just aliases for the passed variables. The following lines show that a procedure returns the changed value even when the parameter is PRIVATE.

```
* Define average temperature in Celsius based on
* daily high and low in Fahrenheit.
  high = 87
  low = 63
  daily_avg = 0

* Call procedure to perform average
  DO tempconv WITH daily_avg, high, low

* Redisplay daily_avg. The fact that it changes
* shows that procedure parameters are aliases
* for the passed variables. In other words,
* they are passed by reference.
  ? daily_avg

RETURN

PROCEDURE TEMPCONV
PARAMETER tempavg, temph, templ
PRIVATE tempavg, temph, templ

* Convert temperature from Celsius to Fahrenheit
  templ = 1.8 * templ + 32
  temph = 1.8 * temph + 32
  tempavg = (templ + temph) / 2

RETURN
```

> **TIP**
> Parameters make calculations in a procedure independent of the variable names and types in the caller. However, beware of changing parameter values. FoxPro assigns changes automatically to the caller's variables.

Matching the Number of Parameters

The caller cannot pass more variables than appear in the procedure's PARAMETER statement. For example, FoxPro cannot pass three variables to a procedure in which the PARAMETER statement expects only two. As there is nowhere to store the third variable, FoxPro displays an error message ("Wrong number of parameters") during compilation.

However, the caller can pass fewer variables than the PARAMETER statement defines. For example, we could pass two parameters to a procedure that accepts three as follows:

```
DO proc1 WITH temperatur,pressure
      .
      .
      .
PROCEDURE proc1
PARAMETER temp,pres,flow
```

Here temperatur's value is passed to 'temp' and pressure's to 'pres'. However, nothing is passed to 'flow'. Therefore, FoxPro sets it to .F.. Note that it does not retain flow's value from a previous call.

> **HINT**
> Always define the PARAMETER statement with all parameters the procedure might need. You do not have to use them in every call.

Although the caller can pass fewer variables, they must still appear sequentially. We cannot skip one as in

```
DO proc1 WITH var1,,var2
```

> **HINT**
> Place optional parameters at the end of the list so you can omit them easily.

Of course, we could pass dummy variables as position holders. However, we might then not know whether a passed variable is valid. We could check it by using a simple TYPE test since unused parameters are set to .F.. Procedure TOT_INCOME in Program 4-3 checks each parameter's type before adding it to total income. You can thus handle cases in which some income types do not occur by just passing dummy variables for them or omitting them from the end of the list.

```
* Program 4-3
* Passing a variable number of parameters

* Set environment
SET TALK OFF
SET STATUS OFF
SET SCOREBOARD OFF
CLEAR

* Initialize income types for year
salary   = 50000
stocks   = 2500
bonds    = 1300
municipl = 2300
taxfree  = 4000

* Calculate total annual income
income = 0
DO TOT_INCOME WITH salary,stocks,bonds,municipl,taxfree
? "Total annual income is: " ;
   + TRANSFORM(income,'$999,999.99')

* Calculate total annual taxable income, omitting the last
* two categories. The unpassed parameters will be of
* logical type in the subroutine.
income = 0
DO TOT_INCOME WITH salary,stocks,bonds
? "Total annual taxable income is: ";
   + TRANSFORM(income,'$999,999.99')

RETURN

PROCEDURE TOT_INCOME
PARAMETER income1,income2,income3,income4,income5

* Add the five parameters if they are numeric
* An unpassed parameter is initialized to .F.
IF TYPE("income1") = 'N'
    income = income + income1
ENDIF
IF TYPE("income2") = 'N'
```

```
        income = income + income2
ENDIF
IF TYPE("income3") = 'N'
        income = income + income3
ENDIF
IF TYPE("income4") = 'N'
        income = income + income4
ENDIF
IF TYPE("income5") = 'N'
        income = income + income5
ENDIF

RETURN

* End of program
```

Program 4-3. Passing a Variable Number of Parameters

Exiting Procedures

The normal way to exit a procedure is via a RETURN statement. Execution continues at the line immediately after the calling DO. However, special exits are sometimes necessary. FoxPro provides the four commands listed in Table 4-3: CANCEL, QUIT, RETURN TO MASTER, and SUSPEND.

Table 4-3. Special Commands to Exit Procedures

Command	Restart Program	Terminate Program	Retain Memory Variables	Terminate FoxPro
CANCEL	no	yes	no	no
QUIT	no	yes	no	yes
RETURN TO MASTER	yes	no	yes	no
SUSPEND	no	yes	yes	no

The CANCEL statement terminates not just the procedure, but also the current program. It returns control to the Command window, releasing all memory variables except system and PUBLIC ones. Currently defined windows remain in memory. If a window, popup, or menu is active during CANCEL, it stays on the screen. This option allows the user to exit an application while remaining in FoxPro. (The runtime version returns to the DOS prompt, releasing everything.)

The QUIT statement also terminates the current program, but it returns control directly to DOS. QUIT releases all variables, menus, windows, and popups. If you use a DOS shell to drive your applications, QUIT returns to it.

The RETURN TO MASTER command transfers control to the command immediately after the highest level call in the main program. It skips all remaining commands in the intermediate level subroutines. We could use it to abort a procedure when a critical error occurs such as inability to access a printer or create a file. If procedures are called from a menu in the main program, RETURN TO MASTER provides a way to return to it from anywhere. Figure 4-3 illustrates how RETURN TO MASTER works.

We can similarly return to an intermediate level by using RETURN TO <procedure>. In Figure 4-3, for example, we could replace RETURN TO MASTER with RETURN TO PROCED_1.

Another use for RETURN TO MASTER or RETURN TO <procedure> is to return to the main or intermediate level menu when the user presses the Esc key during a READ. The following lines trap that key:

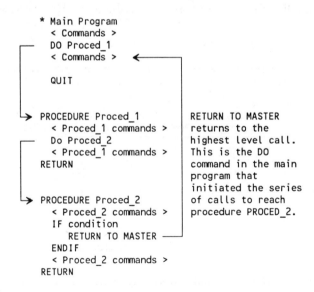

Figure 4-3. Program flow during RETURN TO MASTER.

```
READ
rk = READKEY()
* Code 12 indicates that Esc was pressed without
* READ updating any fields. Code 268 indicates
* it updated at least one field first.
IF (rk = 12 .OR. rk = 268)
   RETURN TO MASTER
ENDIF
```

EXERCISE

Put the above lines into a procedure that a program can call whenever it uses a READ.

Table 4-4 lists common codes recognized by READKEY.

Table 4-4. READKEY Codes

Key	No Update Code	Update Code	Meaning
Backspace Left Arrow Ctrl-H Ctrl-S	0	256	back one character
Right Arrow Ctrl-D Ctrl-L	1	257	ahead one character
Home Ctrl-A	2	258	back one word
End Ctrl-F	3	259	ahead one word
Up Arrow Ctrl-E Shift-Tab Ctrl-R	4	260	back one field
Down Arrow Ctrl-X Tab Ctrl-Enter Ctrl-I Ctrl-J	5	261	ahead one field
PgUp Ctrl-R	6	262	back one screen
PgDn Ctrl-C	7	263	ahead one screen

Table 4-4. READKEY Codes (cont'd.)

Key	No Update Code	Update Code	Meaning
Ctrl-Q Esc	12	268	exit without saving
Ctrl-End Ctrl-W	–	270	exit and save
Enter Ctrl-Right Arrow Ctrl-M	15	271	return or filled
Ctrl-Home Ctrl-]	33	289	toggle menu display
Ctrl-PgUp Ctrl-	34	290	zoom out
Ctrl-PgDn Ctrl-^	35	291	zoom in
F1	36	292	help function key

The SUSPEND command interrupts program execution temporarily and returns control to the Command window. It leaves all variables intact. Some error trapping procedures use it to allow the user to check or change memory variables. We can continue executing the program with the RESUME command or terminate it with CANCEL. Editing a suspended procedure automatically cancels the program. This option is useful mainly during development.

Functions

Not only does FoxPro provide many built-in functions, but it also lets us add our own. User Defined Functions (UDFs), once defined, work just like the built-in ones.

Defining a Function

A function definition resembles a procedure except that it begins with the FUNCTION statement and returns a value to the caller. Its name is the file's name if we save it individually. It can be any legal FoxPro identifier. Of course, we should not duplicate the names of FoxPro's built-in functions. If we do, FoxPro ignores the UDF and continues to use its predefined function. It does not warn us about the conflict or its resolution.

Like a procedure, a function should end with a RETURN statement. However, a function RETURN includes a value derived from a variable or expression. It can be any type except a memo. If we omit the RETURN, the function automatically returns .T..

HINT

Always put a RETURN at the end of procedures and functions. This practice increases readability and simplifies development and maintenance.

Functions can return only one value through the RETURN statement. If we must return more, we must declare them PUBLIC.

Program 4-4 calls a simple function that opens a temporary text file for output. It finds a unique file name, appends the extension TXT to it, and checks the directory to be sure no such file already exists. It then returns the name to the caller via the RETURN statement.

```
* Program 4-4
* Creates an output text file with a unique name

* Set environment
  SET TALK OFF
  SET STATUS OFF
  SET SCOREBOARD OFF
  CLEAR

* Get a unique file name
  ? "A unique file name "+trim(tempfile())+;
    "has been created."

* Direct output to alternate
  SET ALTERNATE ON
* All statements placed here are written to the
* temporary file
  SET ALTERNATE OFF
  CLOSE ALTERNATE

RETURN

FUNCTION tempfile
PRIVATE filenm

* Repeat loop until a valid unique name is found
  DO WHILE .T.
    filenm = SYS(3) + ".TXT"
```

```
    * Test name to insure it is unique
    IF .NOT. FILE(filenm)
      EXIT
    ENDIF
  ENDDO

    * Set alternate to file name
    SET ALTERNATE TO &filenm

RETURN filenm

* End of program
```

Program 4-4. Obtaining a Unique File Name

Passing Parameters to Functions

We specify parameters passed to functions differently than in procedures. We must put parentheses after the function name and place the passed variable names inside them. The function in Program 4-4 does not pass any parameters. However, we still must include the parentheses in the call.

Functions receive information in local variables via a PARAMETER statement. As with procedures, parameters make the function independent of the names used by the caller.

Program 4-5 computes the present value of a future amount. It answers the question, "How much must I invest today to have a specific amount later?" To perform the calculation, we must pass:
- goal amount
- interest rate
- compounding period (annual, monthly, or daily)
- number of periods

Because the calculation is simple, we put the entire expression in the RETURN statement. More complex functions put only the calculated variable there.

```
* Program 4-5
* Passing parameters to a function

* Set environment
  SET TALK OFF
  SET STATUS OFF
  SET SCOREBOARD OFF
  CLEAR
    * Define initial values
```

```
* To have 5000 in 10 years, how much must we
* invest now at 8% compounded monthly?
  goal      = 5000
  rate      = 0.08
  years     = 10
  annl_prds = 12

* Calculate and display present investment
? 'You must invest ' + ;
    TRANSFORM(spv(goal,rate,years,annl_prds),'$99,999.99')+;
    ' today.'

RETURN

FUNCTION spv
* Determine present value of an investment
PARAMETER fv,int,yrs,ppyr
RETURN fv/(1+int/ppyr)**(yrs*ppyr)

* End of program
```

Program 4-5. Passing Parameters to Functions

Like procedures, functions can accept a variable number of parameters. If not enough values are passed, FoxPro initializes the rest to .F..

Even if a function has nothing of significance to return, it must return something, such as a null string. Program 4-6 uses a function to display a message and optionally pause for a key press before continuing. As no return value is needed, it returns a null string.

```
* Program 4-6
* Shows a function that returns a null string to a
* dummy variable

* Set environment
  SET TALK OFF
  SET STATUS OFF
  SET SCOREBOARD OFF
  CLEAR

* Open LENDER file
  USE lender INDEX lender

* Display lenders and current interest rates
  LIST FIELDS l_name,l_currate,l_ratedate OFF
```

```
* Display left justified message. No key press needed
  dum = disp_msg("Lenders with current interest rates",;
                 "L",WROWS()-1,0)

* Display lender names and telephone numbers
  GOTO TOP
  LIST FIELDS l_id,l_name,l_phone OFF
* Display centered message on line 12. Key press needed
  dum = disp_msg("Lender IDs, names, and telephone";
                 + "numbers", "C", WROWS()-1,1)

* Display lender addresses
  GOTO TOP
  LIST FIELDS l_id,l_name,l_city,l_state,l_zip OFF
* Display line right-justified. Key press needed
  dum = disp_msg("Lender addresses","R",WROWS()-1,1)

* Display message at bottom of screen
* Wait for a key press
  ?
  dum = disp_msg("All lists complete","C",WROWS()-1,1)

RETURN

* Begin procedures/functions here

FUNCTION DISP_MSG
PARAMETERS msg,position,line,pause

* Determine position of leftmost character of message
  DO CASE
     CASE position = 'C'
       col = (80-LEN(msg))/2
     CASE position = 'L'
       col = 0
     CASE position = 'R'
       col = (80-LEN(msg))
  ENDCASE

* Display message centered on specified line
  @ line,col SAY msg

* Wait for a keystroke if pause = 1
  IF pause > 0

    * INKEY returns a nonzero value when a key is pressed
      key = 0
      DO WHILE key = 0
        key = INKEY(1)
      ENDDO
  ENDIF
```

```
* No return value, so return a null string
RETURN ""
* End of program
```

Program 4-6. Calling a Function with a Dummy RETURN Variable

Using Functions in Labels or Reports

Of course, we could have written Program 4-6 as a procedure. But suppose we have to use it in a label or report. We cannot issue a DO command in a label definition.

Furthermore, FoxPro does not generate modifiable code during the creation of label or report definitions. However, we can insert calculations into them by using UDFs.

The following expressions define a label for LENDER.DBF using a modified version of the DISP_MSG function in Program 4-6 for 3.5″ labels.

```
DISP_MSG(TRIM(l_id),'R')
DISP_MSG(TRIM(l_NAME),'C')
```

We trim the field variables before passing them to the function. Otherwise, trailing spaces would affect the text position. The first line right justifies bank id. The second one centers bank name. Suppose that we use the two expressions to define two lines in label LENLABEL. Note that we get a syntax error if we validate them in the Label Expression Building dialog. The reason is that you cannot access user defined functions in a program while creating a label. The only way to validate the expressions is through an actual test of the label with the rest of the program.

Program 4-7 shows the modified version of DISP_MSG used to print label LENLABEL.

```
* Program 4-7
* Prints labels using UDF DISP_MSG to center and justify
* text

* Set environment
  SET TALK OFF
  SET STATUS OFF
  SET SCOREBOARD OFF
  CLEAR

* Open database
  USE lender INDEX lender
```

```
* Print labels on screen
LABEL FORM lenlabel

RETURN

* Begin procedures/functions here

FUNCTION DISP_MSG
PARAMETERS msg,position

* Determine position of leftmost character of message
  DO CASE
    CASE position = 'C'
      col = (35-LEN(msg))/2
    CASE position = 'L'
      col = 0
    CASE position = 'R'
      col = (35-LEN(msg))
  ENDCASE

RETURN space(col) + msg

* End of program
```

Program 4-7. Using UDFs in Labels

EXERCISE

Modify the DISP_MSG function in Program 4-7 to accept three arguments:

1. The string
2. Justification flag
3. Label width

The justification flag can have three values: C, L, or R for center, left, or right justification, respectively. Define the label width in characters.

Choosing between Procedures and Functions

We use both procedures and functions extensively throughout this book. In choosing between them, consider the following general guidelines.

We can use a function wherever we can use a variable.

To do calculations in statements where FoxPro expects a variable, use a function. It can perform calculations and then return any type. In fact, functions are the only way to add custom processing to labels and reports. Their ability to return .T. or .F. even allows them to replace logical expressions in VALID clauses. Some common uses for them are:

- General expressions
- VALID clauses
- End point calculations in RANGE clauses
- Label and report expressions
- Logical expressions

Use procedures to divide programs into modules that each perform a single task such as loading, modifying, or saving data.

Use procedures for common tasks called from many places in a program, such as displaying a screen form.

This practice makes maintenance easier and more reliable because changes and corrections occur in just one place.

Use procedures to create general code that other programs can use.

For example, suppose we start each program by checking the system's current time and date so file update times are correct. This code is application-independent, and we do not want to rewrite it each time. Sharing code between applications also promotes consistency.

Sometimes we may need both a function and a procedure to perform similar tasks. We can call procedures in any command line, but only a function can be part of an expression. FoxPro's SEEK command and SEEK() function illustrate this need. We can use the SEEK command to find a specific record as in:

```
USE lender INDEX lender
SEEK 'TN'
DISPLAY
```

On the other hand, we would use the SEEK() function in a VALID clause, as in:

```
@ 10,5 SAY 'Enter lender id' GET l_id VALID SEEK(m->l_id);
      ERROR 'Not a current vendor id'
```

Creating Procedure and Function Libraries

Most applications consist of three parts: a main program, specific procedures and functions, and general procedures and functions. We could save each individual module (program, procedure, or function) as a separate file. For a major application, the result would be a large number of files. The problem is that each call to a new procedure or function requires a separate file and buffer in DOS. Therefore, as the number of nested DO calls increases, we may have to increase the number of FILES and BUFFERS defined in CONFIG.SYS. This reduces the amount of memory available to the program. Even more important is that opening more files slows down the application.

A more efficient structure combines the main program with the specific procedures and functions into one file. Likewise, we combine all general routines into a second file. Figure 4-4 shows the suggested structure.

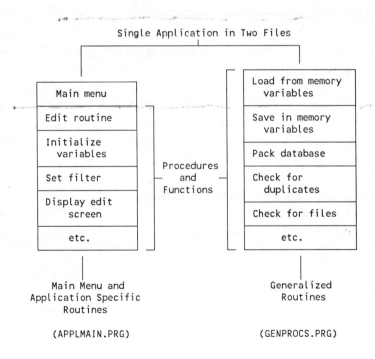

Figure 4-4. Organizing routines for an application.

It is easy to misplace a file when an application involves many of them. File management also is difficult if we store several applications in the same subdirectory. The two file method organizes an application's files.

Another advantage is that storing general routines separately makes them available to any application. In addition, when you change one, the revision is immediately available to all applications that use it.

When we put general procedures in a common file, we must tell FoxPro how to find them. The SET PROCEDURE TO command specifies the name of an auxiliary file. It can contain up to 1,170 individual procedures and functions. If this is not enough, you can use SET PROCEDURE TO to open another file. However, only one auxiliary file can be open at a time.

FoxPro searches for procedures and functions in a specific order. When it executes a DO statement or UDF, it first looks for it in the current file. FoxPro finds procedures and functions stored there the fastest because no additional file access is necessary.

Next it searches the file specified by the current SET PROCEDURE TO. Accessing this file takes slightly longer. However, if it is open, it already has an associated DOS file and buffer. This file should be the general procedure library shown on the right side of Figure 4-4.

FoxPro then examines any previously executed programs in the current application. If we store all application-specific programs in the main file or a general library, it skips this step.

Finally, it searches the current directory for a file with the same name as the procedure. If there are many such files, this search can degrade performance significantly. Unless the routine being sought is in the current or SET PROCEDURE TO file, the search time depends on hard disk access speed.

HINT

To improve performance and organize procedures and functions, store application-specific routines with the main program as a single file. Store general procedures in a library.

HINT

If we use the Project Manager to create an application (APP) or executable (EXE) file, we do not have to worry about combining files. The Project Manager combines them for us to create a single file. However, the above physical file structures are still useful during development.

Summary

This chapter described procedures and functions. They serve as additional routines called from the main program or from one another.

Both procedures and functions help structure applications by dividing code into logical tasks. The resulting modular form is easier to develop and maintain than a single large program. We can pass parameters to make calculations independent of the caller's variable names. A final advantage of procedures and functions is that we can define libraries of common ones and call them from many applications. In later chapters, we use procedures with menus, ON KEY commands, and ON ERROR statements.

The main difference between a procedure and a function is that a function returns a value to the caller. We can put user defined functions anywhere we would put a variable. Thus, they allow us to insert code in places where FoxPro expects single values. They are especially helpful in expanding the capabilities of the RANGE and VALID clauses in GET statements. They also add flexibility in label and report generation.

5

Macros

This chapter describes FoxPro's two types of macros: macro variables and keyboard macros. It examines both and shows how to use them to generalize procedures, provide shorthand, and simulate user input. It also discusses the KEYBOARD command.

Macro Substitution

Macro substitution is a special operation. It substitutes the contents of a memory variable in a command line rather than using it literally. It applies anywhere. The only restriction is that the macro's value must be a string.

Suppose a program prompts the user for a database's name and stores it in a variable. How do we then open it with a USE statement? USE accepts only a literal argument. The solution is macro substitution. Once we have the name in a variable, we can substitute its value. The following lines do the job.

```
ACCEPT "Enter a database name: " TO fname
USE &fname
```

The ampersand (&) preceding fname tells FoxPro to substitute its contents rather than use the literal characters. Without it, FoxPro would try to open the file FNAME.DBF.

Macro substitution works anywhere FoxPro expects a character string. However, the common uses are to generalize a command or an entire procedure. In Program 5-1, macro substitution defines a report destination (screen, printer, or a file), based on the user's selection.

```
* Program 5-1
* Using macro substitution with REPORT FORM to route
* a report to the screen, the printer, or a file
```

```
* Set environment
SET TALK OFF
SET STATUS OFF
SET SCOREBOARD OFF

* Clear screen and define variables
CLEAR
outp_dest = ' '
filenm = SPACE(8)

* Get output destination
@ 5,5 SAY "Route Report to S)creen, P)rinter, or F)ile";
    GET outp_dest PICTURE '@M S,P,F';
    MESSAGE "Press space bar to select destination."
READ

* Define command string segments for each destination
DO CASE
   CASE outp_dest = 'F'
      @ 7,5 SAY "Enter filename" GET filenm PICTURE '@8!'
      READ
      reptgo = 'TO FILE ' + TRIM(filenm) + '.RPT'
   CASE outp_dest = 'P'
     reptgo = 'TO PRINTER'
   CASE outp_dest = 'S'
     reptgo = ''
ENDCASE
* Print report
* (Note: Open database separately if you did
*        not save environment file)
CLEAR
REPORT FORM bankrate ENVIRONMENT &reptgo NOEJECT

* End of program
```

Program 5-1. Using Macro Substitution to Select an Output Destination

When a macro replaces an entire word or string as in the USE example, FoxPro has no difficulty determining where the name ends. The space character or end of line identifies it, just as with other variables and commands.

But suppose we use macro substitution in the middle or even at the beginning of a variable or phrase. A space cannot terminate the macro name without also terminating the variable definition. FoxPro resolves this problem by using a period to end the name. When it performs the substitution, it ignores the period and appends the characters immediately after the command or string. For example, the following variable definitions are equivalent, assuming that item = '1'.

```
prod_id_&item        -   prod_id_1
qtr_&item._gross     -   qtr_1_gross
? '&item.) Reports'  -   ? '1) Reports'
```

Program 5-2 uses macro substitution to build a filter string. It first displays a screen with the fields from LENDER.DBF. It then allows the user to filter on specific ones by entering values for them.

```
* Program 5-2
* Demonstration of macro substitution in creating
* and using a filter

* Set environment
  SET TALK OFF
  SET STATUS OFF
  SET SCOREBOARD OFF

* Open database
  USE lender INDEX lender
  SCATTER memvar BLANK

* Initialize other variables
  t_vrm     = ' '
  t_rrm     = ' '
  t_wrap    = ' '
  filter_str = ' '

* Clear screen and display form
  DO DISP_SCN

* Get filter
  DO FILTER

* Display selected records
  DISPLAY ALL

RETURN

* Specific procedures (listed alphabetically)

PROCEDURE DISP_SCN
* Display screen form
  SET COLOR TO BG+/B
  CLEAR
  @  0,31 SAY "FILTER SET SCREEN"
  @  1, 0 TO 18,79 DOUBLE
  @  3, 1 TO 3,78 DOUBLE
  @  5, 1 TO 5,78
  SET COLOR TO GR+/B
  @  2,29 SAY "MORTGAGE SYSTEM"
  @ 14,47 SAY "Special Financing Offered:"
  SET COLOR TO W+/B
  @  4, 4 SAY "Lender ID"
  @  4,36 SAY "Bank Name"
```

```
      @  7, 6 SAY "Address 1"
      @  9, 6 SAY "City"
      @  9,41 SAY "State"
      @  9,55 SAY "Zip Code"
      @ 11, 6 SAY "Telephone"
      @ 11,33 SAY "Extension"
      @ 13, 6 SAY "Tax ID"
      @ 15, 6 SAY "Current Rate"
      @ 16,13 SAY "As of"
      @ 15,50 SAY "Variable Rate Mortgages"
      @ 16,46 SAY "Renegotiable Rate Mortgages"
      @ 17,61 SAY "Wraparounds"
RETURN

PROCEDURE FILTER
* Set filter on database
   * Get filter fields
      SET COLOR TO ,N/W
      @  4,17 GET m->l_id       PICTURE "!!!"
      @  4,49 GET m->l_name     PICTURE "@X25"
      @  7,17 GET m->l_addr1    PICTURE "@X25"
      @  8,17 GET m->l_addr2    PICTURE "@X25"
      @  9,17 GET m->l_city     PICTURE "@X20"
      @  9,48 GET m->l_state    PICTURE "!!"
      @  9,65 GET m->l_zip      PICTURE "99999-####"
      @ 11,17 GET m->l_phone    PICTURE "(###)999-9999"
      @ 11,44 GET m->l_ext      PICTURE "####"
      @ 13,17 GET m->l_tax_id   PICTURE "99-9999999"
      @ 15,20 GET m->l_currate  PICTURE "#9.9##";
               RANGE 0.0,20.0
      @ 16,20 GET m->l_ratedate PICTURE "@D"
      @ 15,75 GET m->t_vrm      PICTURE "!" ;
               VALID m->t_vrm $ "T, ,F"
      @ 16,75 GET m->t_rrm      PICTURE "!" ;
               VALID m->t_vrm $ "T, ,F"
      @ 17,75 GET m-t_wrap      PICTURE "!" ;
               VALID m->t_vrm $ "T, ,F"
      READ

  * Test for Esc key to exit filter selection.
  * If not, set filter
     IF READKEY() <> 12   && Esc
     * Form filter string by checking which fields have
     * values. Use them to define filter.

       * Check which character fields to add to filter.
       * Place single quotation marks around field values.
       filter_str = filter_str + IIF(.NOT.;
          EMPTY(m->l_id),"l_id='"+TRIM(m->l_id)+"' .AND.","")
       filter_str = filter_str + IIF(.NOT.;
          EMPTY(m->l_name),"l_name='"+TRIM(m->l_name)+"';
          .AND.","")
       filter_str = filter_str + IIF(.NOT.;
          EMPTY(m->l_addr1),"l_addr1='"+TRIM(m->l_addr1)+"';
```

```
   .AND.","")
filter_str = filter_str + IIF(.NOT.;
   EMPTY(m->l_addr2),"l_addr2='"+TRIM(m->l_addr2)+"';
   .AND.","")
filter_str = filter_str + IIF(.NOT.;
   EMPTY(m->l_city),"l_city='"+TRIM(m->l_city)+"';
   .AND.","")
filter_str = filter_str + IIF(.NOT.;
   EMPTY(m->l_state),"l_state='"+TRIM(m->l_state)+"';
   .AND.","")
filter_str = filter_str + IIF(.NOT.;
   EMPTY(m->l_zip),"l_zip='"+TRIM(m->l_zip)+"';
   .AND.","")
filter_str = filter_str + IIF(.NOT.;
   EMPTY(m->l_phone),"l_phone='"+TRIM(m->l_phone)+"';
   .AND.","")
filter_str = filter_str + IIF(.NOT.;
   EMPTY(m->l_ext),"l_ext='"+TRIM(m->l_ext)+"';
   .AND.","")
filter_str = filter_str + IIF(.NOT. ;
   EMPTY(m->l_tax_id),;
   "l_tax_id='"+TRIM(m->l_tax_id)+"' .AND.","")

* Check date fields for addition to filter
IF .NOT. {} = m->l_ratedate
   l_ratedate = DTOC(m->l_ratedate)
   filter_str = filter_str +;
      "l_ratedate=ctod('&l_rate_date') .AND."
ENDIF

* Check numeric fields. Note that
* field values are not quoted.
IF 0 <> m->l_currate
   l_currate = STR(m->l_currate,5,1)
   filter_str = filter_str +;
                "l_currate=&l_currate .AND."
ENDIF

* Add logical fields to filter
IF .NOT. EMPTY(m->t_vrm)
   filter_str = filter_str + ;
      IIF(m->t_vrm='T',"l_vrm .AND.",;
          ".not. l_vrm .AND.")
ENDIF
IF .NOT. EMPTY(m->t_rrm)
   filter_str = filter_str + ;
      IIF(m->t_rrm='T',"l_rrm .AND.",;
          ".not. l_rrm .AND.")
ENDIF
IF .NOT. EMPTY(m->t_wrap)
   filter_str = filter_str + ;
      IIF(m->t_wrap='T',"l_wrap .AND.",;
          ".not. l_wrap .AND.")
ENDIF
```

```
      ENDIF READKEY() <> 12  && Esc = 12

   * Check if filter is defined. If so, set it
   IF EMPTY(filter_str)
      SET FILTER TO

   ELSE
      * Remove last .AND. from filter
      filter_str = SUBSTR(filter_str,1,LEN(filter_str)-6)

      * Set filter
      SET FILTER TO &filter_str
      GOTO TOP

      * Test if any records satisfy filter
      IF EOF()
         DO disp_msg WITH 'No matching records'
         SET FILTER TO
         GO record_no
      ENDIF

   ENDIF '' = TRIM(filter_str)

   ENDIF

RETURN

* End of program
```

Program 5-2. Using Macro Substitution to Create a Filter

Keyboard Macros

Keyboard macros let us record keystrokes and play them back later by pressing a hot key combination. They are especially handy for automating common sequences. We can replace up to 1,024 characters with just one to four keystrokes.

If your application includes long strings or memo fields, macros can customize the user interface. They are stored in a separate file distributed with the application. Popular editing macros are:

- Delete the line at the cursor
- Delete the word at the cursor
- Save the file
- Display the ASCII chart to use a special character
- Insert a line

Once defined, macros are available throughout FoxPro. Some programmers use them to simulate the keystrokes of a favorite editor or word processor.

Defining Macros from the Keyboard

You may prefer to define macros from the keyboard, saving their definitions for later use in applications. To do this, first select the Macro option in the System pulldown menu to display the Keyboard Macro dialog.

The scrollable list in the center shows macros that are already defined. FoxPro provides default definitions for function keys F2 through F9. We cannot redefine F1 and F10. F1 always activates context sensitive help, and F10 always moves the cursor to the leftmost item in the menu bar. Table 5-1 lists the predefined macros and their default actions.

HINT

If a program changes predefined macros, it should restore them before terminating. The fastest way is to restore the default macro set. Changing a macro action affects only its definition in memory.

Table 5-1. Default Function Key Actions

Key	Command	Action
F2	SET	Opens the View window
F3	LIST	Lists records from the current database. Opens the GETFILE window if no database is in use.
F4	DIR	Lists all database files in the current directory.
F5	DISPLAY STRUCTURE	Shows the field definitions of the current database. Opens the GETFILE window if no database is in use.
F6	DISPLAY STATUS	Shows the database open in each area. If an index is also open, it displays the expression. Shows the settings of all SET commands.
F7	DISPLAY MEMORY	Displays the values stored in all memory variables, including system variables. Also shows the definitions of all menus, pads, popups, and windows.
F8	DISPLAY	Shows the current record. Opens the GETFILE window if no database is in use.
F9	APPEND	Enters append mode for the current database. Opens the GETFILE window if no database is in use.

How can we define more macros? In fact, FoxPro lets us define over 250 at a time. Table 5-2 lists all available keys. We can use combinations of letters and function keys with the modifiers Shift, Ctrl, and Alt.

Table 5-2. Available Macro Key Combinations

Key-stroke	Alone	Shift	Ctrl	Alt	Shift/ Ctrl	Shift/ Alt	Alt/ Ctrl	Shift/ Alt/Ctrl	Alt F10
A			X	X	X	X	X	X	X
B			X	X	X	X	X	X	X
C			X	X	X	X	X	X	X
D			X	X	X	X	X	X	X
E			X	X	X	X	X	X	X
F			X	X	X	X	X	X	X
G			X	X	X	X	X	X	X
H			X	X	X	X	X	X	X
I			X	X	X	X	X	X	X
J				X	X	X	X	X	X
K			X	X	X	X	X	X	X
L			X	X	X	X	X	X	X
M			X	X	X	X	X	X	X
N			X	X	X	X	X	X	X
O			X	X	X	X	X	X	X
P			X	X	X	X	X	X	X
Q				X		X	X	X	X
R			X	X	X	X	X	X	X
S				X		X	X	X	X
T			X	X	X	X	X	X	X
U			X	X	X	X	X	X	X
V			X	X	X	X	X	X	X
W			X	X	X	X	X	X	X
X			X	X	X	X	X	X	X
Y			X	X	X	X	X	X	X
Z			X	X	X	X	X	X	X
F1		X	X	X	X	X	X	X	
F2	X	X	X	X	X	X	X	X	
F3	X	X	X	X	X	X	X	X	
F4	X	X	X	X	X	X	X	X	

Table 5-2. Available Macro Key Combinations (cont'd.)

Keystroke	Alone	Shift	Ctrl	Alt	Shift/Ctrl	Shift/Alt	Alt/Ctrl	Shift/Alt/Ctrl	Alt F10
F5	X	X	X	X	X	X	X	X	
F6	X	X	X	X	X	X	X	X	
F7	X	X	X	X	X	X	X	X	
F8	X	X	X	X	X	X	X	X	
F9	X	X	X	X	X	X	X	X	
F10			X		X	X	X	X	
Ins	X	X							
Del	X	X							
Home	X	X	X		X				
End	X	X	X		X				
PgUp	X	X	X		X				
PgDn	X	X	X		X				
Left	X	X	X		X				
Up	X	X							
Right	X	X	X		X				
Down	X	X							

WARNING

Do not use Alt/Ctrl/Del or Shift/Alt/Ctrl/Del as macro keys since they reboot the computer.

If we want even more macros, we can save multiple sets. The potential is unlimited. To save a set, select SAVE from the Keyboard Macro dialog or use the command

```
SAVE MACROS TO filename
```

For example, let's define the macro Alt-T to transpose letters. From the Keyboard Macro dialog, select the New pushbutton. Next press Alt-T to specify the hot key. You need not enter a name; FoxPro calls the macro ALT_T automatically.

Next, tab to the Macro Contents window. Here we can define the macro using <key label> assignments from the Commands & Functions manual and Table 3-9. Note that you must enclose key labels in curly brackets.

Enter the following keystrokes (left column) to complete the definition of ALT_T. It exchanges the character at the cursor position with the one to its right.

{SHIFT+RIGHTARROW}	(Select the character under the cursor)
{ALT+E}	(Open the edit pulldown menu)
T	(Cut the selected character)
{RIGHTARROW}	(Move the cursor one character right)
{ALT+E}	(Open the edit pulldown menu)
P	(Paste the cut character)

Press Ctrl-Enter or tab to the OK button to complete the definition. We can put several macro commands on a line if we wish. Pressing Enter has no effect on the definition process.

TIP

Pressing Enter after a command merely starts the next one on a new line. To insert an Enter keystroke into a macro, you must put it inside curly brackets.

WARNING

When entering a command in a macro definition, remember to include {ENTER} if you normally press it after entering the command from the keyboard. If you forget, the macro will wait for you to press the Enter key when you execute it.

After entering a macro, you can use PLAY MACRO to execute it from a program. For example:

```
PLAY MACRO ALT_T
```

The Keystroke Macro dialog records our keystrokes as we perform an operation if we select the RECORD button. Another way to record keystrokes is to press Shift-F10 while in the command mode. In either case, we still name the macro using direct keystrokes such as Alt-T. However, FoxPro then records all subsequent keystrokes as we enter them. For example, to define the ALT_T macro above, press the actual keys rather than entering their labels. This mode makes generating new macros easier because FoxPro executes the keystrokes as they are recorded.

After entering the keystrokes defining the macro, press Shift-F10 to stop recording. The dialog in Figure 5-1 then appears.

We can also press Shift-F10 to generate a pause in the macro. The options at this point are: Ok, Continue, Discard, and Insert Pause. The first three are obvious. Insert Pause halts the macro temporarily during execution. When we select it, FoxPro provides two options for restarting the macro. KEY TO RESUME displays a box that tells us to press Shift-F10 to resume the macro. The other option is a timed pause. The next example creates macro ALT_I, an editing function that inserts code from a disk file into the currently open file. The required keystrokes are:

{ALT+F}O	(Select OPEN option from File menu)
{BACKTAB}{BACKTAB}	(Move to TYPE option)
{ENTER}F{ENTER}	(Select type FILE)
{BACKTAB}	(Move to ALL FILES option)
<Space>	(Select ALL FILES check box)
{PAUSE KEY}	(Pause to let user select file by highlighting it with the arrow keys and pressing Enter)
{SHIFT+CTRL+END}	(Select entire file)
{ALT+E}C	(Copy selected text to buffer)
{ALT+F}C	(Close second file)
{ALT+E}P	(Paste buffer in original document)

Note that BACKTAB is the label for the shifted Tab key. When the macro pauses during execution, you can select a file from the dialog.

For a timed pause, you must specify its duration in seconds. A typical application is in a demonstration program. You may want screens to advance automatically rather than requiring the user to press a key. The following macro (ALT_P) generates a thirty second pause.

{PAUSE 30.0}	(Generate a 30 second pause)
{ENTER}	(Wait requires Enter)

To use it, insert the following lines in a program:

```
PLAY MACRO ALT_P
WAIT ''
```

Since macros execute only when the program pauses for input, the WAIT statement executes ALT_P.

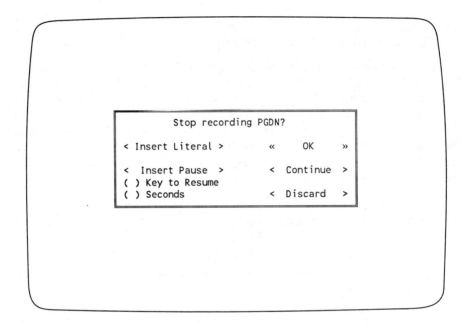

Figure 5-1. Stop Macro Recording dialog.

TIP

We can define a macro at any time by pressing Shift-F10. FoxPro first prompts for the macro's name. It then records all subsequent keystrokes until we press Shift-F10 again. (We can also start the macro recording by selecting the RECORD button in the Keystroke Macro dialog.) Because this method does not display the keystrokes in the Macro Contents window, it is difficult to use for long macros.

Another option in the Stop Recording dialog lets us insert literal keystrokes rather than their macro definitions. Suppose we want to disable the PgDn key for the user. It normally exits a READ statement without forcing him or her to complete other GET requests. To disable it, we could redefine it to do nothing. However, we may also want to retain a hidden option to exit a READ for debugging or testing purposes. Therefore, we redefine Shift-PgDn using the literal definition of PgDn. Now, no one can exit a READ using PgDn, but we can exit using Shift-PgDn.

```
MACRO: PGDN
{RIGHTARROW}          (Move right one character)
{LEFTARROW}           (Move left one character)
MACRO: SHIFT-PGDN
{LITERAL+PGDN}        (Treat next character as a literal)
```

NOTE

To insert a literal while recording keystrokes, you must suspend recording with Shift-F10, select the Insert Literal option, and then resume. If you are using the macro editor, you must enter the characters LITERAL+ before the key label you want to execute.

Removing Keyboard Macro Definitions

The four options to the left of the Keyboard Macro dialog (CLEAR ALL, RESTORE, SAVE, and SET DEFAULT) operate on all current macros in memory. The four to the right (CLEAR, EDIT, NEW, and RECORD) operate on individual macros.

Thus we can remove macro definitions in two ways. CLEAR removes only the currently selected one. CLEAR ALL removes all of them.

Modifying a Keyboard Macro

To edit a macro, specify its name and select EDIT from the Keyboard Macro dialog. This opens the Macro command window. We can now insert into, delete from, and edit the macro using FoxPro's text editor.

Saving a Macro Definition

After defining a set of macros, we can save it in a file. If we restore it in applications written for others, we can control the definitions of keys on their systems. If we do not save the definitions, they remain in effect only during the current session. The next time we run FoxPro, the default set is restored.

We save a macro set from the Keyboard Macro dialog. Macro files have the extension FKY.

Restoring a Macro Definition

When we start FoxPro, it looks for a default macro set called DEFAULT.FKY. (So, if we save our macro definitions under that name, FoxPro will load them automatically.) If it is not present, FoxPro defines function keys F2 through F9 as listed in Table 5-1. We can select the Restore text button from the Keyboard Macro dialog to restore a previously saved macro set. From a program, we restore one with

```
RESTORE MACROS FROM macrofil.fky
```

We can have any number of macro definition files, and we can load more than one. However, a macro with a duplicate name will overwrite one from an earlier set.

Using Keyboard Macros

Once we have defined a macro set, we can use it either from the keyboard or from a program. The PLAY MACRO command executes macros in programs.

If we issue PLAY MACRO from the Command window, it executes immediately. When used in a program, it executes at the next input command such as @...GET, ACCEPT, or INPUT. It then replays the keystrokes. If we issue multiple PLAY MACROs, the macros are replayed in reverse order. That is, the latest one executes first. This works as though they had been pushed onto a stack.

Program 5-3 fills a blank lender record using a macro file. Each macro in LENDER.FKY fills a field with an arbitrary value in response to an input prompt. It then pauses for two seconds so the viewer can see each event occur. This allows us to create a self-running demonstration version of an application.

The complete LENDER.FKY file is on the diskette for this book along with sample DBF and IDX files. The following key sequence shows a typical definition from it; macro ALT_A inserts 987 at the first prompt. The other macros are the same except for the data.

987	(Value to insert at input prompt)
{PAUSE 2.0}	(Insert a 2 second pause)
{ENTER}	(Enter completes input entry)

```
* Program 5-3
* Demonstration of keyboard macros to fill fields
* in a new record

* Set environment
SET TALK OFF
```

```
    SET STATUS OFF
    SET SCOREBOARD OFF

*   Since a Return character appears at the end of each
*   macro, we want SET CONFIRM ON just in case the
*   field value equals the field width. Otherwise,
*   the program will not use the Return until the
*   next input field. It would then skip that field.
    SET CONFIRM ON
    SET BELL OFF

*   Open database
    USE lender INDEX lender
    SCATTER MEMVAR BLANK

*   Clear screen and display form
    DO DISP_SCN

*   Get data using LENDER.FKY
    DO GET_DATA

RETURN

*   Specific procedures (listed alphabetically)

PROCEDURE DISP_SCN
*   Display screen form
    SET COLOR TO BG+/B
    CLEAR
    @   0,23 SAY "LENDER SELF RUNNING DEMONSTRATION"
    @   1, 0 TO 18,79 DOUBLE
    @   3, 1 TO 3,78 DOUBLE
    @   5, 1 TO 5,78
    SET COLOR TO GR+/B
    @   2,29 SAY "MORTGAGE SYSTEM"
    @  14,47 SAY "Special Financing Offered:"
    @  20,14 SAY "(2 second delay between entries)"
    SET COLOR TO W+/B
    @   4, 4 SAY "Lender ID"
    @   4,36 SAY "Bank Name"
    @   7, 6 SAY "Address 1"
    @   8, 6 SAY "Address 2"
    @   9, 6 SAY "City"
    @   9,41 SAY "State"
    @   9,55 SAY "Zip Code"
    @  11, 6 SAY "Telephone"
    @  11,33 SAY "Extension"
    @  13, 6 SAY "Tax ID"
    @  15, 6 SAY "Current Rate"
    @  16,13 SAY "As of"
    @  15,50 SAY "Variable Rate Mortgages"
    @  16,46 SAY "Renegotiable Rate Mortgages"
    @  17,61 SAY "Wraparounds"
RETURN
```

```
PROCEDURE GET_DATA
* Restore macro file
  RESTORE MACROS FROM lender.fky

* Define PLAY MACRO commands in reverse order
* Note reverse order of playing macros
* ALT_P is Wraparound
* ALT_A is Lender ID
  PLAY MACRO ALT_P
  PLAY MACRO ALT_O
  PLAY MACRO ALT_N
  PLAY MACRO ALT_M
  PLAY MACRO ALT_L
  PLAY MACRO ALT_K
  PLAY MACRO ALT_I
  PLAY MACRO ALT_H
  PLAY MACRO ALT_G
  PLAY MACRO ALT_F
  PLAY MACRO ALT_E
  PLAY MACRO ALT_D
  PLAY MACRO ALT_C
  PLAY MACRO ALT_B
  PLAY MACRO ALT_A

* Get filter fields
  SET COLOR TO ,N/W
  @  4,17 GET m->l_id       PICTURE "!!!"
  @  4,49 GET m->l_name     PICTURE "@X25"
  @  7,17 GET m->l_addr1    PICTURE "@X25"
  @  8,17 GET m->l_addr2    PICTURE "@X25"
  @  9,17 GET m->l_city     PICTURE "@X20"
  @  9,48 GET m->l_state    PICTURE "!!"
  @  9,65 GET m->l_zip      PICTURE "99999-####"
  @ 11,17 GET m->l_phone    PICTURE "(###)999-9999"
  @ 11,44 GET m->l_ext      PICTURE "####"
  @ 13,17 GET m->l_tax_id   PICTURE "99-9999999"
  @ 15,20 GET m->l_currate  PICTURE "#9.9##" RANGE 0.0,20.0
  @ 16,20 GET m->l_ratedate PICTURE "@D"
  @ 15,75 GET m->l_vrm      PICTURE "@L"
  @ 16,75 GET m->l_rrm      PICTURE "@L"
  @ 17,75 GET m->l_wrap     PICTURE "@L"
  READ

* Return to default definitions
  RESTORE MACROS FROM default.fky
  RETURN

* End of program
```

Program 5-3. Lender Demonstration Using Macros

TIP
Always restore the default macro set before exiting a program that changes it.

KEYBOARD Command

Macros can customize FoxPro's editing interface. They can also fill fields with literal values as shown in the last example. However, they cannot reference memory or database variables. The KEYBOARD command can stuff the keyboard buffer with both literal strings and variable values. Program 5-4 uses it to fill a blank LENDER record.

The KEYBOARD command stores keystrokes. It plays back strings of characters as if the user had entered them. Note that all terms in it must be the same type. Even if keystrokes represent numeric, date, or logical data, define the value as a string. If a memory variable is not a string, first convert it to one before adding it to the KEYBOARD buffer. KEYBOARD's main limitation is that it cannot store more than 126 characters at a time.

If we can keep all inputs within this limit, we can use KEYBOARD to create self-running demonstration systems as illustrated in Program 5-4.

```
* Program 5-4
* Uses KEYBOARD to create a demonstration

* Set environment
  SET TALK OFF
  SET STATUS OFF
  SET SCOREBOARD OFF

* Since a Return character appears at the end of each
* macro, we want SET CONFIRM ON just in case the
* field value equals the field width. Otherwise,
* the program will not use the Return until the
* next input field. It would then skip that field.
  SET CONFIRM ON
  SET BELL OFF

* Open database file
  USE lender INDEX lender
  SCATTER MEMVAR BLANK
```

```
* Clear screen and display form
  DO DISP_SCN

* Get data using KEYBOARD command
  DO GET_DATA

RETURN

* Specific procedures (listed alphabetically)

PROCEDURE DISP_SCN
* Display screen form
  SET COLOR TO BG+/B
  CLEAR
  @  0,20 SAY "CREATING A DEMO WITH THE KEYBOARD COMMAND"
  @  1, 0 TO 18,79 DOUBLE
  @  3, 1 TO 3,78 DOUBLE
  @  5, 1 TO 5,78
  SET COLOR TO GR+/B
  @  2,29 SAY "MORTGAGE SYSTEM"
  @ 14,47 SAY "Special Financing Offered:"
  @ 20,14 SAY "(No delay between entries)"
  SET COLOR TO W+/B
  @  4, 4 SAY "Lender ID"
  @  4,36 SAY "Bank Name"
  @  7, 6 SAY "Address 1"
  @  8, 6 SAY "Address 2"
  @  9, 6 SAY "City"
  @  9,41 SAY "State"
  @  9,55 SAY "Zip Code"
  @ 11, 6 SAY "Telephone"
  @ 11,33 SAY "Extension"
  @ 13, 6 SAY "Tax ID"
  @ 15, 6 SAY "Current Rate"
  @ 16,13 SAY "As of"
  @ 15,50 SAY "Variable Rate Mortgages"
  @ 16,46 SAY "Renegotiable Rate Mortgages"
  @ 17,61 SAY "Wraparounds"
RETURN

PROCEDURE GET_DATA
* Define KEYBOARD command
* Mix strings with numerics and variable names
cr    = CHR(13)
name  = "Farmer's National Bank" + cr
addr1 = "Box 5C" + cr
addr2 = "523 Main Street" + cr
city  = "Allentown" + cr
KEYBOARD "987"+cr+name+addr1+addr2+city+"PA"+cr+"18503"+cr+;
   "2153782343"+cr+"5432"+cr+"23-5865943"+cr+"10.125"+cr+;
   "022390"+cr+"T"+cr+"F"+cr+"T"+cr
```

```
* Get filter fields
SET COLOR TO ,N/W
  @  4,17 GET m->l_id        PICTURE "!!!"
  @  4,49 GET m->l_name      PICTURE "@X25"
  @  7,17 GET m->l_addr1     PICTURE "@X25"
  @  8,17 GET m->l_addr2     PICTURE "@X25"
  @  9,17 GET m->l_city      PICTURE "@X20"
  @  9,48 GET m->l_state     PICTURE "!!"
  @  9,65 GET m->l_zip       PICTURE "99999-####"
  @ 11,17 GET m->l_phone     PICTURE "(###)999-9999"
  @ 11,44 GET m->l_ext       PICTURE "####"
  @ 13,17 GET m->l_tax_id    PICTURE "99-9999999"
  @ 15,20 GET m->l_currate   PICTURE "#9.9##" RANGE 0.0,20.0
  @ 16,20 GET m->l_ratedate  PICTURE "@D"
  @ 15,75 GET m->l_vrm       PICTURE "@L"
  @ 16,75 GET m->l_rrm       PICTURE "@L"
  @ 17,75 GET m->l_wrap      PICTURE "@L"
READ

RETURN

* End of program
```

Program 5-4. Automatic Field Fill Using the KEYBOARD Command

Summary

This chapter defined two types of FoxPro macros: macro variables and keyboard macros.

Macro variables let us substitute variable information into commands. We can even use them to replace variable names. However, their real power is in generalizing procedures. We ended this section by creating a generalized filter.

Next we examined keyboard macros that store entire keystroke sequences and are activated by simple key combinations. We define them through letter and function keys along with Alt, Ctrl, and Shift. We can use them from the Command window or from application programs.

We ended the chapter by demonstrating the use of both keyboard macros and the KEYBOARD command to store keystrokes for later playback in a program.

data items with a common name; numerical subscripts identify individual elements. Arrays are useful when editing database records. They can also serve as lookup tables during program execution.

FoxPro Arrays

FoxPro supports one- and two-dimensional arrays. You can think of a one-dimensional array as a column or row of values. Similarly, a two-dimensional array as a grid or table of rows and columns. In effect, a one-dimensional array is just a special case of a two-dimensional array. Figure 6-1 shows how to visualize arrays.

We can use each array element as a separate memory variable. We can copy data between it and other memory variables or database fields. We can also use elements directly in calculations.

Although an array has many data values, it counts just once toward FoxPro's memory variable limit. You can thus effectively expand the limit as long as enough memory is available.

Defining and Naming Arrays

Before using an array, we must define and name it. We do this with the DECLARE or DIMENSION command. To declare an array, we must specify two things: its name and its size. We need not specify the type of data it will hold. In fact, each element can contain a different type.

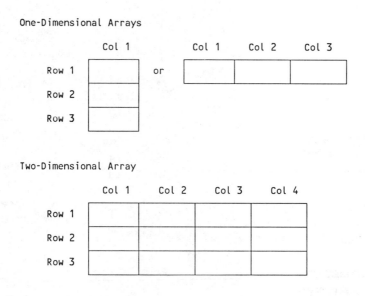

Figure 6-1. Visual representations of arrays.

Array names follow the same conventions as other identifiers. FoxPro arrays can contain up to 3600 elements. To specify one's size, insert it between parentheses or square brackets [] after the name. Typical definitions are:

```
DECLARE bank_id[20]
DIMENSION bank_names[20]
DECLARE bank_rates(20)
DIMENSION rate_date(20)
```

The definition of a two-dimensional array specifies both rows and columns. It involves two numeric parameters between parentheses or square brackets, separated by a comma. Suppose we want to store the above four one-dimensional arrays as a single two-dimensional array. Each array forms a row: bank IDs first, followed by bank names, interest rates, and the dates when they became effective. Since each array has 20 elements, we set the number of columns to 20. Each column then defines information for one bank. The declaration is

```
DECLARE bank_info[4,20]
```

Array bank_info has 80 elements (4 rows of 20). The limit of 3600 elements restricts the size of two-dimensional arrays. For example, the largest square array has 60 columns and 60 rows.

Although an array counts as just one memory variable, FoxPro must allocate enough space for all its elements. The initial declaration defines them as logical variables. However, the actual memory requirements depend on the type of data stored. Character data usually requires the most space. Thus, FoxPro may have enough room to define an array, but not enough to store data in it.

Like other memory variables, arrays are PRIVATE when declared in a program. However, we cannot make one PUBLIC by just putting it in a PUBLIC statement. Instead we must use the PUBLIC ARRAY command, as in

```
PUBLIC ARRAY bank_info[4,20]
```

Remember that we can use PRIVATE variables only in the procedure that defines them or ones it calls. To use an array in a calling procedure, we must declare it with PUBLIC ARRAY.

There is a third way to define an array. The SCATTER command creates a one-dimensional array. It has an element for each field (except memos) in the currently open database.

Although most commands do not differentiate between one and two-dimensional arrays, most situations lend themselves to one or the other. For example, a one-dimensional array is appropriate for tracking the price of a stock. However, a two-dimensional array makes more sense when tracking 50 stocks. In this case, one record might represent one day of stock prices, with each column holding a closing price. In fact, FoxPro databases lend themselves to two-dimensional representations.

FoxPro lets us access arrays using either one-dimensional or two-dimensional nomenclature. It stores elements sequentially in row major order (that is, row 1, then row 2, etc.). Thus a nine element one-dimensional array is the same as a 3 by 3 two-dimensional array. Table 6-1 shows equivalent ways of addressing the elements in array X[9].

Table 6-1. Equivalent Addresses for One- and Two-Dimensional Array Elements

One-Dimensional Representation	Two-Dimensional Equivalent
X[1]	X[1,1]
X[2]	X[1,2]
X[3]	X[1,3]
X[4]	X[2,1]
X[5]	X[2,2]
X[6]	X[2,3]
X[7]	X[3,1]
X[8]	X[3,2]
X[9]	X[3,3]

Redimensioning Arrays

We can redimension an array, thus changing its size. We can also convert a one-dimensional array to two-dimensional and vice versa. During redimensioning, FoxPro tries to preserve element values. If the new array contains more elements than the original, the extra ones are set to .F.. If it contains fewer, the extra ones are lost.

Inserting and Deleting Elements

Not only can we redimension arrays, but we can also delete and insert rows and columns with the ADEL() and AINS() functions. To delete the fourth element of a one-dimensional array or the fourth row of a two-dimensional array, use

```
= ADEL(arrayname,4)
```

Here the second parameter is the row number. To delete the fourth column of a two-dimensional array, include 2 as the third parameter. Now the second parameter is the column number.

```
= ADEL(arrayname,4,2)
```

Deleting a row or column does not change an array's size. It does, however, move the remaining elements, filling the gap. For example, if we delete an element or row, subsequent ones move up one position. The last one is set to .F.. Similarly, if we delete a column, subsequent ones move left one position, and the last one is set to .F..

In the above examples, we used the = operator because we did not need the return value. ADEL() returns 1 if it deletes the specified row or column successfully. Otherwise, it returns -1.

The AINS() function inserts rows and columns into arrays. Like ADEL(), it does not change their size. If we insert a new element into a one-dimensional array or a row into a two-dimensional array, all subsequent elements or rows move down one position. The last element or row is lost. AINS() sets the new elements to .F.. A typical example is

```
= AINS(arrayname,4)
```

To insert a column, include 2 as the third parameter. Inserting a column into a one-dimensional array effectively sets all its elements to .F.. Inserting a column into a two-dimensional array creates a new column initialized to .F.. The command

```
= AINS(arrayname,1,2)
```

inserts a new column 1, moves the old column 1 to column 2, column 2 to column 3, etc. The values from the last column are lost.

Like ADEL(), AINS() returns 1 if it inserts the row or column successfully. Otherwise, it returns -1.

Translating between Element Numbers and Row and Column Subscripts

The AELEMENT() function converts row and column subscripts to the equivalent element number, i.e., the subscript in a one-dimensional array. For example, to get the element number in a 10 by 8 array for the element in the fifth row and second column, use the command

```
elmt_num = AELEMENT(arrayname,5,2)
```

Similarly, the ASUBSCRIPT() function returns the row and column subscripts corresponding to an element number. Given the same two-dimensional array, what row and column correspond to element 50?

```
row = ASUBSCRIPT(arrayname,50,1)   && Get row
col = ASUBSCRIPT(arrayname,50,2)   && Get column
```

We use separate calls to get the row and column values. The third parameter determines whether ASUBSCRIPT() returns the row (1) or column (2) subscript.

Copying Arrays

The ACOPY() function copies an array. It can take up to 5 parameters. The first is the source, and the second the destination. With no other parameters, ACOPY() copies all elements. The order is by element number.

ACOPY() returns the number of elements copied or -1 if it fails. The destination array must be large enough, or FoxPro displays the message:

```
SUBSCRIPT OUT OF BOUNDS
```

To copy only selected elements, we use the third and fourth parameters. The third is the starting point. If the source array is two-dimensional and we want to copy it beginning with the fifth row, we use AELEMENT() to get the element number.

```
numcopied = ACOPY(array1, array2, AELEMENT(array1,5,1))
```

The fourth parameter indicates how many elements to copy. For instance, we can modify the previous example to copy just 10 elements.

```
numcopied = ACOPY(array1, array2, AELEMENT(array1,5,1), 10)
```

Normally, the copy begins at the first element in the destination array. However, the fifth parameter specifies an alternate starting point. This technique allows us to append data to arrays. To copy the 10 elements of array1 in the previous example to the eighth row of array2, use the following command:

```
numcopied = ACOPY(array1, array2, AELEMENT(array1,5,1), 10, ;
                AELEMENT(array2,8,1))
```

Of course, array2 must be large enough to hold all the elements. One way to insure this is to check with the ALEN() function.

Determining the Length of an Array

The ALEN() function returns the number of elements in a one- or two-dimensional array or the number of rows or columns in a two-dimensional array. If we want to copy array1 to array2, we can check whether there is enough room with the following commands.

```
IF ALEN(array1) <= ALEN(array2)
   numcopied = ACOPY(array1,array2)
ENDIF
```

Here ALEN has a single argument. It returns the total number of elements. This test works regardless of how the arrays are dimensioned.

The second parameter must be 0, 1, or 2. A value of 0 returns the total number of array elements, just as in the single-parameter case. A value of 1 returns the number of rows, and 2 the number of columns.

We can combine the options in a complex test that copies a subset of the first array into the middle of the second.

```
a1_start = 4        && First element in array1
a1_count = 10       && Number of elements to copy
a2_start = 8        && First element to replace with copy
IF a1_count <= ALEN(array2) + 1 - a2_start
   numcopied = ACOPY(array1, array2, a1_start, ;
                a1_count, a2_start)
ENDIF
```

Sorting Arrays

The ASORT() function sorts arrays in ascending or descending order. It takes four parameters. The first is the array name. We can sort an entire one- or two-dimensional array by its first column by including just the name, as in

```
success = ASORT(array1)
```

The second parameter is the element or row with which to begin. For example, to sort an array starting with the second element or row, use

```
success = ASORT(array1,2)
```

This command sorts the rest of the array. The third parameter indicates how many rows or elements to sort. For example, to sort 5 rows or elements beginning with the second, use

```
success = ASORT(array1,2,5)
```

The last parameter defines the sort order. If it is zero or omitted, ASORT() performs an ascending sort. A nonzero value indicates a descending sort. The following command sorts five rows beginning with the second in descending order.

```
success = ASORT(array1,2,5,1)
```

How could we perform a descending sort of the entire array beginning with the second element? We cannot omit the third parameter. We could use ALEN() to determine the number of elements or rows. Then we could subtract the number skipped. Fortunately, there is an easier way. Just assign -1 to the third parameter as a placeholder.

```
success = ASORT(array1,2,-1,1)
```

WARNING

To sort the entire array in descending order, use 1 for the second parameter (the first element to sort), not -1.

```
success = ASORT(array1,1,-1,1)
```

In the above examples, we assigned the value returned by ASORT() to the variable *success*. ASORT() returns 1 if it succeeds and -1 if it fails.

Searching an Array for an Expression

ASCAN() searches an array for an expression. Suppose it contains product information. The first column contains the product names. Other columns contain other information such as inventory level, cost, and retail price. The following example uses ASCAN() to locate the row containing the product 'FOXPRO LAN VERSION'.

```
elemt_num = ASCAN(array1,'FOXPRO LAN VERSION')
```

If it finds a match, ASCAN returns the element number. Otherwise, it returns 0. Whether it succeeds depends on the state of SET EXACT. If EXACT is ON, the search text must match the array element precisely in both size and content.

The element number returned by ASCAN for a two-dimensional array does not tell us directly which row of the array to read. However, we can use the ASUBSCRIPT() function to convert it to a row number.

```
row = ASUBSCRIPT(array1,elemt_num,1)
```

ASCAN() also has optional third and fourth parameters. They indicate where to begin and how many elements to search, respectively.

Reading the Directory into an Array

The ADIR() function loads directory information into an array. It requires a two-dimensional array in which each row represents a directory entry. A row must have at least five columns, as defined in Table 6-2. If it does not, ADIR() redefines the array.

Table 6-2. Column Definitions for ADIR() Array

Column	Type	Description
1	Character	Name
2	Numeric	Size
3	Date	Date
4	Character	Time
5	Character	Attributes

The following command loads the current directory information into array1.

```
= ADIR(array1)
```

If we do not want the entire directory, we can use the second parameter to select files. For example, to load program files only, use

```
= ADIR(array1,'*.PRG')
```

We can expand the search by including one or more of the following characters as a third parameter.

```
D - Subdirectories
H - Hidden Files
S - System Files
V - Volume Names
```

For example,

```
= ADIR(array1, 'cust*.*', 'D')
```

returns not only files that begin with CUST, but subdirectories also.

Defaults and Array Initialization

When we declare an array, FoxPro initializes all its elements to .F.. Later they adopt the data type of the information placed in them. A single array may contain numeric, character, logical, or date values. The only type that cannot appear is a memo.

We can initialize arrays in several ways. The fastest one uses a single statement. The following assignments initialize arrays with several variable types.

```
DECLARE bank_id[20],bank_names[20]
DECLARE bank_rates[20],rate_date[20]
bank_id    = " "
bank_names = " "
bank_rates = 0
rate_date  = CTOD('  /  /  ')
```

WARNING

This method works only when SET COMPATIBLE is OFF. If it is ON, the assignment statements redefine the array as a single memory variable.

Two-dimensional arrays often include elements of different types as in BANK_INFO. We then must initialize them individually by column or by row. The following assignments use a FOR...ENDFOR structure to initialize BANK_INFO by row.

```
DECLARE bank_info[4,20]
FOR icnt = 1 TO 20
   bank_info[1,icnt] = " "
   bank_info[2,icnt] = " "
   bank_info[3,icnt] = 0
   bank_info[4,icnt] = CTOD('  /  /  ')
ENDFOR
```

> **WARNING**
>
> If you use FOR...ENDFOR loops to manipulate arrays, watch for program changes that might redimension them.

Using Arrays with Database Files

A common use of arrays is to move elements to or from a database file. FoxPro provides two transfer commands, COPY TO ARRAY and SCATTER. COPY TO ARRAY requires a previously defined array. SCATTER creates one automatically if it does not already exist or is too small.

SCATTER

SCATTER copies fields from the currently open database to individual memory variables or an array. Using the database LENDER.DBF, the following sequence transfers fields from the current record to memory variables. By default, they will have the same names as the database fields.

```
USE lender
SCATTER MEMVAR
```

We can now edit copies of the fields rather than editing them directly. This simplifies corrections and avoids corrupting the database. A variation that creates empty memory variables for each field is useful when adding new records.

```
USE lender
SCATTER BLANK
```

In either case, remember to preface references to memory variables with the m-> qualifier. Otherwise, commands will access the database fields of the same name.

However, to work with all elements as a group, we must load their values into an array with SCATTER. It first checks for an existing array with the specified name. If it finds one, it checks its size. If the array does not exist or is too small, SCATTER creates a new one. Then it copies the value of each field to a separate element. If the array existed and had more elements than SCATTER requires, the extra ones are unaffected.

We need not copy all fields. The FIELDS clause specifies which ones are involved. Without it, SCATTER transfers everything except memos. The following commands transfer four fields from database LENDER to array BANK_INFO.

```
USE lender
SCATTER FIELDS l_id,l_name,l_currate,l_ratedate TO bank_info
```

If a database has a repeating field, storing its values in an array may simplify processing. However, the SCATTER command applies only to the current record.

For example, suppose the database STOCKS contains the following repeating fields, representing the daily closing prices for 10 stocks.

FIELD	CONTENTS
STOCK_1	Daily closing price for stock 1
STOCK_2	Daily closing price for stock 2
STOCK_3	Daily closing price for stock 3
.	.
.	.
.	.
STOCK_10	Daily closing price for stock 10

A program to calculate the total value of all 10 stocks would require a long arithmetic expression to include all the variable names. (Imagine the expression needed in a program tracking 100 stocks!)

```
total = stock_1 + stock_2 + stock_3 + stock_4 + stock_5 ;
        + stock_6 + stock_7 + stock_8 + stock_9 + stock_10
```

Obviously, repetitive commands produce long lines that are difficult to maintain. A better approach uses macro substitution. We can easily generate field names to put the stock number at the end of the price variable. We can then process all ten prices with a single FOR...ENDFOR loop. The equivalent statements are now:

```
* Initialize total to zero
  total = 0

* Begin loop to calculate total
  FOR icnt = 1 TO 10
  * Convert counter to a string
    cnt = LTRIM(STR(icnt,2))
  * Add daily closing price of next stock
    total = total + stock_&cnt
  ENDFOR
```

If we use SCATTER to load the fields into an array, the equivalent lines are:

```
* Initialize total to zero
  total = 0
```

```
* Load database fields for item 1 into memory variables
  SCATTER FIELDS stock_1,stock_2,stock_3,stock_4,;
     stock_5,stock_6,stock_7,stock_8,;
     stock_9,stock_10 TO stock

* Begin loop to calculate total
  FOR icnt = 1 TO 10
  * Calculate total cost of item
    total = total + stock[icnt]
  ENDFOR
```

We wrote a test program to time all three versions using 1600 records with ten stocks each. The version that used a memory variable for each database field and a long arithmetic expression ran the fastest. It took 10 seconds. The macro substitution method required over ten times as long, 110 seconds. Finally, the version using arrays with SCATTER and a FOR...ENDFOR structure took 18 seconds. (Actual times may vary on different system configurations, and all other standard disclaimers also apply.)

TIP

When processing repeating fields, using SCATTER with a FOR...ENDFOR loop may be the best design choice. It is an excellent compromise among factors such as program size, readability, and execution time. But for pure speed, long command lines that avoid macro substitution and loops perform best.

COPY TO ARRAY

The second way to fill an array from a database is with the COPY TO ARRAY command. The main difference between it and SCATTER is that it can transfer multiple records. However, it requires a previously defined array.

With a one-dimensional array, COPY TO ARRAY copies only fields from the first record. If there are excess elements, it leaves them unchanged. If there are too few, it ignores the fields that do not fit.

To copy multiple records, we must use a two-dimensional array. COPY TO ARRAY stores one record in each row. As with one-dimensional arrays, if there are too few columns, it ignores the remaining fields. It also ignores memo fields automatically.

We can limit the fields transferred by using the FIELDS list, as in SCATTER. The following lines load up to 50 rows of bank data into array BANK_INFO. The FIELDS option limits the transfer to just four fields.

```
* Define size of array. It will have up to 50 records
* of 4 elements each. The elements are:
*       bank ID
*       bank name
*       current interest rate
*       date interest rate went into effect
  DECLARE bank_info[50,4]


* Open database
  USE lender INDEX lender


* Copy selected elements into array
  COPY TO ARRAY bank_info FIELDS l_id,l_name,l_currate,;
       l_ratedate
```

We may want to copy as much of the database as possible into the array. The following command lines determine the required size for DIMENSION.

```
* Maximum number of elements in an array is 3600

* First determine number of fields in database
  numflds = FCOUNT()

* Determine maximum number of rows
  numrows = INT(3600/numflds)

* Dimension array
  DECLARE bank_info[numrows,numflds]
```

COPY TO ARRAY also allows a scope clause. With it, FoxPro copies a subset of the database. The options include:

```
NEXT <n>      Next n records from the current position
RECORD <n>    Record n
REST          Rest of the records from the current position
```

We can also use FOR and WHILE clauses. They work the same as in previously discussed commands. Remember that FOR searches all records for the specified condition. On the other hand, WHILE begins at the current record and continues only as long as the condition remains true. For large databases from which we want only a few records, FOR can take much longer than WHILE. However, the records must be sorted or indexed by the fields used in WHILE. For example, suppose we want to copy information only from banks that have interest rates below 10%.

```
  DECLARE bank_info[50,4]


* Open database
  USE lender INDEX lender
```

```
* Copy selected elements into array
  COPY TO ARRAY bank_info FIELDS l_id,l_name,l_currate,;
       l_ratedate FOR l_currate < .10
```

WARNING

Many commands use one or two-dimensional arrays inter-changeably. However, COPY TO ARRAY Is one place where FoxPro makes a distinction. To use it to extract a field from multiple records, we need a two-dimensional array. The following lines will not fill the array date_table:

```
    PUBLIC date_table[20]
    COPY TO ARRAY date_table FIELDS qtrstart
```

Here is the method that works:

```
    PUBLIC date_table[20,1]
    COPY TO ARRAY date_table FIELDS qtrstart
```

GATHER

GATHER is the inverse of SCATTER. It transfers data from memory variables or an array back into the database.

When we use GATHER with MEMVAR, it transfers the values from memory variables with the same names as the database fields. Often we created them originally with SCATTER MEMVAR or SCATTER BLANK. If no memory variable is found for a database field, it is left unchanged.

When GATHER returns an array to a database, it copies each element into sequential fields. If the array has more elements than the database has fields, it ignores the remainder. However, we may not want to return the elements sequentially. In the case of bank_info, suppose the data elements are widely separated in the record structure. Then we must use the FIELDS list. The following command lines show a typical use of SCATTER to first load selected database fields into an array. Then, after some processing steps, GATHER returns them to the same record.

```
    USE lender

* Load database fields for item 1 to memory variables
  SCATTER FIELDS prod_id_1,prod_id_2,prod_id_3,;
      prod_id_4,prod_id_5,prod_id_6,prod_id_7,prod_id_8,;
      prod_id_9,prod_id_10 TO prod_id
  SCATTER FIELDS quant_1,quant_2,quant_3,quant_4,;
      quant_5,quant_6,quant_7,quant_8,quant_9,quant_10;
```

```
          TO quant
     SCATTER FIELDS unit_p_1,unit_p_2,unit_p_3,unit_p_4,;
        unit_p_5,unit_p_6,unit_p_7,unit_p_8,unit_p_9,;
        unit_p_10 TO unit_p
     SCATTER FIELDS tax_1,tax_2,tax_3,tax_4,tax_5,tax_6,;
        tax_7,tax_8,tax_9,tax_10 TO tax

   * Perform calculations in this section

   * Load database fields for item 1 to memory variables
     GATHER FIELDS prod_id_1,prod_id_2,prod_id_3,prod_id_4,;
        prod_id_5,prod_id_6,prod_id_7,prod_id_8,;
        prod_id_9,prod_id_10 FROM prod_id
     GATHER FIELDS quant_1,quant_2,quant_3,quant_4,quant_5,;
        quant_6,quant_7,quant_8,quant_9,quant_10 FROM quant
     GATHER FIELDS unit_p_1,unit_p_2,unit_p_3,unit_p_4,;
        unit_p_5,;unit_p_6,unit_p_7,unit_p_8,unit_p_9,;
        unit_p_10 FROM unit_p
     GATHER FIELDS tax_1,tax_2,tax_3,tax_4,tax_5,tax_6,;
        tax_7,tax_8,tax_9,tax_10 FROM tax
```

WARNING

GATHER replaces values. It is not additive. Therefore, to accumulate values, perform the calculations first, then save the array.

APPEND FROM ARRAY

APPEND FROM ARRAY is the inverse of COPY TO ARRAY. It transfers data from array rows back into new database records in the current area. Each row of a two-dimensional array becomes a record in the database.

If we do not specify a FIELDS list, the first column of the array replaces the first field in the database. Subsequent columns replace sequential fields through the last column or last field, whichever comes first. The FIELDS list allows us to update specific fields, just as in the GATHER command.

HINT

Use COPY TO and APPEND FROM when you must read more than one database record into a table. Use GATHER and SCATTER to access individual records.

Passing Arrays to Procedures

Passing arrays to procedures is just like passing anything else. FoxPro passes parameters by reference. If we change one's value in a procedure, the corresponding variable in the caller also changes. This is because FoxPro passes its memory address, not just its value. In effect, the procedure accesses the original variable's memory location directly.

Saving Arrays

The SAVE TO command stores current memory variables and arrays in a file with the extension MEM. Unless specifically restricted with a LIKE or EXCEPT clause, it saves all variables.

The ALL LIKE option selects specific ones to save. However, rather than providing a list, we use a skeleton as a pattern. Skeletons use the question mark (?) and asterisk (*) as wildcard characters (as in DOS) to define groups of variables. A question mark represents any single character, an asterisk any number of characters, including none. The question mark can appear anywhere in the skeleton, but the asterisk is usually the last or only character. Typical examples are:

`SAVE TO temp ALL LIKE interest`	Saves just the variable INTEREST
`SAVE TO temp ALL LIKE rate?`	Saves variables that begin with RATE and have one character or none afterward such as RATE, RATE1, or RATEA.
`SAVE TO temp ALL LIKE cur*`	Saves all variables that begin with CUR, such as CUR, CURBAL, CURINT, CURPRIN, or CURYR.

The EXCEPT option saves all variables except specific ones. It also uses a pattern for variable names.

`SAVE TO temp EXCEPT interest`	Saves all variables except INTEREST

`SAVE TO temp EXCEPT rate?`	Saves all variables except ones that begin with RATE and have one character or none afterward such as RATE, RATE1, or RATEA.
`SAVE TO temp EXCEPT cur*`	Saves all variables except ones that begin with CUR, such as CUR, CURBAL, CURINT, CURPRIN, or CURYR.

If we name groups of variables with common characters (such as CURBAL, CURINT, CURPRIN, and CURYR), we can include or exclude them from a save to a memory file using wildcards.

Using Arrays as Memory Tables

We can use arrays for any group of related variables. They are easy to process in loops, and they can handle a variety of data types on an element by element basis. One common application is to hold values from a small reference database.

For example, in a point of sale system, the program prompts for a salesperson ID. It is especially important to get the correct value if a commission is involved. We do not need to store all the salesperson's information with each ticket, just his or her ID or name. We can store other information, such as commission rate, first name, and last name, separately.

During data entry, we can validate the name or ID against the salesperson file to insure proper crediting. To do this, the program must perform several steps:

- Open a work area with salesperson data
- Search the records for the salesperson ID or name
- Reopen the original work area to continue sales entry

If there are just a few salespeople, we can reduce search time considerably by saving the information in an array. Then we can validate the name against it without doing any disk accesses.

Program 6-1 uses an array for validation. It first loads the fields from the database EMPLOYEE.DBF into the array STAFF. EMPLOYEE has only three fields: ID, last name, and first name. When the user enters an employee's last name, the program searches the array to validate it and display the full name.

It also uses SOUNDEX() to handle minor misspellings. SOUNDEX() returns a four-character string representing the phonetic equivalent of the string passed to it. This technique cannot handle all misspellings, but it will take care of minor variations such as BROWN and BROWNE.

```
* Program 6-1
* Using an array instead of a database table for validation
* Database used is EMPLOYEE.DBF
* Set environment
  SET TALK OFF
  SET STATUS OFF
  SET EXACT OFF
  SET SCOREBOARD OFF
  CLEAR
  name = SPACE(15)

* Load database file
  USE employee INDEX emplname

* Determine number of fields in array
  ncol = FCOUNT()

* Determine number of rows in array
  nrow = RECCOUNT()

* Dimension array
  DECLARE staff[nrow,ncol]

* Load array
  COPY TO ARRAY staff

* Close database (or use a different one in same area)
  USE

* Display data
  FOR irow = 1 TO nrow
    FOR icol = 1 TO ncol
      ?? staff[irow,icol]+"   "
    ENDFOR
    ?
  ENDFOR
  ?

* Pause to let user read list
  WAIT

* Prompt for name
  CLEAR
  @ 5,5 SAY "Enter a last name: " GET name PICTURE '@15!'
```

```
READ
name = TRIM(name)
```

```
* Loop until name is found or no data left to read
@ 8,5 SAY 'Possible matches include:'
ifind = 0
FOR i = 1 TO nrow

   * Use SOUNDEX() to find possible name matches
   IF SOUNDEX(staff[i,2]) = SOUNDEX(name)
     IF ifind = 0
       ?
       ? '      Emp ID      Employee Name'
     ENDIF
     ? SPACE(5) + staff[i,1] + SPACE(5) + TRIM(staff[i,3]) + ;
          " " + staff[i,2]
     ifind = ifind + 1
   ENDIF
ENDFOR

* End of array encountered without finding name
IF ifind = 0
  @ 8,5 SAY name+" was not found."
  EXIT
ENDIF

* End of program
```

Program 6-1. Using an Array for Lookup Table Validation

The final array example combines several functions and techniques discussed in this chapter. It reads the current directory contents and compares it to an earlier copy. It then lists new files, deleted files, and changed files. This program could help identify virus infections by flagging files that have changed in size or have new times or dates.

```
* Program 6-2
* Using arrays to detect changes in a directory
CLEAR
SET TALK OFF

* Dimension array
* Note that it will be redimensioned
* automatically when used.
  DIMENSION newdir[1,1]

* Load current directory into newdir
```

```
                 = ADIR(newdir)

* If old array exists, load it; otherwise,
* save current array and end
    IF FILE('directry.mem')
      RESTORE FROM directry.mem ADDITIVE
    ELSE
      last = ALEN(newdir)
      rows = ASUBSCRIPT(newdir,last,1)
      cols = ASUBSCRIPT(newdir,last,2)
      DIMENSION olddir[rows,cols]
      = ASORT(newdir)
      = ACOPY(newdir,olddir)
      SAVE TO directry.mem ALL LIKE olddir
      CANCEL
    ENDIF

* In first pass, check for new files
    newfiles = 0
    ? 'New Files:'
    FOR i = 1 TO ALEN(newdir,1)
      filen = newdir[i,1]
      isnew = ASCAN(olddir,filen)
      IF isnew = 0
        ? filen
        newfiles = newfiles + 1
      ENDIF
    ENDFOR
    IF newfiles = 0
      ? 'No new files'
    ENDIF
    ?
    ?

* In second pass, check for deleted files
    delfiles = 0
    ? 'Deleted Files:'
    FOR i = 1 TO ALEN(olddir,1)
      filen = olddir[i,1]
      isdel = ASCAN(newdir,filen)
      IF isdel = 0
        ? filen
        delfiles = delfiles + 1
      ENDIF
    ENDFOR
    IF delfiles = 0
      ? 'No deleted files'
    ENDIF
    ?
    ?

* In third pass, check for files with different sizes
```

```
      dsfiles = 0
      ? 'Files with Different Sizes:'
      FOR i = 1 TO ALEN(newdir,1)
        filen = newdir[i,1]
        newsz = newdir[i,2]
        isold = ASCAN(olddir,filen)
        IF isold > 0
           oldrow = ASUBSCRIPT(olddir,isold,1)
           oldsz  = olddir[oldrow,2]
           IF oldsz # newsz
             ? filen + '  '
             ?? 'Old Size: ' + TRANSFORM(oldsz,'999999999   ')
             ?? 'New Size: ' + TRANSFORM(newsz,'999999999')
             dsfiles = dsfiles + 1
           ENDIF
        ENDIF
      ENDFOR
      IF dsfiles = 0
        ? 'No files with different sizes'
      ENDIF
      ?
      ?


   * The code to check for files with different dates
   * or times is left for the reader as an exercise

   * Save new directory to file
      savedir = 'Y'
      @ WROWS()-1,1 SAY 'Do you want to save the new directory?
           [Y/N]' ;
        GET savedir PICTURE '!' VALID savedir $ 'NY'
      READ
      IF savedir = 'Y'
        last = ALEN(newdir)
        rows = ASUBSCRIPT(newdir,last,1)
        cols = ASUBSCRIPT(newdir,last,2)
        DIMENSION olddir[rows,cols]
        = ASORT(newdir)
        = ACOPY(newdir,olddir)
        ERASE directry.mem
        SAVE TO directry.mem ALL LIKE olddir
      ENDIF

      CLEAR

   RETURN
   * End of program
```

Program 6-2. Using Arrays to Detect Changes in a Directory

Summary

This chapter began by defining arrays and showing how to declare them. We then described how to use them to process records in a database. We also learned how to pass arrays to procedures and save them in memory variable files. Finally, we showed how to use arrays as internal lookup tables instead of referencing small master files.

7

Memo Fields for the Practical Programmer

Memo fields provide valuable facilities for handling text. FoxPro lets us access, edit, and display them just as easily as character fields. In fact, most commands that manipulate character fields work with memos too.

FoxPro also has special commands and functions for memo fields. We can use its text editor to modify their contents in custom windows. This chapter examines techniques needed to use memo fields effectively in everyday applications.

What Is a Memo Field?

Character data fields have a fixed length. They thus occupy the same space per record, regardless of what they contain and even if they are empty. For short fields, the wasted space is of little concern. However, for long ones, it can be significant.

Memo fields can hold variable length text. One record may contain several thousand characters, whereas the next one may have nothing at all. Memo fields use only the space needed to hold the actual data plus a little overhead per record. Therefore, they conserve disk space for information that varies greatly in length or appears only occasionally.

But remember that, although memo fields are related to character fields, they are just cousins. Memo fields can hold any number of characters. Character fields can contain no more than 254. The only limitation on the length of memos is physical disk space. Thus they are essential for storing long text.

The differences do not stop there. Unlike character fields, memo fields can contain anything. They can hold any keyboard character, graphics symbol, or foreign character from the 8-bit ASCII set. This even includes the null character CHR(0). Therefore, memo fields can hold binary data, including programs, scanned or digitized images, and sound.

This chapter focuses on using memo fields to store, edit, and retrieve character information. However, most techniques also work with other data types.

Adding a Memo Field to a Database Structure

We can put a memo field in a database structure just like any other field. We can include it in the initial definition or add it later using MODIFY STRUC-TURE.

FoxPro automatically assigns each memo field a size of 10 characters. Every record in the database requires that much space even if it has no memo data. This space contains a pointer to the information in the memo file (the DBT or FPT file). The pointer is 0 if there is no memo. A database structure may have any number of memo fields. However, all memo data for each database resides in a single file.

Figure 7-1 shows the LENDER file structure with the addition of memo field L_NOTES. Note the automatic size of 10 characters.

Field	Type	Size	Decimal Places
L_ZIP	Character	10	
L_PHONE	Character	13	
L_EXT	Character	4	
L_TAX_ID	Character	10	
L_CURRATE	Numeric	6	3
L_RATEDATE	Date	8	
L_VRM	Logical	1	
L_RRM	Logical	1	
L_WRAP	Logical	1	
L_NOTES	Memo	10	

Figure 7-1. Structure of LENDER.DBF with a memo field.

Calculating the Amount of Space a Memo Uses

We must use memo fields for strings with over 254 characters. But can we save disk space by using them for shorter strings? Yes. The tradeoff depends on several factors, including:

- number of records in the database
- average size of the field versus its maximum size
- percentage of the database that uses a memo field

Suppose that in the LENDER database, l_notes is a character field of length 200. Then if the database has 100 records, it alone would require 20,000 bytes of file space. The result comes from the product

```
maximum character length * number of records
```

Calculating the amount of space required by a memo field is slightly more complex. First, we must know a little about the memo file's structure.

A memo file begins with a 512-byte file header. Each individual memo begins with an 8-byte record header. Text is then added in 64-byte blocks, except for the first one which contains only 56 characters because of the header.

The average memo will thus require a number of blocks given by its length plus 8 bytes (for the header) divided by 64. Unless this number is evenly divisible by 64 (for example, if length plus 8 is 128), an extra block is necessary. We can account for it by adding 63 (block size minus 1) to the adjusted length before dividing. Can you see why?

We must also include the 10-byte memo pointer FoxPro places in each database record. It occupies space given by multiplying the number of records by 10.

Thus, we can estimate the total space required by the memo field with the formula:

```
512 + INT((average memo length + 8 + 63) / 64) * 64 *
    (number of records * usage - 1) +
    average memo length + 8 +
    number of records * 10
```

If the memo is used in all records, it always requires more space than a character field. However, if we use it only 70% of the time, the approaches require the same space. If we use the memo field just one-third of the time, it takes half the space that a character field does.

HINT
If a character field is seldom used, replacing it with a memo field reduces total storage requirements.

Working with Memo Fields from EDIT and BROWSE

We can load memos into strings with the STORE command. We can then work with them just like any character field. Of course, they may be quite long. Let's see how to work with memo fields using the EDIT or BROWSE command from a program.

When we open the Edit window, FoxPro displays the current record's fields along the left edge. Depending on the size of the window and the number of fields per record, we may have to scroll vertically to see everything.

TIP

To determine if a record has a memo, check whether the marker is 'memo' (empty) or 'Memo' (non-empty) in a LIST, DISPLAY, EDIT, or BROWSE.

Note that the memo field l_notes shows only the memo marker, not its contents. We can open a window to display the contents by moving the cursor to it and pressing Ctrl-Home. We can also open it by clicking the mouse twice with the cursor on the marker. Figure 7-2 shows the resulting memo edit window.

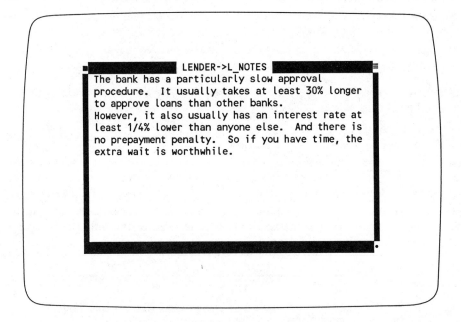

Figure 7-2. Memo edit window.

Once we open this window, we can edit the memo with the FoxPro text editor. We can modify, select, delete, insert, cut, and paste text. We can also perform find and replace operations. Table 7-1 summarizes the editing commands.

To exit, press Ctrl-W. It saves the changes automatically. You can use Esc to exit without saving any changes. A warning box asks if you want to discard them.

Table 7-1. Text Editor Key Commands in the Memo Edit Window

Keystrokes	Definition
Ctrl-A	Select all
Ctrl-C	Copy
Ctrl-D	Do
Ctrl-E	Replace and find again
Ctrl-End	Move the cursor to the end of the memo
Ctrl-F	Find
Ctrl-F1	Cycle windows
Ctrl-F7	Move window
Ctrl-F8	Size window
Ctrl-F10	Zoom window
Ctrl-G	Find again
Ctrl-Home	Move the cursor to the beginning of the memo
Ctrl-K	Continue (repeat Find from current position)
Ctrl-Left Arrow	Move the cursor left one word
Ctrl-M	Resume
Ctrl-R	Redo
Ctrl-Right Arrow	Move the cursor right one word
Ctrl-U	Undo
Ctrl-V	Paste
Ctrl-W	Exit from current edit and save changes
Ctrl-X	Cut
Down Arrow	Move the cursor down one line
End	Move the cursor to the end of the line
Home	Move the cursor to the beginning of the line
Left Arrow	Move the cursor left one character
PgDn	Move the cursor down one text window
PgUp	Move the cursor up one text window
Right Arrow	Move the cursor right one character
Shift-Ctrl-End	Select from cursor to end of text
Shift-Ctrl-Home	Select from cursor to beginning of text
Shift-Ctrl-Left	Select from cursor to beginning of word
Shift-Ctrl-Right	Select from cursor to end of word
Shift-Down Arrow	Select from cursor to same position one line down
Shift-End	Select from cursor to end of line
Shift-Home	Select from cursor to beginning of line
Shift-Left Arrow	Select one character left
Shift-Right Arrow	Select one character right
Shift-Up Arrow	Select from cursor to same position one line up
Up Arrow	Move the cursor up one line

Editing Memo Fields via a Screen Form

Although we can use the BROWSE and EDIT commands in programs, we may prefer a formatted screen. Program 7-1 displays a custom input screen for LENDER. It prompts for the memo field using a GET statement just as with any other variable. The field appears initially as the memo marker. To edit it, move the cursor to the marker and press Ctrl-Home or double click the left mouse button.

```
* Program 7-1
*
* Edits memo fields from a screen form

* Set environment
  SET TALK OFF
  SET BELL OFF
  SET STATUS OFF
  SET SCOREBOARD OFF

* Define memo edit window size and position
  DEFINE WINDOW MEMOEDIT FROM 19,10 TO 21,75 NONE
  SET WINDOW OF MEMO TO MEMOEDIT

* Open procedure file
  SET PROCEDURE TO LENDERP

* Initialize database file
  SELECT 1
  USE lender INDEX lender

* Declare PUBLIC variables
  PUBLIC mL_id,mL_name,mL_addr1,mL_addr2,mL_city,mL_state
  PUBLIC mL_phone,mL_ext,mL_tax_id,mL_currate,mL_ratedate
  PUBLIC mL_vrm,mL_rrm,mL_wrap,mL_zip

* Display screen format
  SET COLOR TO R/N
  @  1, 0 TO 22,79 DOUBLE
  @  3, 1 TO 3,78 DOUBLE
  @  5, 1 TO 5,78
  @  2,29 SAY "MORTGAGE SYSTEM"
  @  4, 4 SAY "Lender ID     "
  @  4,36 SAY "Bank Name     "
  @  7, 6 SAY "Address 1  "
  @  8, 6 SAY "Address 2  "
  @  9, 6 SAY "City       "
  @  9,41 SAY "State  "
  @  9,55 SAY "Zip Code  "
  @ 11, 6 SAY "Telephone Number"
```

```
@ 11,40 SAY "Extension   "
@ 13, 6 SAY "Tax ID      "
@ 15, 6 SAY "Current Rate   "
@ 16,13 SAY "As of  "
@ 15,44 SAY "Variable Rate Mortgages (Y|N)"
@ 16,40 SAY "Renegotiable Rate Mortgages (Y|N)"
@ 17,55 SAY "Wraparounds (Y|N)"
@ 14,41 SAY "Special Financing Offered"
@ 19, 3 SAY "Notes:"

* Process bank records
DO WHILE .T.
   * Display record
   SET COLOR TO BU/N,N/W
   @ 0, 0 SAY "Record: "+SUBSTR(STR(RECNO()+1000000,7),2)
   IF DELETED()
      @ 0,50 SAY "*DELETED*"
   ELSE
      @ 0,50 SAY "          "
   ENDIF
   SET COLOR TO R+/N,N/W
   DO FLDGETS
   CLEAR GETS

   * Display simple menu
   choice = " "
   SET COLOR TO GR+/N,N/W
   @ 24,0 GET choice MESSAGE ;
      "SELECT:  Append  Edit  Delete  Next-Prev-Top-Bottom"+;
      " Quit" PICTURE "!" VALID(choice $ "AEDNPTBQ")
   READ

   * Branch to menu choice
   DO CASE

      * Quit
      CASE choice = 'Q'
         EXIT

      * Add new record
      CASE choice = 'A'

         * Initialize memory variables
         ml_id      = SPACE( 6 )
         ml_name    = SPACE( 25 )
         ml_addr1   = SPACE( 25 )
         ml_addr2   = SPACE( 25 )
         ml_city    = SPACE( 20 )
         ml_state   = SPACE( 2 )
         ml_zip     = SPACE( 10 )
         ml_phone   = SPACE( 13 )
         ml_ext     = SPACE( 4 )
         ml_tax_id  = SPACE( 10 )
```

```
ml_currate  = 0.00
ml_ratedate = DATE()
ml_vrm      = .F.
ml_rrm      = .F.
ml_wrap     = .F.
@ 24,0
@ 24,0 SAY "Press {Ctrl-W} to Exit"

* Read into memory variables
SET COLOR TO R+/N,N/W
DO FLDGETS
READ
* Confirm that user wants to append this record
choice = " "
SET COLOR TO GR+/N,N/W
@ 24,0
@ 24,0 SAY "SELECT:  {A}ccept  {I}gnore";
       GET choice PICTURE "!" VALID( choice $ "AI" )
READ

IF choice = 'A'

   * Add new record
   APPEND BLANK
   MODIFY MEMO l_notes

   * Replace from memory variables
   REPLACE l_id WITH ml_id
   REPLACE l_name WITH ml_name
   REPLACE l_addr1 WITH ml_addr1
   REPLACE l_addr2 WITH ml_addr2
   REPLACE l_city WITH ml_city
   REPLACE l_state WITH ml_state
   REPLACE l_zip WITH ml_zip
   REPLACE l_phone WITH ml_phone
   REPLACE l_ext WITH ml_ext
   REPLACE l_tax_id WITH ml_tax_id
   REPLACE l_currate WITH ml_currate
   REPLACE l_ratedate WITH ml_ratedate
   REPLACE l_vrm WITH ml_vrm
   REPLACE l_rrm WITH ml_rrm
   REPLACE l_wrap WITH ml_wrap
ENDIF

* Edit record
CASE choice = 'E'
  @ 24, 0
  DO FLDGETS
  READ

* Delete record
CASE choice = 'D'
```

```
      IF .NOT. DELETED()
         DELETE
      ELSE
         RECALL
      ENDIF

   * Go to next record
   CASE choice = 'N'
     SKIP
     IF EOF()
        GOTO BOTTOM
     ENDIF

   * Go to previous record
   CASE choice = 'P'
     SKIP -1
     IF BOF()
        GOTO TOP
     ENDIF

   * Go to first record
   CASE choice = 'T'
     GOTO TOP

   * Go to last record
   CASE choice = 'B'
     GOTO BOTTOM

   ENDCASE

ENDDO

* Closing operations
SET COLOR TO R+/N,N/W
CLEAR
SET SCOREBOARD ON
SET BELL ON
SET TALK ON
RETURN
* EOF: LENDER.PRG

PROCEDURE FLDGETS
* Get input data from user
   @  4,17 GET l_id        PICTURE "!!!" ;
      MESSAGE "Enter bank ID"
   @  4,49 GET l_name      PICTURE "@X25" ;
      MESSAGE "Enter bank name"
   @  7,17 GET l_addr1     PICTURE "@X25" ;
      MESSAGE "Enter bank box address"
   @  8,17 GET l_addr2     PICTURE "@X25" ;
      MESSAGE "Enter bank street address"
   @  9,17 GET l_city      PICTURE "@X20" ;
      MESSAGE "Enter bank city"
   @  9,48 GET l_state     PICTURE "!!" ;
      MESSAGE "Enter bank state"
   @  9,65 GET l_zip       PICTURE "99999-####" ;
```

```
             MESSAGE "Enter bank Zip Code"
    @ 11,23 GET l_phone     PICTURE "(###)999-9999" ;
             MESSAGE "Enter bank telephone number"
    @ 11,49 GET l_ext       PICTURE "####" ;
             MESSAGE "Enter bank extension"
    @ 13,17 GET l_tax_id    PICTURE "99-9999999" ;
             MESSAGE "Enter bank tax id"
    @ 15,20 GET l_currate   PICTURE "#9.9##" RANGE 0.0,20.0 ;
             MESSAGE "Enter current mortgage interest rate"
    @ 16,20 GET l_ratedate PICTURE "@D" MESSAGE;
             "Enter the date the interest rate became effective"
    @ 15,75 GET l_vrm       PICTURE "L" MESSAGE;
             "Does the bank offer variable rate mortgages (Y|N)?"
    @ 16,75 GET l_rrm       PICTURE "L" MESSAGE;
             "Does the bank offer renegotiable rate mortgages (Y|N)?"
    @ 17,75 GET l_wrap      PICTURE "L" MESSAGE;
             "Does the bank offer wraparound mortgages? (Y|N)"
    @ 19,10 GET l_notes     MESSAGE;
             "Press Ctrl-Home to open memo window, "+;
             "Ctrl-W to close it"
RETURN

* End of program
```

Program 7-1. Editing LENDER from a Screen Form

Program 7-1 controls the size and position of the memo edit window. It does not overwrite the entire screen, nor does it use the default edit window that usually appears in the upper left corner. In fact, it does not even resemble a window. Rather, it looks like a typical field positioned at the bottom of the input screen. We removed the border by using the keyword NONE in the window definition. The definition also specifies the window's position and size. The following commands define window MEMOEDIT and set the memo edit window to it.

```
    * Define memo edit window size and position
      DEFINE WINDOW MEMOEDIT FROM 19,10 TO 21,75 NONE
      SET WINDOW OF MEMO TO MEMOEDIT
```

When the program first displays the record, all that appears is the memo marker. To display the contents, we must press Ctrl-Home with the cursor on the marker. The program then opens the memo edit window (Figure 7-3).

With the cursor in the window, we can edit its contents. When we press Ctrl-W to close the window, the marker reappears. Thus we have the advantage of quick access to the memo field, while controlling the window's size and position.

The GET statement includes a WINDOW clause specifically to edit memo fields. Of course, we still need the DEFINE WINDOW command. However,

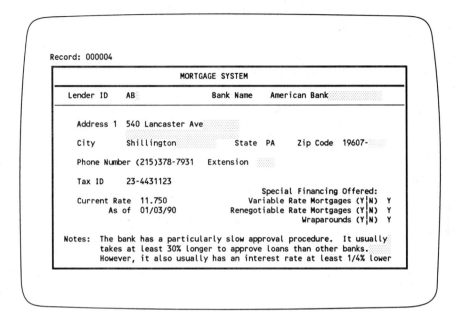

Figure 7-3. LENDER's memo field using window MEMOEDIT.

we do not need SET WINDOW OF MEMO. If GET includes the OPEN keyword, FoxPro opens the window as soon as the program executes it. The new command for procedure FLDGETS is:

```
@ 19,10 GET l_notes OPEN WINDOW memoedit MESSAGE ;
    "Press Ctrl-Home to open memo window, Ctrl-W to close it"
```

Although the command opens the window automatically, we must still press Ctrl-Home to move the cursor into it to edit the memo.

Locating Information in a Memo Field

FoxPro allows us to readily locate text in a memo. Of course, we could load the memo into a string variable and use the **AT** or **SUBSTR** commands to search it. Suppose we want to find information about loan prepayment conditions or penalties. We might search the memo field for the word "prepayment".

```
* Load memo field into memory variable
  STORE l_notes TO tempmemo
* Look for word "prepayment"
  start = AT('prepayment',tempmemo)
```

```
* Print text 50 characters before and after word
  ? SUBSTR(tempmemo,start-50,start+50)
```

However, unless we know which record contains the desired string, we must loop through each one to find it. Unfortunately, we cannot use SEEK or FIND on memo fields. The reason is that they cannot serve as keys, and SEEK and FIND work only on key fields.

On the other hand, we can use LOCATE to search any field, including memos. The following command searches memo field l_notes in all database records for the string "prepayment".

```
LOCATE FOR 'prepayment' $ l_notes
```

LOCATE tests each record until it finds a match or reaches the end of the file. Afterward, we must first check whether it found a valid record.

```
IF FOUND()
   * Valid record found
     < print memo field here >
ENDIF
```

or

```
IF .NOT. EOF()
   * Valid record found
     < print memo field here >
ENDIF
```

Of course, LOCATE finds only the first match. To find others, we must tell the program to continue the search from the current record with the CONTINUE statement. Program 7-2 displays the bank name and memo fields for all records containing prepayment conditions.

```
* Program 7-2
*
* Searches LENDER database for string 'prepayment'
* in memo field L_NOTES

* Set environment
  SET TALK OFF
  SET STATUS OFF
  SET SCOREBOARD OFF
  SET MEMOWIDTH TO 75
  CLEAR

* Open database file
  USE lender INDEX lender

* Locate record matching string
```

```
      LOCATE FOR 'prepayment' $ l_notes

*  Search for string
   DO WHILE .NOT. EOF()

      IF FOUND()
         ?? "Bank: "+l_name
         ?
         ? l_notes
         ?
         WAIT "Press any key to display next matching record"
         CLEAR
         CONTINUE
      ENDIF

   ENDDO

*  End of program
```

Program 7-2. Using LOCATE to Search Memo Fields

Printing Selected Lines from a Memo Field

Program 7-2 lists records containing the string 'prepayment' in the memo field. We can use the SET MEMOWIDTH command to control the display width. However, the program prints the entire memo. For short ones, reading through them to find the desired information is acceptable. However, for longer ones, we need a way to display only the pertinent part.

Two useful functions for dealing with memo fields are MLINE() and MEMLINES(). MLINE() returns a specific line, and MEMLINES() determines the number of lines in the memo.

Of course, the number of lines and the specific one on which text appears depend on how wide they are. A memo displayed with a width of 80 characters occupies fewer lines than it would with only 25 characters. Therefore, the SET MEMOWIDTH command must appear before any read and write commands involving memo fields.

For example, to determine the number of lines in the memo field of the first LENDER record, use the commands:

```
SET MEMOWIDTH TO 50
USE lender
? MEMLINES(l_notes)
```

Note that we specified the memo width even though it is the default (50). This insures the proper setting in case a prior operation changed it. Thus, MEMLINES returns the number of lines required to display the memo in a 50 character window.

We cannot just divide the number of characters in the memo by 50 and round up. Not every line is 50 characters long. FoxPro memos display only whole words on a line. If a word does not fit, FoxPro moves it to the next line. Therefore, almost all lines actually contain fewer than 50 characters.

MLINE() returns a specific line of text from the memo. Again, the SET MEMOWIDTH command determines the first and last word included. Program 7-3 displays any line from the memo field of the selected record. Note that MEMLINES() tests if the memo field exists and restricts line number requests.

```
* Program 7-3
* Uses MLINE() and MEMLINES() to display
* selected lines from LENDER records

* Set environment
  SET TALK OFF
  SET STATUS OFF
  SET SCOREBOARD OFF
  CLEAR

* Open database
  USE lender

* Initialize variables
  showline  = 1
  recnumber = 1

* Get record number
  @ 3,5 SAY 'Enter record number from which to read memo:' ;
        GET recnumber RANGE 1,RECCOUNT() MESSAGE ;
        'Enter a record between 1 and '+STR(RECCOUNT(),4)
  READ
  GOTO recnumber
  maxlines = MEMLINES(l_notes)

* If a memo exists, prompt for line to display.
* Otherwise, report no memo.
  IF maxlines > 0
     @ 5,5 SAY 'Enter line of memo to display' GET showline ;
       RANGE 1,maxlines MESSAGE ;
       'Enter a line number between 1 and '+STR(maxlines,4)
     READ
     @ 7,5 SAY MLINE(l_notes,showline)
  ELSE
```

```
      @ 5,5 SAY 'This record has no memo field'
   ENDIF
   @ 24,0

* End of program
```

Program 7-3. Using MLINE() and MEMLINES() to Display Memo Lines

---

> **TIP**
>
> Always check the line number against MEMLINES() before trying to print a memo field. In a FOR loop, use MEMLINES() as the maximum count.

Program 7-2 searches the memo field of all LENDER records for the text 'prepayment'. It then prints the entire memo along with the bank's name. Unfortunately, a long memo may not fit on the screen. So we would prefer to limit the display to the selected text and a few lines around it. If we can determine which line the desired text is on, we can use MLINE() to produce the display.

FoxPro provides two functions that search memo fields for a text string, ATLINE() and ATCLINE(). The only difference is that ATLINE() is case-sensitive. Program 7-4 is a modification of Program 7-2 that prints four lines before and after the one containing the search string.

```
* Program 7-4
*
* Search LENDER database for string
* 'no prepayment penalty' in memo field L_NOTES
* and display four lines before and after it

* Set environment
   SET TALK OFF
   SET STATUS OFF
   SET SCOREBOARD OFF
   SET MEMOWIDTH TO 50
   CLEAR

* Open database file
   USE lender INDEX lender

* Locate record matching string
```

```
      LOCATE FOR AT('no prepayment penalty',l_notes) <> 0

 *  Search for string
    DO WHILE .NOT. EOF()

      IF FOUND()
         fline = ATCLINE('no prepayment penalty',l_notes) - 4
         ? l_notes
         ? fline
         IF fline < 1
            fline = 1
         ENDIF
         lline = fline + 4
         ? lline
         IF lline > MEMLINES(l_notes)
            lline = MEMLINES(l_notes)
         ENDIF
         ?
         ?? "Bank: "+l_name
         ?
         FOR iline = fline TO lline
            ? MLINE(l_notes,iline)
         ENDFOR
         ?
         WAIT "Press any key to display next matching record"
         CLEAR
         CONTINUE
      ENDIF

    ENDDO

 *  End of program
```

Program 7-4. Using MLINE() to Limit the Number of Lines Displayed

Program 7-4 uses ATLINE() to search for a string. However, the approach does not work if the text is split between lines. ATLINE() will find it only if it is on a single line. Otherwise, it returns 0.

> **TIP**
> Use ATLINE() or ATCLINE() to search for short strings. The longer the string, however, the greater the likelihood of missing occurrences that are split between lines.

Using MLINE() and _MLINE to Read Memos

MLINE() supports a second numeric expression. The optional third parameter is an offset from the beginning of the memo. To display a memo field starting with the tenth character, use

```
? MLINE(memofld,1,9)
```

This command prints one line from the memo beginning with the tenth character (skipping the first nine). It still uses MEMOWIDTH to determine the maximum number of characters per line. Due to word wrap, the actual number of printed characters is usually less.

To display the second line of the memo, use

```
? MLINE(memofld,2,9)
```

To print the second line, MLINE must determine where the first one ended. Starting at the beginning of the memo, it skips the first nine characters. Then it determines how many characters fit on the first line. Only when it knows where that line ends can it determine the start and stop characters for the second line. As you can imagine, printing lines this way from a long memo is inefficient.

FoxPro provides a system memory variable to help solve the problem. Each time MLINE() accesses a line, it stores the offset of the last character in _MLINE. Thus, if we read the first line of a memo with MEMOWIDTH set to 50, _MLINE might be set to 47 to indicate its length.

Now suppose we use _MLINE as the third parameter to MLINE(). It will now skip _MLINE characters from the beginning of the memo. For example, to print the first two lines, we could use

```
? MLINE(memofld,1)
? MLINE(memofld,1,_MLINE)
```

Note that the line number for the second call is 1 because we want to print the first line after the offset.

This technique can read long memo fields efficiently using a loop such as:

```
FOR i = 1 to MEMLINES(memofld)
   ? MLINE(memofld,1,_MLINE)
ENDFOR
```

By using _MLINE to define the offset, we never read more characters than necessary.

Transferring Data to and from Memo Fields

FoxPro lets us transfer memo data to or from external text files. The APPEND MEMO FROM command lets us fill a memo field from a file. It appends the data if the field already contains information. An OVERWRITE option replaces the current contents.

The COPY MEMO TO command saves the memo field in a file. If the file already exists, its contents are lost. The ADDITIVE clause appends the memo. Program 7-5 demonstrates the reading and writing of external files in a personnel system. Here the memo field contains a resume. The main database holds other personal information.

```
* Program 7-5
*
* A personnel system at an employment agency uses memo
* fields to transfer client resumes to and from text
* files.

* Set environment
  SET TALK OFF
  SET BELL OFF
  SET SCOREBOARD OFF

* Initialize database file
  SELECT 1
  USE personel

  PUBLIC mFname,mLname,mAddress,mCity,mState,mZip,mPhone
  PUBLIC mJob_type,mSalary,mRelocation,mBirth_date

* Display screen format
  DO DISPFORM

* Process personnel records with resumes in memo fields
  DO WHILE .T.
    * Display record
    DO DISPREC
    * Display simple menu
    choice = " "
    SET COLOR TO GR+/N,N/W
    @ 24,0 SAY "SELECT:Append/Edit/Delete/Next/Prev/Top/";
           +"Bottom/Memo-append/Copy-memo/Quit";
           GET choice PICTURE "!" ;
           VALID(choice $ "AEDNPTBMCQ")
    READ
    DO CASE
    CASE choice = 'Q'
```

```
      CLOSE MEMO resume
      RELEASE WINDOWS resedit
      EXIT
   CASE choice = 'A'
      * Append record
      DO ADDREC
   CASE choice = 'C'
      * Write memo field into text file
      DO PUTMEMO
   CASE choice = 'E'
      * Edit record
      DO EDITREC
   CASE choice = 'D'
      * Delete record
      IF .NOT. DELETED()
         DELETE
      ELSE
         RECALL
      ENDIF
   CASE choice = 'M'
      * Memo append
      DO APPMEMO
   CASE choice = 'N'
      * Next record
      SKIP
      IF EOF()
         GOTO BOTTOM
      ENDIF
   CASE choice = 'P'
      * Previous record
      SKIP -1
      IF BOF()
         GOTO TOP
      ENDIF
   CASE choice = 'T'
      * Top record
      GOTO TOP
   CASE choice = 'B'
      * Bottom record
      GOTO BOTTOM
   ENDCASE
ENDDO

* Closing operations
   SET COLOR TO W+/N,N/W
   CLEAR
   SET SCOREBOARD ON
   SET BELL ON
   SET TALK ON

RETURN

* EOF:PERSONEL.PRG
```

```
PROCEDURE DISPFORM
   * Display input form
   DEFINE WINDOW resedit FROM 16,2 TO 20,77 NONE
   SET WINDOW OF MEMO TO resedit
   SET COLOR TO W+/B,N/W
   CLEAR
   @  0, 0 SAY SPACE(80)
   @  0,72 SAY DATE()
   SET COLOR TO GR+/B,N/W
   @  1, 0,21,79 BOX "            "
   @  2,27 SAY "MICMINN PERSONNEL SERVICES"
   @  3, 1,3,78 BOX "            "
   SET COLOR TO W+/B,N/W
   @  5, 8 SAY "Applicant's Name:"
   @  7,12 SAY "Home Address:"
   @ 10,14 SAY "Home Phone:"
   @ 12, 7 SAY "Job Type:"
   @ 12,25 SAY "Salary:"
   @ 12,46 SAY "Relocation (Y|N):"
   @ 12,64 SAY "Birth Date:"
   @ 15, 2 SAY "Resume:"
RETURN


PROCEDURE DISPREC
   * Display fields of current record
   SET COLOR TO BG+/B,N/W
   @ 0, 0 SAY "Record: "+SUBSTR(STR(RECNO()+1000000,7),2)
   IF DELETED()
      @ 0,50 SAY "*DELETED*"
   ELSE
      @ 0,50 SAY "            "
   ENDIF
   SET COLOR TO W+/B,N/W
   MODIFY MEMO resume NOWAIT
   SCATTER MEMVAR
   DO SHOWGETS
   CLEAR GETS
RETURN


PROCEDURE EDITREC
   * Edit displayed fields
   DO SHOWGETS
   READ
   @ 24,0
   @ 24,17 SAY "Press Ctrl-W to save memo, Ctrl-Q to abort"
   MODIFY MEMO resume
   @ 24,0
   MODIFY MEMO resume NOWAIT
RETURN


PROCEDURE BLANKREC
   * Initialize memory variables with blanks
   SCATTER MEMVAR BLANK
```

```
      birth_date = DATE()
RETURN

PROCEDURE REPLREC
   * Save memory variables in database
   GATHER MEMVAR
RETURN

PROCEDURE ADDREC
   * Initialize memory variables for database fields
   CLOSE MEMO resume
   DO BLANKREC
   @ 24,0
   @ 24,0 SAY "Press {Ctrl-W} to Exit"
   * Read into memory variables
   SET COLOR TO W+/B,N/W
   DO SHOWGETS
   READ
   * Confirm that user wants to append this record
   choice = " "
   SET COLOR TO GR+/B,N/W
   @ 24,0
   @ 24,0 SAY "SELECT:  {A}ccept  {I}gnore";
          GET choice PICTURE "!" VALID( choice $ "AI" )
   READ
   IF choice = "A"
      * Add new record
      APPEND BLANK
      * Replace from memory variables
      DO REPLREC
   ENDIF
RETURN

PROCEDURE APPMEMO
   * Get file name to load into memo field
   filenm = GETFILE("TXT","Append Resume File:")
   CLOSE MEMO resume
   APPEND MEMO resume FROM &filenm OVERWRITE
   MODIFY MEMO resume NOWAIT
RETURN

PROCEDURE PUTMEMO
   * Get file name into which to write memo field
   filenm = LEFT(trim(lname)+"_____",6)+LEFT(trim(fname)+;
          "__",2)
   filenm = PUTFILE("Text File (.TXT):",filenm,"TXT")
   COPY MEMO resume TO &filenm
RETURN

PROCEDURE SHOWGETS
   * Display current field values
   @  5,27 GET m->Fname
   @  5,38 GET m->Lname
```

```
     @  7,27 GET m->Address
     @  8,27 GET m->City
     @  8,45 GET m->State
     @  8,49 GET m->Zip
     @ 10,27 GET m->Phone FUNCTION "@R (999)999-9999"
     @ 13, 7 GET m->Job_type
     @ 13,25 GET m->Salary PICTURE "9999999.99"
     @ 13,46 GET m->Relocation
     @ 13,64 GET m->Birth_date
  RETURN

  * End of program
```

Program 7-5. Using External Files in a Personnel System

Program 7-5 transfers text files directly to and from memo fields. It also shows a new technique for displaying a memo. Procedure DispForm defines a window called RESEDIT (for 'resume edit') and sets it to the memo window using the commands:

```
     DEFINE WINDOW resedit FROM 16,2 TO 20,77 NONE
     SET WINDOW OF MEMO TO resedit
```

Procedure DISPREC, which displays the current record, uses the command

```
     MODIFY MEMO resume NOWAIT
```

MODIFY MEMO displays the memo's text in the memo window. The NOWAIT keyword tells FoxPro not to wait for editing. The result is to display the memo and continue the program.

In procedure EDITREC, we edit non-memo fields using the READ command. Since the memo field is the last one on the form, we can use READ to get values for the others before dealing with it. When we reach the memo field, we reissue MODIFY MEMO without NOWAIT.

```
     MODIFY MEMO resume
```

This time, FoxPro waits for us to edit the memo field. It cannot execute another command until we close the window. The first line that it executes afterward is another MODIFY MEMO with NOWAIT. This displays the memo again without pausing.

The program's only other special feature is the CLOSE MEMO command executed when we select 'Q' from the main menu. Even though the memo window is open for display only, we still must close it before ending the program. Thus the example shows how to display the memo's contents rather than just the marker.

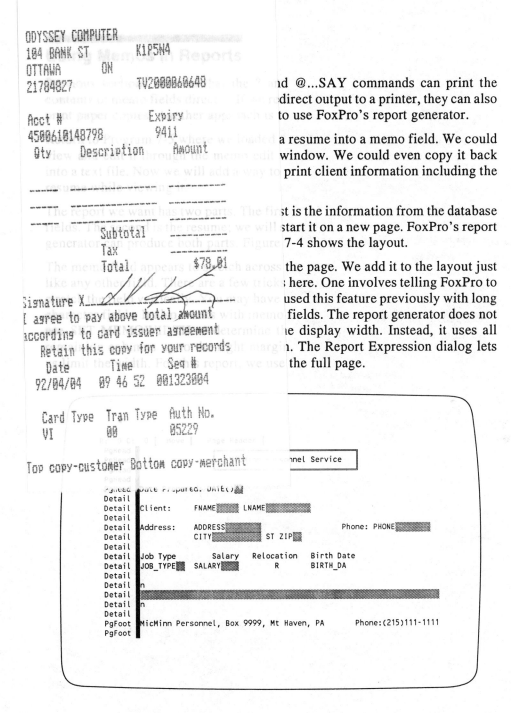

and @...SAY commands can print the contents of memo fields direct. If we redirect output to a printer, they can also use FoxPro's report generator.

a resume into a memo field. We could window. We could even copy it back print client information including the

st is the information from the database start it on a new page. FoxPro's report 7-4 shows the layout.

the page. We add it to the layout just here. One involves telling FoxPro to used this feature previously with long fields. The report generator does not e display width. Instead, it uses all 1. The Report Expression dialog lets the full page.

Figure 7-4. Report layout for employment agency.

The second trick insures that the resume appears on a separate page. The idea is to eject a page by sending ASCII 12 to the printer. So we define the memory variable newpage with that value and put it in the report definition. We insert it immediately before and after the memo.

Now we need add only a few lines of code to Program 7-6 to print the report. First we must revise the main menu to include an Output option as follows:

```
@ 24,0 SAY "SELECT:App/Edit/Del/Next/Prev/Top/";
       +"Bot/Memo-append/Copy-memo/Output/Quit";
       GET choice PICTURE "!" VALID(choice $  AEDNPTBMCOQ")
```

We must also add a few commands in a new CASE option to execute the report. They first close the memo window. Otherwise, the screen echo of the report appears to scroll behind it. Next we clear the entire screen. Then we define the memory variable newpage as the page eject character. We can now print the report with the command

```
REPORT FORM personel NEXT 1 NOEJECT PLAIN TO PRINTER
```

NOEJECT suppresses an initial page eject, and PLAIN eliminates the date and page number from the heading.

After the report prints, we must redisplay the screen form and fill the fields from the current record. We must also reopen the memo window to display the memo. The following commands perform these tasks.

```
CASE option = 'O'
  CLOSE MEMO resume
  CLEAR
  newpage = CHR(12)
  REPORT FORM personel NEXT 1 NOEJECT PLAIN TO PRINTER
  DO DISPFORM
```

HINT
We can also enter and store variable definitions (such as newpage) in the report by opening the Variables option in the Report pulldown menu.

Thus, with the help of the report generator, we have provided an output option by changing one line and adding six. What could be easier?

Of course, we can use memo fields anywhere in a report. We can print a column report from the LENDER database that includes the bank id, bank name, and memo field. Here, the memo field might be only 40 characters wide, but we could again stretch it vertically.

We can control the memo output further using MEMLINE() and MLINE(). We might even write a short UDF (Program 7-6) to print a range of lines. Figure 7-5 shows the associated report layout.

```
R:  0 C:  0 ‖  Move ‖   Page Header ‖
PgHead
PgHead  L_id   L_name                    Notes
PgHead  ------ ------------------------- ----------------------------------
Detail  L_ID   L_NAME                    memoprnt()
Detail
PgFoot
PgFoot
```

Figure 7-5. Report layout for Program 7-6.

```
* Program 7-6
*
* Prints part of a memo field

* Set environment and open databases
  SET TALK OFF
  SET STATUS OFF
  SET SCOREBOARD OFF
  CLEAR
  USE lender

* Set default memo width
  SET MEMOWIDTH TO 50

* Print report
  REPORT FORM lender FOR 'penalty' $ l_notes NOEJECT ;
       TO PRINTER
RETURN
```

```
FUNCTION MEMOPRNT

* Initialize memo string to null
  memostr = ''
* Look for string 'penalty' in note field
  fline = ATCLINE('penalty',l_notes)

* If string found, retrieve text five lines ahead
* of and after it
  IF fline > 0

     * Count back five lines or to line 1
     fline = fline - 5
     IF fline < 1
        fline = 1
     ENDIF

     * Count forward five lines or to last line
     lline = fline + 10
     IF lline > MEMLINE(l_notes)
        lline = MEMLINE(l_notes)
     ENDIF

     * Construct a string from selected memo lines
     FOR iline = fline TO lline
        memostr = memostr + TRIM(MLINE(l_notes,iline))+' '
     ENDFOR
  ENDIF

RETURN memostr

* End of program
```

Program 7-6. Print Selected Memo Lines

The report layout includes two fields from the database and a UDF. The UDF is at the end of the program. It searches for the first occurrence of the string 'penalty' in the memo. Then it counts back five lines and forward five. (A line is 50 characters long, as fixed by SET MEMOWIDTH). In both cases, it checks the boundaries to avoid going outside the memo.

The function then recombines the selected lines into a single memory variable MEMOSTR. It removes extra spaces from the end of each one. The function returns the string to the report which prints it using current field width specifications.

Compressing and Deleting Memo Fields

When we edit a memo field, FoxPro decides whether to replace the old data or append the new data to it. It replaces the old data if the new data fits in the same number of 64-byte blocks. Thus sometimes we can lengthen the memo without changing the file's size. For example, suppose we have the short memo:

```
'The bank loan officer is out on Fridays'
```

It consists of 39 characters plus eight for the record header for a total of 47. Thus it requires only a single 64-byte block. Now suppose we replace it with the memo:

```
'This bank does not make real estate investment loans.'
```

The new string is 53 characters long. With the header, it needs 61 bytes. This still fits in a single 64-byte block. Therefore, FoxPro simply replaces the old memo with the new one. The memo file stays the same size.

Now suppose we change the memo to:

```
'This bank makes all types of private real estate loans, '+
'including VA and FHA loans.'
```

Here the string is too long for the original single block. In fact, it is 91 characters, including the header. So we need two 64-byte blocks.

Finally, suppose the bank has financial problems, and we reduce the memo text to:

```
'This bank has suspended all new loans.'
```

Even though the string has shrunk from 91 characters to 46, the memo field still reserves both 64-byte blocks. FoxPro does not release the second block for reuse. The space is empty, but unavailable.

File space may also become unavailable if we delete a memo. Once we add a memo field to a database record, it becomes a permanent part of the FPT file. We can set the memo field to a null string, but that does not erase its definition from the FPT file. Nor does it reduce the memo file's size.

If you change memo fields often, the file can grow substantially. The only way to reclaim space is to rewrite it. There are three ways to do this.

The first, and by far the easiest, is to PACK the database or issue the PACK MEMO command. The former removes database records marked for deletion and memos no longer referenced. The latter removes only obsolete memos.

The second approach is to create a new database structure. The COPY TO command copies fields from the current database to a second file. It copies all fields, including memos, but only from active records.

The last way to compress a memo file involves modifying the database's structure. When FoxPro creates the new structure, it rewrites the old FPT file, omitting unused references and blocks.

Handling Old Style (DBT) Memo Files

FoxPro can read memo fields created by FoxBASE+, dBASE III PLUS, and dBASE IV (DBT files). In fact, it reads and writes them without converting them to the new FoxPro format. This differs from the way it automatically converts NDX index files to IDX files.

How can we convert old memo files to take advantage of FoxPro's improved memo handling capabilities? There are three ways, and they are the same ones just mentioned for reclaiming unused file space, namely PACKing, creating a new structure, and modifying the structure.

Summary

This chapter began by showing how to add memo fields to database structures. By comparing the needs of strings and memo fields, we saw that memos can save storage space even for short data if they are used in less than 70% of the records.

Then we examined several ways to display and edit memo fields. EDIT and BROWSE provide an easy way to access them. However, we can provide more formatting ability by using the ? and @...SAY statements.

Next we learned how to transfer information between text files and memo fields. We then saw that FoxPro's report generator supports memo fields. We created several reports that printed them. Finally, we used a UDF to display a memo field in a report.

8

FoxPro Does Windows

One of FoxPro's major user interface features is windows. We can display them directly on top of the current screen. Yet when we are through, we can remove them, and the hidden text reappears without our having to write code to restore it. Many FoxPro commands and functions, such as BROWSE, EDIT, GETFILE(), and PUTFILE(), include windows automatically. We can also use them in applications for menus, pick lists, popup dialogs, messages, input prompts, general text screens, and help screens.

This chapter describes how to define and use windows. It also shows how to use the Screen Builder utility to quickly generate standard FoxPro code for windows containing text and input prompts. We can then integrate the code directly into applications.

What Is a Window?

A window is just a rectangle on the screen, used to display information or provide a forum for interaction. Windows may cover text, but do not erase it. When we remove them, the old text reappears. We can nest or overlap windows, and we can remove them individually or all at once. In FoxPro, the only limit on the number of open windows is available memory.

Defining a Window

Before using a window, we must define it. The definition has several parts. Some, such as name and position, are mandatory. Others, such as colors, titles, borders, and special controls, are optional.

We define a window with the DEFINE WINDOW command. It first assigns the window a name, consisting of up to ten characters (letters, numbers, or underscores) beginning with a letter or underscore.

Next come the window's size and position. We must supply the coordinates of the upper left and lower right corners. They include space occupied by the border and are relative to the main screen, even when one window is drawn on top of another. The upper left corner of the window's text area has coordinates 0,0 (row number first). Thus the following command defines window menu1 between screen rows 2 and 10 and columns 5 and 60. After allowing for the border, it has a text area of 7 rows by 54 columns.

```
DEFINE WINDOW menu1 FROM 2,5 TO 10,60
```

A window can have a title. It is a character string that FoxPro automatically centers within the top border. If it is longer than the window's width minus four, FoxPro truncates it.

```
DEFINE WINDOW menu1 FROM 2,5 TO 10,60 TITLE 'MAIN MENU'
```

A window can also have a footer centered in its bottom border.

```
DEFINE WINDOW menu1 FROM 2,5 TO 10,60 FOOTER 'MAIN MENU'
```

There are six types of border: none, single line, double line, panel, custom, and system. The default is single line, unless we change it with SET BORDER. The DOUBLE option (surprisingly enough) produces a double line border. The PANEL option draws a solid border using character 219. NONE means no border. It reassigns the border rows and columns to the text area.

The fifth option is a custom border consisting of eight characters representing each side and corner. They must appear in the following order, delimited with commas: top, bottom, left side, right side, upper left corner, upper right corner, lower left corner, and lower right corner.

Figure 8-1 shows the common options.

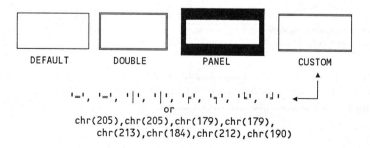

Figure 8-1. Window borders.

If we skip a character in the custom border definition, FoxPro uses the corresponding one from the default border. However, we must retain the commas to position the other characters correctly. Thus, the following definition produces the custom box shown in Figure 8-1 if the default border is a single line.

```
'=', '=', , , 'F', '╕', '╘', '╛'
```

The SYSTEM option emulates system windows. It displays special characters for the CLOSE, GROW, or ZOOM options if we include them in the definition. SYSTEM options do not appear during a READ.

Color and Color Schemes

We can define a window's color attributes either through the COLOR command or by selecting a COLOR SCHEME. The COLOR option includes three attributes: normal text, enhanced text (used in GET fields), and border. This method defines colors as in the SET COLOR TO command. The format is

```
COLOR <standard>,<enhanced>,<border>
```

FoxPro uses the standard color pair for all SAY and ? commands. GET statements use the enhanced colors. For example, to define a window with white text on a blue background, a yellow line on a red border, and black text on cyan for GET statements, use

```
COLOR W+/B, N/BG, GR+/R
```

Table 8-1 lists the color codes. Note that the ones in the right column differ from those in the left by the addition of a plus sign, indicating high intensity (foreground only). For example, either W+/R or W/R+ indicates bright white on a red background. An asterisk after the code makes the foreground characters blink. Thus, sixteen foreground colors are available, but just eight background ones. The color X is useful for secure inputs such as passwords; nothing appears, regardless of the background. Other attributes include U for underlining on a monochrome monitor and I for inverse video.

Table 8-1. Color Attributes

Color	Code	Color	Code
Black	N	Gray	N+
Blue	B	Bright Blue	B+
Red	R	Bright Red	R+
Green	G	Bright Green	G+
Magenta	RB	Bright Magenta	RB+
Cyan	BG	Bright Cyan	BG+
Brown	GR	Yellow	GR+
White	W	Bright White	W+
Blank	X		

We can define color sets of up to 24 schemes in FoxPro to provide consistent combinations for each object across an entire application. FoxPro assigns certain schemes as listed in Table 8-2.

Table 8-2. Color Set Definition

Scheme Number	Color Scheme	Description
1	Usr Winds	User windows
2	Usr Menus	User menus
3	Menu Bar	Menu pads on the system menu bar
4	Menu Pops	Menu popups
5	Dialogs	Dialogs and system messages
6	Dlog Pops	Popup controls and scrollable lists in dialogs
7	Alerts	Alerts
8	Windows	System windows
9	Wind Pops	Menu popups and scrollable lists in windows
10	Browse	Browse window
11	Report	Report layout window
12-16	Schemes 12-16	Reserved
17-24	Schemes 17-24	Available for user applications

To change a color scheme, select the COLOR option in the WINDOW pulldown of the main menu. This opens the dialog in Figure 8-2.

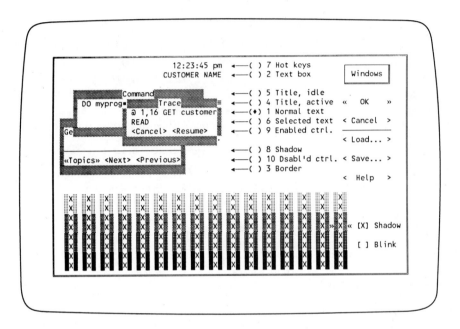

Figure 8-2. Color dialog.

For each object, we can specify color pairs (foreground and background) for up to ten components, including:

Active Title	Border
Disabled Control	Enabled Control
Hot Keys	Inactive Title
Normal Text	Selected Text
Shadow	Text Boxes

Some objects may use fewer pairs or redefine some. In practice, you should emphasize consistency throughout an application. For example, always use the same colors for a particular type of window, menu, or prompt. Applications should not resemble a kaleidoscope. Also, choose colors that work well on both color and monochrome monitors by maximizing contrast.

In an application, we select a color set with SET COLOR SET TO. However, the application must find the set on the particular machine on which it is running. If it must run on different machines, we must transfer the color set definition along with the code. Unfortunately, color sets are stored in files FOXUSER.DBF and FOXUSER.FXP and are not easy to transfer.

Program 8-1 shows an alternate way to define color sets within an application using the SET COLOR OF SCHEME command and SCHEME() function. We use them to redefine the schemes of the current set temporarily. The program saves the current ones in array OLDSCHEME, and replaces them with the ones for the application. Afterward, it restores the old schemes. Thus the application does not permanently change a scheme the user likes or needs for other work.

```
* Program 8-1
* Temporarily redefines color schemes for a program
* without permanently changing the color set on the
* user's machine

* Set environment, clear screen, dimension arrays
SET TALK OFF
CLEAR
DIMENSION oldscheme(11), newscheme(11)

* Define new color schemes in array newscheme
newscheme(1)   = 'RB/BG,R/BG,B+/BG,B/BG,N/BG,RB+/BG*,'+;
                 'B/BG*,N+/N,B+/BG,R+/BG*,+'
newscheme(2)   = 'RB/BG*,R/BG*,B+/BG*,B/BG*,N+/BG*,'+;
                 'RB+/BG*,RB+/BG*,N+/N,B+/BG*,R+/BG*,+'
newscheme(3)   = 'W/BG*,G/BG*,B/BG*,B/BG*,N+/BG*,'+;
                 'RB+/BG*,B+/BG*,N+/N,R+/BG*,N+/BG*,-'
newscheme(4)   = 'W/BG*,G/BG*,B/BG*,B/BG*,N+/BG*,'+;
                 'RB+/BG*,B+/BG*,N+/N,R+/BG*,N+/BG*,-'
newscheme(5)   = 'W+/B*,G+/B,BG+/B*,W+/B*,W/B*,'+;
                 'B+/RB*,N/B*,N+/N,W+/B*,W/B*,+'
newscheme(6)   = 'R+/B,BG+/B,BG+/B,W+/B,W/B,'+;
                 'RB+/B*,G/B,N+/N,W+/B,W/B,+'
newscheme(7)   = 'GR+/RB,W+/RB*,GR+/RB,W+/RB,W/RB,'+;
                 'RB+/R,W+/RB,N+/N,W+/RB,W/RB,+'
newscheme(8)   = 'RB/BG,B+/BG*,B+/BG*,B/BG*,W/BG*,'+;
                 'RB+/BG*,G+/BG,N+/N,B+/BG,N+/BG*,+'
newscheme(9)   = 'RB/BG,B+/BG*,B+/BG*,B/BG*,W/BG*,'+;
                 'RB+/BG*,G+/BG,N+/N,B+/BG,N+/BG*,+'
newscheme(10)  = 'W+/RB*,G+/RB,BG/GR*,B/GR*,G/GR*,'+;
                 'RB/GR*,RB+/RB,N+/N,B/RB*,W/RB*,+'
newscheme(11)  = 'BG+/B*,W+/BG,GR+/BG*,B+/BG*,N+/BG*,'+;
                 'B+/W,G+/B,N+/N,W+/B,N/B*,+'
```

```
* Display window to show color changes
DEFINE WINDOW show1 FROM 5,5 TO 10,45 ;
   TITLE 'COLOR SCHEME DEMO' PANEL CLOSE FLOAT GROW SHADOW
ACTIVATE WINDOW show1
CLEAR
? 'This should be the original scheme.'
WAIT

* Save current schemes in array oldscheme
* and redefine new one
FOR i = 1 TO 11
   oldscheme(i) = scheme(i)
   SET COLOR OF SCHEME i TO &newscheme(i)
ENDFOR

* Display window again
DEFINE WINDOW show2 FROM 7,15 TO 12,55 ;
   TITLE 'COLOR SCHEME DEMO' PANEL CLOSE FLOAT GROW SHADOW
ACTIVATE WINDOW show2
CLEAR
? 'This should be the new color scheme.'
WAIT

* Reset color scheme to original
FOR i = 1 TO 11
   SET COLOR OF SCHEME i TO &oldscheme(i)
ENDFOR

* Display window one last time
DEFINE WINDOW show3 FROM 9,25 TO 14,65 ;
   TITLE 'COLOR SCHEME DEMO' PANEL CLOSE FLOAT GROW SHADOW
ACTIVATE WINDOW show3
CLEAR
? 'Colors should be back to normal now.'
WAIT

* Remove all windows from screen
DEACTIVATE WINDOW ALL

RETURN

* End of program
```

Program 8-1. Redefining Color Schemes in an Application

Special Window Features

CLOSE

The CLOSE option lets the user close a window from the keyboard or by clicking on its upper left corner. FoxPro then removes the definition from memory. We must redefine the window to use it again. With the SYSTEM option, a small close box appears in the upper left corner of the border. However, even without it, clicking on that corner closes the window.

FILL

The FILL option fills the window with a specified character. In practice, extended ASCII values 176, 177, 178, and 219 produce nice effects. They differ in relative percentages of foreground and background color. Character 176 produces a light shade of the foreground color. Characters 177 and 178 add more of it. Finally, character 219 forms a solid block in it.

HINT

The previous section noted that FoxPro supports 16 foreground colors and 8 background colors. By filling a window with character 219, we can effectively define 16 background colors.

FLOAT

FLOAT lets the user move the window to reveal hidden text. It is often used with GROW to expand text windows for help and memo fields.

GROW

GROW lets the user resize the window by moving its lower right corner. Depending on its location, the user may have to move its upper left corner with FLOAT first. We could use GROW to display more text in help and memo field windows. With the SYSTEM border option, its activation character appears in the lower right corner as a small dot.

MINIMIZE

The MINIMIZE option lets the user shrink the window to just the title bar by any of the following methods:
- double clicking on the title bar
- pressing Ctrl-F9
- choosing the ZOOM DOWN option from the Window popup menu

The minimized window stays on the same line as the title bar of the original unless we press the Shift key. Then it is 'docked' or stored along the bottom of the screen. To restore it, use any of the same methods that minimize a window in the first place.

SHADOW

The SHADOW option creates a three-dimensional effect by changing the color of text one character below and to the right of the window. We control the colors used in that area by modifying the Shadow color pair defined in the color dialog. Selecting the same foreground and background colors hides text.

The default for windows turns shadows off. To create them, we need either the SHADOW option or the SET SHADOWS ON command. Subsequent windows have shadows until we use the NOSHADOW option or SET SHADOWS OFF.

ZOOM

The ZOOM option toggles the window from its defined area to full-screen and back. With the SYSTEM option, the ZOOM activation character appears in the upper right corner of the window. It consists of three horizontal lines. Some applications use ZOOM rather than FLOAT and GROW to enlarge help and memo field windows.

IN WINDOW

We can nest windows in two ways. Both require that we draw the outer window first.

Method 1:
Draw the inner window with coordinates that place it inside the outer one's border. Base the coordinates for both on the 0,0 position being the upper left screen corner.

```
DEFINE WINDOW win1 FROM 5,5 TO 20,60 TITLE 'WIN1' ;
    SYSTEM ZOOM GROW FLOAT CLOSE COLOR SCHEME 3
DEFINE WINDOW win2 FROM 6,10 TO 10,30 TITLE 'WIN2' ;
    SYSTEM ZOOM GROW FLOAT CLOSE COLOR SCHEME 4
```

Method 2:
Draw the inner window using the redefined coordinate system established by the outer one. That is, the upper left corner of the outer window becomes the 0,0 position for the inner one. The IN WINDOW clause tells FoxPro which coordinates to use.

```
DEFINE WINDOW win1 FROM 5,5 TO 20,60 TITLE 'WIN1' ;
    SYSTEM ZOOM GROW FLOAT CLOSE COLOR SCHEME 3
```

```
DEFINE WINDOW win3 FROM 6,10 TO 10,30 IN WINDOW win1 ;
    TITLE 'WIN3' SYSTEM ZOOM GROW FLOAT CLOSE ;
    COLOR SCHEME 8
```

In the first method, the windows are independent even though WIN2 appears inside WIN1. It actually only overlays WIN1. We can move it anywhere, even completely outside WIN1.

The second method defines WIN3 as being inside WIN1. Its coordinatcs are defined with respect to WIN1's upper left corner, and it can move only within WIN1. Its borders cannot extend beyond WIN1's.

Managing Windows

FoxPro provides a rich set of commands for managing windows. They allow you to activate, clear, release, deactivate, hide, move, save, and restore windows, as well as customize the border.

Activating Windows

Defining a window does not display it. In fact, we can define all the windows an application needs at the beginning of the program. Then, to use one, we simply activate it. For example,

```
ACTIVATE WINDOW menu1
```

activates a previously defined window menu1. The activated window becomes the default destination for screen output. @...SAY or @...GET commands use its coordinates, not the screen's. The first available output position in its upper left corner is 0,0. If we try to write text outside its coordinates, FoxPro generates an error message.

An ACTIVATE command can apply to several windows. Just separate their names with commas, as in

```
ACTIVATE WINDOW menu1, menu2, menu3
* MENU3 is now active
```

We can activate all defined windows with

```
ACTIVATE WINDOW ALL
* The last window defined is now active
```

Note that only one window can be active and receive text output at a time. FoxPro activates the last window in the list, or the last one defined.

Normally, a newly activated window appears on top. However, we can put it behind others with the BOTTOM option. If we have several overlapping windows, we can return one of them to the top with a command such as

```
ACTIVATE WINDOW menu2 TOP
```

We can also activate a window with the NOSHOW option, allowing us to write text to it without displaying it.

```
                              HINT
    When creating a new window, use the NOSHOW option to add
    all @SAY...GET commands. Then activate the window after-
    ward. It will appear to pop up instantly, and the user does not
    see the fields drawn one at a time.
```

Although FoxPro does not limit the number of windows we can define or activate, there are memory restrictions. In some cases, we may want to have several windows open. For example, suppose the user is selecting options from a series of menus. It is a good practice to keep prior windows open so he or she sees all previous selections. But each open window uses memory. To avoid a run-time "out of memory" error, be sure to close windows unrelated to the current operation or selection.

Removing Windows

Both CLEAR WINDOWS and RELEASE WINDOWS remove windows from the screen. They also release definitions from memory, regardless of whether the windows are displayed.

Deactivating Windows

Deactivating windows removes them from the screen, but not from memory. Programs can no longer direct output to them. However, since they are still in memory, we can display them with the ACTIVATE or SHOW commands without redefining them.

We can DEACTIVATE several windows by listing their names separated by commas, or we can deactivate all of them with the ALL option.

Hiding Windows

Hiding a window removes it from the screen, but not from memory. We can still direct output to it (using ACTIVATE WINDOW NOSHOW). As with

ACTIVATE, we can hide several windows at once or even hide all of them with the ALL option.

The most common use of HIDE WINDOW occurs when we must direct output to the full screen after selecting an option from a window prompt. We do not want to CLOSE the window because we may need it again later.

In the following code example, note that hiding a window does not return output to the main screen. We must activate the screen as well. Otherwise, we just write to the hidden window.

```
* Window definitions
DEFINE WINDOW outpdest FROM 2,5 TO 10,60

* Main program loop
DO WHILE .T.
  * Main menu options

  * Option to print a report
  ACTIVATE WINDOW outpdest
  * Commands appear in window to
  * ask for output destination of
  * file, screen, or printer
  DO REPTOUT

ENDDO
RETURN

PROCEDURE reptout
   HIDE WINDOW outpdest
   ACTIVATE SCREEN
   * Commands to print report
   ACTIVATE WINDOW outpdest
RETURN
```

Moving Windows

The MOVE WINDOW command can move either user-defined or system windows. We can move one to a specific location by using the TO clause with absolute coordinates. We can also move it relative to its current position with the BY clause. In relative moves, negative values mean left or up, positive ones right or down.

Saving and Restoring Windows

Large applications may have more window definitions than we can keep in memory at a time. We can save the rest in a file with the extension WIN.

```
SAVE WINDOW ALL TO BANKLOAN.WIN
```

Then we can restore windows as needed, conserving space by clearing them from memory when we finish using them.

```
RESTORE WINDOW bankname FROM BANKLOAN.WIN
```

We can also use SAVE WINDOW and RESTORE WINDOW to store window definitions in a library. Then changes appear automatically in all applications. We might even want to create a master window file with definitions.

Customizing the Border

The SET BORDER command provides the same options as DEFINE WINDOW. However, it also resets the default definition. For example, suppose we want every window in an application to have a border with single vertical lines and double horizontal ones. We could define the eight character border in each window definition. Or we could define it once by changing the default border with the command

```
SET BORDER TO '=','=','|','|','r','┐','└','┘'
```

At the end of the application, reset the default to a single line using

```
SET BORDER TO
```

Defining Windows for Memos

SET WINDOW OF MEMO specifies a window to be used for editing memo fields. We must still define it first. Thereafter, any @...SAY/GET, APPEND, BROWSE, CHANGE, EDIT, or MODIFY MEMO command can use it. Just press Ctrl-Home while the cursor is in the memo field to display the window. Program 8-2 uses a window to edit a memo field in LENDER. The SYSTEM border, together with the ZOOM option, lets the user expand it to full screen during editing. The close box provides an alternative to Ctrl-W.

```
     * Program 8-2
     *
     * Edits memo fields from a screen form in a memo window

     * Set environment
       SET TALK OFF
       SET BELL OFF
       SET STATUS OFF
       SET SCOREBOARD OFF

     * Define memo edit window size and position
       DEFINE WINDOW MEMOEDIT FROM 18,10 TO 22,76 SYSTEM ;
           CLOSE FLOAT GROW ZOOM COLOR SCHEME 5
```

```
    SET WINDOW OF MEMO TO MEMOEDIT

*   SET PROCEDURE TO LENDERP

*   Initialize database file
    SELECT 1
    USE lender INDEX lender

    PUBLIC ml_id,ml_name,ml_addr1,ml_addr2,ml_city,ml_state
    PUBLIC ml_phone,ml_ext,ml_tax_id,ml_currate,ml_ratedate
    PUBLIC ml_vrm,ml_rrm,ml_wrap,ml_zip

    * Display screen format
    CLEAR
    DO DISPFORM

    * Process bank records
    DO WHILE .T.

      * Display record
      DO DISPREC

      * Display simple menu
      choice = ' '
      @ 24,72 GET choice;
          MESSAGE "SELECT:  Append  Bottom  Delete  Edit  "+;
                  "Next  Prev  Top  Quit";
          PICTURE "!" VALID(choice $ "ABDENPQT")
      READ

      * Branch to menu choice
      DO CASE

        * Quit
        CASE choice = 'Q'
          CLOSE ALL
          EXIT

        * Add new record
        CASE choice = 'A'

          * Initialize memory variables
          DO BLANKREC
          @ 24,0
          @ 24,0 SAY "Press {Ctrl-W} to Exit"

          * Read into memory variables
          DO EDITREC

          * Confirm that user wants to append this record
          choice = ' '
          @ 24,0
          @ 24,0 SAY "SELECT:  {A}ccept  {I}gnore";
```

```
            GET choice PICTURE  ! VALID( choice $  "AI" )
        READ

        IF choice = 'A'

          * Add new record
          APPEND BLANK

          * Replace from memory variables
          DO REPLREC
        ENDIF

   * Edit record
   CASE choice = 'E'
     SCATTER MEMVAR
     @ 24, 0
     DO EDITREC
     DO REPLREC

   * Delete record
   CASE choice = 'D'
     IF .NOT. DELETED()
        DELETE
     ELSE
        RECALL
     ENDIF

   * Go to next record
   CASE choice = 'N'
     SKIP
     IF EOF()
        GOTO BOTTOM
     ENDIF

   * Go to previous record
   CASE choice = 'P'
     SKIP -1
     IF BOF()
        GOTO TOP
     ENDIF

   * Go to first record
   CASE choice = 'T'
     GOTO TOP

   * Go to last record
   CASE choice = 'B'
     GOTO BOTTOM

   ENDCASE

ENDDO
```

```
* Closing operations
  CLEAR
  SET BELL ON
  SET SCOREBOARD ON
  SET TALK ON
RETURN

* Procedures begin here

PROCEDURE DISPFORM
* Display form
  @ 1,0 TO 23,79 DOUBLE
  @ 3,1 TO 3,78 DOUBLE
  @ 5,1 TO 5,78
  @  2,29 SAY "MORTGAGE SYSTEM"
  @  4, 4 SAY "Lender ID     "
  @  4,36 SAY "Bank Name      "
  @  7, 6 SAY "Address 1    "
  @  8, 6 SAY "             "
  @  9, 6 SAY "City         "
  @  9,41 SAY "State   "
  @  9,55 SAY "Zip Code   "
  @ 11, 6 SAY "Telephone   "
  @ 11,33 SAY "Extension   "
  @ 13, 6 SAY "Tax ID       "
  @ 15, 6 SAY "Current Rate   "
  @ 16,13 SAY "As of    "
  @ 15,44 SAY "Variable Rate Mortgages (Y|N) "
  @ 16,40 SAY "Renegotiable Rate Mortgages (Y|N) "
  @ 17,55 SAY "Wraparounds (Y|N) "
  @ 14,47 SAY "Special Financing Offered:"
  @ 18, 3 SAY "Notes:"
RETURN

PROCEDURE DISPREC
* Display record on form
    @  0, 0 SAY "Record: "+SUBSTR(STR(RECNO()+1000000,7),2)
    IF DELETED()
       @ 0,50 SAY "*DELETED*"
    ELSE
       @ 0,50 SAY "         "
    ENDIF
    MODIFY MEMO l_notes NOWAIT
    @  4,17 GET l_id        PICTURE "!!!" ;
           MESSAGE "Enter bank ID"
    @  4,49 GET l_name      PICTURE "@X25" ;
           MESSAGE "Enter bank name"
    @  7,17 GET l_addr1     PICTURE "@X25" ;
           MESSAGE "Enter bank box address"
    @  8,17 GET l_addr2     PICTURE "@X25" ;
           MESSAGE "Enter bank street address
    @  9,17 GET l_city      PICTURE "@X20" ;
           MESSAGE "Enter bank city"
```

```
@  9,48 GET l_state    PICTURE "!!" ;
       MESSAGE "Enter bank state"
@  9,65 GET l_zip      PICTURE "99999-####" ;
       MESSAGE "Enter bank Zip Code"
@ 11,17 GET l_phone    PICTURE "(###)999-9999" ;
       MESSAGE "Enter bank telephone number"
@ 11,44 GET l_ext      PICTURE "####" ;
       MESSAGE "Enter bank extension"
@ 13,17 GET l_tax_id   PICTURE "99-9999999" ;
       MESSAGE "Enter bank tax id"
@ 15,20 GET l_currate  PICTURE "#9.9##" RANGE 0.0,20.0 ;
       MESSAGE "Enter current mortgage interest rate"
@ 16,20 GET l_ratedate PICTURE "@D" ;
       MESSAGE "Enter the date interest rate "+;
               "became effective"
@ 15,75 GET l_vrm      PICTURE "L" ;
       MESSAGE "Does bank offer variable rate "+;
               "mortgages (Y|N)?"
@ 16,75 GET l_rrm      PICTURE "L" ;
       MESSAGE "Does bank offer renegotiable "+;
               "rate mortgages (Y|N)?"
@ 17,75 GET l_wrap     PICTURE "L" ;
       MESSAGE "Does bank offer wraparound "+;
               "mortgages (Y|N)?"
@ 18,10 GET l_notes    ;
       MESSAGE "Press Ctrl-W to close memo window"
   CLEAR GETS
RETURN


PROCEDURE EDITREC
* Edit record values stored in memory variables
   @ 24, 0
   MODIFY MEMO l_notes NOWAIT
   @  4,17 GET m->l_id       PICTURE "!!!" ;
       MESSAGE "Enter bank ID"
   @  4,49 GET m->l_name     PICTURE "@X25" ;
       MESSAGE "Enter bank name"
   @  7,17 GET m->l_addr1    PICTURE "@X25" ;
       MESSAGE "Enter bank box address"
   @  8,17 GET m->l_addr2    PICTURE "@X25" ;
       MESSAGE "Enter bank street address"
   @  9,17 GET m->l_city     PICTURE "@X20" ;
       MESSAGE "Enter bank city"
   @  9,48 GET m->l_state    PICTURE "!!" ;
       MESSAGE "Enter bank state"
   @  9,65 GET m->l_zip      PICTURE "99999-####" ;
       MESSAGE "Enter bank Zip Code"
   @ 11,17 GET m->l_phone    PICTURE "(###)999-9999" ;
       MESSAGE "Enter bank telephone number"
   @ 11,44 GET m->l_ext      PICTURE "####" ;
       MESSAGE "Enter bank extension"
   @ 13,17 GET m->l_tax_id   PICTURE "99-9999999" ;
       MESSAGE "Enter bank tax id"
```

```
      @ 15,20 GET m->l_currate  PICTURE "#9.9##";
              RANGE 0.0,20.0 ;
              MESSAGE "Enter current mortgage interest rate"
      @ 16,20 GET m->l_ratedate PICTURE "@D" ;
              MESSAGE "Enter the date the interest rate "+;
                      "became effective"
      @ 15,75 GET m->l_vrm       PICTURE "L" ;
              MESSAGE "Does bank offer variable rate "+;
                      "mortgages (Y|N)?"
      @ 16,75 GET m->l_rrm       PICTURE "L" ;
              MESSAGE "Does bank offer renegotiable rate "+;
                      "mortgages (Y|N)?"
      @ 17,75 GET m->l_wrap      PICTURE "L" ;
              MESSAGE "Does bank offer wraparound "+;
                      "mortgages (Y|N)?"
      READ
      @ 24,17 SAY "Press Ctrl-W to save memo, "+;
                  "Ctrl-Q to abort memo"
      MODIFY MEMO l_notes
      @ 24, 0
      MODIFY MEMO l_notes NOWAIT
RETURN
PROCEDURE BLANKREC
    SCATTER MEMVAR BLANK
RETURN

PROCEDURE REPLREC
    GATHER MEMVAR
RETURN

* End of program
```

Program 8-2. Using Windows to Edit Memos

Showing Windows

SHOW WINDOW resembles ACTIVATE WINDOW, but it does not redirect output. It can display defined windows, change the order of display, and restore hidden windows. To display a window such as a help window that should not become active, use SHOW rather than ACTIVATE. On the other hand, ACTIVATE menus and memo windows that require user interaction.

Programs 8-3 and 8-4 illustrate the use of windows in a multilevel menu system. Program 8-3 defines the ones used by Program 8-4 and stores them in file PHONE.WIN. Program 8-4 is the menu shell for a telephone report system. It includes options to read captured information, including telephone numbers

called, by line, length of call, and date and time of call. Then the user can select
from the following reports:

calls by extension

calls by trunk line

calls ordered by length

most frequently called numbers

summary of telephone usage

Depending on the report selected, other windows may prompt for information
such as report dates, trunk lines, extension numbers, sort order, and destination.

```
* Program 8-3
*
* Telephone Report for Execuport Phones
* Created By: Michael P. Antonovich
* Date:       April 5, 1990
* Create file PHONE.WIN, containing all windows used by
* telephone system

* Set environment
  SET ECHO OFF
  SET TALK OFF
  SET BELL OFF
  SET STATUS OFF
  SET SCOREBOARD OFF
  SET EXACT OFF

* Define windows
  DEFINE WINDOW main_menu from 5,27 to 13,53 ;
     TITLE 'MAIN MENU' SHADOW
  DEFINE WINDOW rept_menu from 10,10 to 22,50 ;
     TITLE 'AVAILABLE REPORTS' SHADOW
  DEFINE WINDOW period from 7,16 to 15,60 ;
     TITLE 'TIME PERIOD' PANEL COLOR N/BG,BG+/N,B+
  DEFINE WINDOW long_dist from 11,35 to 22,77 ;
     TITLE 'CALL TYPE' PANEL COLOR N/G,W+/GR,GR
  DEFINE WINDOW sort_ordr from 13,1 to 23,40 ;
     TITLE 'SORT ORDER' PANEL COLOR BG+/B,W+/R,R
  DEFINE WINDOW staff_sel FROM 1,1 TO 22,50 ;
     TITLE 'ABC STAFF' PANEL COLOR GR+/R,GR+/N,R+
  DEFINE WINDOW phone_sel from 1,6 to 18,55 ;
     TITLE 'ABC EXTENSIONS' PANEL COLOR GR+/RB,GR+/N,R+
  DEFINE WINDOW destin FROM 2,40 TO 11,78 ;
     TITLE 'REPORT DESTINATIONS' PANEL COLOR W+/RB,RB+/N,W
  DEFINE WINDOW flname FROM 6,50 TO 15,78 ;
     TITLE 'REPORT FILE NAME' PANEL COLOR N/G,G/N,G+
  DEFINE WINDOW inactive FROM 15,15 TO 20,65 ;
     TITLE 'INACTIVE OPTION' PANEL COLOR SCHEME 5
```

```
SAVE WINDOW ALL TO phone.win

RETURN

* End of program
```

Program 8-3. Define and Save Windows

```
* Program 8-4
*
* Telephone Report for Execuport Phones
* Created By: Michael P. Antonovich
* Date:        April 5, 1990
* Window based menu subsystem only
*
* Requires PHONE.WIN file generated in Program 8-3

* Set environment
  SET ECHO OFF
  SET TALK OFF
  SET BELL OFF
  SET STATUS OFF
  SET SCOREBOARD OFF
  SET EXACT OFF
  CLOSE DATABASES
  PRIVATE exited
  exited = .F.
  repttype = 4

* Open databases
  SELECT 3
  USE staff INDEX staff
  SELECT 4
  USE trunks INDEX trunks

* Initialize variables
  last_name  = ""
  first_name = ""
  rept_sel   = .F.
  phone_ext  = ""
  phone_numb = ""
  start_date = CTOD(STR(MONTH(DATE()),2) + '/01/' +;
               STR(YEAR(DATE()),4))
  IF MONTH(DATE()) < 12
    end_date = CTOD(STR(MONTH(DATE())+1,2) + '/01/' +;
```

```
                    STR(YEAR(DATE()),4))-1
  ELSE
     end_date = CTOD('12/31/'+STR(YEAR(DATE()),4))
  ENDIF

* Title page
  SET COLOR TO W+/B
  CLEAR
  cnt = 40
  DO WHILE cnt > 1
     @ 8,cnt SAY REPLICATE('█',(40-cnt)*2+1)
     cnt = cnt - 1
  ENDDO

* Animated title page
  DO TIMEPAUS WITH .1
     @ 7,1 SAY '████████  ████    ████   ████   ████  '+;
     '
     @ 9,1 SAY '██                           ████  '+;
     '

  DO TIMEPAUS WITH .1
     @ 6,1 SAY '██████    ████           ████ ████  '+;
     '
     @ 7,1 SAY '██    ██    ██           ████    ██  '+;
     '
     @ 9,1 SAY '██                           ████  '+;
     '
     @10,1 SAY '██                       ████████  '+;
     '

  DO TIMEPAUS WITH .1
     @ 5,1 SAY '██████    ████           ████  ████  '+;
     '
     @ 6,1 SAY '██    ██    ██           ████    ██  '+;
     '
     @ 7,1 SAY '██    ██    ██           ████    ██  '+;
     '
     @ 9,1 SAY '██                           ████  '+;
     '
     @10,1 SAY '██                           ████  '+;
     '
     @11,1 SAY '██                       ████████  '+;
     '

  @ 8,1 SAY '████  ████    ████  ████ ████  ██  ████  '+;
  '
  DO TIMEPAUS WITH .25
  @ 14,1 SAY '                            Written by: Michael P.'+;
        ' Antonovich'
  @ 16,1 SAY '                                    April  1990'

  DO TIMEPAUS WITH 4
```

```
* Define windows
  RESTORE WINDOW ALL FROM phone.win

  DECLARE staf_rep[14]

* Display main menu
  mainchoice = 'Q'
  DO WHILE .NOT. exited
    CLEAR
    ACTIVATE WINDOW main_menu
    @ 0, 0 SAY "     TELEPHONE LOG SYSTEM"
    @ 2, 0 SAY "     L)oad captured data"
    @ 3, 0 SAY "     R)eport Generation"
    @ 4, 0 SAY "     Q)uit"
    @ 6,10 GET mainchoice PICTURE '!' ;
           VALID m->mainchoice $ 'LRQ';
           MESSAGE 'SELECT Main Choice: Load Data, '+;
                   'Generate Report, Quit';
           ERROR 'You must enter L, R, or Q'
    READ

* Decision branch for main menu
    DO CASE
      CASE m->mainchoice = 'L'
        ACTIVATE WINDOW inactive
        CLEAR
        @ 1,3 SAY "This option is not active. "+;
                  "Try R or Q."
        WAIT
        DEACTIVATE WINDOW inactive
      CASE m->mainchoice = 'R'
        reptchoice = '0'
        ACTIVATE WINDOW rept_menu
          @  1, 3 SAY "   AVAILABLE REPORTS:"
          @  3, 3 SAY " 1 Report by Extension"
          @  4, 3 SAY " 2 Report by Trunk Line"
          @  5, 3 SAY " 3 Report by Longest Call"
          @  6, 3 SAY " 4 Report by Most Frequent Number"
          @  7, 3 SAY " 5 Summary Report"
          @  8, 3 SAY " 0 Cancel Report Option"
          @ 10,10 GET reptchoice PICTURE '!' ;
             VALID m->reptchoice $ '012345';
             MESSAGE 'SELECT a report 1-5 or Quit 0';
             ERROR 'You must enter 0-5'
          READ
        IF m->reptchoice = '0'
          DEACTIVATE WINDOW rept_menu
        ELSE
          DEACTIVATE WINDOW ALL
          DO GETDATA WITH m->reptchoice
        ENDIF
      CASE m->mainchoice = 'Q'
        exited = .T.
```

```
        CLEAR WINDOWS
        CLEAR
    ENDCASE
  ENDDO

RETURN


**** Procedures and functions begin here ****

PROCEDURE GETDATA
PARAMETERS repttype
* Get other information needed to define a report beginning
* with staff members to include

IF m->repttype $ '12345'
  ACTIVATE WINDOW staff_sel
  @  1,1 SAY "      <<< ABC STAFF AND EXTENSIONS >>>"
  @ 18,1 SAY "To select, place a T before the extension."
  icnt = 1
  SELECT 3
  GOTO TOP
  SCAN
    staf_rep[icnt] = rept_sel
    @ icnt+2,3 GET staf_rep[icnt] PICTURE 'L' ;
      MESSAGE "Press T to include this staff member "+;
              "in the report"
    @ icnt+2,8 SAY phone_ext+':  '+first_name+' '+last_name
    icnt = icnt + 1
  ENDSCAN
  READ
  GOTO TOP
  icnt = 1
  SCAN
    REPLACE rept_sel WITH staf_rep[icnt]
    icnt = icnt + 1
  ENDSCAN
ENDIF

* Determine which extension numbers to include in report
IF repttype $ '12345'
  SELECT 4
  GOTO TOP
  ACTIVATE WINDOW phone_sel
  @  1,1 SAY "      <<< ABC PHONE LINES AND NUMBERS >>>"
  @ 13,1 SAY "To select, place a T before the line."
  icnt = 1
  SCAN
    staf_rep[icnt] = rept_sel
    @ icnt+2,3 GET staf_rep[icnt] PICTURE 'L' ;
      MESSAGE "Press T to include this phone extension "+;
              "in the report"
    @ icnt+2,8 SAY trunk_line+' -> '+phone_numb
```

```
      icnt = icnt + 1
    ENDSCAN
    READ
    GOTO TOP
    icnt = 1
    SCAN
      REPLACE rept_sel WITH staf_rep[icnt]
      icnt = icnt + 1
    ENDSCAN
ENDIF

* SELECT time period for report
ACTIVATE WINDOW period
@ 1,1 SAY 'Enter the start date and end date for the'
@ 2,1 SAY 'report. (Default is: CURRENT MONTH)'
@ 4,1 SAY 'Start date: ' GET start_date PICTURE "@D" ;
      VALID m->start_date <= DATE() ;
      MESSAGE 'Enter the first date to appear in the report';
      ERROR 'Date cannot be a future date'
@ 5,1 SAY 'End date:   ' GET end_date PICTURE "@D" ;
      VALID m->end_date >= m->start_date .AND. ;
      m->end_date <= DATE() ;
      MESSAGE 'Enter the last date to appear in the report';
      ERROR 'Date must be after start date and before '+;
            'current date'
READ

* Should report include local or long distance calls or both?
calltype = '1'
IF repttype < '5'
  ACTIVATE WINDOW long_dist
    @ 1, 1 SAY 'Do you want local calls, long distance'
    @ 2, 1 SAY 'calls, or both?  (Default is: BOTH)'
    @ 4,10 SAY '1) LOCAL'
    @ 5,10 SAY '2) LONG DISTANCE'
    @ 6,10 SAY '3) BOTH'
    @ 8,10 GET calltype PICTURE '9' ;
          VALID m->calltype $ '123' ;
          MESSAGE 'Select a call type 1-3';
          ERROR 'You must enter 1-3'
  READ
ENDIF

* SELECT sort order for report
sortorder = 'D'
IF repttype < '6'
  ACTIVATE WINDOW sort_ordr
    @ 1,1 SAY 'You can order the detail phone data'
    @ 2,1 SAY 'either by date or number dialed.'
    @ 3,1 SAY '(Default is: DATE)'
    @ 5,10 SAY 'D)ATE'
    @ 6,10 SAY 'N)UMBER DIALED'
    @ 8,10 GET sortorder PICTURE '!' ;
```

```
            VALID m->sortorder $ 'DN';
            MESSAGE 'Select a sort order for the call report';
            ERROR 'You must enter D or N'
   READ
ENDIF

* SELECT output destination for report
outp_dev = 'S'
ACTIVATE WINDOW destin
@ 1, 1 SAY 'SELECT destination for output:'
@ 3,10 SAY 'F)ile'
@ 4,10 SAY 'P)rinter'
@ 5,10 SAY 'S)creen'
@ 7,10 GET outp_dev PICTURE '!' VALID m->outp_dev $ 'FPS' ;
        MESSAGE 'Select an output destination for the '+;
                'call report';
        ERROR 'You must enter F, P, or S'
READ

DO CASE
  CASE outp_dev = 'F'
    rep_file = SPACE(8)
    ACTIVATE WINDOW flname
    @ 1,1 SAY 'Enter a valid filename:'
    @ 2,1 SAY 'Do not include path or'
    @ 3,1 SAY 'extension.'
    @ 4,1 SAY 'Default extension: RPT'
    @ 6,8 GET rep_file picture '!!!!!!!!!' ;
            MESSAGE 'Enter any valid 8 character filename '+;
                    'for report'
    READ
    DEACTIVATE WINDOW flname
    rep_file = TRIM(m->rep_file)+'.RPT'
    SET PRINTER TO &rep_file
    SET PRINTER ON
  CASE outp_dev = 'S'
  CASE outp_dev = 'P'
    SET CONSOLE OFF
    SET DEVICE TO PRINTER
    SET PRINTER ON
ENDCASE

CLEAR
DEACTIVATE WINDOW destin
DEACTIVATE WINDOW sort_ordr
DEACTIVATE WINDOW long_dist
DEACTIVATE WINDOW period
DEACTIVATE WINDOW staff_sel
DEACTIVATE WINDOW phone_sel

RETURN
PROCEDURE TIMEPAUS
PARAMETER leng
```

```
* Creates a timed pause
start = SECONDS()
DO WHILE SECONDS() < start+leng
ENDDO
RETURN

* End of program
```

Program 8-4. Window-Based Menu Subsystem

Changing Window Size

ZOOM WINDOW changes the size and position of a system or user window. Its first option is the window name. Next comes one of three fixed sizes (MIN, MAX, or NORM), or we can position and size the window with the AT, FROM, SIZE, and TO options.

MIN shrinks the window to show just the title. Conversely, MAX makes it as large as possible. For most windows, the maximum size is the entire screen. However, for a child window (one defined inside another), it is the size of the parent. Only windows defined with MINIMIZE and ZOOM keywords can be resized with MIN and MAX. Finally, NORM returns a window to its original size.

The SIZE clause changes the number of rows or columns in the window. On the other hand, the TO clause moves the lower right corner.

We can also move the upper left corner with the AT or FROM clause.

> **WARNING**
> The AT or FROM clause cannot appear together with the SIZE or TO clause.

Windowing Functions

There are also many windowing functions that we will now describe briefly. We will then show an example using several of them.

WCHILD(windowname,ExpN)

Returns the number of windows defined within the named one. With a numeric expression, it returns the name of the child window at that stack position.

WCOLS(ExpC)

Returns the number of columns in the window specified by ExpC, the active window if no name is specified, or the main screen if ExpC is a null string.

WEXIST(ExpC)

Verifies that a named window has been defined. It returns .T. if it finds the window, .F. if not.

WLCOL(ExpC)

Returns the column of the named or active window's upper left corner relative to the screen coordinates.

WLROW(ExpC)

Returns the row of the named or active window's upper left corner relative to the screen coordinates.

WONTOP(ExpC)

Returns .T. if ExpC is the topmost window. With no parameter, it returns the name of the topmost window.

WOUTPUT(ExpC)

Returns .T. if ExpC is the active window. With no parameter, it returns the name of the active window.

WPARENT(windowname)

Returns the name of the parent of the named window or of the active window if no name is specified.

WROWS(ExpC)

Returns the number of rows in the window specified by ExpC, the active window if no name is specified, or the main screen if ExpC is the null string.

WVISIBLE(ExpC)

Returns .T. if the named window is activated, regardless of whether it is shown.

Program 8-5 uses several window functions to display long strings. Unlike memos that never split words between lines, character fields displayed in windows print up to the rightmost position. The string breaks there even if it is the middle of a word. The rest continues on the next line. Program 8-5 solves this problem with procedure OUTSTRG; it prints a string in a specified window without splitting words.

```
* Program 8-5
*
* Creates two windows and displays text in them.
* It prevents words from being split between lines.
* It pauses at the end of each full window before
* clearing it and printing more text.

* Set environment
  SET TALK OFF
  SET STATUS OFF
  SET SCOREBOARD OFF
  CLEAR

* Define windows and strings to print in them
  DEFINE WINDOW wind1 FROM 5,2 TO 15,25 TITLE 'WINDOW 1'
  DEFINE WINDOW wind2 FROM 10,40 TO 22,60 TITLE 'WINDOW 2'
  str1 = 'Memo fields automatically wrap words that do '+;
         'not fit on the current line. They also stop '+;
         'when the window is full.'
  str2 = 'Character fields normally print up to the edge '+;
         'of the window unless we control them with a '+;
         'procedure like OUTSTRG. '
  str2 = str2 + 'They normally print until the entire'+;
         'string is handled. '
  str2 = str2 + 'However, we may want to have it pause '+;
         'when the window is full before continuing.'

* Activate windows
  ACTIVATE WINDOWS wind1,wind2

* Print string 1 in window 1
  DO OUTSTRG WITH str1,'wind1'
  DO pauseit
* Print string 2 in window 2
  DO OUTSTRG WITH str2,'wind2'
  DO pauseit

CLEAR WINDOWS
CLEAR
RETURN

PROCEDURE pauseit
* Activates screen and waits for user to press any key
```

```
      ACTIVATE SCREEN
      @ 22,79
      WAIT
RETURN


PROCEDURE outstrg
* Writes string in a window without splitting words
PARAMETER strg,winname

* Check if desired window is active
  IF .NOT. WOUTPUT(winname)
  * Check if desired window exists
    IF WEXIST(winname)
      ACTIVATE WINDOW &winname
    ELSE
      ACTIVATE SCREEN
      CLEAR
      ? 'Window: '+ALLTRIM(winname) +;
        ' is undefined.'
      RETURN
    ENDIF
  ELSE
  * Check if active window is on top
    IF .NOT. WONTOP(winname)
      ACTIVATE WINDOW &winname
    ENDIF
  ENDIF

* Print string
  width  = WCOLS()
  height = WROWS()
  irow = 1
  textstrg = strg
  DO WHILE .NOT. EMPTY(textstrg)
    ilen = LEN(textstrg)
    i = width
    IF ilen < i
      i = ilen
    ENDIF
    DO WHILE SUBSTR(textstrg,i,1) # ' ' .AND. i <> ilen
      i = i - 1
      IF i = 0
        i = width
        EXIT
      ENDIF
    ENDDO
    ?? ALLTRIM(LEFT(textstrg,i))
    irow = irow + 1
    IF irow > height - 1
      WAIT "  <<Press a key>>"
      irow = 1
      CLEAR
```

```
     ELSE
        ? ""
     ENDIF
     IF i = ilen
        textstrg = ''
     ELSE
        textstrg = ALLTRIM(SUBSTR(textstrg,i))
     ENDIF
  ENDDO

RETURN

* End of program
```

Program 8-5. Formatting Text Strings in Windows

Screen Builder

Chapter 3 explored commands that collected data interactively from the user. Specifically, it examined variations of the @...SAY/GET command. In the first part of this chapter, we learned how to create and manipulate windows. This section describes how to automate the process with the Screen Builder. We will see how to quickly generate input and output screens that use standard FoxPro commands.

We can use the Screen Builder to define output screens or windows. We can also use it to develop input screens for memory and database variables. They can use all the data validation techniques from Chapter 3. Once we complete the definitions, we can generate standard FoxPro code and integrate it directly into programs.

When defining a screen, we must first name it. Let's create one called PRODUPDT to update information in the database PRODUCTS.DBF.

```
     CREATE SCREEN PRODUPDT
```

CREATE SCREEN opens the screen definition window and adds the SCREEN pulldown menu to the system menu bar.

Like the report generator, the Screen Builder allows freeform entry of text and fields in the layout window. It also supports a Quick Screen option to quickly place fields from currently open databases in either a column or form layout. We can optionally put the name next to the field. Although this option is handy, application developers are unlikely to use it for a final design. Therefore, let's see what powerful features the SCREEN pulldown menu offers.

The first step in creating a screen or window is to define it physically. The Screen Layout option displays the dialog shown in Figure 8-3.

You can use this dialog to define both screens (desktops) and windows. Some options open other dialogs such as Screen Code and READ clauses. For example, when defining a window, the Type option opens a dialog to select its type, attributes, and border as shown in Figure 8-4.

Returning to Figure 8-3, we next define the screen's size and position. The Center option centers windows both vertically and horizontally.

The two Screen Code options let us insert code that executes before displaying the window (Setup...) or after closing it (Cleanup & Procs...). We can include code in the Setup window that opens files, sets relations, sets indexes, and initializes variables. The setup code can also call other procedures and functions. Our product file screen might open the product database with the commands:

```
SELECT 1
USE PRODUCTS
```

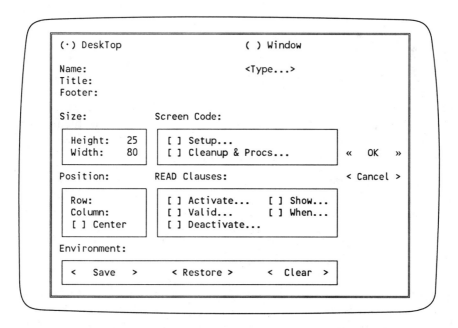

Figure 8-3. Screen layout dialog.

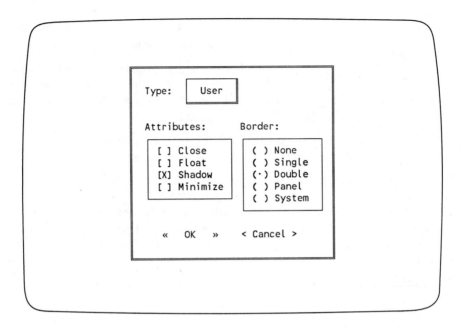

Figure 8-4. Window type dialog.

The Cleanup & Procs option provides similar ability to execute code after closing a window. Typical example tasks are closing files, launching reports, or verifying and appending data entries. Another use is to collect procedures or functions used by several fields in a current screen. For example, they may call the same function to verify input. If we include it with each of them, FoxPro duplicates it unnecessarily. It is better to reference the function in the field validation definition and include its code here.

Each screen also supports five READ clauses. They offer the same capabilities as the READ command. The When clause determines if READ should even execute. The Activate clause provides code that must execute successfully before READ can activate a window and process its GET statements. The Valid clause verifies the input fields before allowing FoxPro to exit the READ. The Deactivate clause must execute successfully before READ can exit the current window. If the program has only one window, the Deactivate clause executes when the Valid clause does. The Show clause executes when the SHOW GETS command executes to refresh SAYs or enable or disable GETs. As with the Screen Codes section, each clause opens an edit window allowing us to enter program code.

WARNING

Although the code for a READ clause should be a function, do not include the FUNCTION statement. FoxPro automatically defines a unique function name for each clause. The same applies to procedures defined for Screen Codes. FoxPro also automatically appends RETURN to procedures and RETURN .T. to functions during compilation. Because READ clauses are functions, we may have to include a RETURN .F. statement in the code when the logical test fails.

The second section of the SCREEN pulldown defines objects we can place on the screen, including:

- boxes and lines
- fields (both database and memory variable)
- text
- pushbuttons
- radio buttons
- check boxes
- popups
- lists

This list includes the @...SAY/GET variations covered in Chapter 3. Except for boxes and text, each object uses dialog boxes to define its parameters completely. Figure 8-5 shows a composite of them. Note that the options in each box are the same ones available in the corresponding @...SAY/GET command.

The third section of the SCREEN pulldown lets us organize the objects. The first two options, Bring to Front and Send to Back, change the stacking order. For example, to place text inside a box, we might decide to draw the box first. But what happens if we make it too small? A better approach is to place the text first, then draw the box over it. Although we can see the text, we cannot select it since it is behind the box. We must send the box to the back to regain access to it.

The Center option places the selected object in the middle of the current line. It provides an excellent way to center titles. We can also change the color of objects. The color option lets us select either the default colors for windows or custom colors by choosing one of the 24 schemes.

The fourth section of the pulldown lets us create and break up groups. They serve several purposes. First, they redefine the order of fields during a READ. Second, they let us move objects as a unit during screen design.

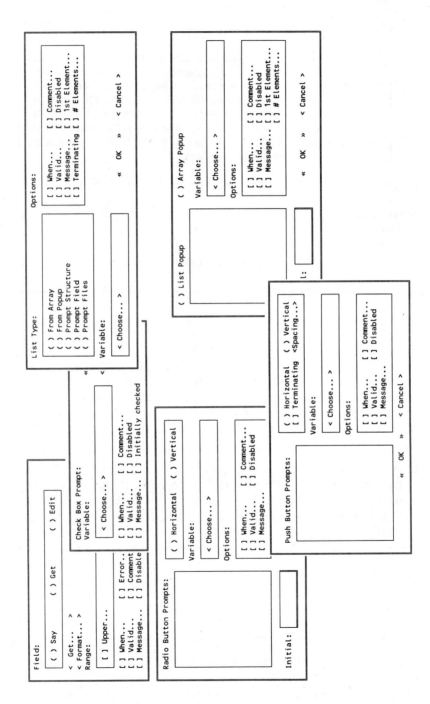

Figure 8-5. @...SAY/GET dialog boxes.

Normally, the READ command accesses GET fields in the order in which they were added to the screen. The Reorder Field option redefines the order from left to right and top to bottom. We can force an individual object to the end of the list by selecting it before choosing this option. We can modify the sequence further by grouping objects. Within a group, objects are ordered left to right and top to bottom even when the fields are scattered. When READ encounters the first object in a group, it proceeds through the others before reading anything else. Thus objects that physically occur after the first one in a group are read only after the entire group is read. Figure 8-6 shows the effect symbolically. Boxes represents GET fields. The dashed line defines the group. The numbers inside the boxes show the read order while the group definition is active.

HINT

The number on the left side of the field always shows the current access order of the screen's GET fields.

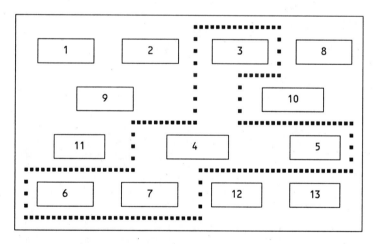

Figure 8-6. Effect of a group definition on READ order.

HINT

To insert a field into a screen or window, you may have to move several objects. Although we could move them individually, it may be easier to group them first, move them as a unit, then ungroup them.

Grouping and ungrouping objects does not change their order during a READ unless we also select the Reorder Fields option.

After completing the screen design, save it using the SAVE option from the FILE pulldown menu. FoxPro automatically assigns screen definitions the extension SCX.

Generating Screen Code

Before we can use screens created with CREATE SCREEN, we must generate code for them. With at least one screen still open in the Screen Design window, select GENERATE from the PROGRAM pulldown menu. This option displays the dialog box in Figure 8-7.

We can generate code for windows and screens by selecting them individually or in combination using the left window of the dialog. If we select more than one, the order in which we select them becomes the order in which the generated program executes them. We can change the order before generating the code by using the Arrange button.

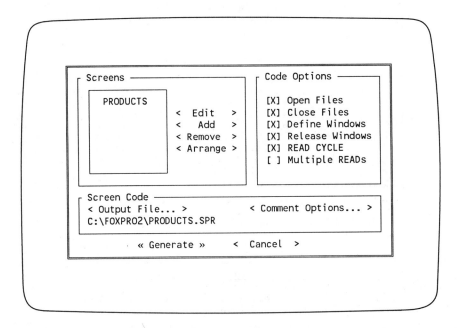

Figure 8-7. Generate dialog.

Code Options

Define Windows

FoxPro uses the information supplied in the Screen Layout dialog to define windows. If we do not select this option, we must supply commands, typically in the Setup option.

Close Files

FoxPro generates commands to close all files at the end of the generated code. If we do not select this option, we must close them explicitly, perhaps in the Cleanup & Procs option.

Open Files

FoxPro uses the environment information saved with the screen to generate code that opens files and indexes and sets relations. If we do not select this option, we must supply code to open files, perhaps in the Setup option.

Multiple Reads

When generating code for a single screen or window, FoxPro groups all GETs under a single READ. However, when generating code for multiple screens, we can choose to perform a READ after all screens (the default) or after each one (multiple READs).

READ Cycle

Determines whether FoxPro generates a READ or a READ CYCLE statement.

Release Windows

FoxPro generates code to release windows at the end of the program. If we do not select it, we must supply the required commands, typically in the Cleanup & Procs section.

Before generating the screen code, check the Comment Options dialog. It defines developer information (name and address) that appears at the beginning of the generated code. It also lets us choose between boxes and asterisks as a commenting style.

Finally, to generate the code, we must supply a program filename. The generated code is ready to run from a DO command. Since it uses standard FoxPro commands, we can use the FoxPro editor to enhance it further or integrate it with other programs.

Summary

This chapter described how to define windows for use in applications. We saw how color schemes help standardize colors. We then used windows for menus and memo fields. Next we used window functions to format string display.

Finally, we took a brief tour of the Screen Builder utility. We saw that it supports all features of the @...GET and READ family of commands for single and multiple screens. Because FoxPro generates actual code for the screens, the utility can save developers considerable time and effort.

9

Controlling Programs with Menus

Any application that asks the user to select an option needs a menu. FoxPro provides commands to create many styles, including:

- ASCII pick lists
- popup menus
- horizontal bar menus
- array menus
- pulldown menus
- component menus

This chapter describes how to define, create, and utilize several styles alone and in combination. Most examples use the same application to simplify comparisons. We also show how to use a database field in a menu. As a variation, we create a menu that lets the user select fields to define a custom report.

We complete the chapter by describing the Menu Builder.

Menu Terminology

First let's review terminology. What are menus? Most people think of them only in terms of major program options such as:

EDIT DATA	LOAD DATA
CREATE REPORT	VIEW DATA

But a menu can help users choose among any set of alternatives. In the report section of a program, it may ask the user if output should be sent to a file, the printer, or the screen. Many programs use the following command to pose the question:

```
@ 18,10 SAY 'Send report to F)ile, P)rinter, or S)creen [FPS]' ;
        GET outpdest VALID outpdest $ 'FPS'
```

Why not ask the user via the menu in Figure 9-1?

This type of menu is called a *popup*. It usually has a border around the options (or *bars*). One is highlighted and is the default, should the user simply press Enter. We can move the highlight with the arrow keys. In some cases, one character of each option is emphasized or underscored. The user can execute it by pressing the key (called a *hot key*). The first character is the default hot key. Of course, we can only use it in practice if each option has a unique beginning. Otherwise, we may want to insert numbers or letters, as shown in Figure 9-2.

Other applications display options horizontally without a surrounding box. Such arrangements are called *menu bars*. The options, also called *menu pads,* are usually single words, but can be phrases. As with popups, we may select an option either via a hot key or by highlighting it and pressing Enter.

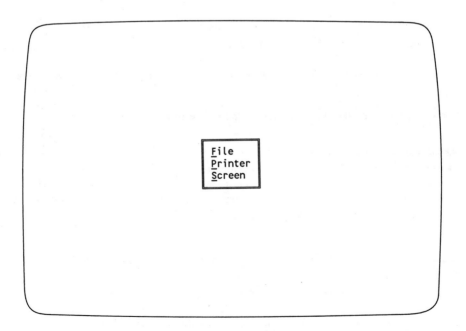

Figure 9-1. Report destination menu.

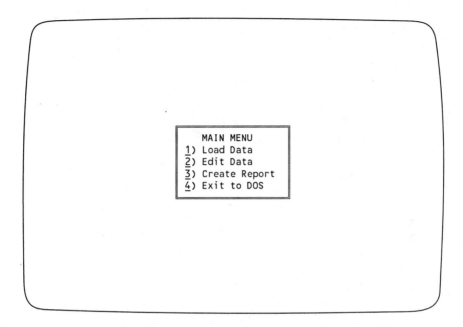

Figure 9-2. Numbered main menu.

Some applications combine the two types. The bar acts as the main menu. As we highlight pads, popups appear below them with related options. In this case, the popups are called *pulldown menus* because they appear to descend from the pads. This is how FoxPro's system menu works.

ASCII Pick Lists

The ASCII pick list is the simplest type of menu. It lists the options, preceding each with a unique identifier. It may be a letter, a digit, or a longer string. To make a selection, the user types the identifier and presses Enter. Generally an @...SAY/GET and READ combination prompts for the choice. Then either a series of IF...ENDIF blocks or a CASE structure implements it. Program 9-1 shows a typical pick list.

```
* Program 9-1
* Multilevel pick list
*
* Loads data about retailers, products, and advertising
* from which it generates reports
*
```

```
* Set environment
  CLEAR ALL
  SET TALK OFF
  SET BELL OFF
  SET SCOREBOARD OFF

* Checks whether all referenced database files exist.
* DBFFILES.DBF stores information about database and
* index files. If an index file does not exist, it
* is generated.
  DO filechek
  CLOSE DATABASES

* Begin main menu
  moption = ' '
  DO WHILE moption # 'Z'

    * Screen
    SET COLOR TO GR+/B
    CLEAR
    SET CLOCK TO 1,68
    @  0,0 TO 20,79 DOUBLE
    @  1,24 SAY 'RETAIL SYSTEM - MAIN MENU'
    @  2, 0 SAY ' ╟───────────────────────────────────────'+;
              '─────────────────────────────────────╢ '


    SET COLOR TO W/B
    moption = 'Z'
    @ 10,25 SAY ' A) Load Retailer Data '
    @ 11,25 SAY ' B) Load Brands/Products Data '
    @ 12,25 SAY ' C) Load Advertisement Data '
    @ 13,25 SAY ' D) Support File Maintenance'
    @ 14,25 SAY ' E) Summary Reports '
    @ 15,25 SAY ' F) Advertisement Report '
    @ 17,25 SAY ' Z) Quit - Exit to DOS '
    choices = 'ABCDEFZ'

    * Get user's choice
    SET COLOR TO GR+
    @ 19,24 SAY "Enter Choice"
    @ 19,21 GET moption PICTURE '!' ;
            VALID moption $ choices
    READ

    * Use choice to branch to procedure
    SET COLOR TO W+/B
    DO CASE
    CASE moption = 'A'
      * Load retailer data
        @ 10,25 SAY '[A) LOAD RETAILER DATA]'
        SET PROCEDURE TO retlload
        DO retlload
```

```
CASE moption = 'B'
  * Load brand and product data
    @ 11,25 SAY '[B) LOAD BRANDS/PRODUCTS DATA]'
    SET PROCEDURE TO brndload
    DO brndload

CASE moption = 'C'
  * Load advertisement data
    @ 12,25 SAY '[C) LOAD ADVERTISEMENT DATA]'
    SET PROCEDURE TO adload
    DO adload

CASE moption = 'D'
  * Use file maintenance program
    @ 13,25 SAY '[D) SUPPORT FILE MAINTENANCE]'
    SET PROCEDURE TO genedit
    DO genedit

CASE moption = 'E'
  * Display submenu of summary reports
    @ 14,25 SAY '[E) SUMMARY REPORTS]'

    * Display secondary menu for summary reports
    @ 12,5 CLEAR TO 19,77
    SET COLOR TO W/B
    option1 = 'Z'
    @ 12,20 SAY ' A) Management Summary '
    @ 13,20 SAY ' B) Region Summary '
    @ 14,20 SAY ' C) District Summary '
    @ 15,20 SAY ' D) Territory Summary '
    @ 16,20 SAY ' Z) Quit - Exit to Main Menu '
    choice1 = 'ABCDZ'

    * Get user's choice from summary reports menu
    SET COLOR TO GR+
    @ 18,24 SAY "Enter Choice"
    @ 18,21 GET option1 PICTURE '!' ;
            VALID option1 $ choice1
    READ

      * Call selected summary report program
      DO CASE
        CASE option1 = 'A'
          @ 12,20 SAY '[A) MANAGEMENT SUMMARY]'
          SET PROCEDURE TO mgmtsum
          DO mgmtsum
        CASE option1 = 'B'
          @ 13,20 SAY '[B) REGION SUMMARY]'
          SET PROCEDURE TO regsum
          DO regsum
        CASE option1 = 'C'
          @ 14,20 SAY '[C) DISTRICT SUMMARY]'
```

```
              SET PROCEDURE TO distsum
              DO distsum
            CASE option1 = 'D'
              @ 15,20 SAY '[D) TERRITORY SUMMARY]'
              SET PROCEDURE TO terrsum
              DO terrsum
        ENDCASE

    CASE moption = 'F'
       @  15,25 SAY '[H) ADVERTISEMENT REPORT]'
       SET PROCEDURE TO addetail
       DO addetail

    CASE moption = 'Z'
       @ 17,21 SAY 'Z) QUIT - EXIT TO DOS'
       SET COLOR TO W+/N
       CLOSE DATABASES
       CLEAR

    ENDCASE

  ENDDO

* End of main procedure
RETURN

**************************************************************

PROCEDURE filechek

DEFINE WINDOW dbcheck FROM 0, 0 TO 23,79 ;
       TITLE 'DATABASE/INDEX CHECK & REINDEX' ;
       SYSTEM FLOAT CLOSE COLOR SCHEME 22

ACTIVATE WINDOW dbcheck
* Begin file check. Initialize counters.
  line_cnt = 99
  file_err = 0

* Open database that lists databases used by program.
* It contains the fields:
*
*    FIELD          DESCRIPTION
*    _____         _____
*    DBFNAME        Database name
*    NDEX           Flag to indicate if database has
*                   an index
*    NDXNAME        Index name
*    NDXKEY         Index key
  SELECT 1
  USE dbffiles

* Loop through records to check each database
  DO WHILE .NOT. EOF()
```

```
dbfname = ALLTRIM(dbfname)
ndxkey  = ndxkey

* If 18 lines already displayed, begin a new screen
IF line_cnt > 18
  line_cnt = 4
  @ 0,  0 CLEAR TO 21,77 COLOR BG+
  @ 0,  0 TO 20,77 DOUBLE
  @ 1, 10 SAY '<< DATABASE AND INDEX FILE CHECK >>' ;
          COLOR GR+/B
  @ 2, 10 SAY 'Filename       Database       Index Name';
             + '       Index' COLOR W+/B
  @ 3, 10 SAY '_____    _____      _____';
             + '       _____' COLOR W+/B
ENDIF

* Set files_ok to .F. and display a message if a file is
* missing; create an index file if none exists.
IF dbfile
  * Check if referenced database exists
  IF .NOT. FILE(m->dbfname + '.dbf')
    @ line_cnt,10 SAY m->dbfname COLOR BG/B
    @ line_cnt,25 SAY 'NOT FOUND' COLOR R+/B
    line_cnt = line_cnt + 1
    file_err = file_err + 1
  ELSE
    ndxname = ALLTRIM(ndxname)

    * Does this database have an index?
    IF ndex
      * If index not found, create it
      IF .NOT. FILE(m->ndxname + '.idx')
        @ line_cnt,10 SAY m->dbfname COLOR BG/B
        @ line_cnt,25 SAY 'FOUND' COLOR G+/B
        @ line_cnt,40 SAY m->ndxname COLOR BG/B
        @ line_cnt,55 SAY 'INDEXING ' COLOR R+/B
        nname = m->ndxname
        SELECT 2
        USE &dbfname
        nkey = LTRIM(TRIM(ndxkey))
        INDEX ON &nkey TO &nname
        @ line_cnt,55 SAY 'REINDEXED' COLOR G+/B
        line_cnt = line_cnt + 1
      ENDIF
    ENDIF
  ENDIF
ENDIF

* Get next database
SELECT 1
SKIP

* Increment line counter.
```

```
      * Check if at bottom of screen.
      IF line_cnt = 18
        @ 22,79
        WAIT 'Press any key for next page'
      ENDIF

  ENDDO

  * Do fatal errors exist (missing database)?
  IF file_err > 0
     @ 12,10 TO 16,70 PANEL COLOR SCHEME 6
     @ 13,11 FILL TO 15,69 COLOR W+/R
     @ 14,20 SAY STR(file_err,2) + ;
             ' FATAL error(s) found. (Missing Files)' ;
             COLOR W+/R
     @ 20,77
     WAIT
     CANCEL
  ELSE
     @ 12,20 TO 16,60 PANEL COLOR SCHEME 6
     @ 13,21 FILL TO 15,59 COLOR W+/G
     @ 14,28 SAY 'A L L   F I L E S   O K' COLOR W+/G
  ENDIF

  CLOSE DATABASES
  DEACTIVATE WINDOW dbcheck
  RELEASE WINDOW dbcheck

RETURN

* End of program
```

Program 9-1. Pick List Menu

Note that options can lead to lower level menus. They also appear in user-defined windows.

Pick lists offer great flexibility in placing options. We can use them to create multi-column menus. On the other hand, although they work well for keyboard entry, they do not readily support a mouse. Besides, unless we expend a lot of effort, their appearance is quite plain. Let's look at FoxPro's other menu options that offer more functionality, better appearance, and mouse support.

Popup Menus

The simplest popup menu uses just two commands: @...PROMPT and MENU TO. The first defines the options and positions them in the screen or window.

We can list them horizontally, vertically, or randomly. Thus, @...PROMPT provides the flexibility of pick lists, but with the advantage of mouse support. MENU TO activates the menu and supports use of a mouse or the arrow keys to select options. The order of the PROMPTs determines the order in which the options are highlighted.

Program 9-2 recreates the main menu from Program 9-1. Note how each PROMPT statement includes a MESSAGE clause. Its text appears centered at the bottom of the screen. (The SET MESSAGE TO command can move it.) As each option is highlighted, FoxPro displays the corresponding message.

We can also control which option is highlighted initially by setting the menu choice variable (moption). Program 9-2 sets it to the seventh or Quit option.

```
* Program 9-2
* Menu using @...PROMPT and MENU TO commands

* Set environment
  CLEAR ALL
  SET TALK OFF
  SET BELL OFF
  SET SCOREBOARD OFF
  SET MESSAGE TO 24 CENTER
  CLOSE DATABASES

* Begin main menu
  DO WHILE .T.
  moption = 7

   * Screen
     SET COLOR TO GR+/B
     CLEAR
     SET CLOCK TO 1,68
     @  0,0 TO 20,79 DOUBLE
     @  1,27 SAY 'RETAIL SYSTEM - MAIN MENU'
     @  2, 0 SAY '‖──────────────────────────────────‖'+;
              '                                                      ‖'
                  '─────────────────────────────────────‖'

     SET COLOR TO W/B
     moption = 'Z'

   * Define prompts
     @ 10,25 PROMPT ' Load Retailer Data ' ;
             MESSAGE 'Data file must have name RETLDATA.DAT'
     @ 11,25 PROMPT ' Load Brands/Products Data ' ;
             MESSAGE 'Data file is an ASCII file BRAND.DAT'
     @ 12,25 PROMPT ' Load Advertisement Data ' ;
             MESSAGE 'Data file is an ASCII file AD.DAT'
     @ 13,25 PROMPT ' Support File Maintenance' ;
```

```
            MESSAGE 'General edit program to support'+;
                    'maintain all files'
@ 14,25 PROMPT ' Summary Reports ' ;
            MESSAGE 'Summary Reports levels: MANAGEMENT, '+;
                    'REGION, DISTRICT, and TERRITORY'
@ 15,25 PROMPT ' Detail Advertisement Report ' ;
            MESSAGE 'Print advertisement details by region'
@ 17,25 PROMPT ' Quit - Exit to DOS ' ;
            MESSAGE 'Exit RETAILER system'

* When user selects a menu option, MENU TO puts an
* integer corresponding to the order of the prompt
* definition in variable moption
MENU TO moption

* Use menu choice to branch to procedure
DO CASE
CASE moption = 1
   SET PROCEDURE TO retlload
   DO retlload

CASE moption = 2
   SET PROCEDURE TO brndload
   DO brndload

CASE moption = 3
   SET PROCEDURE TO adload
   DO adload

CASE moption = 4
   SET PROCEDURE TO genedit
   DO genedit

CASE moption = 5
   * Display secondary menu for summary reports
   @ 12,5 CLEAR TO 19,77
   SET COLOR TO W/B
   @ 12,20 PROMPT ' Management Summary ' ;
           MESSAGE 'Reports advertisements by brand '+;
                   'across regions and districts'
   @ 13,20 PROMPT ' Region Summary ' ;
           MESSAGE 'Reports advertisements by brand '+;
                   'within regions'
   @ 14,20 PROMPT ' District Summary ' ;
           MESSAGE 'Reports advertisements by brand '+;
                   'within districts'
   @ 15,20 PROMPT ' Territory Summary ' ;
           MESSAGE 'Reports advertisements by brand '+;
                   'within territories'
   @ 16,20 PROMPT ' Quit - Exit to MAIN MENU ' ;
           MESSAGE 'Return to RETAILER Main Menu'

  * Variable option1 identifies selected summary
```

```
      * report and calls its procedure
        MENU TO option1
      * Call appropriate program
        DO CASE
           CASE option1 = 1
             SET PROCEDURE TO mgmtsum
             DO mgmtsum
           CASE option1 = 2
             SET PROCEDURE TO regsum
             DO regsum
           CASE option1 = 3
             SET PROCEDURE TO distsum
             DO distsum
           CASE option1 = 4
             SET PROCEDURE TO terrsum
             DO terrsum
        ENDCASE

   CASE moption = 6
      SET PROCEDURE TO addetail
      DO addetail

   CASE moption = 7
      SET COLOR TO W+/N
      CLOSE DATABASES
      CLEAR
      EXIT

   ENDCASE

 ENDDO

* End of main procedure
RETURN

* End of program
```

Program 9-2. Popup Menu Based on MENU TO Command

We can extend the popup menu to include a window automatically by using the @...MENU command. Before opening the menu, we place the options in a one-dimensional array. @...MENU then displays them in a window. We can also include TITLE and SHADOW clauses.

This command can handle more options than it can display. In the next example, the menu has 30 options, but displays only 15 at a time. The user can scroll through them with the cursor keys.

```
@ 1,20 MENU filelist 30,15 TITLE 'FILE LIST' SHADOW
```

The command that retrieves the selected option is

```
READ MENU TO filepick
```

As with the **MENU TO** command, we set filepick as a default when the menu is activated. It returns the relative number of the selected option. Program 9-3 repeats the previous menu with the @...MENU command.

```
* Program 9-3
* Menu using @...PROMPT and MENU TO commands

* Set environment
  CLEAR ALL
  SET TALK OFF
  SET BELL OFF
  SET SCOREBOARD OFF
  SET MESSAGE TO 24 CENTER
  CLOSE DATABASES

* Begin main menu
  DO WHILE .T.
  moption = 1

  * Screen
    SET COLOR TO GR+/B
    CLEAR
    SET CLOCK TO 1,68
    @  0,0 TO 21,79 DOUBLE
    @  1,27 SAY 'RETAIL SYSTEM - MAIN MENU'
    @  2, 0 SAY '‖────────────────────────────────────'+;
              '                                     ‖'

  * Define menu arrays
    DIMENSION mainmenu[7],sub1[5]
    mainmenu[1]  = ' Load \<Retailer Data '
    mainmenu[2]  = ' Load \<Brands/Products Data '
    mainmenu[3]  = ' Load \<Advertisement Data '
    mainmenu[4]  = ' \<File Maintenance '
    mainmenu[5]  = ' \<Summary Reports '
    mainmenu[6]  = ' \<Detail Report '
    mainmenu[7]  = ' \<Quit - Exit to DOS '
    sub1[1] = ' \<Management Summary '
    sub1[2] = ' \<Region Summary '
    sub1[3] = ' \<District Summary '
    sub1[4] = ' \<Territory Summary '
    sub1[5] = ' \<Quit - Exit to Main Menu '

  * Display menu and prompt for user's choice
    @ 12,20 MENU mainmenu,11,6 TITLE ;
            'ADVERTISEMENTS - MAIN MENU' SHADOW
    READ MENU TO moption
```

```
* Use menu choice to branch to procedure
DO CASE
CASE moption = 1
   * Load retailer data
   SET PROCEDURE TO retlload
   DO retlload

CASE moption = 2
   * Load brand and product data
   SET PROCEDURE TO brndload
   DO brndload

CASE moption = 3
   * Load advertisement data
   SET PROCEDURE TO adload
   DO adload

CASE moption = 4
   * Perform general file maintenance
   SET PROCEDURE TO genedit
   DO genedit

CASE moption = 5
   * Display summary report menu
   * Display secondary menu for summary reports
   option1 = 1
   @ 15,35 MENU sub1,5 TITLE 'SUMMARY REPORT MENU' ;
        SHADOW
   READ MENU TO option1

    * Use menu choice to branch to procedure
    DO CASE
       CASE option1 = 1
          * Generate management summary report
          SET PROCEDURE TO mgmtsum
          DO mgmtsum
       CASE option1 = 2
          * Generate region summary report
          SET PROCEDURE TO regsum
          DO regsum
       CASE option1 = 3
          * Generate district summary report
          SET PROCEDURE TO distsum
          DO distsum
       CASE option1 = 4
          * Generate territory summary report
          SET PROCEDURE TO terrsum
          DO terrsum
    ENDCASE

CASE moption = 6
   * Generate advertisement summary report
   SET PROCEDURE TO addetail
```

```
        DO addetail

    CASE moption = 7
        * Close program
        SET COLOR TO W+/N
        CLOSE DATABASES
        CLEAR
        EXIT

    ENDCASE

  ENDDO

RETURN

* End of program
```

Program 9-3. Popup Menu Based on @...MENU Command

In both popup menus, we highlight options to select them. The first letters are default hot keys. As before, we can define others by putting the characters \< ahead of them. Hot key characters appear in a particular color as specified in the color scheme. When the user presses one, the option executes just as if he or she had highlighted it and pressed Enter. There are two restrictions. First, we can define only one hot key per option. Second, each must be unique within a menu. If several options have the same hot key, FoxPro selects the first one.

Another special feature is a horizontal line between options. Just put the characters \- at the beginning of a string in a separate array element. We can also use a slash followed by a space (\ ) to insert a blank line between options.

Horizontal Bar Menus

Horizontal bar menus (also called Lotus-style menus), originally popularized by spreadsheet programs, have become common in many applications. The first step in creating one is to assign a word to each menu choice. FoxPro does not limit the options to one word, but practical considerations of line length usually do.

We define bar options by placing the pads in a two-dimensional array. The first dimension is the text, the second is messages to appear at the SET MESSAGE location. The MENU BAR command installs the array.

The READ MENU BAR TO command activates the menu bar and returns a numeric variable representing the selected pad. Note that it assigns values to two variables. One defines the menu pad selected, and the other the bar selected from the popup. If there is no popup, the second variable is meaningless. Program 9-4 shows our now familiar example using a menu bar for the main options only.

```
* Program 9-4
* Main horizontal bar menu

* Set environment
  CLEAR ALL
  SET TALK OFF
  SET BELL OFF
  SET SCOREBOARD OFF
  SET MESSAGE TO 24 CENTER

* Begin main menu
  DO WHILE .T.
  moption = 1

    * Screen
      SET COLOR TO GR+/B
      CLEAR
      SET CLOCK TO 1,68
      @  0, 0 TO 21,79 DOUBLE
      @  1,24 SAY 'RETAIL SYSTEM - MAIN MENU'
      @  2, 0 SAY '||————————————————————————————————'+;
               '————————————————————————————————||'

    * Define menu arrays
      DIMENSION menubar[4,2],sub1[4],sub3[11]
      menubar[1,1] = 'Load'
      menubar[1,2] = 'Load data from ASCII files'
      menubar[2,1] = 'Edit'
      menubar[2,2] = 'Edit/Maintain database files'
      menubar[3,1] = 'Reports'
      menubar[3,2] = 'Select report'
      menubar[4,1] = 'Quit'
      menubar[4,2] = 'Return to DOS'

    * Display menu and prompt for user's choice
      MENU BAR menubar,4
      level1 = 1
      level2 = 1
      READ MENU BAR TO level1,level2

  @ 22,5 SAY "LEVEL1: "+STR(level1,5)
  @ 23,5 SAY "LEVEL2: "+STR(level2,5)
  WAIT
```

```
    IF LEVEL1 = 4
      EXIT
    ENDIF

    ENDDO

RETURN

* End of program
```

Program 9-4. Main Horizontal Bar Menu

We seldom implement a menu bar alone. Its options usually display pulldown menus. The MENU command lets us define secondary menus and make them appear when the corresponding pads are selected. The basic MENU command structure is

```
MENU <expN1><array><expN2><expN3>
```

The first parameter is the pad to which the pulldown belongs. Next is a one-dimensional array containing the pulldown options. Then comes the number of options. The last parameter specifies how many to display at a time. Note that although we have not specifically asked for a window, the MENU option automatically includes one directly beneath the pad to which it belongs. FoxPro calculates its position and size.

In this case, the READ MENU BAR TO command needs both output variables. The first identifies the selected pad in the horizontal menu, and the second the selected bar in the pulldown. Program 9-5 revises the example menu again to include pulldowns.

```
* Program 9-5
* Array-style menu
* Set environment
  CLEAR ALL
  SET BELL OFF
  SET MESSAGE TO 24 CENTER
  SET SCOREBOARD OFF
  SET TALK OFF

* Begin main menu
  DO WHILE .T.
  moption = 1

  * Screen
    SET COLOR TO GR+/B
    CLEAR
```

```
SET CLOCK TO 1,68
@  0, 0 TO 21,79 DOUBLE
@  1,24 SAY 'RETAIL SYSTEM - MAIN MENU'
@  2, 0 SAY '‖─────────────────────────────'+;
        '                                  ‖'
           └─────────────────────────────┘‖

* Define menu arrays
DIMENSION menubar[4,2],sub1[3],sub3[6]
menubar[1,1] = 'Load'
menubar[1,2] = 'Load data from ASCII files'
menubar[2,1] = 'Edit'
menubar[2,2] = 'Edit/Maintain database files'
menubar[3,1] = 'Reports'
menubar[3,2] = 'Select report'
menubar[4,1] = 'Quit'
menubar[4,2] = 'Return to DOS'

sub1[1] = ' Load retailer data '
sub1[2] = ' Load brand data '
sub1[3] = ' Load advertisement data '

sub3[1] = ' Management Summary Report '
sub3[2] = ' Region Summary Report '
sub3[3] = ' District Summary Report '
sub3[4] = ' Territory Summary Report '
sub3[5] = ' Promoted Code Report '
sub3[6] = ' Advertisement Detail Report '

* Display menu and prompt for user's choice
MENU BAR menubar,4
MENU 1,sub1,3,3
MENU 3,sub3,6,4
level1 = 1
level2 = 1
READ MENU BAR TO level1,level2

* Use menu choices to branch to procedure
DO CASE

* Branch to data load procedure
CASE level1 = 1
  DO CASE
    CASE level2 = 1
      SET PROCEDURE TO retlload
      DO retlload
    CASE level2 = 2
      SET PROCEDURE TO brndload
      DO brndload
    CASE level2 = 3
      SET PROCEDURE TO adload
      DO adload
  ENDCASE
```

```
* Branch to data edit procedure
CASE level1 = 2
  SET PROCEDURE TO genedit
  DO genedit

* Branch to report procedure
CASE level1 = 3
  DO CASE
    CASE level2 = 1
      SET PROCEDURE TO mgmtsum
      DO mgmtsum
    CASE level2 = 2
      SET PROCEDURE TO regsum
      DO regsum
    CASE level2 = 3
      SET PROCEDURE TO distsum
      DO distsum
    CASE level2 = 4
      SET PROCEDURE TO terrsum
      DO terrsum
    CASE level2 = 5
      SET PROCEDURE TO promo
      DO promo
    CASE level2 = 6
      SET PROCEDURE TO addetail
      DO addetail
  ENDCASE

* Exit program
CASE level1 = 4
  SET COLOR TO W+/N
  CLOSE DATABASES
  CLEAR
  EXIT

ENDCASE

ENDDO
RETURN

* End of program
```

Program 9-5. Array-Style Menu

This type of menu is also called *array-style* because it uses arrays to define both horizontal and pulldown menus.

Component Menus

A drawback of array-style menus is their inability to display a message with each option. The component-style menu provides more complete control. We control menu features, their placement, and user interaction.

Defining the Menu Bar

The first step in creating a component menu is defining the main menu bar. We can open menus on the screen or in windows by using the IN WINDOW option. DEFINE MENU assigns the menu a name and attaches an optional message displayed when it is activated.

```
DEFINE MENU ads MESSAGE 'Advertisement Tracking Menu'
```

DEFINE MENU also supports a BAR option that creates a menu bar. Its default position is the top line of the screen or window. The AT LINE option can put it anywhere.

```
DEFINE MENU ads AT LINE 23   && Puts menu at bottom of screen
```

The KEY option adds an event-driven method to activate a menu. To activate it when the user presses Ctrl-M, we could include the separate command

```
ON KEY LABEL CTRL+M ACTIVATE MENU
```

or we could add the KEY option when defining the menu

```
DEFINE MENU mainmenu KEY CTRL+M
```

The MARK option defines a character used to mark selections. It appears just left of each option when it is set. Include the MARGIN option to leave room for the marker.

Next define each PAD. Not only must we supply a display string, but we must also name it and attach it to a specific menu. Optionally, we can specify row and column position rather than accept the default values (left to right across the top row of the screen). Finally, we can include a message clause that appears

---

HINT

The marker defined at any level should be consistent with ones defined at lower levels. For example, if we define the menu level marker as the bullet •, all submenu options should also use it. However, lower level markers take precedence over higher level ones when they differ.

at the SET MESSAGE TO location. Note that it overwrites the DEFINE MENU message.

```
DEFINE PAD reporter OF ads PROMPT '\<REPORTS' AT 0,0
```

The order in which we define pads controls their physical placement and activation order. However, we can change either with the BEFORE and AFTER clauses.

The effect of adding BEFORE and AFTER to DEFINE PAD depends on whether the BAR option appears in DEFINE MENU. Both commands affect the activation order and physical placement of pads. However, the BAR option closes the menu after a selection has been made and its action completed. Without it, the menu remains active until the user presses Esc or the program executes a DEACTIVATE command. In the following example, the pads begin with "QUIT" and end with "GRAPHS".

```
DEFINE MENU mainmenu
DEFINE PAD dataload OF mainmenu PROMPT "LOAD DATA"
DEFINE PAD datentry OF mainmenu PROMPT "DATA ENTRY"
DEFINE PAD rptwrite OF mainmenu PROMPT "REPORTS"
DEFINE PAD grphdisp OF mainmenu PROMPT "GRAPHS"
DEFINE PAD exitmain OF mainmenu PROMPT "QUIT" BEFORE dataload
```

If DEFINE MENU includes the BAR option, BEFORE and AFTER still determine physical placement and activation order. The physical order is the same. Now, however, the menu is deactivated after the user selects a pad.

```
DEFINE MENU mainmenu BAR
DEFINE PAD dataload OF mainmenu PROMPT "LOAD DATA"
DEFINE PAD datentry OF mainmenu PROMPT "DATA ENTRY"
DEFINE PAD rptwrite OF mainmenu PROMPT "REPORTS"
DEFINE PAD grphdisp OF mainmenu PROMPT "GRAPHS"
DEFINE PAD exitmain OF mainmenu PROMPT "QUIT" BEFORE dataload
```

We can define a hot key by preceding it with the usual \<. We can also define a shortcut key or key combination for each pad. The KEY option accepts two parameters. The first defines alternate keystrokes using their key labels. They can be used anytime the menu is active even if the popup to which the command belongs is not visible. For example, to select "QUIT" by pressing Ctrl-Q from any point in the menu, add the following clause to the end of pad EXITMAIN.

```
KEY CTRL+Q
```

Table 3-9 is a list of key labels. Without the BAR option in DEFINE MENU, FoxPro echoes the label to the right of the PAD. Otherwise, the labels do not appear, but the keys still work.

The second KEY parameter displays an alternate text string for the label.

```
KEY CTRL+Q, "^Q"
```

The MARK option defines a single character used to mark selected pads. It works with SET MARK OF PAD.

HINT

The marker option makes sense only if we do not clear or remove the menu or popup as soon as a selection is made. It works best in cascading menus and where the user can select several options from each one.

Defining the Action for a Pad

We can execute a FoxPro command directly upon PAD selection through the ON SELECTION PAD command. It executes any command, even a procedure call. For example, the following command calls procedure FILTER when we select pad FILTER from popup EDITMAIN.

```
ON SELECTION PAD filter OF editmain DO FILTER
```

Program 9-6 shows a menu using the MARK option (with the 'bullet' character) to identify the selected pad. When a pad is selected, the program calls procedure MRKMENU, passing it the menu and pad name as parameters. The first line turns off all pad markers. The second marks the selected pad. The program returns to the menu where another selection can be made. Note the importance here of removing all markers before making more selections.

Before using a menu, we must activate it. The ACTIVATE MENU command names the menu. It also includes a PAD option to specify a default pad.

```
* Program 9-6
* Marking pads in a menu
DEFINE MENU mainmenu MARK '•'
DEFINE PAD dataload OF mainmenu PROMPT "LOAD DATA"
DEFINE PAD datentry OF mainmenu PROMPT "DATA ENTRY"
DEFINE PAD rptwrite OF mainmenu PROMPT "REPORTS"
DEFINE PAD grphdisp OF mainmenu PROMPT "GRAPHS"
DEFINE PAD exitmain OF mainmenu PROMPT "QUIT"

ON SELECTION PAD dataload OF mainmenu ;
     DO mrkmenu WITH MENU(), PAD()
ON SELECTION PAD datentry OF mainmenu ;
     DO mrkmenu WITH MENU(), PAD()
ON SELECTION PAD rptwrite OF mainmenu ;
     DO mrkmenu WITH MENU(), PAD()
ON SELECTION PAD grphdisp OF mainmenu ;
```

```
       DO mrkmenu WITH MENU(), PAD()
ON SELECTION PAD exitmain OF mainmenu cancel

ACTIVATE MENU mainmenu PAD exitmain

RETURN

PROCEDURE mrkmenu
PARAMETER mmenu, mpad

SET MARK OF MENU &mmenu TO .F.
SET MARK OF PAD  &mpad OF &mmenu TO .T.


RETURN
```

Program 9-6. Marking Menu Pads

```
┌─────────────────────────────────────────────┐
│                   EXERCISE                   │
│                                              │
│    Change Program 9-6 to mark multiple options. │
│                                              │
└─────────────────────────────────────────────┘
```

In Program 9-6, all ON SELECTION PAD statements (except QUIT) reference the same procedure with the same parameters. Therefore, we could replace them with a menu level selection statement

```
ON SELECTION MENU mainmenu DO mrkmenu WITH MENU(), PAD()
```

Procedure MRKMENU must then check if the user selected the QUIT pad.

```
IF UPPER(PAD()) = 'EXITMAIN'
   CANCEL
ENDIF
```

```
┌─────────────────────────────────────────────┐
│                    HINT                      │
│  If all pads perform the same action, use ON SELECTION MENU │
│  rather than multiple ON SELECTION PAD commands. If each │
│  pad action is unique, use ON SELECTION PAD.  │
└─────────────────────────────────────────────┘
```

Some options may display lower level menus. The ON PAD command associates a menu pad with a specific popup or menu. The following commands show typical statements that activate popups or bar menus.

```
ON PAD reporter OF ads ACTIVATE POPUP reptpick
ON PAD grapher  OF ads ACTIVATE MENU grphlist
```

Of course, before using a popup, we must define it with DEFINE POPUP. It identifies the name and upper left corner. FoxPro calculates the default size of the popup window based on the number of options, their width, and the size of the screen or window. Alternately, we can include a TO clause to fix the lower right corner and override the automatic calculation.

In either case, we can scroll the popup window with the cursor keys. Adding the SCROLL option displays a scroll bar along its side to help move through long lists. As with DEFINE MENU and DEFINE PAD, we can use the MESSAGE clause to associate a message. The following is a typical POPUP definition.

```
DEFINE POPUP loader FROM 1,0
```

Basic Popup Options

When using popups, we define each option or bar with the DEFINE BAR command. It is identified by a sequential number. The PROMPT clause defines the corresponding text, and a MESSAGE clause displays a brief description of the option. Messages at this level overwrite ones from higher levels.

The SKIP option tells FoxPro to skip a line when the user moves the highlight through the popup. It is used to skip group titles and horizontal lines. We can also disable options by preceding their prompts with a backslash (\). The following bar would still appear, but dimmed to indicate disabling.

```
DEFINE BAR 1 OF mainmenu PROMPT '\GRAPHS'
```

SKIP FOR adds logic to skip an option based on an expression. For example, suppose that a maintenance system limits access to selected users. We can restrict it by testing for specific passwords, user names, or other identifying fields. The following DEFINE BAR command limits access to users in the accounting department.

```
DEFINE BAR...SKIP FOR dept # 'ACCOUNTING'
```

When we define several bars in a menu, their numbers control physical placement. However, we can change the order with the BEFORE and AFTER clauses.

HINT

Use the BEFORE or AFTER clauses to add options to popups if the program later tests for specific bar numbers. This eliminates the need to revise references.

In the following example, we insert a new bar for reports as bar 6, and force it to appear before bar 4. Thus commands that reference bars 4 and 5 need not be changed.

```
DEFINE POPUP mainmenu FROM 1,1 RELATIVE
DEFINE BAR 1 OF mainmenu PROMPT "LOAD DATA"
DEFINE BAR 2 OF mainmenu PROMPT "DATA ENTRY"
DEFINE BAR 4 OF mainmenu PROMPT "GRAPHS"
DEFINE BAR 5 OF mainmenu PROMPT "QUIT"
DEFINE BAR 6 OF mainmenu PROMPT "REPORTS" BEFORE 4
```

Note that there is no bar 3. If we did not include the RELATIVE clause in DEFINE POPUP, the popup would include a blank third line. With the RELATIVE clause, FoxPro does not reserve space for undefined bars.

As with the DEFINE MENU command, we can define hot keys with \< and shortcut keys with the KEY clause for prompts in a popup. Similarly, the MARK option defines a character to mark selected bars when combined with the SET MARK OF BAR command. This feature is useful in cascading menus or in popups that allow multiple selections.

Next we use ON SELECTION POPUP to specify an action when the user selects an option. It can execute any command, but the most common is a DO procedure that determines which bar the user selected and acts on it. Use ON SELECTION POPUP when the actions are similar or need only a few command lines as shown in the next code segment.

```
ON SELECTION POPUP DO SUB1 WITH POPUP(),BAR()
  .
  .
  .
PROCEDURE SUB1
PARAMETER popname, barno

DO CASE
  CASE popname = 'FIRSTPOP'
    DO CASE
      CASE barno = 1
        <code for bar 1 in popup FIRSTPOP>
      CASE barno = 2
        <code for bar 2 in popup FIRSTPOP>
    ENDCASE
  CASE popname = 'SECNDPOP'
    DO CASE
      CASE barno = 1
        <code for bar 1 in popup SECNDPOP>
      CASE barno = 2
        <code for bar 2 in popup SECNDPOP>
    ENDCASE
ENDCASE
RETURN
```

If each bar requires a unique or complex action, use ON SELECTION BAR to execute individual procedures. We can also use ON BAR to activate lower level popups or menus.

Like menus, popups must be activated before we can use them. The ACTIVATE POPUP command includes an AT clause that overrides the row and column position of the upper left corner set by DEFINE POPUP. It also includes a BAR option to specify a default bar number when the popup is activated.

Program 9-7 shows a complete component menu.

```
* Program 9-7
* Component-style menu

* Set environment
  CLEAR ALL
  SET TALK OFF
  SET BELL OFF
  SET SCOREBOARD OFF
  SET MESSAGE TO 24 CENTER

* Define menu components
  DEFINE MENU ads

  DEFINE PAD loaddata OF ads PROMPT '\<LOAD' AT 0,0
  DEFINE PAD editdata OF ads PROMPT '\<EDIT' AT 0,6
  DEFINE PAD reporter OF ads PROMPT '\<REPORTS' AT 0,12
  DEFINE PAD adquiter OF ads PROMPT '\<QUIT' AT 0,21

  ON PAD loaddata OF ads ACTIVATE POPUP loader
  ON SELECTION PAD editdata OF ads DO GENEDIT
  ON PAD reporter OF ads ACTIVATE POPUP REPTPICK
  ON SELECTION PAD adquiter OF ads DO BYENOW

  DEFINE POPUP loader FROM 1,0
  DEFINE BAR 1 OF loader PROMPT ' Load Retailer data '
  DEFINE BAR 2 OF loader PROMPT ' Load Brand data '
  DEFINE BAR 3 OF loader PROMPT ' Load Advertisement data '
  ON SELECTION POPUP loader DO LOADDATA

  DEFINE POPUP reptpick FROM 1,12
  DEFINE BAR 1 OF reptpick PROMPT ;
         ' Management Summary Report '
  DEFINE BAR 2 OF reptpick PROMPT ;
         ' Region Summary Report '
  DEFINE BAR 3 OF reptpick PROMPT ;
         ' District Summary Report '
  DEFINE BAR 4 OF reptpick PROMPT ;
         ' Territory Summary Report '
  DEFINE BAR 5 OF reptpick PROMPT ;
```

```
                   ' Promoted Code Report '
        DEFINE BAR 6 OF reptpick PROMPT ;
                 ' Advertisement Detail Report '
        ON SELECTION POPUP reptpick DO REPTPRNT

           * Screen
             SET COLOR TO GR+/B
             CLEAR
             SET CLOCK TO 1,68
             @  0, 0 TO 21,79 DOUBLE
             @  1,24 SAY 'RETAIL SYSTEM - MAIN MENU'
             @  2, 0 SAY '‖——————————————————————————'+;
                        '————————————————————————————‖'

        * Activate menu
          ACTIVATE MENU ads
          SET COLOR TO W+/N
          CLOSE DATABASES
          CLEAR

        * End of main program
        RETURN


        PROCEDURE LOADDATA

        * Clear all popup marks and mark selected bar
          SET MARK OF POPUP loader TO .F.
          SET MARK OF BAR BAR() OF loader TO .T.

        * Branch to appropriate case
          DO CASE
            CASE BAR() = 1
        *        DO RETLLOAD
            CASE BAR() = 2
        *        DO BRNDLOAD
            CASE BAR() = 3
        *        DO ADLOAD
          ENDCASE
          @ 22,0 CLEAR TO 23,79
        RETURN


        PROCEDURE REPTPRNT

        * Clear all popup marks and mark selected bar
          SET MARK OF POPUP reptpick TO .F.
          SET MARK OF BAR BAR() OF reptpick TO .T.

        * Branch to appropriate case
        DO CASE
```

```
    CASE BAR() = 1
*       DO MGMTSUM
    CASE BAR() = 2
*       DO REGSUM
    CASE BAR() = 3
*       DO DISTSUM
    CASE BAR() = 4
*       DO TERRSUM
    CASE BAR() = 5
*       DO PROMO
    CASE BAR() = 6
*       DO ADDETAIL
ENDCASE
@ 22,0 CLEAR TO 23,79

RETURN


PROCEDURE BYENOW

* Close everything and exit
  DEACTIVATE MENU ads
RETURN

* End of program
```

Program 9-7. Component Menu

Menu Functions

Thirteen functions help identify a user's menu selections. The following summarizes them.

BAR()

BAR() returns the number of the selected option, not its physical order number in the popup. Program 9-7 uses it to determine which procedure to run.

CNTBAR()

CNTBAR() returns the number of bars in a popup.

CNTPAD()

CNTPAD() returns the number of pads in a menu.

GETBAR()

GETBAR() returns the number of a specific bar in any row of a popup. It takes two parameters, the popup name and the physical position of the bar. It is useful when bars are rearranged using the MOVER option in DEFINE POPUP or when DEFINE BAR uses the BEFORE or AFTER clause.

```
* Return bar number of second option
  barno = GETBAR(POPUP(),2)
```

GETPAD()

GETPAD() returns the name of a specific pad in a menu. It takes two parameters, the menu name and the physical position of the pad. It is useful after pads are rearranged with the BEFORE or AFTER clause.

```
* Return pad name of second option in menu
  padname = GETPAD(MENU(),2)
```

MENU()

MENU() returns the name of the currently active menu. If there is none, it returns the null string. It provides a check if a menu is still active, but hidden. It can also identify the active menu when the user makes a selection.

MRKBAR()

MRKBAR() returns .T. if the popup bar is marked. It requires two parameters, the popup name and the bar number.

MRKPAD()

MRKPAD() returns .T. if the menu pad is marked. It requires two parameters, the menu name and the pad name.

PAD()

PAD() returns the name of the last pad chosen from the active menu bar. Like BAR(), it determines the user's selection and provides the basis for branching logic.

POPUP()

POPUP() returns the name of the currently active popup. If there is none, it returns the null string, thus checking if the popup is still active, but hidden. More important, it identifies which popup the user is in.

PRMBAR()

PRMBAR() returns the text of the prompt for a specific bar in a popup. It requires two parameters, the popup name and the bar number.

PRMPAD()

PRMPAD() returns the text of the prompt for a specific pad in a menu. It requires two parameters, the menu name and the pad name.

PROMPT()

PROMPT() returns the character string prompt of the active menu pad or popup. Special options return other information. With the FIELD clause in DEFINE POPUP, PROMPT() returns the contents of the selected field. If we use the FILES clause, it returns the selected full name, including the path name. If we use the STRUCTURE clause, it returns the selected field's name. We will discuss these functions and illustrate their use later.

HIDE/SHOW/RELEASE/DEACTIVATE MENU/POPUP

So far, we have shown how to define and activate menus and popups. Our examples display only the menus, not the rest of the programs they execute. One problem is that if we execute a procedure immediately after a menu selection, screen output appears behind the menus and popups. We must remove them before executing an option.

DEACTIVATE MENU and DEACTIVATE POPUP close menus and popups and remove them from the screen. Unfortunately, they also tell FoxPro to resume execution with the command immediately after the corresponding ACTIVATE command. Of course, we could capture the user's selections with the PAD() and BAR() functions, storing them in memory variables. Then after deactivating the menu, a decision structure could determine where to continue execution. Program 9-8 shows this method.

```
* Program 9-8
* Component menu that deactivates the menu before
* branching to other procedures

* Set environment
  CLEAR
  SET TALK OFF
  SET STATUS OFF
  SET SCOREBOARD OFF

* Define menu structure
  DEFINE MENU toplevel
  DEFINE PAD pad1 OF toplevel PROMPT 'LOAD' AT 0,0
  DEFINE PAD pad2 OF toplevel PROMPT 'REPORTS' AT 0,10
  ON SELECTION PAD pad1 OF toplevel ACTIVATE POPUP pop1
  ON SELECTION PAD pad2 OF toplevel ACTIVATE POPUP pop2

  DEFINE POPUP pop1 FROM 1,0
```

```
      DEFINE BAR 1 OF pop1 PROMPT 'Load Retailers'
      DEFINE BAR 2 OF pop1 PROMPT 'Load Brands/Products'
      DEFINE BAR 3 OF pop1 PROMPT 'Load Advertisements'
      ON SELECTION POPUP pop1 DO GETPICK

      DEFINE POPUP pop2 FROM 1,10
      DEFINE BAR 1 OF pop2 PROMPT 'Weekly Summary'
      DEFINE BAR 2 OF pop2 prompt 'Advertisements by Account'
      DEFINE BAR 3 OF pop2 PROMPT 'Advertisements by Product'
      ON SELECTION POPUP pop2 DO GETPICK

      ACTIVATE MENU toplevel

      CLEAR

      * Decide where to branch depending on selection
      DO CASE
        CASE a_menu = 'TOPLEVEL'
          DO CASE
            CASE a_pad = 'PAD1'
              DO CASE
                CASE a_bar = 1
                  @ 23,0 SAY 'Load Retailers'
*                 DO RETLLOAD
                CASE a_bar = 2
                  @ 23,0 SAY 'Load Brands/Products'
*                 DO BRNDLOAD
                CASE a_bar = 3
                  @ 23,0 SAY 'Load Advertisements'
*                 DO ADLOAD
              ENDCASE
            CASE a_pad = 'PAD2'
              DO CASE
                CASE a_bar = 1
                  @ 23,0 SAY 'Weekly Summary'
*                 DO WKSUMRPT
                CASE a_bar = 2
                  @ 23,0 SAY 'Advertisements by Account'
*                 DO ADACTRPT
                CASE a_bar = 3
                  @ 23,0 SAY 'Advertisements by Product'
*                 DO ADPRDRPT
              ENDCASE
          ENDCASE
      ENDCASE

RETURN

PROCEDURE GETPICK

PUBLIC a_menu, a_pad, a_bar, a_popup

a_menu  = MENU()
```

```
a_pad   = PAD()
a_popup = POPUP()
a_bar   = BAR()

DEACTIVATE MENU toplevel

RETURN

* End of program
```

Program 9-8. Deactivating Menus before Branching

Program 9-8 assumes that we want to make just one menu choice and can then continue execution. This assumption is not always true. We could put the ACTIVATE MENU command in a loop so the program executes it repeatedly. However, we must then begin with the top level menu in each pass.

Suppose instead that we want to execute the procedure called by a choice and then return to the menu where we left off. We could hide the menus, branch to the procedure, and return to the menu afterward. For this, we need the HIDE command. It removes menus and popups from the screen, but keeps them active. Program 9-9 is a revision of Program 9-8 that hides the menus.

```
* Program 9-9
* Component menu system that hides the menu and popup
* before branching to other procedures

* Set environment
  CLEAR
  SET TALK OFF
  SET STATUS OFF
  SET SCOREBOARD OFF

* Define menu structure
  DEFINE MENU toplevel
  DEFINE PAD pad1 OF toplevel PROMPT 'LOAD' AT 0,0
  DEFINE PAD pad2 OF toplevel PROMPT 'REPORTS' AT 0,10
  DEFINE PAD pad3 OF toplevel PROMPT 'QUIT' AT 0,20
  ON SELECTION PAD pad1 OF toplevel ACTIVATE POPUP pop1
  ON SELECTION PAD pad2 OF toplevel ACTIVATE POPUP pop2
  ON SELECTION PAD pad3 OF toplevel DEACTIVATE MENU toplevel

  DEFINE POPUP pop1 FROM 1,0
  DEFINE BAR 1 OF pop1 PROMPT 'Load Retailers'
  DEFINE BAR 2 OF pop1 prompt 'Load Brands/Products'
  DEFINE BAR 3 OF pop1 PROMPT 'Load Advertisements'
  ON SELECTION POPUP pop1 DO GETPICK1
```

```
      DEFINE POPUP pop2 FROM 1,10
      DEFINE BAR 1 OF pop2 PROMPT 'Weekly Summary'
      DEFINE BAR 2 OF pop2 PROMPT 'Advertisements by Account'
      DEFINE BAR 3 OF pop2 PROMPT 'Advertisements by Product'
      ON SELECTION POPUP pop2 DO GETPICK2

      ACTIVATE MENU toplevel

      CLEAR

   RETURN

   PROCEDURE GETPICK1

   HIDE MENU toplevel
   HIDE POPUP pop1

      CLEAR

      * Decide where to branch depending on selection
      DO CASE
        CASE MENU() = 'TOPLEVEL'
          DO CASE
            CASE PAD() = 'PAD1'
              DO CASE
                CASE BAR() = 1
                  @ 23,0 SAY 'Load Retailers'
*                 DO RETLLOAD
                CASE BAR() = 2
                  @ 23,0 SAY 'Load Brands/Products'
*                 DO BRNDLOAD
                CASE BAR() = 3
                  @ 23,0 SAY 'Load Advertisements'
*                 DO ADLOAD
              ENDCASE
          ENDCASE
      ENDCASE

   WAIT
   CLEAR
   DEACTIVATE POPUP pop1

   RETURN

   PROCEDURE GETPICK2
   * Hide menu and popup
   HIDE MENU toplevel
   HIDE POPUP pop2

      CLEAR

      * Decide where to branch depending on selection
      DO CASE
        CASE MENU() = 'TOPLEVEL'
          DO CASE
```

```
             CASE PAD() = 'PAD2'
               DO CASE
                 CASE BAR() = 1
                   @ 23,0 SAY 'Weekly Summary'
     *             DO WKSUMRPT
                 CASE BAR() = 2
                   @ 23,0 SAY 'Advertisements by Account'
     *             DO ADACTRPT
                 CASE BAR() = 3
                   @ 23,0 SAY 'Advertisements by Product'
     *             DO ADPRDRPT
               ENDCASE
           ENDCASE
       ENDCASE

   WAIT
   CLEAR
   DEACTIVATE POPUP pop2

   RETURN

   * End of program
```

Program 9-9. Hiding Menus while Executing Procedures

When we complete a series of menus or popups, the CLEAR or RELEASE command removes them from the screen and from memory. RELEASE PAD releases all or selected pads by name. RELEASE BAR releases all or selected bars by number. Using the EXTENDED option with RELEASE MENUS or RELEASE POPUPS releases all lower level popups, bars, and ON routines.

After releasing pads from a menu or bars from a popup, we may have to restore the original menu. Rather than redefining menus or popups, FoxPro provides an easy way to store their definitions. We can push them onto a stack using the commands:

```
PUSH MENU menuname
PUSH POPUP popupname
```

After adding a copy of the menu or popup to the stack, we can remove pads or bars not currently needed or add new ones. To restore the original menu, just pop it off the stack with the commands:

```
POP MENU menuname
POP POPUP popupname
```

Use RELEASE in error trapping procedures to clear menus, pads, or windows. When a program terminates with an error, it leaves them all open. It is a good practice to release or clear them at the beginning of an error routine.

WARNING

Although we can store multiple menu and popup definitions on the stack, we must remove them in order from latest to earliest.

Other Popup Options

Earlier in this chapter, we introduced the DEFINE POPUP command and used it in the component menu example. It also supports many clauses.

The MOVER option lets the user change the order of the bars interactively. When it is active, the popup includes a double-headed arrow to the left of each bar. To move one, select it and then drag it with the mouse or use Ctrl-UpArrow or Ctrl-DownArrow.

Normally, a popup executes the corresponding ON PAD, ON BAR, or ON SELECTION command as soon as a bar is selected. However, with the MULTI option, we can select multiple bars by holding the Shift key down and pressing Enter, the space bar, or the up or down arrow key (for sequential options). Selecting a bar makes a marker appear to its left.

WARNING

The PROMPT FIELD, PROMPT FILES, and PROMPT STRUC-TURE options do not support MULTI.

HINT

When using the MULTI option, use one of the following com-mands to determine which options were selected and to trigger actions:

```
    ON SELECTION POPUP
```
or
```
    ON SELECTION MENU
```

Do not use ON SELECTION PAD or ON SELECTION BAR since they trigger actions for individual pads or bars.

Popups scroll automatically when there are more bars than fit in the window. However, the SCROLL option adds a scroll bar to help users navigate through long lists.

To define a popup in a window, include the IN WINDOW clause along with its name. Popups also support both TITLE and FOOTER clauses. Three options use file information to define the popup's contents:

> PROMPT FILES
> PROMPT FIELD
> PROMPT STRUCTURE

PROMPT FILES builds a list of files from the default directory. Include the LIKE clause to define a file name skeleton. You can use the standard DOS wildcard characters * and ?. For example, the following clause displays files with a DAT extension.

```
PROMPT FIELD LIKE *.DAT
```

This variation resembles GETFILE(), but it creates a popup list rather than a dialog window.

PROMPT FIELD creates a menu from the specified field's contents. It is often used to validate input data. Suppose a store inventory system prompts for an item by name. We could use SOUNDEX() to search the file. But what if it fails? One solution uses PROMPT FIELD to display a popup list of items. The user can then select a valid one from it.

Program 9-10 illustrates this concept. It first clears the screen and prompts for a product name. It uses SOUNDEX() to compare the name with values in the field prod_name from PRODUCT.DBF. If it finds a match, it displays information about the product. If not, it uses a popup window to display valid names.

```
* Program 9-10
* Uses a popup to display possible field values
* when data is entered incorrectly

* Set environment
  SET TALK OFF
  SET STATUS OFF
  SET SCOREBOARD OFF
  CLEAR

* Open database
  SELECT 1
  USE products INDEX products

* Define popup
  DEFINE POPUP productn FROM 6,28 TO 15,60 ;
    PROMPT FIELD prod_name SHADOW ;
```

```
    MESSAGE "Select a product name" COLOR SCHEME 5
ON SELECTION POPUP productn DO GETPROD

* Prompt for product name
  prodname = SPACE(25)
  @ 5,5 SAY "Enter a product name: " GET prodname
  READ
  LOCATE FOR SOUNDEX(m->prodname) = SOUNDEX(prod_name)
  IF .NOT. FOUND()
    ACTIVATE POPUP productn
  ENDIF
* Display information on selected product
  @ 10,5 SAY "Product data:"
  @ 11,8 SAY "Product code       " + prod_code
  @ 12,8 SAY "Product name       " + prod_name
  @ 13,8 SAY "Manufacturer code  " + manu_code
  @ 14,8 SAY "Average cost       " + STR(avg_cost,6,4)
  @ 15,8 SAY "Sales price        " + STR(sales_price,4,2)
  @ 16,8 SAY "Inventory level    " + STR(prod_inv,5)
RETURN

***********************************************************

PROCEDURE GETPROD
* Read popup choice into variable prodname and close popup
  prodname = PROMPT()
  @ 5,28 SAY m->prodname
  DEACTIVATE POPUP
RETURN

* End of program
```

Program 9-10. Using a Popup to Display Field Values

Note that POPUP works with the @...GET command, not as part of a larger menu system. Of course, we could use similar lists within a traditional menu. The idea is that we can use popups wherever the user must choose among options.

The PROMPT STRUCTURE option takes the current database structure and puts it in a popup. From it, we can select fields. Program 9-11 begins by letting the user select a database with PROMPT FILES. It then writes the structure into a temporary database, FILESTRC.DBF. Next, based on PROMPT STRUCTURE with the original database, the user selects fields to appear in a simple report. We use the temporary database to get other information about fields such as their types and sizes. Then using PROMPT STRUCTURE again, the user builds a filter. Finally, the program sends the custom report to the screen, the printer, or a file.

```
* Program 9-11
* Lets the user select fields for a report and
* a corresponding filter
*

* Set environment
  SET TALK OFF
  SET STATUS OFF
  SET SCOREBOARD OFF
  CLEAR
  CLOSE ALL
  RELEASE MENUS

* Define defaults
  outp_str  = ''
  outp_dev  = 'S'
  filt_str  = ''
  r_width   = 0
  rept_file = SPACE(8)
  rep_file  = SPACE(30)
  done      = .F.
  reptgo    = ''
  ftype     = ''

* Define popup that displays database file
  DEFINE POPUP filepick FROM 5,30 TO 20,50 ;
    PROMPT FILES LIKE *.DBF ;
    MESSAGE 'SELECT A FILE FOR REPORT' ;
    SHADOW COLOR SCHEME 5
  ON SELECTION POPUP filepick DO GETFILE


* Assumes index has same name as database file
  ACTIVATE POPUP filepick
  SELECT 1

* Use index if it exists
  IF FILE(idxfile)
    USE &dbffile INDEX &idxfile
  ELSE
    USE &dbffile
  ENDIF

* Copy structure of selected database to FILESTRC.DBF.
* We will use it later to select fields for the report
* and its filter.
  IF FILE("FILESTRC.DBF")
    ERASE "FILESTRC.DBF"
  ENDIF
  COPY STRUCTURE EXTENDED TO filestrc
  SELECT 2
```

```
USE filestrc
SELECT 1

* Display information defining report at bottom of screen
SET COLOR TO BG+*/N
@ 11,30 FILL TO 13,50
@ 11,30 TO 13,50 double
@ 12,32 SAY "Setting up menus"
SET COLOR TO W+/B
IF FILE(idxname)
   @ 17, 0 SAY "Filter:"
ENDIF
@ 19, 0 SAY "Report:"
@ 21, 0 SAY "Report width is:      "
@ 22, 0 SAY "File destination is: SCREEN"
SET COLOR OF HIGHLIGHT TO N/W

* Define other windows
DEFINE WINDOW filename FROM 10,20 TO 14,47 DOUBLE ;
     COLOR GR+/N,N/W,W+/N
DEFINE WINDOW ichar     FROM 15, 5 TO 17,75 DOUBLE ;
     COLOR GR+/N,N/W,W+/N
DEFINE WINDOW inumber   FROM 15,40 TO 17,75 DOUBLE ;
     COLOR GR+/N,N/W,W+/N
DEFINE WINDOW idate     FROM 15,40 TO 17,75 DOUBLE ;
     COLOR GR+/N,N/W,W+/N
DEFINE WINDOW exists    FROM  2,60 TO  6,78 DOUBLE ;
     COLOR  W+/R,N/W,GR+/R

* Name main menu bar
* Variable coln determines horizontal position of next
* menu pad
DEFINE MENU part_mem MESSAGE 'Main Menu'
coln = 0

* Define Select Field menu beginning with horizontal
* menu pad
DEFINE PAD sel_flds OF part_mem ;
        PROMPT 'Select Fields' AT 0,coln;
        MESSAGE 'Select fields to include in report'
* Assign popup menu for Select Fields pad
ON PAD sel_flds OF part_mem ACTIVATE POPUP pop1
* Define popup menu for Select Fields pad
DEFINE POPUP pop1 FROM 1,coln TO 16,coln+17 ;
        PROMPT STRUCTURE MESSAGE 'Select Fields'
* Set actions
ON SELECTION POPUP pop1 DO FLDSELCT
coln = coln + 15

* Define Set Filter menu pad
DEFINE PAD set_filt OF part_mem ;
        PROMPT 'Set Filter' AT 0,coln MESSAGE ;
        'Select filter for records to include in report'
```

```
* Assign popup menu for Set Filter pad
  ON PAD set_filt OF part_mem ACTIVATE POPUP pop2
* Define popup menu for Set Filter pad
  DEFINE POPUP pop2 FROM 1,coln TO 16,coln+14 ;
        PROMPT STRUCTURE MESSAGE 'Select Filter'
* Set actions
  ON SELECTION POPUP pop2 DO FILTMAKE
  coln = coln + 12

* Define Output Destination menu pad
  DEFINE PAD out_dest OF part_mem ;
        PROMPT 'Output Destination' ;
        AT 0,coln MESSAGE 'Select output destination'
* Assign popup menu for Output Destination pad
  ON PAD out_dest OF part_mem ACTIVATE POPUP pop3
* Define popup menu for Output Destination pad
  DEFINE POPUP pop3 FROM 1,coln ;
        MESSAGE 'Select Output Destination'
* Define possible output destinations
  DEFINE BAR 1 OF pop3 PROMPT 'FILE    ' ;
        MESSAGE 'Send report to a file'
  DEFINE BAR 2 OF pop3 PROMPT 'PRINTER' ;
        MESSAGE 'Send report to the printer'
  DEFINE BAR 3 OF pop3 PROMPT 'SCREEN ' ;
        MESSAGE 'Send report to the screen'
* Set actions
  ON SELECTION POPUP pop3 DO WHEREOUT
  coln = coln + 20

* Define Exit pad of main menu
  DEFINE PAD bye_bye OF part_mem PROMPT 'EXIT' AT 0,coln;
        MESSAGE 'Exit back to DOS'
* Assign popup menu for Exit pad
  ON PAD bye_bye OF part_mem ACTIVATE POPUP pop4
* Define popup menu for Exit
  DEFINE POPUP pop4 FROM 1,coln MESSAGE 'Exit'
* Define ways to exit this program
  DEFINE BAR 1 OF pop4 PROMPT 'Report ' ;
        MESSAGE 'Generate Report'
  DEFINE BAR 2 OF pop4 PROMPT 'Quit' ;
        MESSAGE 'Cancel report and exit to DOS'
  DEFINE BAR 3 OF pop4 PROMPT 'Main' ;
        MESSAGE 'Cancel report and exit to Main Menu'
* Set actions
  ON SELECTION POPUP pop4 DO EXITNOW

* Define relational operator popup and selections used to
* compare a variable to one in filter
  DEFINE POPUP compare FROM 5,32 ;
        MESSAGE 'Select Relational Operator'
  DEFINE BAR 1 OF compare PROMPT ' ='     MESSAGE 'EQUAL'
  DEFINE BAR 2 OF compare PROMPT ' <'     MESSAGE 'LESS THAN'
  DEFINE BAR 3 OF compare PROMPT ' >'     ;
```

```
                 MESSAGE 'GREATER THAN'
       DEFINE BAR 4 OF compare PROMPT ' <= ' ;
                 MESSAGE 'LESS THAN OR EQUAL'
       DEFINE BAR 5 OF compare PROMPT ' >= ' ;
                 MESSAGE 'GREATER THAN OR EQUAL'
       DEFINE BAR 6 OF compare PROMPT ' <> ' ;
                 MESSAGE 'NOT EQUAL'
       ON SELECTION POPUP compare DO COMPSET

     * Define logical operator popup to connect logical
     * expressions in the filter
       DEFINE POPUP nextt FROM 8,40 MESSAGE ;
                 'Select a logical operator to connect expressions'
       DEFINE BAR 1 OF nextt PROMPT 'DONE' ;
                 MESSAGE 'No more expressions'
       DEFINE BAR 2 OF nextt PROMPT '.AND.' ;
                 MESSAGE 'Add logical AND to connect next expression'
       DEFINE BAR 3 OF nextt PROMPT '.OR.'  ;
                 MESSAGE 'Add logical OR to connect next expression'
       ON SELECTION POPUP nextt DO NEXTADD

     * Activate menu system
       @ 11,30 FILL TO 13,50 COLOR W+/B
       @ 11,30 CLEAR TO 13,50
       ACTIVATE MENU part_mem

     * Decide whether to return to DOS or dot prompt
       IF BARR = 2
         QUIT
       ELSE
         RETURN TO MASTER
       ENDIF

     * End of program
       RETURN


     *** P R O C E D U R E S   B E G I N   H E R E ***

     PROCEDURE COMPSET
     * COMPSET selects the relational operators used to compare
     * variables in expressions
       DO CASE
         CASE BAR() = 1
           op = "="
         CASE BAR() = 2
           op = "<"
         CASE BAR() = 3
           op = ">"
         CASE BAR() = 4
           op = "<="
         CASE BAR() = 5
           op = ">="
```

```
       CASE BAR() = 6
          op = "<>"
    ENDCASE

    filt_str = filt_str + op

 * Now prompt for a value to compare based on selected
 * field's type
    DO CASE

       * Prompt for a character string
       CASE ftype = 'C'
          testchar = SPACE(50)
          ACTIVATE WINDOW ichar
          @ 0,1 SAY 'Enter String:' GET testchar PICTURE '@!50'
          READ
          filt_str = filt_str + "'" + TRIM(testchar) + "'"
          DEACTIVATE WINDOW ichar

      * Prompt for a date
       CASE ftype = 'D'
          testdate = CTOD('  /  /  ')
          ACTIVATE WINDOW idate
          @ 0,1 SAY 'Enter Date:' GET testdate PICTURE '@D'
          READ
          filt_str = filt_str + "CTOD('" + DTOC(testdate) + "')"
          DEACTIVATE WINDOW idate

       * Prompt for a numeric value
       CASE ftype = 'N'
          testnum = 0
          ACTIVATE WINDOW inumber
          @ 0,1 SAY 'Enter Number:' GET testnum PICTURE '######'
          READ
          filt_str = filt_str + ALLTRIM(STR(testnum,6))
          DEACTIVATE WINDOW inumber
    ENDCASE

 * Branch to NEXTT to get a logical operator to connect
 * another expression or to end filter construction
    ACTIVATE POPUP nextt

 * Deactivate popup COMPARE
    DEACTIVATE POPUP compare
    SET COLOR TO W+/N
 RETURN


 PROCEDURE EXITNOW
 * Either print report or deactivate menus and exit
 PUBLIC barr

 barr = BAR()
```

```
* Print report before ending program
  IF barr = 1

  * Build list command in variable LISTRPT
    listrpt = 'LIST '

  * Were only some fields selected?
    IF .NOT. EMPTY(outp_str)
      outp_str = LEFT(outp_str,LEN(outp_str)-1)
      listrpt = listrpt + 'FIELDS &outp_str. '
    ENDIF

  * Was a filter defined?
    IF .NOT. EMPTY(filt_str)
      listrpt = listrpt + 'FOR &filt_str. '
    ENDIF

  * Do not print record numbers
    listrpt = listrpt + 'OFF '

  * Where should report be written?
    DO CASE
      CASE outp_dev = 'P'
        listrpt = listrpt + 'TO PRINTER'
      CASE outp_dev = 'F'
        listrpt = listrpt + 'TO FILE &rep_file'
    ENDCASE

    CLEAR
  * Execute LIST expression
    &listrpt

  ENDIF
  DEACTIVATE MENU part_mem

RETURN


PROCEDURE FLDSELCT
* After user selects fields to include in report from
* Select Fields pulldown, this procedure checks the
* field type, builds the field string, and calculates
* the report width

  SELECT 2
  LOCATE FOR field_name = PROMPT()
  DO CASE

  * Character field
    CASE field_type = 'C'
      outp_str = outp_str + TRIM(field_name) + ','
      IF LEN(TRIM(field_name)) > field_len
        r_width = r_width + LEN(TRIM(field_name)) + 1
```

```
        ELSE
          r_width = r_width + field_len + 1
        ENDIF

    * Date field
      CASE field_type = 'D'
        outp_str = outp_str + "DTOC("+TRIM(field_name)+"),"
        IF LEN("DTOC()"+TRIM(field_name)) > 8
          r_width = r_width + LEN(TRIM(field_name)) + 7
        ELSE
          r_width = r_width + 9
        ENDIF

    * Numeric field
      CASE field_type = 'N'
        outp_str = outp_str + "STR("+TRIM(field_name) + ;
                   "," + LTRIM(STR(field_len,3))+"),"
        IF LEN("STR()"+TRIM(field_name)) > field_len
          r_width = r_width + LEN(TRIM(field_name)) + 6
        ELSE
          r_width = r_width + field_len + 1
        ENDIF

    * Logical field
      CASE field_type = 'L'
        outp_str = outp_str + "IIF("+TRIM(field_name)+",;
                   'T','F'),"
        r_width  = r_width + LEN(TRIM(field_name)) + 1

    ENDCASE
    SELECT 1

* Update screen information
  DO REPORTME

RETURN


PROCEDURE FILTMAKE

* Do not try to redefine a filter or define one
* for a file without an index
  IF done .OR. .NOT. FILE(idxfile)
     RETURN
  ENDIF

* Select fields to use in filter
  SELECT 2
  LOCATE FOR field_name = PROMPT()

* Add field to filter definition
  newfield = field_name
  filt_str = filt_str + ALLTRIM(newfield)
```

```
    FTYPE = TRIM(field_type)

* Build comparison string for selected fields
  ACTIVATE POPUP compare
  SELECT 1

* Update screen information with current report definition
  DO REPORTME

RETURN


PROCEDURE GETFILE
* Get user's file selection from popup FILEPICK
  PUBLIC dbffile,idxfile
  dbffile = ALLTRIM(PROMPT())
  idxfile = LEFT(dbffile,LEN(dbffile)-3)+'IDX'
  DEACTIVATE POPUP
RETURN


PROCEDURE NEXTADD
* Select logical operator to connect two expressions
  DO CASE

    * No more expressions
    CASE BAR() = 1
      done = .T.

    * Join last expression to next with AND
    CASE BAR() = 2
      filt_str = filt_str + ' .AND. '

    * Join last expression to next with OR
    CASE BAR() = 3
      filt_str = filt_str + ' .OR. '

  ENDCASE

* Deactivate popup menu
  DEACTIVATE POPUP nextt

RETURN


PROCEDURE WHEREOUT
* Select where to write output
  DO REPORTME
  DO CASE

    * Write output to a file. Get a file name
    CASE BAR() = 1
      whatnow = 'C'
```

```
   * Loop while variable whatnow does not equal 'O'.
   * This test prevents accidentally overwriting files.
     DO WHILE whatnow <> 'O'
       ACTIVATE WINDOW filename
       @  1, 1 SAY "Enter Filename:" GET rept_file ;
              PICTURE '@8!' ;
              MESSAGE "Extension is automatically set "+;
                      "to TXT"
       READ
       rep_file = TRIM(rept_file) + ".TXT"
       whatnow  = 'O'

       * Test if selected file exists
       IF FILE(rep_file)
         ACTIVATE WINDOW exists
         @ 0, 3 SAY "FILE EXISTS!"+CHR(7)
         @ 1, 1 SAY "Overwrite Cancel"
         @ 2, 8 GET whatnow PICTURE "@M O,C" ;
             MESSAGE "Enter O for Overwrite, C to Cancel"
         READ

         * If file is to be overwritten, erase old one first
         IF whatnow = 'O'
           ERASE &rep_file
         ENDIF

         DEACTIVATE WINDOW exists
       ENDIF
       DEACTIVATE WINDOW filename
     ENDDO
     outp_dev = 'F'

   * Send output to printer
     CASE BAR() = 2
       outp_dev = 'P'
   * Send output to screen
     CASE BAR() = 3
       outp_dev = 'S'
 ENDCASE

* Update screen information
  DO REPORTME

* Deactivate popup POP3
  DEACTIVATE POPUP
RETURN


PROCEDURE REPORTME

* Print report definition at bottom of screen
  @ 17, 0 CLEAR TO 18,79
```

```
IF FILE(idxname)
   @ 17, 0 SAY 'Filter: '+filt_str
ENDIF

@ 19, 0 CLEAR TO 21,79
@ 19, 0 SAY "Report: "+LEFT(outp_str,LEN(outp_str)-1)
@ 21, 0 SAY "Report width is: "+STR(r_width,4)
@ 22, 0 SAY "File destination is:"

DO CASE

   CASE outp_dev = 'F'
      reptgo = 'TO FILE ' + rep_file
      @ 22, 0 SAY "File destination is: FILE    "+rep_file ;
              + SPACE(11)

   CASE outp_dev = 'P'
      @ 22, 0 SAY "File destination is: PRINTER"+SPACE(20)
      reptgo = 'TO PRINTER'

   CASE outp_dev = 'S'
      @ 22, 0 SAY "File destination is: SCREEN "+SPACE(20)
      reptgo = ''

   ENDCASE

RETURN

* End of program
```

Program 9-11. Using PROMPT STRUCTURE to Pick Fields

Menu Builder

FoxPro has a utility to create menus. It is similar to the one discussed in the last chapter to create screens. Although it does not support all the flexibility of manually created menus, it can meet many needs. Its main advantages are that it creates error-free menus quickly and it generates modifiable code.

Before creating a menu, we should outline its purpose on paper. Suppose our program must produce a series of reports. Some are part of a family. Others stand by themselves. The program also has a section to load and edit data from two databases. Table 9-1 identifies the basic menu options.

Table 9-1. Menu Structure from Menu Builder Example

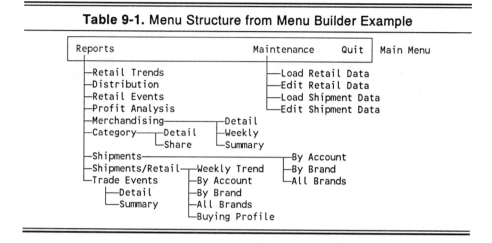

The left column of Table 9-1 represents the primary report menu. It is a popup activated by selecting the Report menu pad. Five of its nine bars identify a second level popup with other reports. Before beginning the menu definition, we open the retail database in area 1 and the shipment database in area 2.

We are now ready to create the menu. First we use the CREATE MENU command to open the Menu Design dialog.

```
CREATE MENU BUSREVUE
```

This command opens the Menu Design window shown in Figure 9-3. Unlike the Screen Design window, it follows a structured sequence to collect information.

We start by defining the pads of the horizontal bar menu. The first field for each one is its prompt text. We can specify a hot key with \<.

We can proceed in one of two ways. We can define the menu by level. That is, we can completely define all pads or bars at one level before moving down. We can also define all pads, menus, and procedures under one top level pad before moving to the next such pad. Either method is fine. If we complete the menu by level (as we will here), we simply press Tab to skip the submenus temporarily.

After defining the prompt text, we must select an action type. A menu pad or bar can perform one of four actions: COMMAND, PAD NAME, PROCEDURE, and SUBMENU.

The COMMAND action allows a pad to execute any single FoxPro command including DO <procedure>. The procedure must be defined elsewhere. When FoxPro generates code from a menu definition, it implements a command with

```
ON SELECTION PAD <pad> <command>
```

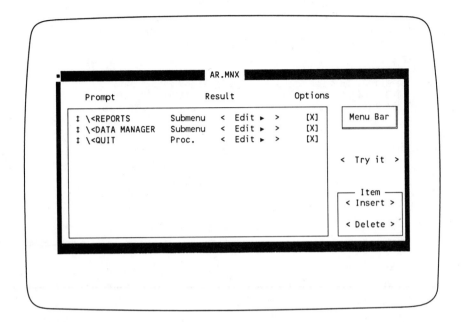

Figure 9-3. Menu design window.

The PAD NAME option lets us supply the name for the menu pad rather than have FoxPro generate one. As a result, it does not generate an action command. Rather, we must edit the code to include an ON SELECTION PAD or ON PAD. We can also define actions through an ON SELECTION MENU. Of course, if there are several named pads, we must determine which one was selected before doing anything.

The PROCEDURE action opens an edit window in which we can enter a series of commands. Although FoxPro treats the code as a procedure, we do not supply a procedure name or statement. Rather, FoxPro generates a unique name for it.

Finally, the SUBMENU type defines a lower level popup that appears when the pad is selected. After SUBMENU is chosen, the next field displays the text button <CREATE> or <EDIT>, depending on whether the menu is new. When we generate the code for a menu, the SUBMENU action generates a command such as

```
ON PAD <pad> OF <menuname> ACTIVATE POPUP <popupname>
```

The last prompt for the menu line is an option box. It opens the dialog shown in Figure 9-4.

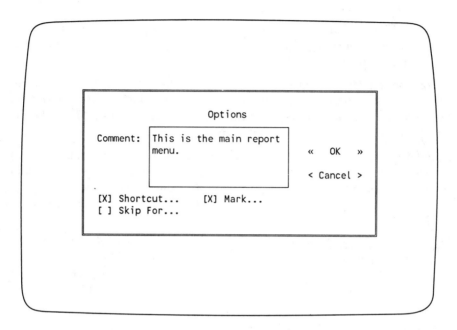

Figure 9-4. Menu line option dialog.

The first prompt is a comment box. We can place text in it to document the menu pad, but it does not appear in the generated code.

The second option is a shortcut command that defines an alternate set of keys to activate the pad or bar. It uses the key label definitions in Table 3-9. In the default menu, the text appears to the right of the popup bars, not with the menu pads. However, we can modify the code to show the shortcut labels.

HINT

The shortcut keys are usually a combination of the Alt key and the hot key letter.

WARNING

The shortcut key does not work if we try to define it with a combination already used by an active macro.

The SKIP FOR option disables a pad or bar if the supplied expression is true. The expression can be anything that returns a logical value, including system or user defined functions.

The last option defines a marker that indicates when a pad or bar is selected. However, it does not appear unless we define a procedure to turn markers on and off as in Program 9-6. We must then call it by choosing the COMMAND or PROCEDURE action when defining the pads or bars.

After defining the pads of the top level menu, we can then define popups opened in lower levels. The bar definitions have the same basic options as the main menu pads. We begin each one by defining its prompt text. Then we assign it one of the four action types. Finally, we can specify the four options shown in Figure 9-4.

At any time while defining the menu, we can test it by selecting the TRY IT pushbutton. It temporarily replaces the System menu with the current menu. To activate it, press the Alt key or use a shortcut key. Alt highlights the first option. We can then use the arrow keys to highlight other pads and select bars from the popups. The shortcut keys execute options directly.

If, in the test mode, we select a popup that executes a procedure or routine outside the menu definition, the menu does not fail. Rather it uses a response dialog box (Figure 9-5) that appears in the center of the screen to display information about the selection. It includes the prompt text and the command that it would execute.

To exit the test mode, select any pad or bar and press Tab to highlight the DONE pushbutton. Pressing the Esc key also causes an exit.

At any point during menu definition, we can open the Menu popup and select General Options. The resulting dialog lets us define global procedures and setup or cleanup code, specify the position of the menu system, and assign a global marker.

The general procedure executes whenever a menu pad is selected. It can be a command, procedure, or program. However, it executes only if there is no procedure for the specific pad. It generates the command

```
ON SELECTION MENU <menuname> <command>
```

WARNING

Do not include a PROCEDURE statement with this code. Fox-Pro generates its own unique name if you enter more than one line of code.

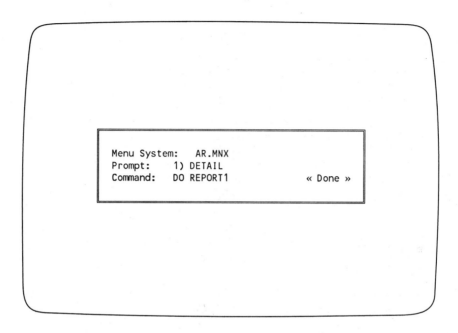

```
Menu System:    AR.MNX
Prompt:     1) DETAIL
Command:    DO REPORT1              « Done »
```

Figure 9-5. Response dialog box.

The Setup code executes before the menu begins. It typically defines the environment, opens files, sets relations, and defines variables. For example, we can use it to open databases in different areas.

The Cleanup code executes after the menu selection is made. It may execute code based on the pad or bar selected. Neither it nor the Setup code produces separate procedures. Rather, they are inserted at the beginning and end of the menu code, respectively.

The Mark option defines a global marker for the menu. Although we can define individual markers by pad, popup, or bar, most menus use a common one. This option does not set markers. You must do that with a separate procedure using the SET MARK command.

The Location option provides four ways to display the menu. All are variations on the use of FoxPro's system menu. The Replace button replaces the current system menu with the new menu. Append adds the new one to the system menu (much as the MENU pad appears in the CREATE MENU or MODIFY MENU mode.).

HINT

If the system menu line lacks enough room for system pads and our pads, we can use the SET SYSMENU command to include only selected system pads. The following line uses only the EDIT, FILE, and WINDOW pads.

```
SET SYSMENU TO _msm_edit, _msm_file, _msm_windo
```

BEFORE and AFTER insert the new menu between pads of the existing one. We will show at the end of this section how to modify the generated menu to make it independent of the system menu.

The Menu Options bar in the Menu pulldown lets us define options specific to individual menus or popups. They include adding a procedure, defining a color scheme, and specifying a marker.

For example, to execute a specific routine when we execute a popup, first display the popup in the Menu Design window. Then select the Menu Options dialog. (Actually, the word Menu is replaced with the popup name.) Do not begin the procedure with a PROCEDURE statement. The menu generator assigns a random name to it and then references it with the command

```
ON SELECTION POPUP <popupname> DO <command>
```

WARNING

FoxPro executes only one action when a menu selection is made, the one defined at the lowest level. Thus, when we select a bar, FoxPro executes the action defined at the bar level. Only if no such action exists does it execute the popup level action. This rule applies, regardless of whether the action is a procedure, command, or another submenu.

The color scheme definition applies to either the entire menu system or to the current popup, depending on where we specify it. Similarly, the mark option defines a marker for the current and lower levels. Suppose we define the diamond character (ASCII 04) as the marker at the main menu level, but the bullet (ASCII 249) at a popup level. The bullet supersedes the diamond in the popup.

Generating Menu Code

After completing the menu definition, save it using the SAVE option in the FILE menu or press Ctrl-W. To generate code for the menu, select GENERATE from the PROGRAM menu. Program 9-12 shows the result of generating the menu described in this section.

Besides selecting an output file name, we can define several comment options. They include the developer's name and address, commenting style, and home directory.

The home directory determines how the generated code references databases and other files. It uses a minimal path based on their current location and the home directory path which defaults to the current directory. For example, if all referenced files are in the specified home directory, no path appears in the generated USE statements.

```
                           HINT
If the program will run from the directory containing the data
files, set the home directory to the data/program directory. If the
data directory is a subdirectory of the program directory, set the
home directory to the program directory. If the data directory is
unrelated to the program directory (a different drive or a dif-
ferent tree branch), set the home directory to either the root or
the program directory. The basic rule is: set the home directory
to the program directory.
```

```
*
*
*  03/30/91              AR.PRG                 08:39:55
*
*
*
*  Michael P. Antonovich
*
*  Copyright (c) 1991 MicMinn Associates
*  Box 6020
*  Wyomissing, PA  19610
*
*  Description:
*  This program was automatically generated by GENMENU.
*
*
```

```
*
*
*                       Setup Code
*
*
```

```
* Set environment
  SET TALK OFF
  CLEAR


* Open databases
  CLOSE DATABASES ALL

  SELECT 1
  USE RETAIL INDEX RETAIL
  SELECT 2
  USE SHIPMENT INDEX SHIPMENT
*
* ┌──────────────────────────────────────────────────────────┐
* │                    Menu Definition                       │
* │                                                          │
* └──────────────────────────────────────────────────────────┘
*

SET SYSMENU TO
SET SYSMENU AUTOMATIC

DEFINE PAD _pu60iknbn OF _MSYSMENU PROMPT "\<REPORTS";
     KEY CTRL+R, "CTRL+R"
DEFINE PAD _pu60iknr2 OF _MSYSMENU PROMPT "\<DATA MANAGER";
     KEY CTRL+D, "CTRL+D"
DEFINE PAD _pu60ikns4 OF _MSYSMENU PROMPT "\<QUIT";
     KEY CTRL+Q, "CTRL+Q"
ON PAD _pu60iknbn OF _MSYSMENU ACTIVATE POPUP reports
ON PAD _pu60iknr2 OF _MSYSMENU ACTIVATE POPUP datamanage
ON SELECTION PAD _pu60ikns4 OF _MSYSMENU;
     DO _pu60iko41 IN AR.PRG


DEFINE POPUP reports MARGIN RELATIVE SHADOW COLOR SCHEME 4
DEFINE BAR 1 OF reports  PROMPT "\<1) TREND" ;
     KEY ALT+E, "ALT+E"
DEFINE BAR 2 OF reports  PROMPT "\<2) DISTRIBUTION" ;
     KEY ALT+H, "ALT+H"
DEFINE BAR 3 OF reports  PROMPT "\<3) EVENTS" ;
     KEY ALT+P, "ALT+P"
DEFINE BAR 4 OF reports  PROMPT "\<4) PROFIT ANALYSIS" ;
     KEY ALT+V, "ALT+V"
DEFINE BAR 5 OF reports  PROMPT "\<5) MERCHANDISING..."
DEFINE BAR 6 OF reports  PROMPT "\<6) CATEGORY..."
DEFINE BAR 7 OF reports  PROMPT "\<7) SHIPMENT"
DEFINE BAR 8 OF reports  PROMPT "\<8) SHIPMENT/MOVEMENT..."
DEFINE BAR 9 OF reports  PROMPT ;
     "\<9) TRADE EVENT ANALYSIS..."
ON SELECTION BAR 1 OF reports REPORT FORM REPORT5
ON SELECTION BAR 2 OF reports REPORT FORM REPORT8
ON SELECTION BAR 3 OF reports REPORT FORM REPORT16
ON SELECTION BAR 4 OF reports REPORT FORM REPORT22
ON BAR 5 OF reports ACTIVATE POPUP _pu50ysoo2
ON BAR 6 OF reports ACTIVATE POPUP _pu50yspg9
ON BAR 7 OF reports ACTIVATE POPUP _pu30riip2
ON BAR 8 OF reports ACTIVATE POPUP _pu30rpa1p
```

```
ON BAR 9 OF reports ACTIVATE POPUP _pu30rqqro

DEFINE POPUP _pu50ysoo2 MARGIN RELATIVE SHADOW COLOR SCHEME 4
DEFINE BAR 1 OF _pu50ysoo2  PROMPT "1) DETAIL" ;
     KEY ALT+A, "ALT+A"
DEFINE BAR 2 OF _pu50ysoo2  PROMPT "2) WEEKLY" ;
     KEY ALT+B, "ALT+B"
DEFINE BAR 3 OF _pu50ysoo2  PROMPT "3) SUMMARY" ;
     KEY ALT+C, "ALT+C"
DEFINE BAR 4 OF _pu50ysoo2  PROMPT "4) RESPONSE MATRIX" ;
     KEY ALT+F, "ALT+F"
ON SELECTION BAR 1 OF _pu50ysoo2 REPORT FORM REPORT1
ON SELECTION BAR 2 OF _pu50ysoo2 REPORT FORM REPORT2
ON SELECTION BAR 3 OF _pu50ysoo2 REPORT FORM REPORT3
ON SELECTION BAR 4 OF _pu50ysoo2 REPORT FORM REPORT6

DEFINE POPUP _pu50yspg9 MARGIN RELATIVE SHADOW COLOR SCHEME 4
DEFINE BAR 1 OF _pu50yspg9  PROMPT "1) DETAIL" ;
     KEY ALT+D, "ALT+D"
DEFINE BAR 2 OF _pu50yspg9  PROMPT "2) SHARE" ;
     KEY ALT+G, "ALT+G"
ON SELECTION BAR 1 OF _pu50yspg9 REPORT FORM REPORT4
ON SELECTION BAR 2 OF _pu50yspg9 REPORT FORM REPORT7

DEFINE POPUP _pu30riip2 MARGIN RELATIVE SHADOW COLOR SCHEME 4
DEFINE BAR 1 OF _pu30riip2  PROMPT "1) BY ACCOUNT" ;
     KEY ALT+J, "ALT+J"
DEFINE BAR 2 OF _pu30riip2  PROMPT "2) BY BRAND" ;
     KEY ALT+K, "ALT+K"
DEFINE BAR 3 OF _pu30riip2  PROMPT "3) ALL BRANDS" ;
     KEY ALT+L, "ALT+L"
ON SELECTION BAR 1 OF _pu30riip2 REPORT FORM REPORT10
ON SELECTION BAR 2 OF _pu30riip2 REPORT FORM REPORT11
ON SELECTION BAR 3 OF _pu30riip2 REPORT FORM REPORT12

DEFINE POPUP _pu30rpa1p MARGIN RELATIVE SHADOW COLOR SCHEME 4
DEFINE BAR 1 OF _pu30rpa1p  PROMPT "1) WEEKLY" ;
     KEY ALT+I, "ALT+I"
DEFINE BAR 2 OF _pu30rpa1p  PROMPT "2) BY ACCOUNT" ;
     KEY ALT+M, "ALT+M"
DEFINE BAR 3 OF _pu30rpa1p  PROMPT "3) BY BRAND" ;
     KEY ALT+N, "ALT+N"
DEFINE BAR 4 OF _pu30rpa1p  PROMPT "4) ALL BRANDS" ;
     KEY ALT+O, "ALT+O"
DEFINE BAR 5 OF _pu30rpa1p  PROMPT "5) BUYING PROFILE" ;
     KEY ALT+S, "ALT+S"
ON SELECTION BAR 1 OF _pu30rpa1p REPORT FORM REPORT9
ON SELECTION BAR 2 OF _pu30rpa1p REPORT FORM REPORT13
ON SELECTION BAR 3 OF _pu30rpa1p REPORT FORM REPORT14
ON SELECTION BAR 4 OF _pu30rpa1p REPORT FORM REPORT15
ON SELECTION BAR 5 OF _pu30rpa1p REPORT FORM REPORT19

DEFINE POPUP _pu30rqqro MARGIN RELATIVE SHADOW COLOR SCHEME 4
```

```
DEFINE BAR 1 OF _pu30rqqro   PROMPT "1) DETAIL" ;
     KEY ALT+Q, "ALT+Q"
DEFINE BAR 2 OF _pu30rqqro   PROMPT "2) SUMMARY" ;
     KEY ALT+R, "ALT+R"
ON SELECTION BAR 1 OF _pu30rqqro REPORT FORM REPORT17
ON SELECTION BAR 2 OF _pu30rqqro REPORT FORM REPORT18

DEFINE POPUP datamanage MARGIN RELATIVE SHADOW COLOR SCHEME 4
DEFINE BAR 1 OF datamanage   PROMPT "\<1) LOAD DATA" ;
     KEY CTRL+L, "CTRL+L"
DEFINE BAR 2 OF datamanage   PROMPT "\<2) EDIT DATA" ;
     KEY CTRL+E, "CTRL+E"
ON SELECTION BAR 1 OF datamanage DO LOADDATA
ON SELECTION BAR 2 OF datamanage DO EDITDATA
```

```
*
*   ┌────────────────────────────────────────────────┐
*   │ _PU60IKO41  ON SELECTION PAD                     │
*   │                                                  │
*   │ Procedure Origin:                                │
*   │                                                  │
*   │ From Menu: AR.PRG,          Record:   39         │
*   │ Called By: ON SELECTION PAD                      │
*   │ Prompt:    QUIT                                  │
*   │                                                  │
*   └────────────────────────────────────────────────┘
```

```
PROCEDURE _pu60iko41
* Close databases
  CLOSE DATABASES ALL

* Restore default system menu
  SET SYSMENU TO DEFAULT
  CLEAR

* End of program
```

Program 9-12. Generated Menu for Business Review System

Generating a Non-System Menu

The generator assumes that the new menu replaces the existing system menu, appends to it, or inserts into it. However, we may want a separate menu. Since FoxPro generates modifiable code, we can edit the result. In this case, we must eliminate the system menu related lines:

```
SET SYSMENU TO
SET SYSMENU AUTOMATIC
```

at the beginning. They clear the default pads from the system menu and tell FoxPro to keep it active during program execution.

We should also remove the line that restores the system menu to its defaults.

```
SET SYSTEM TO DEFAULT
```

Next we insert a line to define the menu using DEFINE MENU. All pads that previously referred to the system menu, _MSYSMENU, must now refer to the new one. Finally, we need a command to activate the menu. Program 9-13 is a revision of Program 9-12 that creates a free-standing menu.

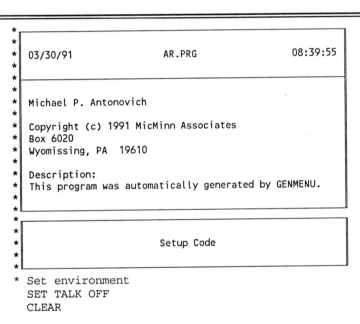

```
*
*
*   03/30/91              AR.PRG                08:39:55
*
*
*
*
*   Michael P. Antonovich
*
*   Copyright (c) 1991 MicMinn Associates
*   Box 6020
*   Wyomissing, PA  19610
*
*   Description:
*   This program was automatically generated by GENMENU.
*
*
*
*
*                         Setup Code
*
*
*
*   Set environment
    SET TALK OFF
    CLEAR

*   Open databases
    CLOSE DATABASES ALL

*   SELECT 1
*   USE RETAIL INDEX RETAIL
*   SELECT 2
*   USE SHIPMENT INDEX SHIPMENT
```

```
*
*
*                      Menu Definition
*
*
```

```
*   Make sure system menu is set to default and is not active
*   during program execution.
    SET SYSMENU TO DEFAULT
    SET SYSMENU OFF
```

```
* Initialize variable
  rptwidth = 0

* For a system menu style menu use:
*     DEFINE MENU AR BAR
  DEFINE MENU AR MARK '^D'

DEFINE PAD _pu60iknbn OF ar PROMPT "\<REPORTS";
    KEY CTRL+R, "CTRL+R"
DEFINE PAD _pu60iknr2 OF ar PROMPT "\<DATA MANAGER";
    KEY CTRL+D, "CTRL+D"
DEFINE PAD _pu60ikns4 OF ar PROMPT "\<QUIT";
    KEY CTRL+Q, "CTRL+Q"
ON PAD _pu60iknbn OF ar ACTIVATE POPUP reports
ON PAD _pu60iknr2 OF ar ACTIVATE POPUP datamanage
ON SELECTION PAD _pu60ikns4 OF ar;
    DO _pu60iko41

DEFINE POPUP reports MARGIN RELATIVE SHADOW COLOR SCHEME 4
DEFINE BAR 1 OF reports  PROMPT "\<1) TREND" ;
    KEY ALT+E, "ALT+E"
DEFINE BAR 2 OF reports  PROMPT "\<2) DISTRIBUTION" ;
    KEY ALT+H, "ALT+H"
DEFINE BAR 3 OF reports  PROMPT "\<3) EVENTS" ;
    KEY ALT+P, "ALT+P"
DEFINE BAR 4 OF reports  PROMPT "\<4) PROFIT ANALYSIS" ;
    KEY ALT+V, "ALT+V"
DEFINE BAR 5 OF reports  PROMPT "\<5) MERCHANDISING..."
DEFINE BAR 6 OF reports  PROMPT "\<6) CATEGORY..."
DEFINE BAR 7 OF reports  PROMPT "\<7) SHIPMENT"
DEFINE BAR 8 OF reports  PROMPT "\<8) SHIPMENT/MOVEMENT..."
DEFINE BAR 9 OF reports  PROMPT "\<9) TRADE EVENT ANALYSIS..."
ON SELECTION BAR 1 OF reports REPORT FORM REPORT5
ON SELECTION BAR 2 OF reports REPORT FORM REPORT8
ON SELECTION BAR 3 OF reports REPORT FORM REPORT16
ON SELECTION BAR 4 OF reports REPORT FORM REPORT22
ON SELECTION BAR 5 OF reports DO GETREPT WITH POPUP(), BAR()
ON BAR 6 OF reports ACTIVATE POPUP _pu50yspg9
ON BAR 7 OF reports ACTIVATE POPUP _pu30riip2
ON BAR 8 OF reports ACTIVATE POPUP _pu30rpa1p
ON BAR 9 OF reports ACTIVATE POPUP _pu30rqqro

DEFINE POPUP _pu50ysoo2 FROM 5,rptwidth MARGIN RELATIVE
SHADOW
COLOR SCHEME 4
DEFINE BAR 1 OF _pu50ysoo2  PROMPT "1) DETAIL" ;
    KEY ALT+A, "ALT+A"
DEFINE BAR 2 OF _pu50ysoo2  PROMPT "2) WEEKLY" ;
    KEY ALT+B, "ALT+B"
DEFINE BAR 3 OF _pu50ysoo2  PROMPT "3) SUMMARY" ;
    KEY ALT+C, "ALT+C"
DEFINE BAR 4 OF _pu50ysoo2  PROMPT "4) RESPONSE MATRIX" ;
    KEY ALT+F, "ALT+F"
```

```
ON SELECTION BAR 1 OF _pu50ysoo2 REPORT FORM REPORT1
ON SELECTION BAR 2 OF _pu50ysoo2 REPORT FORM REPORT2
ON SELECTION BAR 3 OF _pu50ysoo2 REPORT FORM REPORT3
ON SELECTION BAR 4 OF _pu50ysoo2 REPORT FORM REPORT6

DEFINE POPUP _pu50yspg9 MARGIN RELATIVE SHADOW COLOR SCHEME 4
DEFINE BAR 1 OF _pu50yspg9  PROMPT "1) DETAIL" ;
     KEY ALT+D, "ALT+D"
DEFINE BAR 2 OF _pu50yspg9  PROMPT "2) SHARE" ;
     KEY ALT+G, "ALT+G"
ON SELECTION BAR 1 OF _pu50yspg9 REPORT FORM REPORT4
ON SELECTION BAR 2 OF _pu50yspg9 REPORT FORM REPORT7

DEFINE POPUP _pu30riip2 MARGIN RELATIVE SHADOW COLOR SCHEME 4
DEFINE BAR 1 OF _pu30riip2  PROMPT "1) BY ACCOUNT" ;
     KEY ALT+J, "ALT+J"
DEFINE BAR 2 OF _pu30riip2  PROMPT "2) BY BRAND" ;
     KEY ALT+K, "ALT+K"
DEFINE BAR 3 OF _pu30riip2  PROMPT "3) ALL BRANDS" ;
     KEY ALT+L, "ALT+L"
ON SELECTION BAR 1 OF _pu30riip2 REPORT FORM REPORT10
ON SELECTION BAR 2 OF _pu30riip2 REPORT FORM REPORT11
ON SELECTION BAR 3 OF _pu30riip2 REPORT FORM REPORT12

DEFINE POPUP _pu30rpa1p MARGIN RELATIVE SHADOW COLOR SCHEME 4
DEFINE BAR 1 OF _pu30rpa1p  PROMPT "1) WEEKLY" ;
     KEY ALT+I, "ALT+I"
DEFINE BAR 2 OF _pu30rpa1p  PROMPT "2) BY ACCOUNT" ;
     KEY ALT+M, "ALT+M"
DEFINE BAR 3 OF _pu30rpa1p  PROMPT "3) BY BRAND" ;
     KEY ALT+N, "ALT+N"
DEFINE BAR 4 OF _pu30rpa1p  PROMPT "4) ALL BRANDS" ;
     KEY ALT+O, "ALT+O"
DEFINE BAR 5 OF _pu30rpa1p  PROMPT "5) BUYING PROFILE" ;
     KEY ALT+S, "ALT+S"
ON SELECTION BAR 1 OF _pu30rpa1p REPORT FORM REPORT9
ON SELECTION BAR 2 OF _pu30rpa1p REPORT FORM REPORT13
ON SELECTION BAR 3 OF _pu30rpa1p REPORT FORM REPORT14
ON SELECTION BAR 4 OF _pu30rpa1p REPORT FORM REPORT15
ON SELECTION BAR 5 OF _pu30rpa1p REPORT FORM REPORT19

DEFINE POPUP _pu30rqqro MARGIN RELATIVE SHADOW COLOR SCHEME 4
DEFINE BAR 1 OF _pu30rqqro  PROMPT "1) DETAIL" ;
     KEY ALT+Q, "ALT+Q"
DEFINE BAR 2 OF _pu30rqqro  PROMPT "2) SUMMARY" ;
     KEY ALT+R, "ALT+R"
ON SELECTION BAR 1 OF _pu30rqqro REPORT FORM REPORT17
ON SELECTION BAR 2 OF _pu30rqqro REPORT FORM REPORT18

DEFINE POPUP datamanage MARGIN RELATIVE SHADOW COLOR SCHEME 4
DEFINE BAR 1 OF datamanage  PROMPT "\<1) LOAD DATA" ;
     KEY CTRL+L, "CTRL+L"
DEFINE BAR 2 OF datamanage  PROMPT "\<2) EDIT DATA" ;
```

```
     KEY CTRL+E, "CTRL+E"
ON SELECTION BAR 1 OF datamanage DO LOADDATA
ON SELECTION BAR 2 OF datamanage DO EDITDATA

ACTIVATE MENU AR
```

```
*
*   ┌──────────────────────────────────────────────────┐
*   │                                                  │
*   │ _PU60IKO41  ON SELECTION PAD                     │
*   │                                                  │
*   │ Procedure Origin:                                │
*   │                                                  │
*   │ From Menu:  AR.PRG,            Record:   39      │
*   │ Called By:  ON SELECTION PAD                     │
*   │ Prompt:     QUIT                                 │
*   │                                                  │
*   └──────────────────────────────────────────────────┘
```

```
PROCEDURE _pu60iko41
* Close databases
  CLOSE DATABASES ALL

* Restore default system menu
  DEACTIVATE MENU AR
  RELEASE MENUS ALL
RETURN
```

```
*
*   ┌──────────────────────────────────────────────────┐
*   │                                                  │
*   │ GETREPT      ON SELECTION PAD                    │
*   │                                                  │
*   │ Procedure Origin:                                │
*   │                                                  │
*   │ From Menu:  AR.PRG,                              │
*   │ Called By:  ON SELECTION PAD                     │
*   │ Prompt:     MERCHANDISING                        │
*   │                                                  │
*   └──────────────────────────────────────────────────┘
```

```
PROCEDURE GETREPT
PARAMETER mpopup,mbar

* Convert bar number to a string
  nbar = ALLTRIM(STR(mbar))

* Mark selection in first popup
  IF UPPER(mpopup) = 'REPORTS'
    SET MARK OF POPUP &mpopup TO .F.
    SET MARK OF BAR &nbar OF &mpopup TO .T.
  * Determine maximum width of popup
    FOR i = 1 to cntbar(mpopup)
      rptwidth = MAX(rptwidth,LEN(PRMBAR(mpopup,i)))
    ENDFOR
```

```
    * Move popup before activating it
      MOVE POPUP _pu50ysoo2 TO 5,rptwidth+3
      ACTIVATE POPUP _pu50ysoo2
    ENDIF

    * Clear marks before returning to menu
      SET MARK OF POPUP &mpopup TO .F.
    RETURN
```

Program 9-13. Free Standing Menu

Now we can modify this menu further by adding features discussed at the beginning of this chapter, but not readily available through the menu creation utility.

EXERCISE

Program 9-13 modified the fifth bar in the first popup to mark the bar selection before opening the submenu for Merchandising reports. Modify the other bars that have submenus.

Summary

This chapter examined menus ranging from simple ASCII pick lists to full featured bar and popup menus. We used menus to select major branches in programs and to choose among simple alternatives such as report destinations.

Later we used menus to offer choices based on data derived directly from a database rather than preprogrammed options. We used this feature as a powerful way to validate input data against a master file.

With a slight modification of the popup window, we created a program that lets the user select any database file. Then by displaying its fields in a popup, we were able to pick display fields and define a filter for a custom report.

We ended the chapter by examining the Menu Builder utility. Its main advantage is that it creates error-free menus quickly and generates code that we can enhance further in applications.

10

Importing and Exporting Data

After creating a database, we must load it with data. We could use an input form and enter the data manually. However, this is time consuming and error prone. If the data is already in another file, a more reliable method is to transfer it electronically. The main difficulty is translating it into a form that FoxPro can import. Only a few other programs can create DBF files. In most cases, an ASCII file is the best approach. Exporting data raises similar issues.

This chapter examines ways to transfer data to and from databases. FoxPro can read and write formats used in several major software products. However, it cannot possibly handle all known types. Therefore, we will describe ways of transferring data to and from ASCII files. Finally, for difficult situations, we show how to use low-level file functions.

Transfers between Database Files

The easiest way to create a database is by copying from an existing one. For example, we may create a subset to distribute selected data from a master file. The COPY TO command is the mechanism.

Before using it, we must open the master database. If we do not include the FIELDS option, FoxPro copies all fields. It transfers them directly without doing any calculations or string manipulations.

Suppose we want a subset of the company master database for a division. We can use a FOR clause to extract the desired records. COPY TO also supports a WHILE clause that we can use instead if the database is ordered or indexed

331

appropriately. When using WHILE, be sure to move the pointer to the first division record before copying.

HINT

The WHILE clause is faster than FOR because it reads only records satisfying the extraction criteria. The FOR clause scans the entire database.

Without FOR or WHILE, COPY TO copies all records unless we specify a scope. Valid ones are:

ALL	(default) all records in the database
NEXT(n)	next n records beginning with the current one
RECORD(n)	specific record number
REST	all records from the current one through the end of the database

With NEXT and REST, the specific records copied depend on the active index and the current pointer position.

Figure 10-1 shows the structure of a sales file for a chain of stores. It tracks shipments received and units sold from each store, department, and manufacturer by product number.

Field	Type	Size	Decimal Places
DATE	Date	8	
STORE_ID	Character	3	
DEPARTMENT	Character	3	
PRODUCT	Character	10	
MANUF_ID	Character	8	
REC_UNITS	Numeric	4	
REC_COST	Numeric	7	
SOLD_UNITS	Numeric	4	
SOLD_COST	Numeric	7	2
RETURNS	Numeric	4	
DAMAGED	Numeric	4	2
ITEM_UPC	Character	15	

Figure 10-1. Sales master database structure.

When a store manager requests information, we need not provide the entire file. Rather, we extract his or her store's records with a command such as

```
COPY TO STORE407 FOR STORE_ID = '407'
```

This command copies all fields for records with store id 407. Some reports may need only a few fields. For example, one might list the number of returned or damaged items by manufacturer. The following command extracts this information for manufacturer BIGTOP_TOYS.

```
COPY TO SHIPCHECK FIELDS date, rec_units, rec_cost, ;
       returns, damaged, item_upc ;
       FOR manuf_id = 'BIGTOP_TOYS' ;
          .AND. .NOT. EMPTY(damaged) ;
          .AND. .NOT. EMPTY(returns)
```

COPY TO lets us protect the master database by creating distribution files with only the required information. It also has another benefit. The resulting file is smaller than the master, so programs execute faster and operations require less disk space.

While copying all or part of a database, we can also copy its structural compound index file (the one with the same name) by including the CDX or PRODUCTION keyword. We must copy other (independent) compound index files separately.

COPY TO (or EXPORT) can create many common file types directly (see Table 10-1). A later section covers writing data to ASCII delimited files for programs that cannot read any of them.

Suppose we want to append records to a database. APPEND FROM copies records into the currently active one. We can limit it to specific fields, and we can specify a FOR clause to copy selected records. The following command appends records from file STORE407 with dates after September 1, 1990.

```
APPEND FROM STORE407 FOR DATE >= {09/01/1990}
```

APPEND FROM can handle the file types listed in Table 10-2.

IMPORT can read the same file types as APPEND FROM. However, it creates an entirely new database. For example, the following command creates SHUTTLE.DBF from a Lotus file SHUTTLE.WK1.

```
IMPORT FROM shuttle.wk1 TYPE WK1
```

Table 10-1. File Types Created by COPY TO or EXPORT

File Type	Origin or Significance
DIF	Data Interchange Format (DIF) used by VisiCalc
FOXPLUS	FoxBASE+ has the same database structure as FoxPro, but a different memo structure. Use this option to create FoxBASE+ files that include memos.
MOD	Microsoft Multiplan Version 4.01
SDF	System Data Format, an ASCII text file with fixed record length and a carriage return-line feed combination at the end of each record
SYLK	Symbolic Link Interchange format used by Microsoft Multiplan
WK1	Lotus 1-2-3 Version 2.x
WKS	Lotus 1-2-3 Version 1A
WR1	Lotus Symphony Versions 1.1 and 1.2
WRK	Lotus Symphony Version 1.0
XLS	Microsoft Excel Version 2

Table 10-2. File Types Read by APPEND FROM

File Type	Origin or Significance
DIF	Data Interchange Format (DIF) used by VisiCalc.
FW2	Ashton-Tate's Framework II
MOD	Microsoft Multiplan Version 4.01
PDOX	Borland's Paradox Version 3.5
RPD	Ashton-Tate's RapidFile Version 1.2
SDF	System Data Format, an ASCII text file with fixed record length and a carriage return-line feed combination at the end of each record
SYLK	Symbolic Link Interchange format used by Microsoft Multiplan
WK1	Lotus 1-2-3 Version 2.x
WK3	Lotus 1-2-3 Version 3.x
WKS	Lotus 1-2-3 Version 1A
WR1	Lotus Symphony Versions 1.1 and 1.2
WRK	Lotus Symphony Version 1.0
XLS	Microsoft Excel Version 2

> **HINT**
>
> FoxPro expects the first record in a spreadsheet to define field names. It defines the field structure from the spreadsheet's column widths and types. Similarly, it writes the field names to the first row of spreadsheet files and defines the column widths and types based on the field structure. Of course, it transfers only values, not equations.

> **WARNING**
>
> Some spreadsheets require numeric columns to be one character wider than the largest number. For example, to display numbers in the range 100 to 999 requires a column width of 4.

FoxPro reads database and index files from FoxBASE, dBASE III, and dBASE IV. It automatically converts indexes into FoxPro (IDX) indexes without changing the original files. However, FoxPro will not create indexes for other programs. And although we can create indexes with the extension NDX using the command

```
INDEX = NDX
```

they are still FoxPro indexes.

Importing ASCII Files

The data we want to load may not be in a format FoxPro can read directly. It may be in an ASCII file instead. The APPEND FROM command reads several styles, namely:

```
DELIMITED
DELIMITED WITH BLANK
DELIMITED WITH <delimiter>
DELIMITED WITH TAB
SDF (System Data Format)
```

Importing SDF Files

SDF files resemble output reports. In fact, that is often exactly what they are. All records are the same length. Furthermore, each field always has the same size and position. The fields from a record must appear on one line, ending with a carriage return and line feed. Individual fields are not delimited. Figure 10-2 shows part of an SDF file containing data for LENDER.DBF. We can append it to the database with

```
APPEND FROM lender.txt TYPE SDF
```

The example SDF file contains six fields. They must be the first ones in the database structure and in the specified order. Also, each must occupy the same number of character positions in the SDF file as in the database's field definition. For example, if the first database field is 12 characters, APPEND FROM loads it with the first 12 characters of each record in the SDF file. Because there are no delimiters, FoxPro counts characters to identify fields.

Can we skip fields? Yes! We can use the FIELDS clause to load selected ones. We can even change the order. This ability is useful, as the SDF file may not have fields arranged as in the database. Figure 10-3 shows the same data as Figure 10-1 but with a different field order. We can append it to the database with the command

```
APPEND FROM lender.txt FIELDS l_id, l_name, l_address, ;
       l_zip, l_state, l_city TYPE SDF
```

```
AB      American Bank           540 Lancaster Ave      Schilington   PA19607
BS      Berkshire Savings       1 Centre Plaza         Canyon Forge  PA19552
GBL     Gulf Bank and Loan      1000 Court Street      Chester       PA18443
GS      Golden Savings          954 Platinum Place     Silver Lake   PA17554
HNB     Hamilton National Bank  543 St James Road      Reading       PA19603
KPB     Knowers Private Bank    Granite Hill Corp Ctr  Boslin        PA19322
MAB     Merchants Assoc Bank    Wyomissing Plaza       Wyomissing    PA19610
MCB     Meridian Century Bank   14 Broadcasting Road   Mount Penn    PA19605
MPA     My Personal Account Bank My Place              Hometown      PA19111
NBP     National Bank of Potts  Centre Plaza Tower     Provident     PA19002
PF      Pacific Financial       24 Hill Ave            San Tego      PA19221
PHF     Philadelphia Finance    1500 Benter Avenue     East Lawn     PA19609
PNB     Piper National Bank     938 5th Avenue         Robison       PA19221
TT      Traveler's Trust        3rd & Washington       Mogenville    PA18998
```

Figure 10-2. Example SDF data file.

```
AB    American Bank          540 Lancaster Ave     19607PASchilington
BS    Berkshire Savings      1 Centre Plaza        19552PACanyon Forge
GBL   Gulf Bank and Loan     1000 Court Street     18443PAChester
GS    Golden Savings         954 Platinum Place    17554PASilver Lake
HNB   Hamilton National Bank 543 St James Road     19603PAReading
KPB   Knowers Private Bank   Granite Hill Corp Ctr 19322PABoslin
MAB   Merchants Assoc Bank   Wyomissing Plaza      19610PAWyomissing
MCB   Meridian Century Bank  14 Broadcasting Road  19605PAMount Penn
MPA   My Personal Account Bank My Place            19111PAHometown
NBP   National Bank of Potts Centre Plaza Tower    19002PAProvident
PF    Pacific Financial      24 Hill Ave           19221PASan Tego
PHF   Philadelphia Finance   1500 Benter Avenue    19609PAEast Lawn
PNB   Piper National Bank    938 5th Avenue        19221PARobison
TT    Traveler's Trust       3rd & Washington      18998PAMogenville
```

Figure 10-3. Example SDF data file with a different field order.

WARNING

The APPEND FROM command does not check for duplicate records. Thus we will end up with two copies of each record if we accidentally load the SDF file twice.

Importing Delimited Files

To handle applications that cannot create SDF files, FoxPro can also read delimited files. Delimiters indicate where fields begin and end, so they can vary in length. The most common way to delimit data is to put commas between fields and double quotation marks around character fields. Each record must still end with a carriage return and a line feed. Figure 10-4 shows delimited data; you can load it into the current database with the command

```
APPEND FROM lender.txt TYPE DELIMITED
```

What if the character data includes double quotation marks? Then we cannot use them as delimiters without confusing FoxPro. So we must choose another

```
"AB","American Bank","540 Lancaster Ave","Schilington","PA","19607"
"BS","Berkshire Savings","1 Centre Plaza","Canyon Forge","PA","19552"
"GBL","Gulf Bank and Loan","1000 Court Street","Chester","PA","18443"
"GS","Golden Savings","954 Platinum Place","Silver Lake","PA","17554"
"HNB","Hamilton National Bank","543 St James Road","Reading","PA","19603"
"KPB","Knowers Private Bank","Granite Hill Corp Ctr","Boslin","PA","19322"
"MAB","Merchants Assoc Bank","Wyomissing Plaza","Wyomissing","PA","19610"
"MCB","Meridian Century Bank","14 Broadcasting","Mount Penn","PA","19605"
"MPA","My Personal Account Bank","My Place","Hometown","PA","19111"
"NBP","National Bank of Potts","Plaza Tower","Provident","PA","19002"
"PF","Pacific Financial","24 Hill Ave","San Tego","PA","19221"
"PHF","Philadelphia Finance","1500 Benter Avenue","East Lawn","PA","19609"
"PNB","Piper National Bank","938 5th Avenue","Robison","PA","19221"
"TT","Traveler's Trust","3rd & Washington","Mogenville","PA","18998"
```

Figure 10-4. Example delimited data.

character and identify it in the DELIMITED WITH clause. The following command appends data using a vertical bar as the delimiter:

```
APPEND FROM lender.txt DELIMITED WITH |
```

Note that we do not enclose the delimiter in quotation marks. Also, commas must still separate fields.

We can also separate them with blanks or tabs. However, do not use more than one, as multiple commas, spaces, or tabs all indicate skipped fields. The following commands load files using blanks or tabs:

```
APPEND FROM lender.txt DELIMITED WITH BLANK
APPEND FROM lender.txt DELIMITED WITH TAB
```

WARNING

Do not use DELIMITED WITH BLANK when the data contains strings with embedded spaces. This format does not enclose character fields in quotation marks. Therefore, FoxPro treats each word as a separate field, causing misalignment.

Exporting ASCII Files

We can create ASCII files from FoxPro databases to transfer data to other applications such as graphics programs or spreadsheets. The COPY TO command can write the same types of ASCII files that APPEND FROM reads, namely SDF and delimited files.

Exporting SDF Files

SDF files created by COPY TO resemble reports. Each record appears on a separate line of equal length. Within each line, the database structure determines the field lengths and positions. FoxPro automatically places a carriage return and line feed at the end. Figure 10-5 shows the COPY TO command and the SDF file created from the LENDER.DBF file.

```
USE lender INDEX lender
COPY TO lender1.txt TYPE SDF
```

Some applications require delimited files rather than SDF files. They have commas between fields and double quotation marks around character strings. However, as with APPEND FROM, COPY TO can enclose strings in any character. We can also choose among commas, spaces, and tabs as field separators. Typical variations are:

```
COPY TO lender.txt DELIMITED
COPY TO lender.txt DELIMITED WITH |
COPY TO lender.txt DELIMITED WITH BLANK
COPY TO lender.txt DELIMITED WITH TAB
```

Generating Files from Multiple Databases

We can use JOIN to combine databases. It requires a FOR clause to define the fields from the primary database that establish the connection. Only when they match the index value of the secondary database does JOIN combine the fields into a single record.

The FIELDS clause tells FoxPro which fields to copy to the joined database. Otherwise, it copies all fields from both databases.

To combine more databases, we use a series of JOINs. Later we can produce SDF or delimited ASCII files containing data previously stored in several databases.

AB	American Bank	540 Lancaster Ave	Schilington	PA19607	(215)378-7931	23-443112311.7501990103TTT
BS	Berkshire Savings	1 Centre Plaza	Canyon Forge	PA19552		
GBL	Gulf Bank and Loan	1000 Court Street	Chester	PA18443		
GS	Golden Savings	954 Platinum Place	Silver Lake	PA17554	0.000	FFF
HNB	Hamilton National Bank	543 St James Road	Reading	PA19603	(215)376-729712	23-123444310.0001990104FTT
KPB	Knowers Private Bank	Granite Hill Corp Ctr	Boslin	PA19322		
MAB	Merchants Assoc Bank	Wyomissing Plaza	Wyomissing	PA19610	(215)374-224623	23-111222312.0001990102FFT
MCB	Meridian Century Bank	14 Broadcasting Road	Mount Penn	PA19605	(215)776-2234144	23-643833211.5001989230FFF
MPA	My Personal Account Bank	My Place	Hometown	PA11111	(111)111-1111	11-1111111 5.0001990312FFF
NBP	National Bank of Potts	Centre Plaza Tower	Provident	PA19002		
PF	Pacific Financial	24 Hill Ave	San Tego	PA19221	(619)332-1823265	98-234435612.5001990105TTT
PNB	Piper National Bank	938 5th Avenue	Robison	PA19221		
PHF	Philadelphia Finance	1500 Benter Avenue	East Lawn	PA19609	(215)775-3452	23-968459311.2501990228FTF
TT	Traveler's Trust	3rd & Washington	Mogenville	PA18998		

Figure 10-5. Example SDF file created with COPY TO.

Reading Structured Files

Not all applications can read and write files in SDF or delimited format. Some may store dates differently, or include commas in numbers. In such cases, we cannot use APPEND FROM.

WARNING

FoxPro interprets T or F in an ASCII file as a logical value. It also converts dates in the YYYYMMDD format to a valid date type. However, it cannot convert dates in other formats such as MM/DD/YYYY. APPEND FROM cannot read numeric data if it contains commas.

Figure 10-6 shows part of a report from a construction company. The site manager wants to analyze the data further. However, it is not in SDF format because the dates are formatted improperly. Furthermore, the numbers include commas, and the overtime column contains 'YES' or 'NO' rather than 'T' or 'F'.

ACCOUNT	DATE	LABOR	MATERIAL	OTHER	TOTAL	OVERTIME
2100120000	09/14/1990	298,775	50,762	11,914	361,451	NO
2100210000	08/01/1990	228,631	170,428	10,896	409,955	NO
2100830004	02/18/1990	32,106	10,261	6,971	49,338	YES
2100890000	01/11/1990	13,145	8,641	3,375	25,161	NO
2106122004	06/24/1990	57,623	377,611	8,036	443,270	NO
2106141404	05/10/1990	37,225	32,039	1,944	71,208	NO
2106141406	10/22/1990	25,266	21,104	746	47,116	NO
2106145004	09/30/1990	90,998	28,274	29,384	148,656	YES
2106245004	03/19/1990	14,406	32,669	15,522	62,597	NO
2106540011	07/28/1990	1,665	1,314	62	3,041	NO
2106540012	04/16/1990	1,651	61	2,708	4,420	NO
2106900000	08/03/1990	19,346	13	3,605	22,964	NO
2300112000	07/14/1990	313,640	25,904,011	319,251	26,536,902	YES
2300112011	01/05/1990	71,144	5,156	71	76,371	NO
2300150000	11/10/1990	8,935	42,809	15,119	66,863	NO
2300210000	12/15/1990	671,497	3,281,840	34,872	3,988,209	NO
2300210011	05/09/1990	36,769	27,996	499	65,264	NO
2300260000	04/30/1990	5,603	4,897	44,807	55,307	NO
2300282024	02/28/1990	2,368	19	2,004	4,391	YES
2300289000	08/04/1990	34,998	310,271	380	345,649	NO
2300290000	07/18/1990	125,908	1,005,297	118,267	1,249,472	NO
2300613100	03/21/1990	692	1,258	212,528	214,478	NO
2300620000	09/12/1990	45,835	73,523	4,753	124,111	NO
2300631000	08/06/1990	597,919	295,647	57,720	951,286	NO
2300652000	04/17/1990	29,804	36,512	1,437	67,753	YES

Figure 10-6. Example ASCII file for Program 10-1.

Program 10-1 creates a temporary file consisting of a single 80-character field and loads the raw report data into it. Next, it scans each record, parsing the string into individual fields. Some, such as numerics, require special processing to remove commas.

```
* Program 10-1
* Loads ASCII file into a temporary database.
* Then it rereads the data and parses it into
* individual fields.

* Set environment
  SET TALK OFF
  SET STATUS OFF
  SET SCOREBOARD OFF
  CLOSE ALL
  CLEAR

* Get input data file name
  infile = SPACE(50)
  infile = GETFILE('','Select input ASCII file')

* Define record length large enough for ASCII file
  inlen = 80

* Create temporary file
  IF FILE('tempstru.dbf')
     ERASE tempstru.dbf
  ENDIF
  tempfile = SYS(3)
  USE construc
  COPY STRUCTURE EXTENDED TO tempstru
  USE tempstru
  DELETE ALL
  PACK
  APPEND BLANK
  REPLACE field_name WITH 'STRING'
  REPLACE field_type WITH 'CHARACTER'
  REPLACE field_len  WITH m->inlen
  CLOSE DATABASES
  CREATE &tempfile FROM tempstru
  CLOSE databases
  ERASE tempstru.dbf
  USE &tempfile
  APPEND FROM &infile TYPE SDF

* Scan temporary file, parse data, and load it into
* construc.dbf
  SELECT 2
  USE construc
  DELETE ALL
```

```
PACK
SELECT 1
USE &tempfile

SCAN
SELECT 1
   arecord  = string
   account  = SUBSTR(arecord,1,10)
   chardate = '{'+SUBSTR(arecord,12,10)+'}'
   date     = &chardate
   labor    = getnum(SUBSTR(arecord,22,11))
   material = getnum(SUBSTR(arecord,33,12))
   other    = getnum(SUBSTR(arecord,45, 9))
   total    = getnum(SUBSTR(arecord,54,12))
   overtime = IIF(SUBSTR(arecord,67,3) = 'YES',.T.,.F.)
   SELECT 2
   APPEND BLANK
   GATHER MEMVAR
ENDSCAN

* Close all databases and erase temporary database
CLOSE DATABASES
ERASE &tempfile..dbf

RETURN

***************PROCEDURES AND FUNCTIONS*******************

FUNCTION getnum
PARAMETER snum

* Converts a string to a number by removing commas and
* other incidentals. It does this by reading one
* character at a time and comparing it to a valid list.
* It passes only valid characters to the variable news
* so it can use VAL to convert news to a numeric.
news = ''
snum = ALLTRIM(snum)
sign = IIF(LEFT(snum,1) = '-', -1, 1)
lenstr = LEN(snum)
FOR i = 1 TO lenstr
   IF SUBSTR(snum,i,1) $ '1234567890.'
     news = news + SUBSTR(snum,i,1)
   ENDIF
ENDFOR
RETURN sign * VAL(news)

* End of program
```

Program 10-1. Loading Data via a Temporary Database

Low-Level Commands and Data Transfers

Program 10-1 assumes enough disk capacity for another copy of the raw data. For large files, this may not be available. Then we must read and parse the data simultaneously. Low-level functions (see Chapter 2) let us do exactly that. They provide programmers with more control over reading and writing ASCII files than COPY TO or APPEND FROM.

Program 10-2 uses low-level functions to read an ASCII file. After some initialization, it asks the user for the file's name. As the program uses GETFILE to display available files, we know the name is valid and the file exists.

The program next tries to open the file in read-only mode. We will not write to it, so write buffers are unnecessary. Even though we know the name is valid, we still check FOPEN's return value just in case FoxPro has a problem opening the file.

The program then loops through the file reading each record. The FEOF() in the DO WHILE statement detects end of file. FGETS() reads the entire record into a memory variable and parses it as in Program 10-1. However, since we can control the actual number of bytes read at one time with either FGETS() or FREAD(), we can get exactly the number of characters needed for each field.

Program 10-1 consists of two steps. First it reads the data and writes it to a temporary file. Then it reads it again before writing the final record. Program 10-2 reads the data and processes it immediately before writing it to CONSTRUC.DBF. Its main advantages are reduced disk storage needs and less string manipulation.

After we finish reading the raw data, FCLOSE() closes the ASCII file. Thus, Program 10-2 can read the same input as Program 10-1, but without requiring a temporary file.

```
* Program 10-2
* Reads ASCII file using low-level functions

* Set environment
  SET TALK OFF
  SET STATUS OFF
  SET SCOREBOARD OFF
  CLOSE ALL
  CLEAR
  DEFINE WINDOW ferr FROM 15,5 TO 20,75 ;
      TITLE 'LOW-LEVEL FILE ERROR ENCOUNTERED' ;
      DOUBLE SHADOW COLOR SCHEME 5

* Get input data file name
```

```
    infile = SPACE(50)
    infile = GETFILE('','Select input ASCII file')

* Open ASCII file to check length
    filenum = FOPEN(infile)
    IF m->filenum < 0
      DO filerror
    ENDIF

* Loop through ASCII file
* Parse data and load it into CONSTRUC.DBF
    SELECT 1
    USE construc
    DELETE ALL
    PACK

    DO WHILE .NOT. FEOF(filenum)
      account  = ALLTRIM(FGETS(filenum,11))
      chardate = '{'+FGETS(filenum,10)+'}'
      date     = &chardate
      labor    = getnum(FGETS(filenum,11))
      material = getnum(FGETS(filenum,12))
      other    = getnum(FGETS(filenum, 9))
      total    = getnum(FGETS(filenum,12))
      overtime = IIF(ALLTRIM(FGETS(filenum)) = 'YES',.T.,.F.)
      APPEND BLANK
      GATHER MEMVAR
    ENDDO

* Close all databases and erase temporary database
    = FCLOSE(filenum)

RETURN


***************PROCEDURES AND FUNCTIONS*****************

FUNCTION getnum
PARAMETER snum

* Converts a string to a number by removing commas and
* other incidentals. It does this by reading one
* character at a time and comparing it to a valid list.
* It passes only valid characters to the variable news
* so it can use VAL to convert news to a numeric.
    news = ''
    snum = ALLTRIM(snum)
    sign = IIF(LEFT(snum,1) = '-', -1, 1)
    lenstr = LEN(snum)
    FOR i = 1 TO lenstr
      IF SUBSTR(snum,i,1) $ '1234567890.'
        news = news + SUBSTR(snum,i,1)
      ENDIF
    ENDFOR
RETURN sign * VAL(news)
```

```
PROCEDURE FILERROR
* Checks for file errors
  ACTIVATE WINDOW ferr
  xerr = FERROR()
  DO CASE
    CASE xerr = 2
      @ 1,3 SAY 'FILE NOT FOUND'
    CASE xerr = 4
      @ 1,3 SAY 'TOO MANY FILES OPEN (OUT OF HANDLES)'
    CASE xerr = 5
      @ 1,3 SAY 'ACCESS DENIED'
    CASE xerr = 6
      @ 1,3 SAY 'INVALID FILE HANDLE'
    CASE xerr = 8
      @ 1,3 SAY 'OUT OF MEMORY'
    CASE xerr = 25
      @ 1,3 SAY 'SEEK ERROR (CANNOT SEEK BEFORE START '+;
              'OF FILE)'
    CASE xerr = 29
      @ 1,3 SAY 'DISK FULL'
    CASE xerr = 31
      @ 1,3 SAY 'ERROR OPENING FILE OR GENERAL FAILURE '+;
              '(EOF ENCOUNTERED)'
  ENDCASE

  WAIT 'Press any key to continue'
  DEACTIVATE WINDOW
  EXIT

RETURN

* End of program
```

Program 10-2. Reading Data with Low-Level File Functions

As a final example of using low-level functions, Program 10-3 formats a FoxPro program. It first renames the file by changing its extension to OLD. It then reads one line at a time, looking for FoxPro keywords. It capitalizes them, while forcing all other characters not in strings or remarks to lowercase. After reformatting the string, it writes it to a new file with the same name as the original. Program 10-3 uses FGETS() to read strings and FPUTS() to write reformatted ones. It gets FoxPro keywords from the file PROWORDS.FXD.

```
* Program 10-3
* Uses low-level functions to read a PRG file, parse
* each command to capitalize FoxPro keywords,
* and write a new version.
```

```
* Set environment
SET TALK OFF
SET STATUS OFF
SET SCOREBOARD OFF
CLOSE ALL
CLEAR
DEFINE WINDOW ferr FROM 15,5 TO 20,75 DOUBLE ;
    COLOR SCHEME 5 SHADOW ;
    TITLE 'LOW-LEVEL FILE ERROR ENCOUNTERED'

* First check if the temporary file FOXWORDS.DBF exists
* from a previous execution of this program.
*
* If it does not, create a new database file. Since
* there is no direct way to do this, use a series of steps:
*
*     - open any database
*     - copy its structure to FOXWSTRU.DBF
*     - delete all records from FOXWSTRU so we can
*       redefine it
*     - add a single record with three fields:
*           'STRING'     -> field_name
*           'CHARACTER' -> field_type
*           15           -> field_len
*     - create FOXWORDS.DBF from this structure
*
* Next, append the records from PROWORDS.FXD to the new
* database. Lines that begin with an asterisk are comments
* that must be removed. Lines that begin with !, @, or %
* affect how the command appears in the cross reference
* produced by FoxDoc. Remove the markers.
*
    IF .NOT. FILE('foxwords.dbf')
      USE lender
      COPY STRUCTURE EXTENDED TO foxwstru
      USE foxwstru
      DELETE ALL
      PACK
      APPEND BLANK
      REPLACE field_name WITH 'STRING'
      REPLACE field_type WITH 'CHARACTER'
      REPLACE field_len WITH 15
      CLOSE DATABASES
      CREATE foxwords FROM foxwstru
      CLOSE DATABASES
      ERASE foxwstru.dbf
      USE foxwords
      APPEND FROM prowords.fxd TYPE SDF
      DELETE ALL FOR LEFT(string,1) = '*'
      REPLACE ALL string WITH RIGHT(string,LEN(string)-1) ;
      FOR LEFT(string,1) $ '!@%'
```

```
      PACK
      INDEX ON string TO foxwords
   ENDIF

* Get input data file name
   infile = SPACE(50)
   infile = GETFILE('PRG','Select FoxPro Source Program')
   oldfile = LEFT(infile,LEN(infile)-4)+'.Z_Z'
   RENAME &infile TO &oldfile

* Scan temporary file, parse data, and load it into
* construction database file
   SELECT 1
   USE foxwords INDEX foxwords

* Open program file and read through it a line at a time
   prgfile = FOPEN(oldfile,0)
   newfile = FCREATE(infile,0)
   IF newfile < 0 .OR. prgfile < 0
     DO FILERROR
   ENDIF
   SELECT 1
   cr = CHR(0)
   strout = ''

* Check for end of file
   DO WHILE .NOT. FEOF(prgfile)
     testword = ''
     charin = FGETS(prgfile,1)

   * Check for a remark line
     IF charin = '*'
       testword = charin + FGETS(prgfile)
       wrotechars = FPUTS(newfile,testword)
       IF wrotechars = 0
         DO FILERROR
       ENDIF
       LOOP
     ENDIF

   * Look for specific characters indicating the end
   * of a word
     DO WHILE .NOT. (charin $ ',=+-*/^( ') .AND. ;
             ASC(charin) # 0
       testword = testword + charin

     * Beginning with a single quotation mark
       IF charin = "'"
         strout = strout + charin
         testword = ' '
         DO WHILE .T.
           charin = FGETS(prgfile,1)
           strout = strout + charin
```

```
          IF charin = "'"
             EXIT
          ENDIF
       ENDDO
    ENDIF

  * Beginning with a double quotation mark
    IF charin = '"'
       strout = strout + charin
       testword = ' '
       DO WHILE .T.
          charin = FGETS(prgfile,1)
          strout = strout + charin
          IF charin = '"'
             EXIT
          ENDIF
       ENDDO
    ENDIF
    charin = FGETS(prgfile,1)

  ENDDO

* Check if word is a FoxPro keyword. If so, make all
* characters uppercase. Otherwise, make them
* lowercase.
  SEEK UPPER(m->testword)
  IF FOUND()
     strout = strout + UPPER(m->testword)
  ELSE
     strout = strout + LOWER(m->testword)
  ENDIF
* Check for end of line. If found, write reformatted
* line to disk. Otherwise, just append last character
* to output string.
  IF ASC(charin) = 0
     wrotechars = FPUTS(newfile,strout)
     IF wrotechars = 0
        DO FILERROR
     ENDIF
     strout = ''
  ELSE
     strout = strout + charin
  ENDIF

ENDDO

* Close all databases and erase temporary database
  CLOSE DATABASES
  = FCLOSE(prgfile)
  = FCLOSE(newfile)

RETURN

***************PROCEDURES AND FUNCTIONS*******************
```

```
PROCEDURE FILERROR
* Checks for file errors
  ACTIVATE WINDOW ferr
  xerr = FERROR()
  DO CASE
     CASE xerr = 2
       @ 1,3 SAY 'FILE NOT FOUND'
     CASE xerr = 4
       @ 1,3 SAY 'TOO MANY FILES OPEN (OUT OF HANDLES)'
     CASE xerr = 5
       @ 1,3 SAY 'ACCESS DENIED'
     CASE xerr = 6
       @ 1,3 SAY 'INVALID FILE HANDLE'
     CASE xerr = 8
       @ 1,3 SAY 'OUT OF MEMORY'
     CASE xerr = 25
       @ 1,3 SAY 'SEEK ERROR (CAN'T SEEK BEFORE '+;
                  'START OF FILE)'
     CASE xerr = 29
       @ 1,3 SAY 'DISK FULL'
     CASE xerr = 31
       @ 1,3 SAY 'ERROR OPENING FILE OR GENERAL FAILURE '+;
                  '(EOF ENCOUNTERED)'
  ENDCASE

  WAIT 'Press any key to continue'
  DEACTIVATE WINDOW ferr
  EXIT

RETURN

* End of program
```

Program 10-3. Formatting FoxPro Programs with Low-Level File Functions

---

Summary

This chapter examined ways to transfer data to and from database files. We saw that the simplest method moves it between databases directly. Another simple transfer involves an ASCII file. Unfortunately, although the COPY TO and APPEND FROM commands make working with ASCII files easy, they do require specific formats.

For ASCII files in other formats, we must manipulate individual bytes. We examined two ways to perform these more difficult transfers. The first appends data into a temporary database from which we parse the individual fields. The second involves reading and writing ASCII files directly using low-level functions.

11

FoxPro File Structures

This chapter describes FoxPro's major file structures. Its purpose is to provide information required to use FoxPro files from other languages. The structures examined include:

DBF	Database files
FPT	Memo files
FRX	Report files
IDX	Index files
LBX	Label files
MEM	Memory variable files

Database Files

The most important FoxPro structure is the database (DBF) file that contains the data. It consists of two parts, header and database records. Let's start with the header.

DBF Header – Part 1

The header consists of two parts. The first (Table 11-1) is always 32 bytes long.

File Type

A FoxPro database can be of two types. If it has at least one memo field, the value is F5h; otherwise, it is 03h. Values other than those listed in Table 11-1 cause FoxPro to report

```
Not a database file.
```

Table 11-1. Structure of the First Part of the DBF Header

Byte Number	Description
1	File type identifier
	03 – DBF without memo (FoxBASE+ / FoxPro / dBASE III PLUS / dBASE IV)
	83 – DBF with memo (FoxBASE+ / dBASE III PLUS)
	8B – dBASE III with memo
	F5 – FoxPro with memo
2-4	Date of last update (YYMMDD)
5-8	Number of records in file
9-10	Offset to start of data
11-12	Size of record
13-28	Not used
29	Flag for compound index
30-32	Not used

Last Update Date

The date is in hexadecimal. The first byte contains the last two digits of the year, the second the month, and the third the day. For example, the three bytes

    5A   0A   0B

identify the last update as occurring on October 11, 1990 (5A = 90, 0A = 10, and 0B = 11). If you have trouble with hexadecimal conversions (most people do unless they have 16 fingers), you should buy either a calculator or a computer utility (such as PC Tools) that does base conversions. Both are widely available at low cost.

Number of Records in the Database

This number includes ones marked for deletion, but not packed. FoxPro stores the value in byte-reversed format with the least significant byte first. Therefore, the four bytes

    3B   01   00   00

mean 13B hexadecimal or 305 decimal. The RECCOUNT() function gets its return value from here. That is why it is wrong if the database contains deleted records that have not been packed. They are still in the file (gone but not forgotten!). Only after packing will RECCOUNT() return the correct result.

Offset to Start of Data

This is the offset (in reversed form) from the beginning of the file to the first data record. For example, the two bytes 41 02 indicate that the first record begins 0241h or 577 decimal bytes from the beginning of the file.

Record Length

The record is one byte larger than the sum of the field sizes because of the deletion flag.

Compound Index Flag

The 29th byte is a flag indicating the presence of a structural compound index. If that index is deleted via the DOS DELETE or ERASE command, FoxPro displays the message

```
STRUCTURAL CDX FILE NOT FOUND
```

the next time we try to open the database. To delete a compound index properly, open the database and issue the command

```
DELETE TAG ALL
```

It clears the flag as well as deleting the index.

Other Bytes

FoxPro does not use the rest of part 1. It is generally all zeros (null characters).

DBF Header – Part 2

The second part of the header depends on the number of fields in the database. It uses 32 bytes per field, organized as shown in Table 11-2. There is also a single terminator byte (0D hex or 13 decimal) at the very end.

Table 11-2. Field Definition Structure

Byte Number	Description
1-11	Field name
12	Field type
13-14	Offset of field from beginning of record
15-16	Not used
17-18	Field length [non-numeric fields]
17	Field length [numeric fields]
18	Field decimals [numeric fields]
19-32	Not used

Field Name

Although FoxPro limits field names to ten characters, the structure provides room for eleven. The last (rightmost) one must be null (zero). If the name has less than ten characters, the first one to its right must be null. We can either pad the remaining bytes (with nulls) or ignore them.

Field Type

The field type is one of five ASCII values listed in Table 11-3.

Table 11-3. Field Type Values

Type	ASCII Character	Decimal	Hex
Character	C	67	43
Date	D	68	44
Logical	L	76	4C
Memo	M	77	4D
Numeric	N	78	4E

Field Length

The field length definition depends on the data type. For character fields, two bytes at positions 17 and 18 define the size (in reversed format). Memo, date, and logical fields need only the first byte to define their sizes, which are fixed at 10, 8, and 1, respectively. For numeric data, the first byte specifies the total number of digits, and the second the number of decimal places.

Remaining Bytes

The field definition does not use the rest of the 32 bytes. They usually contain nulls (zeros).

Determining the End of Field Definitions

FoxPro does not store the number of field definitions in the header. There are three ways to determine when we have read all the fields. The first is to sum the lengths. The last field has been read when the total equals the record length stored in the header minus 1 for the deletion flag. The second method is to look for 0D (hex) or 13 decimal as the first character after a field definition. It separates the header from the beginning of the data. Remember the extra byte when determining the size of a DBF header. The third method counts the total number of bytes read and compares it to the data offset value in the first part of the header.

Database Data

The actual data begins immediately after the header's terminator byte. The first byte of each record is its deletion flag. If it is 20h (an ASCII space), the record is active. If it is 2Ah (an ASCII asterisk), the record has been marked for deletion.

The next byte is the first byte of the first field. There are no separators between fields, as there is no need for them. The record definition section specifies each field's exact size and position.

Character Fields

Character fields are the easiest to read. Each byte, arranged from left to right, holds one character. To determine the field's contents, just convert the hexadecimal values to ASCII. Use FoxPro's ASCII table in the System pulldown.

Date Fields

Dates are also easy to interpret. Each occupies eight bytes. The first four are the year, followed by two for the month and two for the day. The bytes are ASCII digits (30-39 hex correspond to 0-9 decimal). For example, the date August 4, 1988 appears as:

Y	Y	Y	Y	M	M	D	D	(format)
31	39	38	38	30	38	30	34	(hex)
1	9	8	8	0	8	0	4	(decimal)

Amazingly enough, the digits are in normal order.

Logical Fields

FoxPro stores logical values using the ASCII characters F and T. That is, it stores a logical false as 46h, and true as 54h.

Memo Fields

Memo fields use 10 bytes in each record. If the field is empty, all ten are 20h (an ASCII space). If a memo exists, ASCII characters define its position (in 64-byte blocks) in the FPT file. If the ten bytes are:

20	20	20	20	20	20	20	20	33	38	(hex)
–	–	–	–	–	–	–	–	3	8	(decimal)

the memo data begins after the 38th 64-byte block.

Numeric Fields

FoxPro stores numeric fields as individual ASCII numbers. It defines the number of digits through the database structure. For example, suppose we define a numeric field to store investment interest rates as six characters with three decimal places. Furthermore, the number we want to store is 11.725. It appears as:

```
31   31   2E   37   32   35     (hex)
 1    1    .    7    2    5      (decimal)
```

Note the decimal point (2Eh in ASCII). Unused positions to the left of it are blank filled (character 20h). Ones to the right are zero filled (character 30h). Therefore, a value of 8.5 appears as:

```
20   38   2E   35   30   30     (hex)
 _    8    .    5    0    0      (decimal)
```

End-of-File Character

After the last record, FoxPro places an end-of-file character (1Ah). Remember this extra byte when determining the size of a DBF file. Note that it differs from the end of header character (0Dh).

Example DBF File

> **EXERCISE**
>
> Before proceeding to another file type, let's examine a hexadecimal dump of a few sectors of LENDER.DBF. Figure 11-1 defines its structure and contents. See if you can confirm the following information.

Header Contents	Value	Byte
Does the file have a memo field?	Yes	01
Last update date	10/13/90	02-04
Number of records in file	14	05-08
Offset to start of data	577	09-10
Size of record	178	11-12

Database Structure:

Field	Type	Size	Decimal Places
L_ID	C	6	
L_NAME	C	25	
L_ADDR1	C	25	

L_ADDR2	C	25	
L_CITY	C	20	
L_STATE	C	2	
L_ZIP	C	10	
L_PHONE	C	13	
L_EXT	C	4	
L_TAX_ID	C	10	
L_CURRATE	N	6	3
L_RATEDATE	D	8	
L_VRM	L	1	
L_RRM	L	1	
L_WRAP	L	1	
L_NOTES	M	10	
N_NOTES	M	10	

First Record Contents:

Field	Value	Offset
L_ID	AB	1
L_NAME	American Bank	7
L_ADDR1	540 Lancaster Ave	32
L_ADDR2		57
L_CITY	Shillington	82
L_STATE	PA	102
L_ZIP	19607	104
L_PHONE	(215)378-7931	114
L_EXT		127
L_TAX_ID	23-4421123	131
L_CURRATE	11.750	141
L_RATEDATE	01/03/1990	147
L_VRM	T	155
L_RRM	T	156
L_WRAP	T	157
L_NOTES		158
N_NOTES		168

```
Sector 1:
 Dec  Hex
0000(0000) F5 5A 0A 0D 0E 00 00 00 41 02 B2 00 00 00 00 00
0016(0010) 00 00 00 00 00 00 00 00 00 00 00 00 00 00 00 00
0032(0020) 4C 5F 49 44 00 00 0B D3 34 D3 55 43 01 00 00 00
0048(0030) 06 00 00 00 00 00 00 00 00 00 00 00 00 00 00 00
0064(0040) 4C 5F 4E 41 4D 45 00 D3 34 D3 55 43 07 00 00 00
0080(0050) 19 00 00 00 00 00 00 00 00 00 00 00 00 00 00 00
0096(0060) 4C 5F 41 44 44 52 31 00 34 D3 55 43 20 00 00 00
0112(0070) 19 00 00 00 00 00 00 00 00 00 00 00 00 00 00 00
0128(0080) 4C 5F 41 44 44 52 32 00 34 D3 55 43 39 00 00 00
0144(0090) 19 00 00 00 00 00 00 00 00 00 00 00 00 00 00 00
0160(00A0) 4C 5F 43 49 54 59 00 00 34 D3 55 43 52 00 00 00
0176(00B0) 14 00 00 00 00 00 00 00 00 00 00 00 00 00 00 00
0192(00C0) 4C 5F 53 54 41 54 45 00 34 D3 55 43 66 00 00 00
0208(00D0) 02 00 00 00 00 00 00 00 00 00 00 00 00 00 00 00
0224(00E0) 4C 5F 5A 49 50 00 45 00 34 D3 55 43 68 00 00 00
0240(00F0) 0A 00 00 00 00 00 00 00 00 00 00 00 00 00 00 00
0256(0100) 4C 5F 50 48 4F 4E 45 00 34 D3 55 43 72 00 00 00
0272(0110) 0D 00 00 00 00 00 00 00 00 00 00 00 00 00 00 00
0288(0120) 4C 5F 45 58 54 00 45 00 34 D3 55 43 7F 00 00 00
0304(0130) 04 00 00 00 00 00 00 00 00 00 00 00 00 00 00 00
0320(0140) 4C 5F 54 41 58 5F 49 44 00 D3 55 43 83 00 00 00
0336(0150) 0A 00 00 00 00 00 00 00 00 00 00 00 00 00 00 00
0352(0160) 4C 5F 43 55 52 52 41 54 45 00 55 4E 8D 00 00 00
0368(0170) 06 03 00 00 00 00 00 00 00 00 00 00 00 00 00 00
0384(0180) 4C 5F 52 41 54 45 44 41 54 45 00 44 93 00 00 00
0400(0190) 08 00 00 00 00 00 00 00 00 00 00 00 00 00 00 00
0416(01A0) 4C 5F 56 52 4D 00 44 41 54 45 00 4C 9B 00 00 00
0432(01B0) 01 00 00 00 00 00 00 00 00 00 00 00 00 00 00 00
0448(01C0) 4C 5F 52 52 4D 00 44 41 54 45 00 4C 9C 00 00 00
0464(01D0) 01 00 00 00 00 00 00 00 00 00 00 00 00 00 00 00
0480(01E0) 4C 5F 57 52 41 50 00 41 54 45 00 4C 9D 00 00 00
0496(01F0) 01 00 00 00 00 00 00 00 00 00 00 00 00 00 00 00

Section 2:
 Dec  Hex
0000(0000) 4C 5F 4E 4F 54 45 53 00 54 45 00 4D 9E 00 00 00
0016(0010) 0A 00 00 00 00 00 00 00 00 00 00 00 00 00 00 00
0032(0020) 4E 5F 4E 4F 54 45 53 00 54 45 00 4D A8 00 00 00
0048(0030) 0A 00 00 00 00 00 00 00 00 00 00 00 00 00 00 00
0064(0040) 0D 20 41 42 20 20 20 20 41 6D 65 72 69 63 61 6E
0080(0050) 20 42 61 6E 6B 20 20 20 20 20 20 20 20 20 20 20
0096(0060) 20 35 34 30 20 4C 61 6E 63 61 73 74 65 72 20 41
0112(0070) 76 65 20 20 20 20 20 20 20 20 20 20 20 20 20 20
0128(0080) 20 20 20 20 20 20 20 20 20 20 20 20 20 20 20 20
0144(0090) 20 20 20 53 68 69 6C 6C 69 6E 67 74 6F 6E 20 20
0160(00A0) 20 20 20 20 20 20 20 50 41 31 39 36 30 37 20 20
0176(00B0) 20 20 20 28 32 31 35 29 33 37 38 2D 37 39 33 31
0192(00C0) 20 20 20 20 32 33 2D 34 34 33 31 31 32 33 31 31
0208(00D0) 2E 37 35 30 31 39 39 30 30 31 30 33 54 54 54 20
0224(00E0) 20 20 20 20 20 20 20 33 37 20 20 20 20 20 20 20
0240(00F0) 20 33 38
```

Figure 11-1. Hexadecimal dump of a DBF file.

Index Files

FoxPro supports three types of indexes:

- Standard single-key
- Compact single-key
- Compound multiple-key

Single-key index files use IDX as their extension, multiple-key ones use CDX. We analyze the standard single-key structure first, then the compound multiple-key structure.

Standard Index Header

Standard index files begin with the 512-byte header described in Table 11-4.

Table 11-4. Standard Index Header

Byte Number	Description
1-4	Pointer to root node
5-8	Pointer to free node list (next available 512-byte block). -1 or FF FF FF FF if no list is present.
9-12	Size of file in bytes
13-14	Length of the key in bytes
15	Flag – 0 Standard index file only
	1 Index file with UNIQUE
	8 Conditional index file
	9 Conditional and UNIQUE file
16	Not used
17-236	Index expression
237-456	For condition expression
457-512	Not used

Pointer to Root Node

This hexadecimal byte-reversed value is where FoxPro begins its search through the index. It represents the number of bytes from the beginning of the index file to the start of the root node.

Pointer to Free Node List

This value is often -1 (FF FF FF FF), indicating no free node list. When one is present, the pointer specifies the next available 512-byte block. It is used only when that block is not at the end of the index file.

Size of Index File

The size is in bytes. For example, a value of 00 1E 00 00 in byte-reversed notation defines the file size as 1E00 hex or 7680 bytes.

Length of Key

If we define the key using a 20 character last name, these bytes are:

```
    14   00   (hex)
```

Note that 0014 hex = 20 decimal.

Index Options

This field specifies whether the index uses special features, namely UNIQUE and FOR.

UNIQUE tells FoxPro to include only records with unique keys. It does not prevent the user from adding records with duplicate keys to the database. They just will not appear in the index. If we have SET UNIQUE ON before defining the index, or if we include the UNIQUE option in the INDEX command, FoxPro adds 1 to this byte.

FoxPro supports a FOR condition option during index definition. When we use one, FoxPro adds 8 to byte 15 of the index header.

If we use both features in a definition, FoxPro adds 1 and 8 and puts 9 in byte 15. Of course, if we use neither, the byte is zero.

Key Expression

The next 220 bytes contain the key field expression, an ASCII null-terminated string. The expression type is not stored. FoxPro determines it when it uses the key.

Conditional Expression

The conditional expression used by the FOR clause also occupies a maximum of 220 bytes. The FOR clause indexes a subset of the database without requiring a separate SET FILTER expression. FoxPro stores the conditional clause as an ASCII null-terminated string.

Remainder of Header

The rest of the header is neither used nor specified. Since it may contain random values, we should ignore it.

Standard Nodes

FoxPro stores index data in 512-byte segments called *nodes*. The first 12 bytes form a header (Table 11-5). It contains the node's type (index, root, leaf, or leaf and root), number of keys, and pointers to its predecessor and successor.

Root Node

The root node is the first one FoxPro jumps to when it begins searching for a
key value in the index. The root node can contain:

- Key values along with pointers to the DBF file for small files
  having short index values (Figure 11-2). The number in
  parentheses identifies the node type.

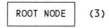

Figure 11-2. Root node.

- Key values that point to other nodes called *leaf nodes* that
  contain values less than or equal to the one in the root node.
  The values in the leaf nodes point to corresponding records
  in the DBF file (Figure 11-3).

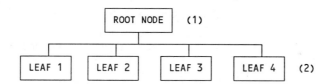

Figure 11-3. Root and leaf nodes.

- Key values that point to other nodes called *index nodes*. They
  contain values less than or equal to the one in the root node.
  They in turn point to other index nodes or leaf nodes that contain values less than or equal to their contents (Figure 11-4).

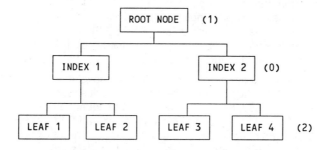

Figure 11-4. Root, index, and leaf nodes.

(The numbers in parentheses in Figures 11-1 through 11-3 indicate the node type value for each level. See Table 11-5 for definitions.)

Index Node

FoxPro uses index nodes when there are more leaf node references than a single root node can hold. In such cases, the root node splits the references. The pointer associated with each value in the index node refers to another node in the index file. It is called an *intra-index pointer*.

Leaf Node

The leaf node is the lowest level. All key values from the database occur in one somewhere in the index file. Each value in a leaf node points to a corresponding record in the DBF file.

Table 11-5. Node Header

Byte	Description
1-2	Type of Node: 0 *Index node* – Contains key values and points to other index or leaf nodes
	1 *Root node* – The first node searched by FoxPro. Contains references to index or leaf nodes.
	2 *Leaf node* – Contains key values and points to records in DBF file.
	3 *Leaf and root node* – Occurs with small files where all keys fit into one 256-byte segment.
3-4	Number of keys in this 512-byte node. FoxPro must fit an entire key within a node; it cannot split values between nodes. This restriction limits the theoretical size of a key.
5-8	Points to the prior node on the same level (in terms of bytes from the beginning of the file). Leaf nodes point to prior leaf nodes, and index nodes to prior index nodes. The first node on any level has the value FF FF FF FF. Other nodes define the number of bytes from the beginning of the file to the start of the prior node.
9-12	Points to the next node on the same level in terms of bytes from the beginning of the file. Leaf nodes point to subsequent leaf nodes, and index nodes to subsequent index nodes. The last node at any level has the value FF FF FF FF. Nodes need not appear in order. Therefore, always use the next node value to read the database sequentially.

Index Data

The actual index data follows the node header. It consists of sets of key values and pointers. The values are the data from the database. FoxPro stores them in sorted order. In a leaf node, the four bytes after each value point to the database record to which it belongs. In other nodes, they contain an intra-index pointer to another index node that contains values less than or equal to the current node's.

Figure 11-5 shows the hexadecimal dump of the first 768 bytes of the LENDER.IDX file. The index uses the six-character field L_ID. UNIQUE was active when we created it. The file contains 1024 bytes divided into two 512-byte segments. The root node begins after the 512-byte header. It has a type of 03h since it is the only node needed in this small index. It has 14 key values so it is therefore both a root and a leaf node. The first record in index order is lender AB which also happens to be the first record in the database. See if you can derive this information on your own.

Compound Indexes

Table 11-6 shows the header structure for a compound index. It defines the type of index along with the sizes of the key and FOR clause. The key and FOR clause occupy a separate 512-byte segment immediately after the header.

Table 11-6. Compound Index Header

Bytes	Description
1-4	Pointer to root node
5-8	Pointer to free node list (-1 if absent)
9-12	Reserved
13-14	Key length
15	Index options: 1 – unique 8 – FOR clause 32 – compact index 64 – compound index
16	Reserved
17-502	Reserved
503-504	Ascending or descending: 0 – ascending 1 – descending
505-506	Reserved
507-508	FOR expression length
509-510	Reserved
511-512	Key expression length

Table 11-7 defines a compound interior node. It may be an index or root node; it is the same as a standard index node described in Table 11-5.

```
Segment 1:
Dec  Hex
0000(0000) 00 02 00 00 FF FF FF FF 00 04 00 00 06 00 00 00
0016(0010) 4C 5F 49 44 00 00 00 00 00 00 00 00 00 00 00 00
0032(0020) 00 00 00 00 00 00 00 00 00 00 00 00 00 00 00 00
0048(0030) 00 00 00 00 00 00 00 00 00 00 00 00 00 00 00 00
0064(0040) 00 00 00 00 00 00 00 00 00 00 00 00 00 00 00 00
0080(0050) 00 00 00 00 00 00 00 00 00 00 00 00 00 00 00 00
0096(0060) 00 00 00 00 00 00 00 00 00 00 00 00 00 00 00 00
0112(0070) 00 00 00 00 00 00 00 00 00 00 00 00 00 00 00 00
0128(0080) 00 00 00 00 00 00 00 00 00 00 00 00 00 00 00 00
0144(0090) 00 00 00 00 00 00 00 00 00 00 00 00 00 00 00 00
0160(00A0) 00 00 00 00 00 00 00 00 00 00 00 00 00 00 00 00
0176(00B0) 00 00 00 00 00 00 00 00 00 00 00 00 00 00 00 00
0192(00C0) 00 00 00 00 00 00 00 00 00 00 00 00 00 00 00 00
0208(00D0) 00 00 00 00 00 00 00 00 00 00 00 00 00 00 00 00
0224(00E0) 00 00 00 00 00 00 00 00 00 00 00 00 00 00 00 00
0240(00F0) 00 00 00 00 00 00 00 00 00 00 00 00 00 00 00 00
0256(0100) 00 00 00 00 00 00 00 00 00 00 00 00 00 00 00 00
0272(0110) 00 00 00 00 00 00 00 00 00 00 00 00 00 00 00 00
0288(0120) 00 00 00 00 00 00 00 00 00 00 00 00 00 00 00 00
0304(0130) 00 00 00 00 00 00 00 00 00 00 00 00 00 00 00 00
0320(0140) 00 00 00 00 00 00 00 00 00 00 00 00 00 00 00 00
0336(0150) 00 00 00 00 00 00 00 00 00 00 00 00 00 00 00 00
0352(0160) 00 00 00 00 00 00 00 00 00 00 00 00 00 00 00 00
0368(0170) 00 00 00 00 00 00 00 00 00 00 00 00 00 00 00 00
0384(0180) 00 00 00 00 00 00 00 00 00 00 00 00 00 00 00 00
0400(0190) 00 00 00 00 00 00 00 00 00 00 00 00 00 00 00 00
0416(01A0) 00 00 00 00 00 00 00 00 00 00 00 00 00 00 00 00
0432(01B0) 00 00 00 00 00 00 00 00 00 00 00 00 00 00 00 00
0448(01C0) 00 00 00 00 00 00 00 00 1E 8B 1E 1A 8B 80 3F 00
0464(01D0) 74 11 8A 16 24 8B 30 F6 89 D8 E8 3F 1E C7 06 66
0480(01E0) 12 00 00 83 3E C2 34 00 74 0C 83 3E DA 17 00 7E
0496(01F0) 05 9A 92 DB D2 28 9A 2B D9 D2 28 9A 0D 50 D2 28

Segment 2:
Dec  Hex
0000(0000) 03 00 0E 00 FF FF FF FF FF FF FF FF 41 42 20 20
0016(0010) 20 20 00 00 00 01 42 53 20 20 20 20 00 00 00 02
0032(0020) 47 42 4C 20 20 20 00 00 00 03 47 53 20 20 20 20
0048(0030) 00 00 00 04 48 4E 42 20 20 20 00 00 00 05 4B 50
0064(0040) 42 20 20 20 00 00 00 06 4D 41 42 20 20 20 00 00
0080(0050) 00 07 4D 43 42 20 20 20 00 00 00 08 4D 50 41 20
0096(0060) 20 20 00 00 00 09 4E 42 50 20 20 20 00 00 00 0A
0112(0070) 50 46 20 20 20 20 00 00 00 0B 50 4E 42 20 20 20
0128(0080) 00 00 00 0C 50 53 20 20 20 20 00 00 00 0D 54 54
0144(0090) 20 20 20 20 00 00 00 0E 00 00 00 00 00 00 00 00
0160(00A0) 00 00 00 00 00 00 00 00 00 00 00 00 00 00 00 00
0176(00B0) 00 00 00 00 00 00 00 00 00 00 00 00 00 00 00 00
0192(00C0) 00 00 00 00 00 00 00 00 00 00 00 00 00 00 00 00
0208(00D0) 00 00 00 00 00 00 00 00 00 00 00 00 00 00 00 00
0224(00E0) 00 00 00 00 00 00 00 00 00 00 00 00 00 00 00 00
0240(00F0) 00 00 00 00 00 00 00 00 00 00 00 00 00 00 00 00
```

Figure 11-5. Hexadecimal dump of an IDX file.

Table 11-7. Compound Interior Node

Bytes	Description
1-2	Type of node: 0 – Index node 1 – Root node 2 – Leaf node 3 – Leaf and root node
3-4	Number of keys in this 512-byte node
5-8	Pointer to the prior node on the same level (in bytes from the beginning of the index file)
9-12	Pointer to the next node on the same level (in bytes from the beginning of the index file)
13-512	Key information

Table 11-8 defines a compound exterior node. FoxPro uses it to store the index data. The major changes are fields that define the mask and the number of bits used for record numbers, duplicate counts, and a trail count. The index data itself is split. The compacted record number, duplicate count, and trailing bytes begin at byte 21. However, the corresponding key entries appear at the logical end of the node in reverse order.

Table 11-8. Compound Exterior Node

Bytes	Description
1-2	Type of node: 0 – Index node 1 – Root node 2 – Leaf node 3 – Leaf and root node
3-4	Number of keys in this 512-byte node
5-8	Pointer to the prior node on the same level (in bytes from the beginning of the index file)
9-12	Pointer to the next node on the same level (in bytes from the beginning of the index file)
13-14	Available free space in node
15-18	Record number mask
19	Duplicate count number mask
20	Trail count mask
21	Number of bits used by record number
22	Number of bits used by duplicate count number
23	Number of bits used by trail count
24	Number of bytes required to store the record number, duplicate count, and trail count values
25-512	Key information

Memo Files

FoxPro stores memo data separately from the database in a file with the database's name but an FPT extension. It does not restructure memo files from other systems automatically as it does index files. Instead, it keeps the original format until you do one of the following:

- Modify the parent database's structure
- Copy the database with COPY TO
- Pack the memo file with PACK or PACK MEMO

Memo File Header

The memo file begins with a 512-byte header. However, it contains only two pieces of information as shown in Table 11-9. Both values are hexadecimal numbers in normal left-to-right order.

Table 11-9. Memo File Header

1-4	Number of data blocks in memo file, or location of next free block
5-8	Size of data block

FoxPro uses a data block of only 64 bytes, as compared to 512 in dBASE and Clipper. It can thus use memo fields efficiently for shorter entries. You can change the block size by manually changing the value in the header, but we will assume the default size for simplicity.

Memo Data

Each individual memo starts with an 8-byte header, leaving only 56 characters in the first block for text. The header consists of two fields. The first contains the bytes 00 00 00 01, indicating a new memo value. The second is the memo's length. For example, a value of 00 00 00 F2 means the memo is 242 characters long. Note that although the value is stored in hex, it is not byte-reversed! Together with the 8-byte header, this memo requires four 64-byte blocks or 256 bytes.

Figure 11-6 shows part of the LENDER memo file. The overall header indicates there are forty 64-byte blocks. The first memo contains the following text (240 characters):

The bank has a particularly slow procedure to approve loans. It usually takes at least 30% longer to get loans approved here. However they usually have a rate at least 1/4% better than anyone else. So if you have time, it's worth the wait.

It is followed by a 59 character memo:

American Bank Mortgage Loan System is offering 10.5% loans.

Note that this memo needs two blocks because its length (59 characters) plus 8 (for the header) exceeds 64.

```
Section 1:
 Dec  Hex
0000(0000) 00 00 00 28 00 00 00 40 00 00 00 00 00 00 00 00
0016(0010) 00 00 00 00 00 00 00 00 00 00 00 00 00 00 00 00
0032(0020) 00 00 00 00 00 00 00 00 00 00 00 00 00 00 00 00
0048(0030) 00 00 00 00 00 00 00 00 00 00 00 00 00 00 00 00
0064(0040) 00 00 00 00 00 00 00 00 00 00 00 00 00 00 00 00
0080(0050) 00 00 00 00 00 00 00 00 00 00 00 00 00 00 00 00
0096(0060) 00 00 00 00 00 00 00 00 00 00 00 00 00 00 00 00
0112(0070) 00 00 00 00 00 00 00 00 00 00 00 00 00 00 00 00
0128(0080) 00 00 00 00 00 00 00 00 00 00 00 00 00 00 00 00
0144(0090) 00 00 00 00 00 00 00 00 00 00 00 00 00 00 00 00
0160(00A0) 00 00 00 00 00 00 00 00 00 00 00 00 00 00 00 00
0176(00B0) 00 00 00 00 00 00 00 00 00 00 00 00 00 00 00 00
0192(00C0) 00 00 00 00 00 00 00 00 00 00 00 00 00 00 00 00
0208(00D0) 00 00 00 00 00 00 00 00 00 00 00 00 00 00 00 00
0224(00E0) 00 00 00 00 00 00 00 00 00 00 00 00 00 00 00 00
0240(00F0) 00 00 00 00 00 00 00 00 00 00 00 00 00 00 00 00
0256(0100) 00 00 00 00 00 00 00 00 00 00 00 00 00 00 00 00
0272(0110) 00 00 00 00 00 00 00 00 00 00 00 00 00 00 00 00
0288(0120) 00 00 00 00 00 00 00 00 00 00 00 00 00 00 00 00
0304(0130) 00 00 00 00 00 00 00 00 00 00 00 00 00 00 00 00
0320(0140) 00 00 00 00 00 00 00 00 00 00 00 00 00 00 00 00
0336(0150) 00 00 00 00 00 00 00 00 00 00 00 00 00 00 00 00
0352(0160) 00 00 00 00 00 00 00 00 00 00 00 00 00 00 00 00
0368(0170) 00 00 00 00 00 00 00 00 00 00 00 00 00 00 00 00
0384(0180) 00 00 00 00 00 00 00 00 00 00 00 00 00 00 00 00
0400(0190) 00 00 00 00 00 00 00 00 00 00 00 00 00 00 00 00
0416(01A0) 00 00 00 00 00 00 00 00 00 00 00 00 00 00 00 00
0432(01B0) 00 00 00 00 00 00 00 00 00 00 00 00 00 00 00 00
0448(01C0) 00 00 00 00 00 00 00 00 00 00 00 00 00 00 00 00
0464(01D0) 00 00 00 00 00 00 00 00 00 00 00 00 00 00 00 00
0480(01E0) 00 00 00 00 00 00 00 00 00 00 00 00 00 00 00 00
0496(01F0) 00 00 00 00 00 00 00 00 00 00 00 00 00 00 00 00
```

Figure 11-6. Hexadecimal dump of an FPT file.

```
Section 2:
 Dec  Hex
0000(0000) 00 00 00 01 00 00 00 F2 54 68 65 20 62 61 6E 6B
0016(0010) 20 68 61 73 20 61 20 70 61 72 74 69 63 75 6C 61
0032(0020) 72 6C 79 20 73 6C 6F 77 20 70 72 6F 63 65 64 75
0048(0030) 72 65 20 74 6F 20 61 70 70 72 6F 76 65 20 6C 6F
0064(0040) 61 6E 73 2E 20 20 49 74 20 75 73 75 73 61 6C 6C 79
0080(0050) 20 74 61 6B 65 73 20 61 74 20 6C 65 61 73 74 20
0096(0060) 33 30 25 20 6C 6F 6E 67 65 72 20 74 6F 20 67 65
0112(0070) 74 20 6C 6F 61 6E 73 20 61 70 70 72 6F 76 65 64
0128(0080) 20 68 65 72 65 2E 20 20 48 6F 77 65 76 65 72 20
0144(0090) 74 68 65 79 20 75 73 75 61 6C 6C 79 20 68 61 76
0160(00A0) 65 20 61 20 72 61 74 65 20 61 74 20 6C 65 61 73
0176(00B0) 74 20 31 2F 34 25 20 62 65 74 74 65 72 20 74 68
0192(00C0) 61 6E 20 61 6E 79 6F 6E 65 20 65 6C 73 65 2E 20
0208(00D0) 20 53 6F 20 69 66 20 79 6F 75 20 68 61 76 65 20
0224(00E0) 74 69 6D 65 2C 20 69 74 27 73 20 77 6F 72 74 68
0240(00F0) 20 74 68 65 20 77 61 69 74 2E 65 00 9A 88 9A 00
0256(0100) 00 00 00 01 00 00 00 3B 41 6D 65 72 69 63 61 6E
0272(0110) 20 42 61 6E 6B 20 4D 6F 72 74 67 61 67 65 20 4C
0288(0120) 6F 61 6E 20 53 79 73 74 65 6D 20 69 73 20 6F 66 66
0304(0130) 66 65 72 69 6E 67 20 31 30 2E 35 25 20 6C 6F 61
0320(0140) 6E 73 2E 89 D0 9A 88 9A 00 00 8B 46 FC 8B 56 FE
0336(0150) 9A C0 26 43 2D A1 FC 16 89 46 FA C7 06 FC 16 00
0352(0160) 00 31 C0 31 F6 EB 07 89 82 E6 FB 46 46 40 3B 45
0368(0170) 12 7C F4 31 C0 50 8B 4D 12 31 C0 31 D2 8D 9E E6
0384(0180) 00 00 00 01 00 00 00 06 0D 0A 0D 0A 0D 0A 9A 3B
0400(0190) 50 00 00 9A BF 9F 81 1F 9A 25 28 43 2D 83 3E DE
0416(01A0) 14 00 74 08 A1 4C 50 9A BF 4F 00 00 8B 55 08 8B
0432(01B0) 45 0A 8B 5E F8 89 17 89 47 02 C7 06 E2 14 00 00
0448(01C0) 00 00 00 01 00 00 00 34 54 68 69 73 20 69 73 20
0464(01D0) 74 68 65 20 62 65 73 74 20 72 61 74 65 20 79 6F
0480(01E0) 75 20 77 69 6C 6C 20 65 76 65 72 20 67 65 74 20
0496(01F0) 61 72 6F 75 6E 64 20 74 6F 77 6E 2E 00 00 00 00
```

Figure 11-6. Hexadecimal dump of an FPT file (cont'd.)

Memory Variable Files

Memory variable files have no overall header. Instead, each variable has its own structure as shown in Table 11-10. A special marker (1A hex) indicates the end of the entire file.

Table 11-10. Memory Variable File Structure

Byte Number	Description
1-11	Variable name
12	Variable type
13-16	Not used
17-18	Length of variable value if non-numeric. If numeric, byte 17 is the number of digits, and byte 18 the number of decimals.
19-32	Not used
33-	Variable value

How Variables Are Stored

FoxPro stores character strings in ASCII null-terminated form. Thus, a string with 25 characters actually occupies 26 bytes.

It stores logical variables as either zero for false or one for true. Note the difference from the ASCII F or T used in database files.

Dates use an eight byte IEEE format (see the reference at the end of the chapter) to define a day number. The first defined date is 2299161 (that well-known day, Friday, October 15, 1582—don't ask me why!). The format is equivalent to C's double type that can represent magnitudes from 1.7×10^{-308} to $1.7 \times 10^{+308}$ with 15-digit accuracy. The first four bits define the sign and exponent. The rest define the significant digits.

Numeric values also use an eight byte IEEE format (regardless of how FoxPro displays them) as specified by bytes 17 and 18.

Figure 11-7 shows a memory variable file with four variables. Can you identify their names, types, and values?

```
A = 'Federal Finance loan rate:'
B = 10.24
C = .T.
D = {10/13/90}
```

```
0000(0000) 41 00 00 00 00 00 00 00 00 00 00 43 00 00 00 00
0016(0010) 1B 00 00 00 00 00 00 00 00 00 00 00 00 00 00 00
0032(0020) 46 65 64 65 72 61 6C 20 46 69 6E 61 6E 63 65 20
0048(0030) 6C 6F 61 6E 20 72 61 74 65 3A 00 42 00 00 00 00
0064(0040) 00 00 00 00 00 00 4E 00 00 00 00 0D 02 00 00 00
0080(0050) 00 00 00 00 00 00 00 00 00 00 00 7B 14 AE 47 E1
0096(0060) 7A 24 40 43 00 00 00 00 00 00 00 00 00 00 4C 00
0112(0070) 00 00 00 01 00 00 00 00 00 00 00 00 00 00 00 00
0128(0080) 00 00 00 01 44 00 00 00 00 00 00 00 00 00 00 44
0144(0090) 00 00 00 00 00 00 00 00 00 00 00 00 00 00 00 00
0160(00A0) 00 00 00 00 00 00 00 00 99 AD 42 41 45 00 00 00
0176(00B0) 00 00 00 00 00 00 00 00 4E 00 00 00 00 10 05 00 00
0192(00C0) 00 00 00 00 00 00 00 00 00 00 00 00 79 06 0D FD
0208(00D0) 13 DC F3 BF 1A 00 EC 98 D7 12 89 2C 1F 0D 01 00
0224(00E0) 43 4F 4D 50 52 45 53 53 48 4C 50 20 00 00 00 00
0240(00F0) 00 00 00 00 00 00 F7 9A D7 12 BC 2C 0B 17 00 00
```

Figure 11-7. Hexadecimal dump of a MEM file.

Label Files

Label information is stored in two ways. General definitions, called layouts, go in the FOXUSER file. Labels defined for specific applications have the extension LBX. They are actually database files. Before considering how to store label information in a database, let's examine the physical definition of a label as illustrated in Figure 11-8.

Label Remark

We identify label formats with a remark up to 60 characters long. It does not actually print. Rather, it identifies a specific layout when stored as a general definition in FOXUSER. Predefined layouts included with FoxPro are:

3½" × 15/16" × 1"	6½" × 3⅝" Envelope
3½" × 15/16" × 2"	9⅞" × 7⅛" Envelope
3½" × 15/16" × 3"	3" × 5" Rolodex
4½" × 17⁄16" × 1"	4" × 2¼" Rolodex
3²⁄10" × 11/12" × 3" (Cheshire)	2" × 4" Rolodex

Label Height

The label height is the number of printable lines with the printer's current setting.

Left Margin

The left margin is the number of characters from the leftmost printable position on a page to the label's first column.

Label Width

The label width is the number of characters across it with the printer's current setting.

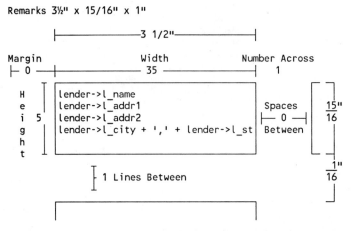

Note that there is a 1/16" vertical gap between labels that is unusable.

Figure 11-8. Label defined by records in Figure 11-9.

Number of Labels across the Page

Forms with only one label across the page are called *one-up forms.* Narrow labels often have two, three, or more across.

Spaces between Labels

The number of spaces between labels is meaningful only for forms having more than one label across a page. It defines the distance between the last printable character of one label and the first printable one of the next. Note the term printable character, not last printed character.

Lines between Labels

The number of lines between labels does not refer to the physical space between them. Rather it defines the distance between the last printable line of one label and the first printable one of its successor.

Now we can examine how FoxPro stores this information in a database (Table 11-11).

Table 11-11. Label File Database Structure

Field	Field Name	Type	Size	Description
1	OBJTYPE	N	2	Object Type
2	OBJCODE	N	2	Object Code
3	NAME	M	10	Name
4	EXPR	M	10	Expression
5	STYLE	M	10	Style
6	HEIGHT	N	3	Height
7	WIDTH	N	3	Width
8	LMARGIN	N	3	Left Margin
9	NUMACROSS	N	3	Number of Labels Across
10	SPACESBET	N	3	Number of Spaces between Horizontal Labels
11	LINESBET	N	3	Number of Lines between Labels Vertically
12	ENVIRON	L	1	Save Environment
13	ORDER	N	3	Order
14	UNIQUE	L	1	Unique Flag
15	TAG	M	10	Tag

FoxPro uses 15 fields to define all label characteristics through five record or object types as listed in Table 11-12.

Table 11-12. Label Object Types	
2	Database Information
3	Index Information
4	Relation Information
19	Label Expressions
30	Label Physical Definition

Let's look at the information required by each type.

FoxPro includes only the first three object types if the environment is saved with the label. Otherwise, the user must open all files and set relations before running it.

Object Type 2: Database Information

The OBJCODE field defines the work area of the open database. The memo field NAME stores the database name. The ORDER field defines which index to use for multiple indexes. Finally, TAG contains the database alias name.

Object Type 3: Index Information

The OBJCODE field defines the work area of the open index. The NAME memo field stores the index name, and EXPR the index expression. UNIQUE is .T. if we define the index to log only unique key values. Finally, the TAG field holds the FOR expression when defined by the index.

Object Type 4: Relation Information

This type occurs only if the label opens multiple databases and defines relations between them. The work area for the database into which the relation is defined is stored in OBJCODE. Memo field EXPR stores the relation expression.

Object Type 19: Label Expressions

Each line in the label generates one record of this type even if it is blank. The label expression appears in field EXPR, and style codes in STYLE.

Object Type 30: Label Physical Description

The label remark or expression appears in the memo field NAME. The label's height in lines and width in characters appear in fields HEIGHT and WIDTH, respectively. LMARGIN defines the left margin in characters. LINESBET, NUMACROSS, and SPACESBET are the numbers of lines between labels vertically, labels across a page, and spaces between horizontal labels, respectively. Finally, the ENVIRON field is .T. if the label saves the current environment.

Figure 11-9 displays selected records used to define the label in Figure 11-8. Since all expression records have similar contents, we show just one.

Report Files

Report files have the extension FRX, but, like labels, are actually database files. Before considering their contents, let's examine the physical structure of a report.

FoxPro includes three bands in each report automatically: page header, detail, and page footer. They correspond to column headers, detailed data, and page summary information, respectively. It prints the page header and page footer bands on each page. Within a page, it repeats the detail band as many times as possible for each record in the database that satisfies the selection criteria. If there are no criteria, it prints all records.

However, we can add bands. A title band prints once at the beginning of a report. Similarly, a summary band prints once at the end.

The final two bands are group bands. They always appear in pairs and include a header and a footer. They relate records through a common field value. For

Field	Physical Label	First line	...	Database	Index
OBJTYPE	30	19		2	2
OBJCODE				1	1
NAME	3 1/2" 15/16" x 1			LENDER.DBF	LENDER.IDX
EXPR		lender->l_name			
STYLE		B			
HEIGHT	5				
WIDTH	35				
LMARGIN	0				
NUMACROSS	1				
SPACESBET	0				
LINESBET	1				
ENVIRON	T				
ORDER				1	
UNIQUE					T
TAG				LENDER	

Figure 11-9. Records used to define the label in Figure 11-8.

example, a group band definition in a company report might use department number or name. Accounting group bands might use a code of accounts field. We use group bands to calculate report subtotals. FoxPro supports up to 20 nested groups in a report.

Reports consist of ten basic structures or objects. FoxPro defines each using up to 32 fields although no single one uses more than half that number. The objects are:

Page layout   Character string (text)
Database definition   Group
Index definition   Box
Relation definition   Field
Band definition   Variable

The page layout object together with the band and group objects control the report's overall appearance. The database, index, and relation definition objects identify data used by the report and how to read it. The remaining objects define temporary variables or position fields, text strings, or boxes. Although the objects can appear in any order, if two overlap, their record order determines which appears on top. Records defined later overlay ones defined earlier.

The following section describes each object in more detail.

Object Type 1: Page Layout

The page layout object (Table 11-13) defines basic information about the output page.

Table 11-13. Report Page Layout Object

Field	Description
OBJTYPE	Page layout identifier: 1
OBJCODE	Version identifier: 0
HEIGHT	Page length
WIDTH	Page width
ENVIRON	Save the environment flag
EJECTBEFOR	Page eject before start of report
EJECTAFTER	Page eject at end of report
PLAIN	Determines if page and date appears on each page
SUMMARY	Display group summary only
OFFSET	Left margin
TOPMARGIN	Top margin
BOTMARGIN	Bottom margin

Five fields define the report page text area: HEIGHT, WIDTH, OFFSET, TOPMARGIN, and BOTMARGIN. HEIGHT defines the most lines that can appear on a page. WIDTH defines the most characters across the page. It assumes a non-proportional font. Both values depend on the current font.

The OFFSET defines the left margin or printer offset. On printers that adjust paper position horizontally, this setting must consider the current position.

TOPMARGIN and BOTMARGIN define the number of lines to skip at the top and bottom of the page, respectively. Some printers, such as laser printers, have an unprintable region around each border. These fields skip additional lines.

When set to .T., the ENVIRON field opens databases and indexes automatically and sets relations.

Fields EJECTBEFOR and EJECTAFTER provide page ejects during printing before or after the report.

Setting PLAIN to .T. suppresses page headers on all except the first page.

To suppress detail lines, set the SUMMARY field to .T.. Then only summary lines from group footers appear in the report.

Object Type 2: Database Definition

The database definition object uses the five fields listed in Table 11-14.

Table 11-14. Report Database Definition Object

Field	Description
OBJTYPE	Database definition identifier: 2
OBJCODE	Work area
NAME	Database file name
ORDER	Index number for compound indexes
TAG	Database alias

OBJCODE defines the database's work area. The memo field NAME stores its name. The ORDER field defines which index to use from multiple indexes. Finally, TAG contains the database's alias name. FoxPro generates this record only if the report saves the environment.

Object Type 3: Index Definition

The index definition object uses the six fields listed in Table 11-15.

Table 11-15. Report Index Definition Object

Field	Description
OBJTYPE	Index definition identifier: 3
OBJCODE	Work area
NAME	Index file name
EXPR	Index expression
UNIQUE	Index unique records only
TAG	For expression

OBJCODE defines the open index's work area. The NAME memo field stores its name, and EXPR its expression. UNIQUE is .T. if we define the index to log only unique key values. Finally, the TAG field holds the FOR expression when defined by the index. FoxPro generates this record only if the report saves the environment.

Object Type 4: Relation Definition

Table 11-16 shows the fields used to define relations.

Table 11-16. Report Relation Definition Object

Field	Description
OBJTYPE	Relation definition identifier: 4
OBJCODE	Work area
EXPR	Relation expression

The work area for the database into which the relation is defined is in OBJCODE. The memo field EXPR stores the relation expression. FoxPro generates this record only if the report saves the environment.

Object Type 5: Text

The text object displays all strings except data fields and boxes. They include titles, headers, and other text. Text can appear in any band and can vary in length, even spanning multiple lines. Text object definitions use the ten fields listed in Table 11-17.

Table 11-17. Report Text Object

Field	Description
OBJTYPE	Text identifier: 5
OBJCODE	SAY type: 0
EXPR	SAY expression
VPOS	Row of first character
HPOS	Column of first character
HEIGHT	Number of rows in SAY
WIDTH	Number of columns across SAY
STYLE	Text style
FLOAT	Allows text to float with stretched fields
COMMENT	Internal documentation memo field

All text objects have an object code of 0 since they are written with the @...SAY command.

The EXPR field contains the text string to print. It begins at row VPOS and column HPOS. The height and width of the text area are in fields HEIGHT and WIDTH, respectively. Text strings wrap to multiple lines automatically if HEIGHT is greater than 1.

FoxPro supports the following styles:

STYLE	CODE
BOLD	B
ITALIC	I
SUBSCRIPT	L
SUPERSCRIPT	R
UNDERLINE	U

FoxPro inserts style codes in the database, not the actual printer commands. To use styles, you must have a driver for your printer.

FLOAT moves text so it always appears one line below other report fields even as they stretch vertically.

COMMENT opens a memo field for internally documenting the text string. It does not appear in the final report.

Object Type 7: Box

The box object draws lines and boxes on the report. The fields required to define it appear in Table 11-18.

Table 11-18. Report Box Object

Field	Description
OBJTYPE	Box identifier: 7
OBJCODE	Box type: 4 – Single line
	5 – Double line
	6 – Panel
	7 – Custom character
VPOS	Row of upper left corner
HPOS	Column of upper left corner
HEIGHT	Height of box in rows
WIDTH	Width of box in columns
STYLE	Box style
COMMENT	Internal documentation memo field
BOXCHAR	Character used to draw box border
FILLCHAR	Character used to fill inside of box
FLOAT	Allows box to float with stretched fields

Box objects have codes of 4, 5, 6, or 7 that define border styles listed in Table 11-18.

The next four fields define the box's position and size. Its upper left corner is anchored at row VPOS and column HPOS. Its height and width are in fields HEIGHT and WIDTH, respectively.

FoxPro supports the styles noted previously for text objects. The FLOAT and COMMENT fields are also the same.

BOXCHAR defines a custom character for the box type. Note that unlike the SET BORDER command that specifies each side and corner, it defines a single character for the entire border. We can also define a second character, FILLCHAR, as a background or fill character. Good values (as noted earlier) are CHR(176), CHR(177), CHR(178), and CHR(219).

Object Type 8: Field

The field object resembles the text object. It prints values from database fields or memory variables.

Table 11-19. Report Field Object

Field	Description
OBJTYPE	Field identifier: 8
OBJCODE	Field type: 0
EXPR	SAY expression
VPOS	Row of first field character
HPOS	Column of first field character
HEIGHT	Number of rows in field output
WIDTH	Number of columns across field output
STYLE	Text style
PICTURE	Format string to display field value
COMMENT	Internal documentation memo field
FLOAT	Float field when other fields stretch
STRETCH	Stretch field if longer than WIDTH
NOREPEAT	Do not repeat field value if it has not changed
TOTALTYPE	Totaling option: 0 – None
	1 – Count
	2 – Sum
	3 – Average
	4 – Lowest
	5 – Highest
	6 – Standard deviation
	7 – Variance
RESETTOTAL	Total reset point: 0 – Report
	1 – Page
	2 – Column
	3-22 – Group

All fields defined via the report generator have an object code of 0 since they are written with the @...SAY command.

The EXPR field contains the field or field expression to print. It can be any valid FoxPro expression. It begins at row VPOS and column HPOS. The height and width of the output area are in HEIGHT and WIDTH, respectively. We can print text and memo fields in fixed size areas, or we can allow them to stretch vertically by setting STRETCH to .T..

The styles and FLOAT and COMMENT fields are the same as for text objects.

The PICTURE field stores a format string for the field. It can contain any codes used in the PICTURE clause of the @...SAY command.

If NOREPEAT is .T., FoxPro suppresses the output of the field if its value is the same as in the prior record.

TOTALTYPE is usually applied to numeric data. It provides the totaling options listed in Table 11-18. FoxPro can count records using any field. However, it calculates the sum, average, lowest or highest value, standard deviation, and variance of numeric fields only.

RESETTOTAL tells FoxPro when to reset counters used in totaling to zero. Table 11-19 lists possible reset point values.

Object Type 9: Band

FoxPro's report generator defines reports via bands. Table 11-20 defines the database fields used to specify a band.

Table 11-20. Report Band Object

Field	Description
OBJTYPE	Band identifier: 9
OBJCODE	Band type: 0 – Title
	1 – Page header
	2 – Not used
	3 – Group header
	4 – Detail
	5 – Group footer
	6 – Not used
	7 – Page footer
	8 – Summary
EXPR	Group expression
HEIGHT	Height of band in rows
PAGEBREAK	Send a page break at start of band
SWAPHEADER	Swap the header and group header
SWAPFOOTER	Swap the footer and group footer

The field OBJCODE defines the band level. Previously we described how FoxPro uses bands to divide a report into logical sections. Most bands are independent. However, group bands must include a header and footer band for each group definition. The order in which bands appear in the database is controlled first by their OBJCODE values. However, since a report can have several group bands, we need a way to determine their order. Basically, they are nested so the outermost one corresponds to the highest level group. For example, a report that groups employees alphabetically by city and state would define state as the highest level. For a group band, EXPR contains the expression defining the group. When its value changes, FoxPro prints the footer band. If there are more records, it prints the group header and then detail lines that satisfy the new group value.

The default height for bands inserted while interactively defining a report is one line. But we can set it to anything to include box, field, and text objects.

We can tell FoxPro to start a new page when the group value changes by setting PAGEBREAK to .T..

When we define group bands, we can tell FoxPro to display the group header or footer instead of the page header or footer. SWAPHEADER and SWAP-FOOTER control this option.

Object Type 18: Variable

We can define variables within the report by selecting the Variables option in the Report pulldown menu. Although the definition itself does not physically appear on the report, it does generate a separate record in the report file. Table 11-21 defines the fields for user defined variables.

Table 11-21. Report Variable Object

Field	Description	
OBJTYPE	Variable identifier: 18	
NAME	Variable name	
EXPR	Variable expression	
TAG	Initial value	
TOTALTYPE	Totaling option:	0 – None
		1 – Count
		2 – Sum
		3 – Average
		4 – Lowest
		5 – Highest
		6 – Standard deviation
		7 – Variance
RESETTOTAL	Total reset point:	0 – Report
		1 – Page
		2 – Column
		3-22 – Group

A common use of a variable in a report is to calculate a derived field. For example, in a point-of-sale system, we may store the cost of individual items sold and a logical flag to indicate whether they are taxable. However, we need not store the sales tax amount. Rather, we can include a variable definition in the report such as:

```
sales_tax = IIF(taxable, sale_amt * tax_rate, 0)
```

Then we could use the variable SALES_TAX in the detail report lines and sum it to obtain the total tax due.

The above equation determines both the NAME field (SALES_TAX) and the EXPR field (the expression).

We can set the initial value stored in the TAG field to anything, but it is typically 0. It is also used at the reset point defined by RESETTOTAL.

TOTALTYPE can be applied to any variable, but it usually appears with numeric data. It provides the totaling options listed in Table 11-20.

EXERCISE

Figure 11-10 shows a report layout using the file LENDER.DBF. Generate the report and then compare the resulting database records to the definitions in this section.

```
R: 0 C  0 | Move |  Page Header |
PgHead                              LENDER REPORT
PgHead
PgHead
Detail  L_ID   L_NAME                    Tax ID: L_TAX_ID
Detail                                   Phone: L_PHONE
Detail  Address: L_ADDR1                    Ext: L_EX
Detail           L_ADDR2
Detail           L_CITY              L_   L_ZIP
Detail
Detail  Current Rate:  L_CURR as of L_RATEDA
Detail
Detail  Variable Rate Loans: IIF
Detail  Renegotiable Loans:   IIF
Detail  Wraparound Loans:     IIF
Detail
Detail  Other Information:
Detail      L_NOTES
Detail  - - - - - - - - - - - - - - - - - - - - - - - -
Detail
PgFoot
Summary Report Date: DATE()        Average interest rate:  L_CURR
```

Figure 11-10. Lender report.

Summary

This chapter examined six important FoxPro file structures: database, index, memo, memory variable, label, and report files. We can use the detailed information provided here to transfer data between FoxPro and the outside world, combine FoxPro with other languages such as C, and diagnose and repair damaged files.

Reference

The IEEE format appears in "IEEE Standard for Binary Floating-Point Arithmetic, ANSI/IEEE Std 754-1985," IEEE, 345 E. 47th St., New York, NY 10017.

12

Using FoxPro File Structures from C

This chapter develops C programs that read and write specific FoxPro file formats described in Chapter 11. Using C to access FoxPro files gives programmers the flexibility to create calculation intensive programs in a general purpose language while performing data management functions in FoxPro. It also provides a faster, more dependable way for external programs to access databases than via ASCII dumps. Some databases change rapidly, making ASCII versions quickly obsolete. On the other hand, C applications that access FoxPro databases directly always read current data.

This chapter contains four major examples of reading and writing FoxPro files from C programs. The first reads a database file, including the header and the fields of the first record. The second creates a database file and appends several records to it from definitions stored in an ASCII file. The third example builds on the first by using an index file to read database records sequentially. It also uses memo pointers to retrieve memo fields. The final example reads a memory variable file and adds one field of each type.

We wrote the examples using Borland's Turbo C. Other compilers may require minor changes.

Appendix C lists references on C for programmers unfamiliar with the language.

Reading a Database

Before reading a file from C, we must open it and define a *file handle*. The handle identifies the file for later accesses. For example,

```
dbf_file = open('MYFILE.DBF', O_RDONLY|O_BINARY);
```

opens the file MYFILE.DBF as read only and binary. Open is a function that returns an integer file handle. It opens the file with the read-only flag (O_RDONLY) and the binary flag (O_BINARY). The latter avoids the translation of carriage return-line feed combinations into a single line feed, as is characteristic of ASCII (text) files. It also insures that read functions process the end-of-file character (hex 1A) without stopping.

The key to reading the database file is the header. It consists of two parts, as described in Tables 11-1 (general information) and 11-2 (field definitions).

An easy way to read the header is via C structures. They bundle values of different types into a unit for easier handling. The one needed to read the first part of the header is:

```
typedef struct
   {
     char filetype;
     char lastchange[3];
     long numrecs;
     unsigned firstbyte;
     unsigned reclength;
     char fill[20];
   } DBF_HEAD;
```

This structure defines a new data type, DBF_HEAD, with six elements (called *members*). The first five correspond to specific data values in the header. The last is a filler to account for unused bytes. Next, we define a variable using the data type with the command

```
DBF_HEAD dbf_head;
```

This statement defines a new variable, dbf_head, using the structure DBF_HEAD. Note that C is a case-sensitive language, so the two names differ. Now use dbf_head as an input buffer to read the header.

```
read(dbf_file, (char *)&dbf_head, sizeof(dbf_head))
```

The read command uses the handle to identify the open file. It then reads the number of bytes specified by sizeof(dbf_head) and stores them in dbf_head.

To be more specific, it puts the first byte of the database in dbf_head.filetype. It puts the next three bytes in the three-element array dbf_head.lastchange. Both fields are of type character. The next member, dbf_head.numrecs, is a long integer and therefore requires four bytes. Following it are two integer values of two bytes each. They are dbf_head.firstbyte and dbf_head.reclength, respectively. FoxPro does not use the rest of the first 32 bytes. (We do not care if the database has a compound index.) Therefore, we simply assign a character array as a filler for it. Compare this structure to the header definition in Table 11-1.

The second part of the header is also easy to read. It defines each field in the database using 32-byte blocks. The only problem is determining how many fields to read. Before solving the problem, let's quickly review the FoxPro structure used to define fields (Table 11-2).

Again we must define a C structure to hold the information. The following lines define both it and the variable names.

```
typedef struct
   {
    char name[11];
    char type;
    long offset;
    union
      {
      unsigned char_len;
      struct
        {
         char nonchar_len;
         char numeric_dec;
        } number_type;
      } length;
    char fill2[14];
   } DBF_FIELDS;
DBF_FIELDS dbf_fields;
```

The main new feature here is the union. It lets us interpret one set of bytes in two ways. For character fields, bytes 17 and 18 together contain the field length as an unsigned integer. For all other types, byte 17 alone is the field length. For numeric fields, byte 18 is the number of decimal places.

We then use a loop to read the field definitions. But when should we stop? There are several ways to find the end of the header information, namely:

- Read each field definition, summing the lengths. Stop when the sum equals the record length stored in the header minus 1 (for the deletion flag).
- Read until the first byte of the 32-byte structure is \x0D (hex 13). We must then move the file pointer back 31 bytes to access the first database record. Remember that the last header block consists of a single byte with the data following immediately after it.
- Count the number of bytes read in the header. When it equals dbf_head.firstbyte minus one for the header/data separator (\x0D), we have read all the field definitions.

As we read each field definition, we store the information in arrays for later reference.

Do not use a predefined structure to read the data record. Using one would lock the program into a specific file format. Rather, define a character array variable as a buffer. Its size depends on the record length found in the header. The malloc function assigns space to the buffer based on the length passed to it.

```
char *recval;
recval = malloc(dbf_head.reclength);
```

The two statements create recval as a character pointer and assign it enough bytes to hold the entire record.

Next read dbf_head.reclength bytes from the database and store them in the buffer. Then parse it using the field information to reconstruct each value.

Program 12-1 follows the above steps to open and read the header and first record of a FoxPro database. It consists of three functions besides main():

- RDBFHDR reads the DBF header (first 32 bytes)
- RFLDDEF reads the field definitions
- RDBFDATA reads the first record of the database

It also includes many print statements to display the information it reads. To run it, first compile it, then execute it with the command

```
CHAP1201 filename.DBF
```

where filename.DBF can be any DBF file.

```
/* Program 12-1 (CHAP1201.C)
   Reads header and structure of a DBF file,
   then the first record
   Written in Turbo C, other compilers may require changes.

*/

#include <alloc.h>
#include <fcntl.h>
#include <io.h>
#include <math.h>
#include <stdio.h>
#include <stdlib.h>
#include <string.h>

/* Structure of DBF file header

       filetype    - identifies whether file has memos
       lastchange  - date file was last updated
       numrecs     - number of records in file
       firstbyte   - offset to first data byte
       reclength   - number of bytes in each record
```

```
      fill        - filler */
typedef struct
  {
    char filetype;
    char lastchange[3];
    long numrecs;
    unsigned firstbyte;
    unsigned reclength;
    char fill[20];
  } DBF_HEAD;


/* FoxPro repeats this header for each field saved

      name        - field name
      type        - field type - C,D,L,M,N
      offset      - field offset from beginning of record
      char_len    - length of character field (2 bytes)
      nonchar_len - length of non-character field
      numeric_dec - number of decimal places in numeric
      fill2       - filler   */

typedef struct
  {
    char name[11];
    char type;
    long offset;
    union
      {
      unsigned char_len;
      struct
        {
          char nonchar_len;
          char numeric_dec;
        } number_type;
      } length;
    char fill2[14];
  } DBF_FIELDS;
DBF_HEAD dbf_head;
DBF_FIELDS  dbf_fields;

char field_names[250][11];   /* Array of DBF field names */
char field_types[250];       /* Array of DBF field types */
int  field_cnt = 0;          /* Counts fields */
int  field_length[250];      /* Array of DBF field sizes */
int  field_offset[250];      /* Array of field offsets */
int  dbf_file;               /* Integer DBF file handle */
void rdbfhdr(void);
void rflddef(void);
void rdbfdata(void);
```

```
/* Main procedure begins here */
main(argc,argv)

int argc;           /* Number of command line parameters */
char *argv[];       /* Passed command line */

{
  /* Check for file name passed as argument */
  if (argc != 2)
    {
      printf("Usage: %s dbf_file.dbf\n\n",argv[0]);
      exit(1);
    }

  dbf_file = open(argv[1], O_RDONLY|O_BINARY);

  /* Try to open memory file */
  if (dbf_file == -1)
    {
      printf("Error opening memory file %s\n",argv[1]);
      exit(1);
    }

  /* Call procedures that read header, field definitions,
     and data */
  rdbfhdr();
  rflddef();
  rdbfdata();

  return;
}

void rdbfhdr(void)
/* _____

          PROCEDURE RDBFHDR

  Reads database header information
  and displays it
  _____ */
{
/* Read first 32 bytes of DBF header */

  if (read(dbf_file, (char *)&dbf_head, sizeof(dbf_head))
      != sizeof(DBF_HEAD))
    {
      printf("\nProblem reading database header.\n");
      exit(1);
    }
  switch (dbf_head.filetype) {
    case '\003':
      printf("\nDBF file (dBASE III/IV/FoxBase/FoxPro) ");
      printf("without memos");
```

```
          break;
      case '\203':
          printf("\nFoxBase DBF with memo");
          break;
      case '\213':
          printf("\ndBASE IV with memo");
          break;
      case '\365':
          printf("\nFoxPro with memo");
  }
  printf("\nDate of last update: %d/%d/19%d",
             dbf_head.lastchange[1], dbf_head.lastchange[2],
             dbf_head.lastchange[0]);
  printf("\nNumber of records:    %d",dbf_head.numrecs);
  printf("\nFirst byte:           %d",dbf_head.firstbyte);
  printf("\nRecord length:        %d",dbf_head.reclength);

  return;
}


void rflddef(void)
/* _____

          PROCEDURE RFLDDEF

  Reads field definitions for database and
  displays them
  _____ */
{
  int field_dec = 0;   /* Number of decimals in
                          numeric fields */
  int field_len;       /* Field length */
  int i;               /* FOR loop counter */

  printf("\n\nField Definition Section:");

/* Loop through second part of header reading each field
  definition */
  for (i = 1; i < dbf_head.reclength;)
  {
  if (read(dbf_file, (char *)&dbf_fields,
      sizeof(dbf_fields)) != sizeof(DBF_FIELDS))
    {
      printf("\nProblem reading database record ");
      printf("definition.\n");
      exit(1);
    }

  ++field_cnt;

  printf("\nFIELD %3d: %-10s",field_cnt,dbf_fields.name);
  strncpy(field_names[field_cnt],dbf_fields.name,11);
```

```
       printf("   TYPE: %c",dbf_fields.type);
       field_types[field_cnt] = dbf_fields.type;
       printf("   OFFSET: %3d",dbf_fields.offset);
       field_offset[field_cnt] = dbf_fields.offset;

       field_dec = 0;
       switch (dbf_fields.type) {
         case 'C' :
           field_len = dbf_fields.length.char_len;
           breal;
         case 'D' :
           field_len = dbf_fields.length.number_type.nonchar_len;
           break;
         case 'L' :
           field_len = dbf_fields.length.number_type.nonchar_len;
           break;
         case 'M' :
           field_len = dbf_fields.length.number_type.nonchar_len;
           break;
         case 'N' :
           field_len = dbf_fields.length.number_type.nonchar_len;
           field_dec = dbf_fields.length.number_type.numeric_dec;
       }
       printf("   LENGTH: %3d",field_len);
       printf("   DECIMALS: %1d",field_dec);
       field_length[field_cnt] = field_len;
       i += field_len;
       }
     return;
}

void rdbfdata(void)
/* _____

               PROCEDURE RDBFDATA

     Reads records for database and displays fields
     _____ */
{
     int i,j;            /* FOR loop counter */
     char *recval;       /* Record string */
     char achar[2];
     char tempfield[250];

     printf("\n\nRecord Section:");
     printf("\nRecord 1:");

/* Jump to beginning of data section using data offset */
     if (lseek(dbf_file,(long)dbf_head.firstbyte,0) == -1)
       printf("\nCannot find the beginning of the data.\n");

/* Read and display first record in database */
     recval = malloc(dbf_head.reclength);
```

```
/* Is record marked for deletion? */
   if (recval[0] == '\x2A')
     printf("\nThis record is marked for deletion.");
   printf("\n%d",recval[0]);
/* Display field information */
   for (i = 1; i <= field_cnt; i++)
   {
       printf("\nField: %-10s",field_names[i]);
       printf("  Type: %c",field_types[i]);
       printf("  Offset: %3d",field_offset[i]);
       printf("  Length: %2d",field_length[i]);
       for (j = field_offset[i];
            j < field_offset[i]+field_length[i]; j++)
       tempfield[j-field_offset[i]] = recval[j];
       tempfield[field_length[i]] = '\0';
       printf("  Value: %s",tempfield);
   }

   return;
}
```

Program 12-1. Reading a Database

Creating a Database

Creating a database is just as easy as reading one. It requires both structural information and the actual data records.

For example, we could use an ASCII file organized as shown in Figure 12-1. It contains sections for header and record data. Each ends with a line containing the word STOP. The first section defines the fields for the new database. The first ten characters are the field name. The eleventh is left blank intentionally. The next one is the field type. Another blank character separates it from the field length defined by the next three characters. Finally, after another blank, the last character defines the number of decimal places for numeric variables. The blanks are included for readability only. Note that each field in the ASCII file has a fixed length.

Two data lines follow the first STOP. The order in which fields appear and the number of columns in each of them follow the definitions in the header. For example, the field L_ID uses the first six columns, followed by a 25 column value for L_NAME. Thus, our program must read the ASCII file by looping through the first section, storing the field definitions. It stops when it reaches a line beginning with 'STOP'.

```
L_ID        C    6 0
L_NAME      C   25 0
L_ADDR      C   25 0
L_CITY      C   20 0
L_STATE     C    2 0
L_ZIP       C   10 0
L_RATE      N    6 3
L_RATEDATE  D    8 0
L_WRAP      L    1 0
STOP
CB     City Bank          100 Main Court       Yourtown      PA19999-999910.75419901112F
FS     Financial Savings  15 West Hill Road    Vienna        PA18888-888811.12519901108T
STOP
```

Figure 12-1. ASCII file used to create a database.

What do we know at this point? We obviously know the complete field definition of the database. But what about the first part of the header? Since there are no memo fields, we know the type is \x03. We also know the date of the last update. It is the current system date. By counting the number of fields and multiplying by 32 and adding 33 (32 for the first header section and 1 for the header terminator byte), we can calculate the offset to the beginning of the data. Similarly, we know the record size if we sum the field lengths and add one for the deletion flag. In fact, the only field we do not know is the number of records. We will not know it until we read the second half of the ASCII file. However, we can set it to zero for now. We will show how to correct it later.

To write the header, we use the same structures used to read the database in Program 12-1 (DBF_HEAD and DBF_FIELDS). We can then write entire units with one call. Of course, we must loop through the field definitions to write each one separately. Remember to end the header with the terminator \x0D before proceeding.

Next we read the data records from the ASCII file. In this example, each line corresponds to a record. Furthermore, each value is already the exact length of its database field. Therefore, we can read the entire line into a buffer variable and then write it to the file. The only change is that we must put a byte at the beginning of each record to identify it as active. Therefore, initialize the buffer variable with character \x20. Then just concatenate the ASCII string to it.

A separate variable counts the number of records added to the database. When we reach the second STOP, we must do two things to complete the file. First, add an end-of-file marker as the last byte. Second, insert the correct number of records into the header. The lseek() function moves the file pointer.

Program 12-2 creates a new database this way. Note that the command line requires both the ASCII file and the DBF file as arguments. Also note that we open the database with the create option (O_CREAT). We also use the read and write option (O_RDWR) and the binary option (O_BINARY). The permission flags (S_IREAD and S_WRITE) determine the file attribute settings. Since we must read and write the database later, we include both.

```c
/* Program 12-2
   Creates a new DBF file from data in an ASCII
   file. Requires both file names as
   arguments. It also adds two records to
   the database.

   Written using Turbo C, other compilers may require changes
*/

#include <alloc.h>
#include <fcntl.h>
#include <io.h>
#include <math.h>
#include <stdio.h>
#include <stdlib.h>
#include <string.h>
#include <sys\stat.h>

/* Structure of FoxPro memory file field header,
   repeated for each memory variable saved */

typedef struct
   {
      char filetype;
      char lastchange[3];
      long numrecs;
      unsigned firstbyte;
      unsigned reclength;
      char fill[20];
   } DBF_HEAD;

typedef struct
   {
      char name[11];
      char type;
      long offset;
      union
```

```
      {
      unsigned char_len;
      struct
        {
        char nonchar_len;
        char numeric_dec;
        } number_type;
      } length;
    char fill2[14];
  } DBF_FIELDS;

typedef struct
  {
    int  da_year;
    char da_day;
    char da_mon;
  } DATE;

DBF_HEAD dbf_head;
DBF_FIELDS dbf_fields;
DATE d;

char field_names[250][11];    /* Array of DBF field names */
char field_types[250];        /* Array of DBF field types */
int  field_cnt = 0;           /* Counts number of fields */
int  field_length[250];       /* Array of DBF field lengths */
int  field_offset[250];       /* Array of DBF field offsets */
int  field_decimal[250];      /* Number of decimal positions
                                  for numeric fields */
int  dbf_file;                /* Integer DBF file handle */
int  totlength;               /* Length of record */
int  bytecnt = 32;            /* Bytes to beginning of data */
int  fieldcnt;                /* Number of fields */
void wdbfhdr(void);

main(argc,argv)

int  argc;                    /* Number of parameters in
                                  command string */
char *argv[];                 /* Passed command string */

{
  char buffer[110];           /* Input buffer */
  char formatstr[110];        /* Write buffer */
  char flag[4];               /* Loop flag */
  char endoffile[2];          /* End of file marker */
  FILE *dbfdata;              /* Input data file */

  /* Check for file names passed as arguments */
  if (argc != 3)
    {
    printf("Usage: %s dbf_data.dat dbf_file.dbf\n\n",argv[0]);
    exit(1);
```

```
        }

/* Parse file names */
    if ((dbfdata = fopen(argv[1], "rt")) == NULL)
        {
          printf("\nCannot open input data file\n");
          exit(1);
        }

/* Open new database file */
    dbf_file = open(argv[2],O_RDWR|O_CREAT|O_BINARY,
                    S_IREAD|S_IWRITE);
    if (dbf_file == -1)
        {
         printf("Error opening new database file: %s\n",
                argv[2]);
         exit(1);
        }

/* Read field definitions */
    fieldcnt = 0;
    while (fgets(buffer,20,dbfdata) != NULL)
        {
          strncpy(flag,buffer,4);
          flag[4] = '\0';
          if (strcmp(flag,"STOP") == 0) break;
          ++fieldcnt;
          bytecnt += 32;
          sscanf(buffer,"%10s %c %3d %d", field_names[fieldcnt],
            &field_types[fieldcnt], &field_length[fieldcnt],
            &field_decimal[fieldcnt]);
          totlength += field_length[fieldcnt];
        }

    totlength++;

/* Write database header */
    wdbfhdr();

/* Read data records and add to database */
    while (fgets(buffer,110,dbfdata) != NULL)
        {
          printf("\nB:%s",buffer);
          strncpy(flag,buffer,4);
          flag[4] = '\0';
          if (strcmp(flag,"STOP") == 0) break;
          dbf_head.numrecs++;
          formatstr[0] = '\x20';
          formatstr[1] = '\0';
          strcat(formatstr,buffer);
          write(dbf_file,&formatstr,dbf_head.reclength);
        }
```

```
/* Add end of file marker */
   strcpy(endoffile,"\x1A");
   write(dbf_file,endoffile,1);

/* Correct number of records in header */
   if (lseek(dbf_file,0L,SEEK_SET) == 0)
     write(dbf_file,&dbf_head,sizeof(dbf_head));

/* Close file */
   close(dbf_file);

   return;
}

void wdbfhdr(void)
/* _____

           PROCEDURE WDBFHDR

   Writes database header information
   _____ */
{
   int  i;
   int  offset;
   char yr;

/* No memo field in this database example */
   dbf_head.filetype = '\003';

/* Get current date */
   getdate(&d);
   yr = d.da_year - 1900;
   dbf_head.lastchange[0] = yr;
   dbf_head.lastchange[1] = d.da_mon;
   dbf_head.lastchange[2] = d.da_day;
   dbf_head.numrecs = 0;
   dbf_head.firstbyte = bytecnt + 1;
   dbf_head.reclength = totlength;
   strset(dbf_head.fill,'\x20');

   write(dbf_file,&dbf_head,sizeof(dbf_head));

/* Loop to write data for each field */

   offset = 1;
   for (i = 1; i <= fieldcnt; i++)
     {
       strncpy(dbf_fields.name,field_names[i],11);
       dbf_fields.type = field_types[i];
       if (field_types[i] == 'C')
         dbf_fields.length.char_len = field_length[i];
       else
```

```
      {
      dbf_fields.length.number_type.nonchar_len =
         field_length[i];
      dbf_fields.length.number_type.numeric_dec =
         field_decimal[i];
      }
   dbf_fields.offset = offset;
   offset += field_length[i];
   strset(dbf_fields.fill2,'\x20');

   write(dbf_file,&dbf_fields,sizeof(dbf_fields));
   }

   yr = '\xd';
   write(dbf_file,&yr,1);

   return;
}
```

Program 12-2. Creating and Adding Records to a Database

Reading a Database Using an Index

Reading a database sequentially using an index extends the concepts developed in Program 12-1. The example also includes routines to read memo values, not just their pointers.

We start by reading the database header information. If the database has a memo field, we also open the memo file. Although it has a 512 byte header, only the first eight are meaningful. The structure MEMO_HEAD loads this data.

```
typedef struct
   {
   char memo1;    /* Number of data blocks in memo */
   char memo2;
   char memo3;
   char memo4;
   char memo5;    /* Size of a data block */
   char memo6;
   char memo7;
   char memo8;
   char fillm[504];
   } MEMO_HEAD;
```

The first four bytes define the number of data blocks in the memo file. FoxPro stores them with the most significant byte first. (Normal integers have their least significant byte first, so we now have reversed byte reversal!) The structure helps separate the bytes so we can calculate the integer value using the following equation.

```
memoblks = memo_head.memo4 + 256 * (memo_head.memo3 +
           256 * (memo_head.memo2 +
           256 * (memo_head.memo1)));
```

The second set of four bytes define the size of a data block. The default is 64 bytes. FoxPro also stores this value with the most significant byte first. The product of the data block size and the number of data blocks equals the file size.

After opening the database and memo files, open the index file and read its header. It consists of 512 bytes as defined in Table 11-4. The program reads it into the C structure INDX_HEAD.

```
typedef struct
  {
    long root_node;      /* Pointer to root node */
    long free_node;      /* Pointer to free node list */
    long filesz;         /* Index file size in bytes */
    int  keysize;        /* Key size */
    char indxoptn;       /* Index option flag */
    char fill3;          /* Filler */
    char keyexp[220];    /* Key expression */
    char forexp[220];    /* For expression */
    char fill4[56];      /* Filler */
  } INDX_HEAD;
```

The main value we need from the header is the key size. If we intend to read the database sequentially, the location of the root node is not the only way to find the first key pointer. The first key is almost always in the data block immediately after the header information. We can save time by looking for it directly rather than tracing through the root pointers. Let's see how to read the index under this assumption.

The index blocks, also called nodes, each contain 512 bytes. The first 12 form a header (Table 11-5). The first two bytes identify the node type. The next two contain the number of keys. Both fields are integers. Following them are two long integers. The first is the position of the previous node in terms of number of bytes from the beginning of the index file. If it is -1 (FF FF FF FF), we have found the first node. The second long integer identifies the next node in sequence. If it is -1, we have reached the last node.

Thus, we could read sequential blocks of 512 bytes until we find a leaf node in which the previous node value is -1. By using its keys, we can locate the first record in the database. After we finish processing the key pointers in this node, we can use the next node pointer to find the next set. We continue the process until the next node value is -1.

There is a minor complication. The index file consists of three different types of nodes: root, index, and leaf. Root and index nodes contain pointers to other nodes, whereas leaf nodes contain pointers to database records. Therefore, we want to read only leaf nodes, those of type 2 or 3.

After finding the first leaf node, read the key information to get the database record pointer. The first part of the information is the key value itself. It has little significance in our current exercise, but is useful when performing a seek. Therefore, skip it and focus on the pointer. It consists of four bytes with the most significant one first. Again, use a C structure to read the bytes individually and calculate the pointer value.

```
typedef struct
  {
    char ptr1;       /* Pointer value */
    char ptr2;
    char ptr3;
    char ptr4;
  } PTR_DATA;

PTR_DATA ptr_data;

indexptr = ptr_data.ptr4 + 256 * (ptr_data.ptr3 +
        256 * (ptr_data.ptr2 + 256 * (ptr_data.ptr1)));
```

The pointer identifies which record in the database to read. The database header contains the position of the first data byte and the record length. With these three pieces of information, we can move the pointer to the first byte of any record using the following equation.

```
dbfptr = dbf_head.firstbyte + dbf_head.reclength *
        (indexptr - 1);
```

As in Program 12-1, we use a buffer to read the record. If the database has a memo field with a nonzero pointer value, we must also read the memo file. The pointer consists of ten bytes representing an ASCII number. Therefore, we read them into a buffer and use the atoi function to convert them into an integer. The result tells us which block of the memo file to begin reading. It must always be less than or equal to the number of blocks in the file as stored in the memo header. To find the relative position from the beginning of the file to the start of the memo, we multiply the pointer value by the memo block size (also in the header).

Each memo begins with an eight byte header consisting of two long integers. The second one is its length. Because memo values must use contiguous blocks, we can define a character buffer to read it with a single command.

Program 12-3 uses the techniques just described to read a database in sequential order, including any memo field values. It requires just one command line argument.

```
CHAP1203 filename
```

Note that the example assumes the same root name for all three files—database, index, and memo. It then appends the proper extensions.

```
/* Program 12-3 (CHAP1203.C)

   Reads header and structure of a DBF file, then
   reads the records including memo fields using the
   index file to determine the sequence

   Written using Turbo C, other compilers may require
   changes

*/

#include <alloc.h>
#include <fcntl.h>
#include <io.h>
#include <math.h>
#include <stdio.h>
#include <stdlib.h>
#include <string.h>

/* Structure of DBF file header

     filetype    - identifies whether file has memos
     lastchange  - date file was last updated
     numrecs     - number of records in file
     firstbyte   - offset to first data byte
     reclength   - number of bytes in each record
     fill        - filler */

typedef struct
   {
     char filetype;
     char lastchange[3];
     long numrecs;
     unsigned firstbyte;
     unsigned reclength;
     char fill[20];
   } DBF_HEAD;

/* FoxPro repeats this header for each field saved

     name        - field name
     type        - field type - C,D,L,M,N
```

```
    offset       - field offset from beginning of record
    char_len     - length of character field (2 bytes)
    nonchar_len  - length of non-character field
    numeric_dec  - number of decimal places in numeric
    fill2        - filler   */

typedef struct
   {
     char name[11];
     char type;
     long offset;
     union
        {
        unsigned char_len;
        struct
           {
              char nonchar_len;
              char numeric_dec;
           } number_type;
        } length;
     char fill2[14];
   } DBF_FIELDS;

/* Structure of memo file header */
typedef struct
   {
     char memo1;        /* Number of data blocks in memo */
     char memo2;
     char memo3;
     char memo4;
     char memo5;        /* Size of a data block */
     char memo6;
     char memo7;
     char memo8;
     char fillm[504];   /* Filler */
   } MEMO_HEAD;

/* Structure of memo value header */
typedef struct
   {
     char data1;        /* Type of memo field */
     char data2;
     char data3;
     char data4;
     char data5;        /* Size of a memo field */
     char data6;
     char data7;
     char data8;
   } MEMO_DATA;

/* Structure of index header */
typedef struct
   {
```

```
      long root_node;       /* Pointer to root node */
      long free_node;       /* Pointer to free node list */
      long filesz;          /* Index file size in bytes */
      int  keysize;         /* Key size */
      char indxoptn;        /* Index option flag */
      char fill3;           /* Filler */
      char keyexp[220];     /* Key expression */
      char forexp[220];     /* For expression */
      char fill4[56];       /* Filler */
   } INDX_HEAD;

/* Structure of index node header */
typedef struct
   {
      char secttype;        /* Type of sector */
      char fill5;           /* Filler */
      int  numkeys;         /* Number of keys in sector */
      long priornode;       /* Prior node sequentially */
      long nextnode;        /* Next node sequentially */
   } NODE_HEAD;

/* Structure of pointer value */
typedef struct
   {
      char ptr1;            /* Pointer value */
      char ptr2;
      char ptr3;
      char ptr4;
   } PTR_DATA;


DBF_HEAD     dbf_head;
DBF_FIELDS   dbf_fields;
MEMO_HEAD    memo_head;
MEMO_DATA    memo_data;
INDX_HEAD    indx_head;
NODE_HEAD    node_head;
PTR_DATA     ptr_data;

char field_names[250][11];  /* Array of DBF field names */
char field_types[250];      /* Array of DBF field types */
int  field_cnt = 0;         /* Number of fields */
int  field_length[250];     /* Array of DBF field lengths */
int  field_offset[250];     /* Array of DBF field offsets */
int  dbf_file;              /* Integer DBF file handle */
int  dbf_memo;              /* Integer FPT file handle */
int  indx_file;             /* Integer IDX file handle */
int  memoblks;              /* Number of memo file blocks */
int  blksize;               /* Memo file block size */
long dbfptr;                /* Pointer from index file to
                               DBF record */
void rdbfdata(long recordnum);
void rdbfhdr(void);
void rdbindex(void);
```

```
void rflddef(void);

/* Main procedure begins here */
main(argc,argv)

int argc;                   /* Number of command string
                               parameters */
char *argv[];               /* Passed command string */

{
  char dbffile[50];         /* Buffer for DBF name */
  char dbfmemo[50];         /* Buffer for FPT name */
  char idxfile[50];         /* Buffer for IDX name */

  /* Check for file name passed as argument */
  if (argc != 2)
    {
      printf("Usage: %s dbf_file\n\n",argv[0]);
      exit(1);

    }

  /* Try to open specified DBF file */
  strcpy(dbffile,argv[1]);
  strcat(dbffile,".DBF");
  dbf_file = open(dbffile, O_RDONLY|O_BINARY);
  if (dbf_file == -1)
    {
      printf("Error opening database file %s\n",argv[1]);
      exit(1);
    }

  /* Read DBF header */
    rdbfhdr();
    rflddef();

  if (dbf_head.filetype == '\365')
   {
    /* Try to open corresponding memo file */
      strcpy(dbfmemo,argv[1]);
      strcat(dbfmemo,".FPT");
      dbf_memo = open(dbfmemo,O_RDONLY|O_BINARY);
      if (read(dbf_memo,(char *)&memo_head,
          sizeof(memo_head)) != sizeof(MEMO_HEAD))
     {
       puts("\nProblem reading memo header.\n");
       exit(1);
     }
     memoblks = memo_head.memo4 + 256 * (memo_head.memo3 + 256
         * (memo_head.memo2 + 256 * (memo_head.memo1)));
     blksize  = memo_head.memo8 + 256 * (memo_head.memo7 + 256
         * (memo_head.memo6 + 256 * (memo_head.memo5)));
   }
```

```
    /* Try to open corresponding index file */
    strcpy(idxfile,argv[1]);
    strcat(idxfile,".IDX");
    indx_file = open(idxfile,O_RDONLY|O_BINARY);

    /* Call procedure to read index file */
    rdindex();

    return 0;
}

void rdindex(void)
/* _____

            PROCEDURE RDINDEX

    Reads index file for a database
    and displays records sequentially
    _____ */
{
  char      indxptr[5];    /* Index pointer string */
  char      *cvar;         /* Buffer for index pointer */
  int       indexptr;      /* Index pointer value */
  int       i;             /* Loop counter */
  unsigned cvarsz;         /* Size of index pointer buffer */

/* Read 512 byte IDX header */
  if (read(indx_file, (char *)&indx_head,
      sizeof(indx_head)) != sizeof(INDX_HEAD))
    {
      printf("\nProblem reading index header.\n");
      exit(1);
    }

/* Read first node */
  while (read(indx_file,
         (char *)&node_head,sizeof(node_head)) > 0)
    {
      if (node_head.secttype == '\0')
        continue;
      if (node_head.secttype == '\1')
        continue;
      if (node_head.priornode > 0)
        continue;

/* Read keys in first node */
      printf("\nKey Size:         %d",indx_head.keysize);
      printf("\nSector Type:      %d",node_head.secttype);
      printf("\nNumber of Keys:   %d",node_head.numkeys);
      printf("\nPrior Node:       %ld",node_head.priornode);
      printf("\nNext Node:        %ld",node_head.nextnode);
      for (i = 0; i < node_head.numkeys; i++)
        {
```

```
        cvarsz = indx_head.keysize;
        cvar = malloc(cvarsz+1);
        read(indx_file,cvar,cvarsz);
        cvar[cvarsz] = '\0';
        printf("\nKey Value: %s",cvar);
        read(indx_file,(char *)&ptr_data,sizeof(ptr_data));
        indexptr = ptr_data.ptr4 + 256 * (ptr_data.ptr3 + 256
            * (ptr_data.ptr2 + 256 * (ptr_data.ptr1)));
        printf("\nRead DBF record: %d",indexptr);
        dbfptr = dbf_head.firstbyte + dbf_head.reclength
            * (indexptr - 1);

        /* Call procedure that reads dbf data */
        rdbfdata(indexptr);
      }

      /* Is there another node? */
      if (node_head.nextnode == -1)
        break;
      lseek(indx_file,node_head.nextnode,0);
    }

return;
}

void rdbfhdr(void)
/* _____

        PROCEDURE RDBFHDR

    Reads database header information
    and displays it
    _____ */
{
/* Read first 32 bytes of DBF header */

  if (read(dbf_file, (char *)&dbf_head,
      sizeof(dbf_head)) != sizeof(DBF_HEAD))
    {
    printf("\nProblem reading database header.\n");
    exit(1);
    }

  switch (dbf_head.filetype) {
    case '\003':
      printf("\nDBF file (dBASE III/IV/FoxBase/FoxPro) ");
      printf("without memos");
      break;
    case '\203':
      printf("\nFoxBase DBF with memo");
      break;
    case '\213':
      printf("\ndBASE IV with memo");
```

```
        break;
      case '\365':
        printf("\nFoxPro with memo");
    }
    printf("\nDate of last update: %d/%d/19%d",
            dbf_head.lastchange[1], dbf_head.lastchange[2],
            dbf_head.lastchange[0]);
    printf("\nNumber of records:     %d",dbf_head.numrecs);
    printf("\nFirst byte:            %d",dbf_head.firstbyte);
    printf("\nRecord length:         %d",dbf_head.reclength);

    return;
}


void rflddef(void)
/* _____

            PROCEDURE RFLDDEF

    Reads field definitions for database and displays them
    _____ */
{
    int field_dec = 0;   /* Stores number of decimals in
                            numeric fields */
    int field_len;       /* Stores field length */
    int i;               /* FOR loop counter */

    printf("\n\nField Definition Section:");

/* Loop through second part of header reading each field
    definition */
    for (i = 1; i < dbf_head.reclength;)
      {
        if (read(dbf_file, (char *)&dbf_fields,
            sizeof(dbf_fields)) != sizeof(DBF_FIELDS))
        {
         printf("\nProblem reading database record ");
         printf("definition.\n");
         exit(1);
        }

        ++field_cnt;

        printf("\nFIELD %3d: %-10s",field_cnt,dbf_fields.name);
        strncpy(field_names[field_cnt],dbf_fields.name,11);

        printf("  TYPE: %c",dbf_fields.type);
        field_types[field_cnt] = dbf_fields.type;

        printf("  OFFSET: %3d",dbf_fields.offset);
        field_offset[field_cnt] = dbf_fields.offset;

        field_dec = 0;
        switch (dbf_fields.type) {
```

```
        case 'C' :
          field_len = dbf_fields.length.char_len;
          break;
        case 'D' :
          field_len =
            dbf_fields.length.number_type.nonchar_len;
          break;
        case 'L' :
          field_len =
            dbf_fields.length.number_type.nonchar_len;
          break;
        case 'M' :
          field_len =
            dbf_fields.length.number_type.nonchar_len;
          break;
        case 'N' :
          field_len =
            dbf_fields.length.number_type.nonchar_len;
          field_dec =
            dbf_fields.length.number_type.numeric_dec;
      }
      printf("  LENGTH: %3d",field_len);
      printf("  DECIMALS: %1d",field_dec);
      field_length[field_cnt] = field_len;
      i += field_len;
    }
  return;
}


void rdbfdata(long recordnum)
/* _____

            PROCEDURE RDBFDATA

    Reads records for database and displays fields
    _____  */
{
  int      i,j;              /* FOR loop counter */
  char     memosize[4];      /* Size of memo in bytes */
  char     memosize1;
  char     memosize2;
  char     memosize3;
  char     memosize4;
  long     memojump;         /* Start byte for memo data */
  unsigned cvarsz;           /* Size of memo field value */
  char     *recval;          /* Record string */
  char     *cvar;            /* Buffer for memo field */
  char     achar[2];
  char     memotype[4];      /* Memo type */
  char     tempfield[250];

  printf("\n\nRecord Section:");
  printf("\nRecord %d:",recordnum);
```

```
/* Jump to beginning of data section using data offset */
   if (lseek(dbf_file,dbfptr,0) == -1)
     printf("\nCannot find the beginning of the data.\n");

/* Read and display first record in database */
   recval = malloc(dbf_head.reclength);
   read(dbf_file,recval,dbf_head.reclength);

/* Is record marked for deletion? */
   if (recval[0] == '\x2A')
     printf("\nThis record is marked for deletion.");
   printf("\n%d",recval[0]);

/* Display field information */
   for (i = 1; i <= field_cnt; i++)
   {
      printf("\nField: %-10s",field_names[i]);
      printf("  Type: %c",field_types[i]);
      printf("  Offset: %3d",field_offset[i]);
      printf("  Length: %2d",field_length[i]);
      for (j = field_offset[i];
           j < field_offset[i]+field_length[i]; j++)
        tempfield[j-field_offset[i]] = recval[j];
      tempfield[field_length[i]] = '\0';

      if (field_types[i] == 'M') {
/* If memo field has a value, get and display it */
         if (atoi(tempfield) > 0)
         {

/* Calculate number of bytes from beginning of file to
   start of data */
         memojump = blksize * atoi(tempfield);
         lseek(dbf_memo,memojump,SEEK_SET);

/* Read memo header */
         if (read(dbf_memo, (char *)&memo_data,
             sizeof(memo_data)) != sizeof(MEMO_DATA))
           {
             puts("\nProblem reading memo data.\n");
             exit(1);
           }
         cvarsz = memo_data.data8 + 256 * (memo_data.data7 + 256
              * (memo_data.data6 + 256 * (memo_data.data5)));
         cvar = malloc(cvarsz+1);
         read(dbf_memo,cvar,cvarsz);
         cvar[cvarsz] = '\0';
         printf("\nMemo:  %s",cvar);
         free(cvar);
      }
    else
      {
        puts("No Memo Value");
```

```
      printf("  Value: %s",tempfield);
    }
  }
  else
    printf("  Value: %s",tempfield);
  }

return;
}
```

Program 12-3. Reading a Database with an Index

> **EXERCISE**
>
> Using index pointers, revise Program 12-3 to start with the root node and use node pointers to search for the first node.

Reading and Writing Memory Variable Files

Unlike the files discussed previously, memory variable files lack overall headers. However, each variable has a small header (Table 11-10) that identifies it.

We use the C structure MEM_HEAD to read the variable header.

```
typedef struct
  {
    char mvarname[11];
    char mvartype;
    char mvarfilla[4];
    char mvarlen;
    char mvardec;
    char mvarfillb[14];
  } MEM_HEAD;

MEM_HEAD mem_head;
```

FoxPro stores most memory variables differently in MEM files than in DBF files, as noted in Chapter 11. In fact, it stores only character fields in the same way, as ASCII characters.

Logical variables appear as 1 for true and 0 for false rather than ASCII T or F. They still occupy only a single byte.

Both numeric values and dates use the IEEE format for storing numbers in eight bytes. (We need not worry about the exact format since Turbo C also reads floats using it.) FoxPro converts dates to an integer day number. As noted in Chapter 11, the first defined date is the mysterious day number 2299161 (Friday, October 15, 1582). FoxPro then increments the number for each subsequent day.

Program 12-4 reads and displays the variables stored in a memory variable file passed to it using the command

```
CHAP1204 filename.MEM
```

It then adds one variable of each type: character, date, logical, and numeric. The trickiest variable to add is a date, as we must determine the proper day number. For example, our program saves the variable DFIELD with a date of December 31, 1990 which is day number 2448257 (obviously!).

One last reminder—memory variable files require a terminating marker (1A hex).

```
/* Program 12-4 (CHAP1204.C)

   Reads a memory variable file (MEM) and appends the
   variable LANDVALUE

   Written using Turbo C, other compilers may require changes
*/

#include <alloc.h>
#include <fcntl.h>
#include <io.h>
#include <math.h>
#include <stdio.h>
#include <stdlib.h>
#include <string.h>

/* Structure of memory file field header, repeated
   by FoxPro for each variable saved. */
typedef struct
   {
     char mvarname[11];
     char mvartype;
     char mvarfilla[4];
     char mvarlen;
     char mvardec;
     char mvarfillb[14];
   } MEM_HEAD;

MEM_HEAD mem_head;
```

```
/* Integer file handle for memory variable file */
int mem_file;

/* Main procedure begins here */
main(argc,argv)

int argc;        /* Number of parameters in command string */
char *argv[];    /* Passed command string */

{
  int      mem_file;
  char     logic;
  double   num;
  char     *cvar;
  char     buffer[250];
  char     endoffile[2];
  unsigned cvarsz;

/* Check for file name passed as argument */
  if (argc != 2)
    {
      printf("Usage: %s mem_file.mem\n\n",argv[0]);
      exit(1);
    }

/* Try to open memory variable file */
  mem_file = open(argv[1], O_RDWR|O_BINARY);
  if (mem_file == -1)
    {
      printf("Error opening memory variable file %s\n",
             argv[1]);
      exit(1);
    }

/* Loop to read each memory variable saved */
  while (read(mem_file, (char *)&mem_head,
         sizeof(MEM_HEAD)) == sizeof(MEM_HEAD))
    {

      /* Determine which memory variable was just read */
      switch (mem_head.mvartype) {
        case 'C':
          {
          cvarsz = mem_head.mvarlen + mem_head.mvardec * 256;
          cvar = malloc(cvarsz);
          read(mem_file,cvar,cvarsz);
          printf("\n%-10s  %s",mem_head.mvarname,cvar);
          free(cvar);
          break;
          }
        case 'D':
          {
          read(mem_file, (char *)&num,8);
```

```
                    printf("\n%-10s   %10.0f",mem_head.mvarname,num);
                    break;
                    }
                case 'L':
                    {
                    cvarsz = 1;
                    cvar = malloc(cvarsz);
                    read(mem_file,cvar,cvarsz);
                    if (cvar == '\1')
                        printf("\n%-10s   TRUE",mem_head.mvarname);
                    else
                        printf("\n%-10s   FALSE",mem_head.mvarname);
                    free(cvar);
                    break;
                    }
                case 'N':
                    {
                    read(mem_file,(char *)&num,8);
                    printf("\n%-10s   %e",mem_head.mvarname,num);
                    break;
                    }
                }
        }

    /* Back up over current end-of-file marker */
      lseek(mem_file,-1L,SEEK_CUR);

    /* Add a string variable */
      strcpy(mem_head.mvarname,"CFIELD");
      mem_head.mvartype = 'C';
      cvar = malloc(25);
      strcpy(cvar,"This is a test field\0");
      mem_head.mvarlen = strlen(cvar)+1;
      mem_head.mvardec = 0;
      write(mem_file,&mem_head,sizeof(mem_head));
      write(mem_file,cvar,mem_head.mvarlen);
      free(cvar);

    /* Add a logical variable */
      strcpy(mem_head.mvarname,"LFIELD");
      mem_head.mvartype = 'L';
      mem_head.mvarlen = 1;
      mem_head.mvardec = 0;
      logic = '\1';
      write(mem_file,&mem_head,sizeof(mem_head));
      write(mem_file,&logic,1);

    /* Add a date of 12/31/90 */
      strcpy(mem_head.mvarname,"DFIELD");
      mem_head.mvartype = 'D';
      mem_head.mvarlen = 0;
      mem_head.mvardec = 0;
      num = 2448257;
```

```
    write(mem_file,&mem_head,sizeof(mem_head));
    write(mem_file,&num,8);

/* Add a numeric value of 3.141592654 */
    strcpy(mem_head.mvarname,"PI");
    mem_head.mvartype = 'N';
    mem_head.mvarlen  = 11;
    mem_head.mvardec  = 9;
    num = 3.141592654;
    write(mem_file,&mem_head,sizeof(mem_head));
    write(mem_file,&num,8);

/* Add end of file marker */
    strcpy(endoffile,"\x1A");
    write(mem_file,endoffile,1);

    close(mem_file);

    return;
}
```

Program 12-4. Reading and Writing Memory Variable Files

Summary

In this chapter, we learned how to use the following FoxPro file types from C programs:

> database (DBF) files
> memo (FPT) files
> index (IDX) files
> memory variable (MEM) files

Using the concepts presented here, we can read or write any FoxPro file whose structure we defined in the previous chapter. We can use FoxPro file structures in C applications even if they do not interface with FoxPro at all. Of course, we get the most benefit by integrating FoxPro and C in systems where FoxPro handles data management chores and C performs other types of operations.

13

Running External Programs

By running external programs from FoxPro, programmers can combine its data handling features with existing software. The combination of FoxPro and a powerful general-purpose language such as C provides a high performance hybrid for application development.

Previous chapters covered FoxPro's data handling and data management capabilities. FoxPro also has a rich variety of numeric functions. They range from mathematical functions such as trigonometric functions, logarithms, and exponentials to business functions such as present and future value. With the tremendous capabilities of FoxPro's own language, you may ask why we need external commands.

One reason is to avoid reinventing the wheel. If we already have a tested program that performs a function, why rewrite it in FoxPro? A second reason is that, whereas FoxPro is fast at data handling and management tasks, other languages have a speed advantage for purely mathematical functions. A third reason is to integrate FoxPro data with graphical or other non-FoxPro applications. We will examine several ways to combine FoxPro with external programs.

RUN Command

Suppose you have a series of programs written and compiled in another language. Together they form an application system. However, we must run each one separately. We could use FoxPro to create a main menu that integrates the system for users.

Program 13-1 runs four programs from a checking account system. It is a menu shell that displays the names of programs compiled in other languages. The user selects one to execute. FoxPro then uses the RUN command to open a DOS shell in which to run it. (A DOS shell puts a second copy of DOS in the computer's free memory. It can then execute a second program without exiting from the first one.) When it finishes, FoxPro closes the shell and returns control to the next statement.

```
* Program 13-1
*
* Executes four external programs from a checking
* account system via a FoxPro menu

* Set environment
  SET TALK OFF
  SET BELL OFF
  SET SCOREBOARD OFF
  SET MESSAGE TO 24 CENTER
  CLEAR

* Define window for menu
  DEFINE WINDOW main FROM 8,20 TO 16,60 SHADOW COLOR SCHEME 7

* Loop through main menu unless exit option is selected
  DO WHILE .T.
     CLEAR
     @ 0,0 TO 23,79 DOUBLE
     @ 2,5 SAY PADC('*** CHECKING ACCOUNT SYSTEM ***',70)
     ACTIVATE WINDOW main

     * Define menu options
     @ 1,5 PROMPT '\<Write/Print a check' ;
          MESSAGE 'Run program CKPRT.EXE'
     @ 2,5 PROMPT '\<Find/View a check' ;
          MESSAGE 'Run program CKFNDVEW.EXE'
     @ 3,5 PROMPT '\<Reconcile checking account' ;
          MESSAGE 'Run program CKRCNCLE.EXE'
     @ 4,5 PROMPT '\<Print check history' ;
          MESSAGE 'Run program CKHISTRY.EXE'
     @ 5,5 PROMPT '\<Exit checking system' ;
          MESSAGE 'Return to FoxPro command window'

     moption = 5

     MENU TO moption

     DEACTIVATE WINDOW ALL

     * Execute external programs in response to user selection
```

```
DO CASE
   CASE moption = 1
      RUN 'CKPRT.EXE'
   CASE moption = 2
      RUN 'CKFNDVEW.EXE'
   CASE moption = 3
      RUN 'CKRCNCLE.EXE'
   CASE moption = 4
      RUN 'CKHISTRY.EXE'
   CASE moption = 5
      CLEAR
      CANCEL
   ENDCASE

   ENDDO

   RETURN

   * End of program
```

Program 13-1. Running External Programs from a FoxPro Menu

This menu is simple, but the concept applies to multilevel menus that call external programs. A more elaborate example could have some options executing FoxPro procedures.

In the simplest approach, we call each compiled program with the RUN command. It opens a DOS shell that shares memory with the transient part of DOS. When DOS boots, part of it loads into a protected area. The rest loads into high RAM. However, some large programs, especially ones that run in shells, overwrite this area. When the external program ends, the protected part of DOS recognizes that some of the transient part is missing. It tries to reinstall it using COMMAND.COM. If it cannot find COMMAND.COM, it halts the computer, which must then be rebooted. Therefore, we must first tell DOS where to find COMMAND.COM by setting the COMSPEC environment variable. We define it with the DOS SET command as in

```
SET COMSPEC=C:\DOS
```

This command tells DOS that COMMAND.COM is in directory DOS on drive C. Although we can enter it at any time, the best place for it is in AUTO-EXEC.BAT. To see if COMSPEC has been set or to determine its value, type SET from the DOS prompt.

Of course, the DOS shell has limited memory when called from a FoxPro program. Not only does the application take memory, but so does the original copy of DOS, as well as FoxPro or its runtime. RUN also uses memory to create the DOS shell. Finally, the specified program must load there as well. Things could become quite claustrophobic if it were not for FOXSWAP.

FOXSWAP is a memory management utility supplied with FoxPro for executing large external programs. It operates by storing part of the current application as well as FoxPro on disk while it runs the external program. FoxPro uses FOXSWAP to execute FoxView, FoxDoc, and FoxGraph. You can also use it to run programs. To do so, just put FOXSWAP between the RUN command and the program's name as in

```
RUN FOXSWAP TYPE filename > PRN:
```

In an application, the line executes the DOS TYPE command to print the file on the printer. By integrating this approach with Program 13-1, we can use FOXSWAP to run large programs.

DOS versions 4.0 and higher include the utility MEM.EXE. It reports the total memory in the computer as well as the amount available to a program. Novell users can run the network command SYSMAP to get a similar report. We can use it to determine the effect of FOXSWAP. In my system, I have 523K of available memory after loading DOS. With FoxPro loaded (but no application), I have only about 234K of free memory when I use the command

```
RUN C:\DOS\MEM
```

However, if I include FOXSWAP, I have 506K of available space.

```
RUN FOXSWAP C:\DOS\MEM
```

Thus I regain all but 17K of system memory. (Available memory in your system will depend on DOS version, device drivers, and other configuration settings.) As you can see, FOXSWAP makes almost all the original memory available to external programs.

We can control how much memory FOXSWAP recovers by using the /N option with RUN. N is the amount of memory in K (kilobytes) to allocate. For example, if we have a program that requires 300K, we can use the command

```
RUN /300 c:\myprog
```

If the amount is unknown, a value of 0 tells FOXSWAP to make available as much memory as possible. Why not always specify that amount? Because nothing is free. FOXSWAP causes a noticeable delay in program execution while it copies the application and FoxPro to and from disk. The more memory it swaps, the longer and more obvious the delay becomes.

Integrating External Programs with Database Systems

So far, we have called utilities or other standalone programs from FoxPro. However, a more powerful technique combines the data entry and data handling capabilities of FoxPro with the speed of a compiled C application.

For example, Program 13-2 (written in FoxPro) serves as the data entry and data handling part of a simple linear regression system written in C. It asks the user to either create a new data file or edit an existing one. In either case, it stores the information partly in a memory variable file and partly in a database. (We could also store data in a memo field.)

It then executes a compiled version of Program 13-3 (written in C). This program reads the files created by FoxPro and performs the linear regression calculations. After printing the results, it returns control to FoxPro.

```
* Program 13-2
*
* Linear regression using FoxPro to perform data entry and
* database management for external programs

* Set environment
  SET TALK OFF
  SET BELL OFF
  SET SCOREBOARD OFF
  SET MESSAGE TO 24 CENTER
  CLOSE ALL
  CLEAR

* Initialize variables
  lrtitle = SPACE(40)
  lrdvar  = SPACE(40)
  lrivar  = SPACE(40)
  memfile = SPACE(50)

* Define window for menu
  DEFINE WINDOW main FROM 7,20 TO 12,50 SHADOW COLOR SCHEME 7
  DEFINE WINDOW instr FROM WROW()-6,2 TO WROW()-1,78
         COLOR SCHEME 5

* Loop through main menu unless exit option is selected
  DO WHILE .T.
     CLEAR
     @ 0,0 TO 23,79 DOUBLE
```

```
       @ 2,5 SAY PADC('*** L I N E A R   R E G R E S S I O N '+;
          '***',70)
       ACTIVATE WINDOW main

    * Define menu options
       @ 0, 2 SAY 'Perform regression on a:'
       @ 1, 5 PROMPT '\<New file' ;
          MESSAGE 'Create a new linear regression case'
       @ 2, 5 PROMPT '\<Existing file' ;
          MESSAGE 'Modify data from an existing regression case'
       @ 3, 5 PROMPT '\<Quit LR system' ;
          MESSAGE 'Quit linear regression system.'
       moption = 1
       MENU TO moption

       DEACTIVATE WINDOW ALL

    * Get name for a new file
       IF moption = 1
          filenm = 'LRDATA.DBF'
          filenm = ALLTRIM(PUTFILE(;
            'Select file name to save data', filenm,'DBF'))
          IF FILE(filenm)
            LOOP
          ENDIF
          CREATE &filenm FROM lrmstr
          USE &filenm
          memfile = LEFT(m->filenm,LEN(m->filenm)-3) + 'MEM'
       ENDIF

    * If existing file, get its name
       IF moption = 2
          filenm = SPACE(50)
          filenm = ALLTRIM(GETFILE('DBF',;
                      'Pick a linear regression data set'))
          USE &filenm
       * Parse DBF file name to get memory variable name
          memfile = LEFT(m->filenm,LEN(m->filenm)-3) + 'MEM'
          RESTORE FROM &memfile ADDITIVE
       ENDIF

    * Quit linear regression system
       IF moption = 3
          CLEAR
          CANCEL
       ENDIF

    * Prompt for title information for problem
       CLEAR
       @ 0, 0 TO 23,79 DOUBLE
       @ 1, 5 SAY PADC('Linear Regression Title Information:';
```

```
            ,70) COLOR GR+
  @  5, 3 SAY "ENTER THE FOLLOWING TITLE INFORMATION:"
  @  7, 6 SAY "Title of regression problem:" ;
        GET m->lrtitle;
        MESSAGE "Enter a title for the regression data set"
  @  9, 6 SAY "Dependent variable:          " ;
        GET m->lrdvar ;
        MESSAGE "Enter a name for the dependent variable"
  @ 11, 6 SAY "Independent variable:        " ;
        GET m->lrivar ;
        MESSAGE "Enter a name for the independent variable"
  READ
  IF FILE(memfile)
    ERASE &memfile
  ENDIF
  SAVE TO &memfile ALL LIKE LR*

* Edit data
  CLEAR
  ACTIVATE WINDOW instr
  @ 0,1 SAY "Use the ^X & ^Y keys to select different "+;
            "data sets."
  @ 1,1 SAY "Ctrl-N appends a new line."
  @ 2,1 SAY "Ctrl-T marks a data pair for deletion "+;
            "(^G appears on record's left)."
  @ 3,1 SAY "Esc or Ctrl-End exits the edit window and "+;
            "begins regression."
  ACTIVATE SCREEN
  BROWSE FIELDS x = RECNO() :R :H='Data Pair', ;
      lr_x_value :H="Independent Variable", ;
      lr_y_value :H="Dependent Variable" ;
      TITLE "DATA PAIRS FOR LINEAR REGRESSION"
  DEACTIVATE WINDOW ALL
  CLEAR
  PACK

* Execute C program

  lrname = LEFT(m->filenm,LEN(m->filenm)-4)
  RUN FOXSWAP LR &lrname
  WAIT
  CLEAR
ENDDO

RETURN

* End of program
```

Program 13-2. Linear Regression—FoxPro Part

```
/* Program 13-3 (CHAP1303.C)
                L I N E A R   R E G R E S S I O N
Linear regression is a mathematical procedure to
determine the best fit line through a series of
points. In this simplified example, it examines the
relationship between two variables. It calculates the
coefficients for the line

                    y = a + b * x
where:   a is the intercept
         b is the slope
         x is the independent variable
         y is the dependent variable
It then calculates a series of statistics that determine
how well the line fits the data.

The program reads the data files created by FoxPro, first
the memory variable file, then the database file. Much of
the logic is already set for more complex expressions.

For more information on linear regression and related
statistics, see:
  Applied Linear Statistical Models
  by John Neter, William Wasserman, Michael Kutner
  published by Richard D. Irwin Inc. (Homewood, IL)
  Copyright 1974

*/

#include <alloc.h>
#include <conio.h>
#include <fcntl.h>
#include <float.h>
#include <io.h>
#include <math.h>
#include <stdio.h>
#include <stdlib.h>
#include <string.h>

/* Structure of memory file field header, repeated by FoxPro
   for each memory variable saved  */

typedef struct
   {
      char mvarname[11];
      char mvartype;
      char mvarfilla[4];
      char mvarlen;
      char mvardec;
      char mvarfillb[14];
   } MEM_HEAD;
```

```
/* Structure of database file header */

typedef struct
   {
     char filetype;
     char lastchange[3];
     long numrecs;
     unsigned firstbyte;
     unsigned reclength;
     char fill[20];
   } DBF_HEAD;

/* Structure of database record */

typedef struct
   {
     char delflag;
     char xstr[15];
     char ystr[15];
   } DBF_REC;

DBF_HEAD dbf_head;
DBF_REC  dbf_rec;
MEM_HEAD mem_head;

main(argc,argv)

int argc;
char *argv[];

{
   int dbf_file, dfe, dfr, dfr1, dfr2, dft, i, j, k, l, m;
   int mem_file, nrecs;
   float cmc, cod, dw, factor1, factor2, fvalue, msr, mse,
         p, see, ss, sse, ssr, ssto, swap, s1, s2, ycalc;
   float b[4][4], beta[4], c[4][4], coef[4][4], erry[101];
   float sumx2[101][4], sumy2[101], sumx[4], tvalue[4],
         x[101];
   float xz[101][4], y[101];
   char  *cvar, *dbfname, *memname;
   char  lrdvar[41],lrivar[41],lrtitle[41],srecs[20];
   unsigned cvarsz;

   /* Check for file name passed as argument */
   if (argc != 2)
     {
       printf("Usage: %s filename    ",argv[0]);
       printf("[DO NOT INCLUDE AN EXTENSION]\n\n");
       exit(1);
     }

   /* Display title */
   clrscr();
```

```
printf("SIMPLE LINEAR REGRESSION WITH ");
printf("ONE INDEPENDENT VARIABLE");

/*  This section reads three memory variables saved by
    Program 13-2.

    It was written using Borland's Turbo C, other compilers
    may require changes.
*/

strcpy(memname,argv[1]);
strcat(memname,".MEM");

/* Try to open memory variable file */
mem_file = open(memname, O_RDONLY|O_BINARY);
if (mem_file == -1)
   {
     printf("Error opening memory file %s\n",memname);
     exit(1);
   }

/* Loop to read each memory variable saved */
while (read(mem_file, (char *)&mem_head,
       sizeof(MEM_HEAD)) == sizeof(MEM_HEAD))
   {
     cvarsz = mem_head.mvarlen + mem_head.mvardec * 256;
     cvar = malloc(cvarsz);
     read(mem_file,cvar,cvarsz);

     /* Determine which memory variable was just read */
     if (strcmp(mem_head.mvarname,"LRTITLE") == 0)
        strcpy(lrtitle,cvar);
     if (strcmp(mem_head.mvarname,"LRDVAR") == 0)
        strcpy(lrdvar,cvar);
     if (strcmp(mem_head.mvarname,"LRIVAR") == 0)
        strcpy(lrivar,cvar);
     free(cvar);
   }

printf("\n\nLinear Regression Title: %s",lrtitle);
printf("\nIndependent Variable:    %s",lrivar);
printf("\nDependent Variable:      %s",lrdvar);

/*
   This section reads the data pairs for regression saved
   by Program 13-2.

   It was written using Borland's Turbo C, other compilers
   may require changes.
*/

strcpy(dbfname,argv[1]);
strcat(dbfname,".DBF");
```

```
/* Try to open database file */
dbf_file = open(dbfname, O_RDONLY|O_BINARY);

if (dbf_file == -1)
  {
    printf("Error opening database file %s\n",dbfname);
    exit(1);
  }

/* Read database header */
if (read(dbf_file, (char *)&dbf_head,
    sizeof(dbf_head)) != sizeof(DBF_HEAD))
  {
    printf("\nProblem reading database header\n");
    exit(1);
  }

/* Jump to beginning of data using offset from header */
if (lseek(dbf_file,(long)dbf_head.firstbyte,0) == -1)
  {
    printf("\nCannot find the beginning of the data\n");
    exit(1);
  }

ltoa(dbf_head.numrecs,srecs,10);
nrecs = atoi(srecs);              /* Number of data points */
dfr = 1;                   /* Regression degrees of freedom */
dfr1 = dfr+1;
dfr2 = dfr+2;

/* Initialize arrays */
for(i = 1; i < nrecs + 1; i++)
  {
    x[i] = 0;
    sumy2[i] = 0;
    for(j = 1; j <= dfr1; j++)
      xz[i][j] = 0;
    for(j = 1; j <= dfr2; j++)
      sumx2[i][j] = 0;
  }

/* Loop through database reading each record and assigning
   values to array. Variable x holds data points. */
printf("\n\nData sets to be used in regression:");
x[1] = 1;
for(i = 1; i <= nrecs; i++)
  {
    read(dbf_file,(char *)&dbf_rec,dbf_head.reclength);
    x[dfr1] = atof(dbf_rec.xstr);               /* x value */
    x[dfr2] = atof(dbf_rec.ystr);               /* y value */
    printf("\nX VALUE: %f",x[dfr1]);
    printf("\nY VALUE: %f\n",x[dfr2]);
    y[i] = x[dfr2];          /* Array of observed y values */
```

```
      /* Calculate sum of x squared, sum of x * y, and
         y squared */
      for(j = 1; j <= dfr1; j++)
        {
          xz[i][j] = x[j];
          for(k = 1; k <= dfr2; k++)
            sumx2[j][k] += x[j] * x[k];
          sumy2[j] = sumx2[j][dfr2];          /* sum of x*y  */
        }
      /* sum of y squared */
      sumy2[dfr2] += x[dfr2] * x[dfr2];
    }

 /* Set up arrays b and c with all zero elements except
    main diagonal. This calculation determines a factor
    used in standard error for each regression coefficient.
    Use array b to determine next action, but perform it
    on both b and c. */
 for(i = 1; i <= dfr1; i++)
   {
     for(j = 1; j <= dfr1; j++)
       {
       b[i][j] = 0;
       for(k = 1; k <= dfr1; k++)
         b[i][j] += xz[k][i] * xz[k][j];
       c[i][j] = 0;
       }
     /* Put a 1 in all diagonal elements of array c */
     c[i][i] = 1;
   }

 /* Solve matrix working through diagonal */
 for(i = 1; i <= dfr1; i++)
   {
     for(j = i; j <= dfr1; j++)
       {
       if (b[j][i] == 0)
         {
           /* This problem has no solution */
           if (i == j)
           {
             printf("\nSingular matrix");
             exit(1);
           }
         }
       else
         {
           /* Swap rows /*
           for(k = 1; k <= dfr1; k++)
             {
               swap    = b[i][k];
               b[i][k] = b[j][k];
               b[j][k] = swap;
```

```
               swap    = c[i][k];
               c[i][k] = c[j][k];
               c[j][k] = swap;
             }

         /* Normalize row to diagonal element */
         factor1 = 1.0 / b[i][i];
         for(k = 1; k <= dfr1; k++)
            {
              b[i][k] *= factor1;
              c[i][k] *= factor1;
            }

         /* Subtract multiple of current row from all
            others */
         for(m = 1; m <= dfr1; m++)
            {
              if (m != i)
                 {
                   factor1 = -b[m][i];
                   for(k = 1; k <= dfr1; k++)
                      {
                        b[m][k] += factor1 * b[i][k];
                        c[m][k] += factor1 * c[i][k];
                      }
                 }
            }
         j = dfr1;
       }
    }
  }

/* Sum of x */
for(i = 2; i <= dfr1; i++)
  sumx[i] = sumx2[1][i];

/* Solve for regression coefficients */
for(i = 1; i <= dfr1; i++)
  {
    j = 1;
    while (sumx2[j][i] == 0)
       {
         j++;
         if (j > dfr1)
            {
              printf("\n\nNO UNIQUE SOLUTION!");
              exit(1);
            }
       }

    /* Normalize row to diagonal element */
    factor2 = 1.0 / sumx2[i][i];
    for(k = 1; k <= dfr2; k++)
```

```
        sumx2[i][k] *= factor2;

    /* Subtract multiple of current row from all others */
    for(j = 1; j <= dfr1; j++)
      if (j != i)
        {
        factor2 = -sumx2[j][i];
        for(k = 1; k <= dfr2; k++)
          sumx2[j][k] += factor2 * sumx2[i][k];
        }
  }

/* Calculate coefficients and coefficient statistics */
p = 0;
for(i = 2; i <= dfr1; i++)
  p += sumx2[i][dfr2] * (sumy2[i] - sumx[i] *
      sumy2[1]/nrecs);

/* Total sum of squares */
ssto = sumy2[dfr2] - sumy2[1] * sumy2[1] / nrecs;

/* Degrees of freedom error */
dfe = nrecs - dfr - 1;

/* Retrieve coefficients from array */
for(i = 1; i <= dfr1; i++)
  coef[i][dfr2] = sumx2[i][dfr2];

/* Standard error of estimate */
see = pow(fabs((ssto - p)/dfe),.5);

/* Coefficient of determination */
cod = p/ssto;

/* Coefficient of multiple correlation */
cmc = pow(cod,.5);

ss = pow(fabs(1.0 - cod)*ssto/dfe,.5);

/* Calculate standard error and t-value */
for(i = 1; i <= dfr1; i++)
  {
    beta[i] = ss * pow(c[i][i],.5);
    if (fabs(beta[i]) < 1.0E-8)
      beta[i] = 1.0E-8;

    /* Student-t is calculated by dividing the coefficient
       by its standard error */
    tvalue[i] = coef[i][dfr2]/beta[i];
  }

/* Print report */
```

```
/* The first part prints a table containing
   the coefficients of the equation:
              y = constant + a * x  */
printf("\n                   COEFFICIENT    ");
printf("STANDARD ERROR     T-VALUE");
printf("\nConstant     %15.4f %15.4f %15.4f",
       coef[1][dfr2],beta[1],tvalue[1]);
for(i = 2; i <= dfr1; i++)
  printf("\nIndependent %15.4f %15.4f %15.4f",
         coef[i][dfr2],beta[i],tvalue[i]);

/* The coefficient of determination (r-squared) is the
   square of the correlation coefficient. Its range is
   zero to one. A value of .85 means that 85% of the
   variance in the dependent variable can be explained by
   the regression equation */
printf("\n\nCoefficient of determination:         %15.4f",
       cod);

/* The correlation coefficient is a measure of association.
   Its range is from -1 to 1. -1 indicates a perfect
   negative correlation (when the independent variable goes
   up, the dependent variable goes down). A perfect
   positive correlation has a value of +1. A value
   of zero indicates no correlation.   */
printf("\nCoefficient of multiple correlation:   %15.4f",
       cmc);

/* The standard error of estimate measures the amount of
   variability in points around the calculated regression
   line. It is the standard deviation between the actual
   points and the regression line.   */
printf("\nStandard error of estimate:           %15.4f",
       see);

/* ANOVA stands for ANalysis Of VAriance. It tries to
   show the amount of variation of calculated values from
   actual due to the regression (explained) and to residuals
   (unexplained). The more variation that can be explained
   by the regression, the greater the F-value (the ratio of
   explained to unexplained variance)  A good general rule
   of thumb is that a regression is significant if the
   F-value is greater than 30.

   A residual is the difference between the actual point and
   the value calculated by the regression line.   */

printf("\n\nANOVA Table:");
printf("\n                      SUM OF    DEGREES      ");
printf("MEAN");
printf("\n                      SQUARES   FREEDOM      ");
printf(" SQ ");
```

```
    ssr = cod * ssto;        /* Regression sum of squares */
    sse = (1-cod) * ssto;    /* Error sum of squares */
    dft = dfe + dfr;         /* Degrees of freedom total */
    msr = ssr / dfr;         /* Regression mean square */
    mse = sse / dfe;         /* Error mean square */
    if (mse == 0)
      mse = 1.0E-8;
    fvalue  = msr / mse;

    printf("\n REGRS    %15.4f   %d    %15.4f",ssr,dfr,msr);
    printf("\n RESID    %15.4f   %d    %15.4f",sse,dfe,mse);
    printf("\n TOTAL    %15.4f   %d",ssto,dft);

/* The Durbin-Watson Test tests the correlation in the
   residuals. In simple terms, it measures the tendency of
   the error between the calculated value and the actual
   value of a data point to influence the error of the next
   point. A value of zero indicates no autocorrelation,
   small values indicate a positive autocorrelation, and
   large values indicate a negative autocorrelation. */

    for(i = 1; i <= nrecs; i++)
      {
      /* Determine calculated y */
        ycalc = sumx2[1][dfr2];
        for(k = 2; k <= dfr1; k++)
          ycalc += sumx2[k][dfr2] * pow(xz[i][k],(k-1));

      /* Calculate error between actual and calculated y */
        erry[i] = y[i] - ycalc;
      }

    s1 = 0;
    s2 = 0;
    for(i = 2; i <= nrecs; i++)
      {
      s1 += (erry[i] - erry[i-1]) * (erry[i] - erry[i-1]);
      s2 += erry[i] * erry[i];
      }
    s2 += erry[1] * erry[1];
    if (s2 == 0)
      s2 = 1.0E-8;
    if (fabs(s1) < 1.0E-8)
      s1 = 0;
    dw = s1 / s2;
    printf("\n\nDurbin Watson statistic for ");
    printf("%d points is: %15.4f",nrecs,dw);

}
```

Program 13-3. Linear Regression—C Part

Loading Binary Files

Program 13-2 runs an external EXE file from FoxPro by using RUN to load it each time it is needed. The delay is minimal if it is called just once. However, suppose we call it many times. Then the repeated loading has a large effect. FoxPro provides a way to load binary files into memory once, and then call them repeatedly using the LOAD and CALL commands.

Binary files loaded by FoxPro must have the extension BIN. They are not the same as executable (EXE) files. However, we can convert some EXE files generated from assembly language programs to BIN files using the DOS utility EXE2BIN. Rules to follow when creating or using binary files with FoxPro are:

- The first executable instruction must have a zero offset from the beginning of the file. Do not reserve memory there for temporary storage.
- Do not change the lengths of variables passed as arguments. The information may not be passed back to FoxPro correctly.
- Restore the SS and CS registers to their original values before exiting the routine or it will not return to FoxPro.
- Use a far return when CALLing the routine from FoxPro. If EXIT terminates the routine, use RUN to execute it rather than CALL.
- The program cannot use any external space. Therefore, if it needs temporary storage, provide for it in the assembly language program itself.

The LOAD command copies a binary file into memory. FoxPro can have up to sixteen such files in memory at a time, provided there is enough room. A file can be as large as 32K. Once the files are loaded, we can call any of them by name using CALL.

Suppose we create a program called XWHEREIS.ASM to locate a file in any directory on the current drive. After assembling the source to an EXE module, we can use the utility EXE2BIN to convert it to a binary file:

```
EXE2BIN XWHEREIS.EXE
```

Now we can load the converted file into our application with the command

```
LOAD XWHEREIS
```

The LOAD command has a single option, SAVE. It copies the contents of video RAM when the binary file finishes executing and puts it on FoxPro's desktop. FoxPro then treats the information exactly like something it wrote. So it will not erase the information when we move a window over it. When we remove the window, the text reappears just like other text written by FoxPro. Of course, the CLEAR command removes all text at any time.

The LOAD command just reads the binary file into memory. To execute it, we must CALL it. We must follow CALL with its name, even if only one binary file has been loaded. Along with the name, we can pass a character string as a parameter. It serves the same purpose as options on a command line of an EXE file. We can also pass memory variables of any type from the application, as long as the binary file has instructions to interpret them.

Like LOAD, CALL supports the SAVE and NOSAVE options. They override ones used with LOAD. Therefore, to save the screen generated by the binary file, use the SAVE option with CALL rather than with LOAD.

Program 13-4 is a small routine that prompts for a file name. It then uses FILE() to check whether the file exists. If not, the program calls the binary procedure XWHEREIS to check all directories in the current drive. The SAVE option allows the user to view possible locations for the file before entering the name again.

```
* Program 13-4
*
* Prompts for a file name and determines whether it exists

* Set environment
  SET TALK OFF
  SET STATUS OFF
  SET SCOREBOARD OFF
  CLEAR

* Prompt for a file name
  DO WHILE .T.
     filenm = SPACE(40)
     @ 5,10 SAY "Enter a file name: " GET m->filenm ;
            PICTURE "@S20"
     READ
     filenm = ALLTRIM(m->filenm)

     * If file exists, exit loop and continue program
     IF FILE(m->filenm)
        EXIT
     ENDIF

     * File not found. Check if it is in another directory.
     CLEAR
     @ WROWS()-3,0 SAY 'File &filenm. was not found. '+;
       'Looking in other directories.'
     CALL xwhereis WITH filenm SAVE
```

```
WAIT 'If correct, enter one of above at prompt. '+;
  'Press any key to continue.'
CLEAR

ENDDO

* Rest of program would continue here
RETURN
```

Program 13-4. Calling a Binary File

RELEASE Command

As we use more utilities with our applications, we may find the limitation of
sixteen binary files restrictive. Or we may find that we do not have enough
memory to load even sixteen because of their size. In either case, we must
actively manage which binary files we load concurrently. To load others, we
must remove some from memory. The RELEASE command removes the named
modules. Typical examples are:

```
RELEASE MODULE XWHEREIS
RELEASE MODULE DUMTERM, LINREG
```

Interfacing with FoxGraph

The last external program we will discuss here is FoxGraph. It produces 15
types of two-dimensional graphs and 32 types of three-dimensional graphs. It
contains a Data Manager that reads the file types listed in Table 13-1.

Table 13-1. File Types Read by FoxGraph

Extension	File Type or Origin
3DT	FoxGraph files
ASC	Boeing Calc files
DAT	ASCII files
DIF	DIF (spreadsheet) files
SLK	SYLK (Multiplan) files
WKS	Lotus 1-2-3 Version 1A
WK1	Lotus 1-2-3 Version 2

FoxGraph cannot read FoxPro databases directly. However, it provides the utility GPRO.PRG that lets a user select information from them to build ASCII files that it can read. We can execute GPRO directly from a FoxPro program with a DO statement

```
DO GPRO
```

The interface includes features to help the user select fields, create titles, and pick other options for the graph. We could employ it in other applications where we want the user to control the selection of graph parameters.

FoxGraph's Tagged ASCII File Structure

Rather than use GPRO.PRG, we may want the application to generate an ASCII file directly for FoxGraph. Thus we need to know how to format it. FoxGraph's tagged ASCII file consists of two parts, a data part and a data definition part. They can appear in either order, but they should not be split.

Data Definition Section

The data definition consists of tagged parameter strings. Each specifies where in the data section to find an item of the graph definition, either headers or data. It is surrounded by quotation marks and begins and ends with two percentage signs (%%). The parameter name is followed by row and column numbers, representing its position in the data section. Table 13-2 describes all parameter string types.

Table 13-2. FoxGraph Parameter String Definitions

Column_Headers: <row>, <column>

Designates headers for individual columns. If any are skipped, FoxGraph leaves the corresponding column definitions blank. For example,

```
"%%Column_Headers: 5, 2%%"
```

indicates that the column headers are on line 5 beginning with the second field. FoxGraph keeps reading across the line until it finds the number of headers defined by the data area.

Column_Title: <row>, <column>

Designates the column title. If it is absent, FoxGraph assumes that the graph has no column title. For example,

```
"%%Column_Title: 4, 1%%"
```

indicates that the column title is the first field of the fourth line.

Lower_Bottom_Right: <row>, <column>

Designates the last data point. If we omit it, FoxGraph assumes that the last data value it finds is the end of the range. For example,

```
"%%Lower_Bottom_Right: 10, 7%%"
```

indicates that the last data point is the seventh field of the tenth line.

Row_Headers: <row>, <column>

Designates headers for the rows. If any are skipped, FoxGraph leaves the corresponding row definitions blank. For example,

```
"%%Row_Headers: 6, 1%%"
```

indicates that the row headers are in the first field beginning with line 6. FoxGraph will keep reading the first field of subsequent lines until it finds headers for the number of rows defined by the data area.

Row_Title: <row>, <column>

Designates the row title. If it is absent, FoxGraph assumes that the graph has no row title. For example,

```
"%%Row_Title: 3, 1%%"
```

indicates that the row title is the first field of the third line.

Subtitle: <row>, <column>

Designates the subtitle. If it is absent, FoxGraph assumes that the graph has no subtitle. For example,

```
"%%Subtitle: 2, 1%%"
```

indicates that the subtitle is the first field of the second line.

Title: <row>, <column>

Designates the title. If it is absent, FoxGraph assumes that the graph has no title. For example,

```
"%%Title: 1, 1%%"
```

indicates that the title is the first field of the first line.

Upper_Top_Left: <row>, <column>

Designates the first data point. If we omit it, FoxGraph assumes that the first data value it finds is the beginning of the range. For example,

```
"%%Upper_Top_Left: 6, 2%%"
```

indicates that the first data point is the second field of the sixth line.
FoxGraph will keep reading data beginning in the second field of
subsequent rows until it reaches the Lower_Bottom_Right position.

Data Section

The data section includes both header information and data to be plotted. We
must enclose header information in quotation marks and separate individual
strings with commas or put them on separate lines. Commas alone separate
numeric data values.

If you do not provide a data definition section, FoxGraph expects the data to
be organized as follows:

- The first row contains the graph title, followed by the
  row heading.
- The second row contains the graph subtitle, followed
  by the column heading.
- The third row contains the column headers.
- The rest of the lines contain the data, one row per line.
- Each line begins with the row header.

In all the above discussions, a row means a line in the ASCII file. A column
means an individual string or a data point separated from other columns by a
comma.

Sample ASCII File for FoxGraph

Figure 13-1 contains a sample ASCII file for FoxGraph. It is a simple graph
plotting student scores for projects, examinations, and class participation. The
numbers, when summed, provide an evaluation of each student's overall class
performance. Figure 13-2 shows a bar chart of the cumulative results.

Suppose we store the ASCII file under the name SAMPLE.DAT in directory
SCHOOL. To execute FoxGraph with it from FoxPro, use the command

```
RUN FOXSWAP FOXGRAPH /D:\SCHOOL\SAMPLE.DAT
```

```
"FoxPro Programmer's Class"
"Instructor: M.P. Antonovich"
""
"Student"
"","AARON","ALEX","JOHN","LAURA","RAY","SANDY"
"1st Project", 94, 88, 90, 72, 92, 60
"Midterm", 90, 96, 82, 89, 62, 78
"2nd Project", 97, 94, 98, 68, 84, 86
"Participation", 89, 83, 93, 55, 70, 84
"Final Examination", 91, 70, 80, 46, 60, 89
"%%Title: 1, 1%%"
"%%Subtitle: 2, 1%%"
"%%Row_Title: 3, 1%%"
"%%Column_Title: 4, 1%%"
"%%Column_Headers: 5, 2%%"
"%%Row_Headers: 6, 1%%"
"%%Upper_Top_Left: 6, 2, 1%%"
"%%Lower_Bottom_Right: 10, 7, 1%%"
```

Figure 13-1. Sample ASCII file for FoxGraph.

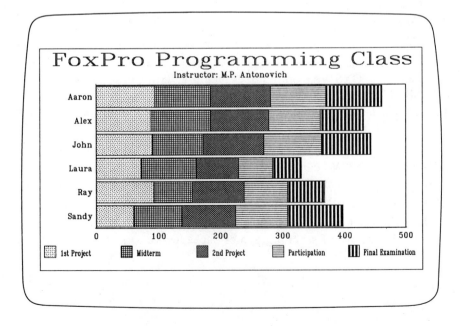

Figure 13-2. FoxGraph bar chart of data in Figure 13-1.

API—The Next Step

The next step in integrating FoxPro with other languages uses the External Routine API (Application Program Interface). It lets developers do the following:

- Link external routines written in Watcom C or 80x86 assembly language directly to FoxPro code
- Use external routines as if they were FoxPro functions rather than via CALL or RUN commands
- Access multiple external routine libraries simultaneously
- Access FoxPro's memory management, input/output, memo fields, dialogs, menus, event handlers, and video output routine from external programs.
- Manipulate FoxPro windows directly
- Execute FoxPro commands
- Evaluate FoxPro expressions

A detailed examination of these features is beyond the scope of this book. In fact, they deserve a entire book on their own. The key at this point in our learning of FoxPro is to master the basic techniques, knowing that these powerful features are there if we need them.

Summary

This chapter showed several ways in which FoxPro supports external programs. We can run utilities or entire programs from an application using the RUN command. The FOXSWAP option frees memory, letting us run large programs. With this ability, we can combine the best features of FoxPro, namely its data entry and data handling functions, with the best features of other languages such as C or Pascal.

From assembly language routines, we can also create binary files that we load into memory once. We can then execute them repeatedly with a CALL statement. The main advantage of memory resident binary files is that no time is lost reading a disk drive when we call them.

Finally we showed the ASCII file format needed to transfer data to FoxGraph. FoxGraph is just one of several graphics packages we can use to display data.

14

Networking FoxPro

This chapter examines FoxPro/LAN, FoxPro's multiuser version. Although a single user can run FoxPro on a network, you must use FoxPro/LAN to realize the full advantages of the environment. It supports multiple users in two basic ways:

- It creates and maintains separate configuration and resource files for each user to customize his or her interface.

- It supports additional program commands that lock records and entire files, allowing users to obtain exclusive control over them.

FoxPro or FoxPro/LAN?

FoxPro and FoxPro/LAN have the same basic features. The main difference is that FoxPro/LAN supports multiple users accessing database files concurrently. Of course, we could copy shared files and distribute them. However, when a file is updated, some users may not receive or may not install the new version. If updates are frequent, they may even install them in the wrong order.

Networks eliminate this risk by providing a single directory from which users can access common files. Any changes they make are immediately available to everyone. This eliminates the need to copy files to and from diskettes, and reduces the chance of error or loss of data. So why not just run FoxPro on a network? Without the support provided by FoxPro/LAN, the integrity of the databases cannot be insured.

Suppose two people are running applications that access a company's inventory file. One loads a record specifying 100 widgets and reduces it by four to reflect a sale. But before it can be saved, the other accesses the same record to add 500 from a new shipment. How many widgets will the record report are in inventory?

Without locking, the answer could be 96 or 600 (quite a difference!). It depends on who saves his or her modifications last. If the salesperson saves 96 widgets first, the receiving clerk overwrites it with 600. Thus the electronic inventory contains four more widgets than it should. On the other hand, if the clerk saves the 600 widgets first, the electronic inventory has 500 fewer than it should. The key point is that neither result is correct.

The problem occurs because two people accessed a record for editing at the same time. The purpose of locks is to prevent this from happening. The idea is to lock the inventory file or record to stop others from editing it. Thus when the first person reads 100 widgets as the current inventory, no one else can change it until he or she saves the new value of 96 and removes the lock. Only then can the second person add the 500 items received. The inventory thus has the correct value of 596 widgets; the locks protect data integrity.

If you share database files on a network, you need the locking features of FoxPro/LAN.

Installing FoxPro/LAN

FoxPro/LAN comes with an installation program similar to FoxPro's. It installs on any network drive and works with major network software that supports NETBIOS. Most of the installation is automatic. However, we must create two sets of files for each user:

```
CONFIG.FP
FOXUSER.DBF, FOXUSER.IDX, FOXUSER.FPT
```

The first is FoxPro's configuration file CONFIG.FP. It customizes the environment for each user. We can put copies of it on his or her local drive or network root drive.

HINT

If users execute programs from different machines, put CONFIG.FP on their network root drives. Conversely, if they always use the same machine, put it on their local drives.

Besides the parameters described in Chapter 1, the configuration file should also contain path references to four major directories:

> overlay file
> editor work file
> sort work file
> program work file

The first path points to the directory containing FoxPro/LAN. The other three can point to directories on network or local drives. The primary consideration here is access time. The local drive is typically faster than network drives because of the extra time required to transfer data across the network, but this is not always true. Network drives could have very high transfer rates, especially if they are large capacity drives with SCSI interfaces and caching. Several utilities can test drive transfer rates. Test your network before assigning the directories. Assigning them to the fastest drives improves FoxPro's performance.

HINT

If you lack a utility to test your computer's disk transfer rates, assume that the local drives are faster.

Related to the configuration file are the resource files FOXUSER.DBF, FOXUSER.FPT, and FOXUSER.IDX. They contain information about FoxPro's appearance and information for some utilities. FOXUSER.DBF stores the color sets, window positions and sizes, and diary entries for the calendar. Although it is a database, we cannot access it without first issuing the command

```
SET RESOURCE OFF
```

We can then edit it just like any other database. For example, we can copy a color set MYCOLORS to a temporary database MYSETUP with the commands:

```
SET RESOURCE OFF
USE foxuser INDEX foxuser
COPY TO mysetup FOR ALLTRIM(id) = 'colorset' .AND.;
   ALLTRIM(name) = 'mycolors'
USE
SET RESOURCE ON
```

To add this color set to another user's configuration file, enter:

```
SET RESOURCE OFF
USE foxuser INDEX foxuser
APPEND FROM mysetup
USE
SET RESOURCE ON
```

As with CONFIG.FP, the ideal location for the resource files may be in a network directory. This choice allows users to log in from any station and still access them.

FoxPro/LAN includes a program ADDUSER that creates CONFIG.FP from CONFIG.DEF. It also creates the resource files from DEFUSER.DBF. If there are common settings needed for all users, you should establish them in these source files before running ADDUSER. Alternately, you may find it more convenient to copy the files from an existing user, editing them for individual changes. If you decide not to run ADDUSER, you must also manually modify the person's AUTOEXEC file or login script to include the following environment variable definition:

```
SET FOXPROCFG = H:\USERDIR\CONFIG.FP
```

FOXPROCFG tells FoxPro where to find the configuration file. In this example, it is on the H drive in directory USERDIR.

If we have multiple configuration files, we can override the one set by the environment variable when executing FoxPro by including the -C parameter. The full pathname of the file must appear. For example, we can change the configuration file's name with

```
FOXPROLN -CH:\MIKE\MYCONFIG.MPA
```

The configuration file sets the drive and directory for all subsequent work files, resource files, and of course, the FoxPro system overlays themselves.

Exclusive versus Shared Files

A major concern in multiuser systems is insuring that only one user can write to a file or record at a time. One way to do this is to open database files for exclusive use. No other user or application can then read or write them. Furthermore, an application will stop if any database file needed exclusively is already open.

This is a brute force way of programming network applications. We use it only when we must prevent all other applications and users from reading or writing a file. Five database actions require such exclusivity. They are:

- INSERT
- MODIFY STRUCTURE
- PACK
- REINDEX
- ZAP

They do not work unless we open the files exclusively. As you can see, they all involve major restructuring of the database or its indexes.

There are three ways to open files exclusively. The first is by default because EXCLUSIVE is initially ON by default for FoxPro/LAN. (We can change this in the CONFIG.FP file with the command EXCLUSIVE = OFF.)

The second uses the SET EXCLUSIVE command. Once it is ON, all subsequently opened files are exclusive to the application. Setting it OFF opens subsequent files as shared, but ones opened earlier remain exclusive. The following commands open two files for exclusive use and two for shared.

```
SET EXCLUSIVE ON
SELECT 1
USE manufact INDEX manufact
SELECT 2
USE brand INDEX brand
SET EXCLUSIVE OFF
SELECT 3
USE inventry INDEX inventry
SELECT 4
USE sales INDEX sales
```

We can get the same effect with the EXCLUSIVE clause of the USE command:

```
SET EXCLUSIVE OFF
SELECT 1
USE manufact INDEX manufact EXCLUSIVE
SELECT 2
USE brand INDEX brand EXCLUSIVE
SELECT 3
USE inventry INDEX inventry
SELECT 4
USE sales INDEX sales
```

Sometimes we need a file opened exclusively only briefly. Suppose our application edits a database. For most features, we need lock only the edited record. However, suppose one function marks records for deletion. We will typically want to pack the database when we exit the edit mode. However, PACK requires exclusive control. Must we open the file initially in exclusive mode to accommodate it?

The solution is to open the file in shared mode for the editing part of the program. Then reopen it in exclusive mode to pack it. The following sequence shows the logic.

```
SET EXCLUSIVE OFF
USE lender INDEX lender
.
.
* Editing routine appears here
.
.
USE lender INDEX lender EXCLUSIVE
PACK
USE lender INDEX lender
```

Network Flags

Besides using SET EXCLUSIVE, we may have to consider other restrictions on opening files imposed by the network itself.

Some networks, such as Novell, allow the system administrator to assign rights to directories and files. For example, he or she can define a directory in which all files can be read, but users cannot create a new file or even write to an existing one. Network rights override anything assigned by FoxPro. Therefore, if the network defines a directory as read only, FoxPro cannot edit files in it even if the program opens them exclusively. Besides directory rights, networks set flags on a file-by-file basis, designating each one as shareable or non-shareable. In most systems, the default for a new file is non-shareable. If its flag is not changed, only one FoxPro user can access it at a time. The Novell command to make all files in a directory shareable is

```
FLAG *.* s
```

To check the shared flag of database files, use

```
FLAG *.dbf
```

Automatic Locking

As we mentioned, the default for FoxPro/LAN is to open files exclusively. Do we lose automatic data protection if we open them as shared? No. In fact, many FoxPro commands (Table 14-1) include automatic locking.

Table 14-1. Commands Providing Automatic Locks

Command	Lock
APPEND	File
APPEND BLANK	File header
APPEND FROM	File
APPEND FROM ARRAY	File
APPEND MEMO	Record
BROWSE	Record
CHANGE	Record
DELETE	Record
DELETE NEXT 1	Record
DELETE RECORD n	Record n
DELETE (NEXT n, ALL, REST)	File
EDIT	Record
GATHER	Record
MODIFY MEMO	Record
READ	Record
RECALL	Record
RECALL NEXT 1	Record
RECALL RECORD n	Record n
RECALL (NEXT n, ALL, REST)	File
REPLACE	Record
REPLACE NEXT 1	Record
REPLACE RECORD n	Record n
REPLACE (NEXT n, ALL, REST)	File
UPDATE	File

SET REPROCESS TO

SET REPROCESS TO tells FoxPro to keep trying to set the lock until it succeeds or another condition is met. If the database or record is already in use when FoxPro tries to set an automatic lock, its response depends on the current value of SET REPROCESS TO and ON ERROR. Table 14-2 lists the options.

Table 14-2. SET REPROCESS TO Values

Value	Meaning
-2	Continue trying to lock indefinitely or until Esc is pressed
-1	Continue trying to lock indefinitely. Will not stop when Esc is pressed.
0	Error routine takes precedence over locking
n	Limits retries to n where n is between 1 and 32,000
n SECONDS	Limits retries to n seconds where n is between 1 and 32,000
AUTOMATIC	Same as -2

Values of SET REPROCESS that let the Esc key interrupt further locking attempts also open a window to display:

```
'Attempting to lock... Press ESC to Cancel'
```

The user can cancel the lock operation by pressing Esc. Doing so executes the ON ERROR procedure if one is defined. Even if none exists, FoxPro still displays an alert box. It allows the user to cancel the program, suspend it, or ignore the error. Although we can choose to ignore errors generated by pressing the Esc key, we should not ignore ones generated by file locks. Doing so skips only the current write operation. The program will stop again when the next command tries to write to the file.

Program 14-1 appends data to a database. If the file cannot be accessed due to a record or file lock, SET REPROCESS TO AUTOMATIC keeps trying to apply the lock.

```
* Program 14-1
*
* Uses SET REPROCESS TO to keep trying to set locks

* Set environment
  SET TALK OFF
  SET BELL OFF
  SET STATUS ON
  SET SCOREBOARD OFF
  SET EXCLUSIVE OFF
  SET REPROCESS TO AUTOMATIC

* Open lender database
```

```
    SELECT 1
    USE lender INDEX lender

*   Append from SDF file LENDER.DAT
    APPEND FROM lender.dat TYPE SDF

    RETURN

*   End of program
```

Program 14-1. Using SET REPROCESS TO AUTOMATIC

This program displays

```
    Attempting to lock... Press ESC to Cancel.
```

while trying to set the lock. If we press the Esc key, it displays

```
    Record is in use by another
```

or
```
    File is in use by another
```

If we cancel the lock attempt with Esc, the program does not append anything.

The main difference between the -1 setting and others is that it prevents the user from canceling the operation with the Esc key. It will not execute an ON ERROR routine. The only way to stop the process other than with a successful lock is to reset or turn off the computer. Use the -1 option for applications that cannot be interrupted for any reason. The -2 setting also tells FoxPro to continue trying to set a lock. It opens a window with the message

```
    'Waiting for lock...'
```

The default setting for SET REPROCESS is 0. It also tries to set file and record locks indefinitely. The main difference from -1 is that an ON ERROR routine, if defined, takes precedence over repeated locking attempts. Therefore, if we change the statement

```
    SET REPROCESS TO AUTOMATIC
```

in Program 14-1 to

```
    SET REPROCESS TO 0
```

it will branch to an ON ERROR procedure if the first attempt to set the lock fails.

We can also limit the attempts or time allowed to set a lock. The maximum number of attempts can range from 1 to 32,000. The following command tries up to 1000 times:

```
SET REPROCESS TO 1000
```

The SECONDS option tells FoxPro to keep trying to set the lock for a specified number of seconds. The following command tries for up to 5 minutes (300 seconds):

```
SET REPROCESS TO 300 SECONDS
```

NOTE

FoxPro cannot retry a lock more than 18.3 times per second.

ON ERROR

ON ERROR traps many kinds of errors, not just network-related ones. When FoxPro encounters an error during program execution, it tries to determine its cause and assigns a number to it. Without ON ERROR, FoxPro displays an alert box, giving the user a choice to cancel the program, suspend it, or ignore the error. However, the user may be able to recover from some errors. For example, an incorrect file name or path is easy to correct. Likewise, the failure of a lock need not cause the program to fail. To let users correct error conditions during program execution, use ON ERROR.

ON ERROR redirects the program to a named procedure when an error occurs. Once there, the function ERROR() returns a number identifying the error. Appendix B lists all FoxPro errors; Table 14-3 lists ones specifically associated with network applications.

Table 14-3. Network-Related Errors

Error Number	Error Message
108	File is in use
109	Record is in use
110	Exclusive open of file is required
111	Cannot write to a read-only file
124	Invalid printer redirection
130	Record is not locked

Users cannot recover from some errors. The best solution is to terminate the program after noting the error number and message.

> **WARNING**
>
> FoxPro does not consider the failure of FLOCK(), LOCK(), or RLOCK() to be an error. Rather, it just returns .F. from the function. The programmer must check the value and provide code that responds to the problem.

For some network errors, we can help the user recover and continue processing. Suppose that a program uses SET REPROCESS TO 300 SECONDS along with an ON ERROR statement. If FoxPro fails to set a lock after 5 minutes, the lock command fails and ON ERROR executes an error procedure. The procedure, recognizing that the error was a failure to set a lock, might open a window to ask the user to either cancel the program or keep trying the lock. If we want the program to try again, we can exit the error procedure with a RETRY command. If we want it to continue by skipping the line that caused the error, we use a normal RETURN. However, after most errors, we will want to CANCEL the program. After several failed attempts at locking the record or file, it may also be necessary to cancel. After all, someone may have gone on vacation and left the file locked.

Program 14-2 adds an ON ERROR routine to Program 14-1. It tests only for network errors. If an error is due to inability to set a lock, the program asks the user whether to retry or cancel. If the user elects to retry, FoxPro repeats the lock command for another five minutes (SET REPROCESS TO 300 SECONDS). Note that the user cannot press Esc to stop locking attempts when we SET REPROCESS with a fixed time or a fixed number of retries. We must wait until the program returns to the ON ERROR routine.

```
* Program 14-2
*
* Appends data to LENDER using SET REPROCESS TO to set
* locks and ON ERROR to exit the program if the lock
* cannot be set

* Set environment
SET TALK OFF
SET BELL OFF
SET STATUS ON
SET SCOREBOARD OFF
SET EXCLUSIVE OFF
SET REPROCESS TO 300 SECONDS              && 5 minutes
ON ERROR DO ERRTRAP WITH error()
```

```
DEFINE WINDOW errshow FROM 10,10 TO 15,60 ;
    TITLE 'ERROR DETECTED' SHADOW COLOR SCHEME 7
DEFINE POPUP nowhere FROM 5,60 SHADOW COLOR SCHEME 4
DEFINE BAR 1 OF nowhere PROMPT '\<Retry Lock' ;
    MESSAGE 'Re-execute the lock command'
DEFINE BAR 2 OF nowhere PROMPT '\<Cancel Program' ;
    MESSAGE 'Cancel the program. Lock cannot be set'
ON SELECTION POPUP nowhere DO GETWHERE

* Open database
SELECT 1
USE lender INDEX lender

* Append from SDF file LENDER.DAT
APPEND FROM lender.dat TYPE SDF

RETURN


PROCEDURE ERRTRAP
PARAMETER errnum

* This procedure is called by ON ERROR. It tries to identify
* the error and, if possible, give the user a chance to
* retry the lock command. Other errors display messages
* before terminating the program.

PUBLIC exit, retry
exit  = .F.
retry = .F.

ACTIVATE WINDOW errshow
DO CASE

  * File in use
  CASE errnum = 108
    @ 0,1 SAY 'File in use'
    ACTIVATE SCREEN
    ACTIVATE POPUP nowhere

  * Record in use
  CASE errnum = 109
    @ 0,1 SAY 'Record in use by another'
    ACTIVATE SCREEN
    ACTIVATE POPUP nowhere

  * Exclusive open of file is required
  CASE errnum = 110
    @ 0,1 SAY 'Exclusive open required'
    exit = .T.
```

```
    * Cannot write to a read-only file
    CASE errnum = 111
      @ 0,1 SAY 'Cannot write to a read-only file'
      exit = .T.

    * Invalid printer redirection
    CASE errnum = 124
      @ 0,1 SAY 'Invalid printer redirection'
      exit = .T.

    * Record not locked
    CASE errnum = 130
      @ 0,1 SAY 'Record is not locked'

    * Non-network error
    OTHERWISE
      @ 0,1 SAY 'ERROR: ' + STR(errnum,4) + ;
                ' Not network related'
  ENDCASE

  DEACTIVATE WINDOW errshow

  * If exit option from POPUP NOWHERE was selected,
  * variable exit is set to .T.
  IF exit
    CANCEL
  ENDIF

  * If retry option from POPUP NOWHERE was selected,
  * variable retry is set to .T.
  IF retry
    RETRY
  ENDIF

RETURN


PROCEDURE GETWHERE

* Gets choice from POPUP nowhere
  barr = BAR()
  DO CASE
    CASE barr = 1
      retry = .T.
    CASE barr = 2
      exit = .T.
  ENDCASE

  DEACTIVATE POPUP
```

```
RETURN

* End of program
```

Program 14-2. Appending Data Using ON ERROR
and SET REPROCESS TO

Setting Manual Locks

FoxPro/LAN does not normally set locks for the read-only commands in Table 14-4. The idea is that since they do not write to the database, the file does not need a lock. FoxPro tries only to protect the database from simultaneous updates. However, a problem arises when others change the file during extensive processing or reporting. Failure to set locks can lead to inconsistencies between sections of a report or procedure.

Table 14-4. Commands That Do Not Set Locks

AVERAGE	JOIN
CALCULATE	LABEL
COPY TO	LIST
COPY TO ARRAY	REPORT
COUNT	SORT
DISPLAY	SUM
INDEX	TOTAL

The SET LOCK ON command adds the commands in Table 14-4 to the automatic file locking list. Locking files while executing them is the only way to ensure that no changes occur. However, automatic locks may not do the job.

Suppose we have a report program that uses information from the LENDER file. It first computes the average interest rate for lenders and displays it. While the AVERAGE command executes, FoxPro sets an automatic lock. If the program next uses the LIST command to display detailed lender information, it also sets a lock. However, between AVERAGE and LIST, the database is not locked. If someone has been waiting with an edited record during the average calculation, FoxPro saves it then. Thus the average displayed at the beginning of the report could differ from the one calculated from the detailed listing. Although the probability of such a discrepancy occurring is low, a good program guards against it.

The problem is that an automatic lock lasts only as long as the command does. Consider Program 14-3. When it starts, it displays a bank record from LENDER. This step requires no locks. Next it prompts for a lender ID. Then using SEEK, it finds a matching record and scatters the fields to memory variables. Since SCATTER is only a read operation, FoxPro does not set an automatic lock. After editing the fields, it gathers them back to the record. During the GATHER command, the record is locked. The program then loops, looking for another lender ID.

```
* Program 14-3
*
* Edits lender data
* Sets automatic locks and ON ERROR routines
* Set environment
  SET TALK OFF
  SET BELL OFF
  SET STATUS ON
  SET SCOREBOARD OFF
  SET EXCLUSIVE OFF
  SET REPROCESS TO 0
  ON ERROR DO ERRTRAP WITH ERROR()

* Define windows and popups
  DEFINE WINDOW getlendr FROM  5, 5 TO  8,30 ;
      TITLE 'LENDER SELECT' SHADOW COLOR SCHEME 5
  DEFINE WINDOW errshow  FROM 10,10 TO 15,60 ;
      TITLE 'ERROR DETECTED' SHADOW COLOR SCHEME 7
  DEFINE POPUP nowhere FROM 5,60 SHADOW COLOR SCHEME 4
  DEFINE BAR 1 OF nowhere PROMPT '\<Retry Lock' ;
      MESSAGE 'Re-execute the lock command'
  DEFINE BAR 2 OF nowhere PROMPT '\<Cancel Program' ;
      MESSAGE 'Cancel the program. Lock cannot be set'
  ON SELECTION POPUP nowhere DO getwhere

* Open database and display first record
  SELECT 1
  USE lender INDEX lender
  DO DISPFORM
  SCATTER MEMVAR
  DO EDITREC
  CLEAR GETS

* Select a lender
  DO WHILE .T.
     lenderno = '    '
     ACTIVATE WINDOW getlendr
     @ 0,2 SAY 'Enter a Lender ID'
     @ 1,10 GET m->lenderno PICTURE '!!!!'
     READ
```

```
      SEEK m->lenderno
      IF FOUND()
        DEACTIVATE WINDOW getlendr
        EXIT
      ENDIF
    ENDDO

* Display selected record, edit it, and replace changes
   SCATTER MEMVAR
   DO EDITREC
   READ
   GATHER MEMVAR

RETURN


PROCEDURE DISPFORM

* Display record form
   SET COLOR TO BG/N
   @ 1,0 TO 22,79 DOUBLE
   @ 3,1 TO 3,78 DOUBLE
   @ 5,1 TO 5,78
   @  2,29 SAY "MORTGAGE SYSTEM"
   @  4, 4 SAY "Lender ID     "
   @  4,36 SAY "Bank Name     "
   @  7, 6 SAY "Address 1   "
   @  9, 6 SAY "City          "
   @  9,41 SAY "State   "
   @  9,55 SAY "Zip Code  "
   @ 11, 6 SAY "Telephone   "
   @ 11,33 SAY "Extension   "
   @ 13, 6 SAY "Tax ID      "
   @ 15, 6 SAY "Current Rate   "
   @ 16,13 SAY "As of   "
   @ 15,44 SAY "Variable Rate Mortgages (Y|N) "
   @ 16,40 SAY "Renegotiable Rate Mortgages (Y|N) "
   @ 17,55 SAY "Wraparounds (Y|N) "
   @ 14,47 SAY "Special Financing Offered:"

RETURN


PROCEDURE EDITREC

* Edit current record
   SET COLOR TO BU/N,N/W
   @ 0, 0 SAY "Record: "+SUBSTR(STR(RECNO()+1000000,7),2)
   IF DELETED()
      @ 0,50 SAY "*DELETED*"
   ELSE
      @ 0,50 SAY "            "
   ENDIF
```

```
    SET COLOR TO BG+/N,N/W
    @  4,17 GET m->l_id        PICTURE "!!!" ;
           MESSAGE "Enter bank ID"
    @  4,49 GET m->l_name      PICTURE "@X25" ;
           MESSAGE "Enter bank name"
    @  7,17 GET m->l_addr1     PICTURE "@X25" ;
           MESSAGE "Enter bank box address"
    @  8,17 GET m->l_addr2     PICTURE "@X25" ;
           MESSAGE "Enter bank street address"
    @  9,17 GET m->l_city      PICTURE "@X20" ;
           MESSAGE "Enter bank city"
    @  9,48 GET m->l_state     PICTURE "!!" ;
           MESSAGE "Enter bank state"
    @  9,65 GET m->l_zip       PICTURE "99999-####" ;
           MESSAGE "Enter bank Zip Code"
    @ 11,17 GET m->l_phone     PICTURE "(###)999-9999" ;
           MESSAGE "Enter bank telephone number"
    @ 11,44 GET m->l_ext       PICTURE "####" ;
           MESSAGE "Enter bank extension"
    @ 13,17 GET m->l_tax_id    PICTURE "99-9999999" ;
           MESSAGE "Enter bank tax id"
    @ 15,20 GET m->l_currate   PICTURE "#9.9##" RANGE 0.0,20.0;
           MESSAGE "Enter current mortgage interest rate"
    @ 16,20 GET m->l_ratedate PICTURE "@D" MESSAGE ;
           "Enter the date the interest rate became effective"
    @ 15,75 GET m->l_vrm       PICTURE "L" MESSAGE ;
           "Does bank offer variable mortgages? (Y|N)"
    @ 16,75 GET m->l_rrm       PICTURE "L" MESSAGE ;
           "Does bank offer renegotiable mortgages? (Y|N)"
    @ 17,75 GET m->l_wrap      PICTURE "L" MESSAGE;
           "Does bank offer wraparound mortgages? (Y|N)"

RETURN

PROCEDURE ERRTRAP
PARAMETER errnum

* This procedure is called by ON ERROR. It tries to identify
* the error and, if possible, give the user a chance to
* retry the lock command. Other errors display a message
* before terminating the program.

    PUBLIC exit, retry
    exit  = .F.
    retry = .F.

    ACTIVATE WINDOW errshow
    DO CASE
      CASE errnum = 108
        @ 0,1 SAY 'File in use'
        ACTIVATE SCREEN
        ACTIVATE POPUP nowhere
      CASE errnum = 109
```

```
                @ 0,1 SAY 'Record in use by another'
                ACTIVATE SCREEN
                ACTIVATE POPUP nowhere
            CASE errnum = 110
                @ 0,1 SAY 'Exclusive open required'
                exit = .T.
            CASE errnum = 111
                @ 0,1 SAY 'Cannot write to a read-only file'
                exit = .T.
            CASE errnum = 124
                @ 0,1 SAY 'Invalid printer redirection'
                exit = .T.
            CASE errnum = 130
                @ 0,1 SAY 'Record cannot be locked'
                exit = .T.
            OTHERWISE
                @ 0,1 SAY 'ERROR: ' + STR(errnum,4) + ;
                          ' Not network related'
        ENDCASE
        WAIT WINDOW

        DEACTIVATE WINDOW errshow

        IF exit
           CANCEL
        ENDIF
        IF retry
           RETRY
        ENDIF

    RETURN

    PROCEDURE GETWHERE

    * Gets choice from POPUP nowhere
      barr = BAR()
      DO CASE
        CASE barr = 1
          retry = .T.
        CASE barr = 2
          exit = .T.
      ENDCASE

      DEACTIVATE POPUP

    RETURN

    * End of program
```

Program 14-3. Using Automatic Locks to Edit Lender Data

One problem is that Program 14-3 does not stop the user from modifying a locked record until it tries to save the changes. But this is a minor annoyance compared to the fact that the lock is not in place long enough to protect the data. Between the time we scatter the fields and the time we gather them back to the database, several minutes could elapse. During that period, a second user might edit the record. Whoever saves it first loses his or her edits. This situation is worse than if there were no locking at all because the programmer thinks that the data is protected.

To solve the problem, we must apply manual locks. FoxPro locks the current file with the FLOCK() function. Unlike SET EXCLUSIVE ON which prevents other users from having any access to a file, FLOCK() only locks the file to write commands or locking functions. Others can open the file and view records without even knowing that a lock exists.

FLOCK() returns .T. if the lock succeeds. We can simulate the SET REPROCESS TO -1 logic by testing its value in a loop structure as follows:

```
DO WHILE .NOT. FLOCK()
ENDDO
```

HINT

Be careful when using ON ERROR and FLOCK() together. FoxPro does not consider the failure to set a lock to be an error. Therefore, it does not execute the ON ERROR procedure when a lock fails. It does return .F. if the lock fails after the SET REPROCESS period or if we press Esc during an attempt. However, we must then handle the logic for the failed lock manually.

FLOCK() locks the current database. We can lock ones in other areas by specifying their aliases or area numbers as parameters (i.e., FLOCK(lender) or FLOCK('1')). This ability is important when locking related files. Locking the primary file in a relation does not affect the others. We must lock each separately with FLOCK().

Of course, we may not need to lock the entire file. In Program 14-3, we only need to lock the edited record. Specifically, we want to lock it from when we scatter its fields to memory variables until after we gather their edited values.

RLOCK() and LOCK() lock the current record in the current database. Like FLOCK(), they return .T. if they succeed. If you do not use SET REPROCESS or have only set it to a fixed number of tries, you must check the return value to determine whether the program can continue.

We must remove locks after completing the file or record operation to avoid delaying other users or applications. Setting a new lock automatically releases the previous one. However, rather than waiting for the next lock, use the UNLOCK command to release locks as soon as possible.

UNLOCK uses IN along with a database alias to release locks in related files. However, it may be faster to release all locks in all areas at once with UNLOCK ALL.

Program 14-4 extends Program 14-3 to use record locks to protect the data from the time it loads memory variables until it saves the edited values with GATHER.

```
* Program 14-4
*
* Updates lender data. Sets manual locks.

* Set environment
  SET TALK OFF
  SET BELL OFF
  SET STATUS ON
  SET SCOREBOARD OFF

* FoxPro will try to set manual locks for up to 5 minutes.
* The ON ERROR is ignored when a timed function fails to
* lock the file or record. Therefore, you must test the
* function value.
  SET EXCLUSIVE OFF
  SET REPROCESS TO 300 SECONDS            && 5 minutes
  ON ERROR DO ERRTRAP WITH ERROR()

* Define windows and popups
  DEFINE WINDOW getlendr FROM 5,5 TO 8,30 ;
      TITLE 'LENDER SELECT' SHADOW COLOR SCHEME 5
  DEFINE WINDOW errshow FROM 10,10 TO 15,60 ;
      TITLE 'ERROR DETECTED' SHADOW COLOR SCHEME 7

  DEFINE POPUP rtrycncl FROM 5,60 SHADOW COLOR SCHEME 4
  DEFINE BAR 1 OF rtrycncl PROMPT '\<Retry Lock' ;
      MESSAGE 'Re-execute the lock command'
  DEFINE BAR 2 OF rtrycncl PROMPT '\<Cancel Program' ;
      MESSAGE 'Cancel the program. Cannot set the lock'
  ON SELECTION POPUP rtrycncl DO getwhere

* Open database and display first record
  SELECT 1
  USE lender INDEX lender
```

```
      DO DISPFORM
      SCATTER MEMVAR
      DO EDITREC
      CLEAR GETS

* Select lender
      DO WHILE .T.
         lenderno = '    '
         ACTIVATE WINDOW getlendr
         @ 0,2 SAY 'Enter a Lender ID'
         @ 1,10 GET m->lenderno PICTURE '!!!!'
         READ
         SEEK m->lenderno
         IF FOUND()
            lockset = RLOCK()
            IF .NOT. lockset
               DO NOLOCK
            ENDIF
            DEACTIVATE WINDOW getlendr
            EXIT
         ENDIF
      ENDDO

* Display selected record, edit it, and replace changes
      SCATTER MEMVAR
      DO EDITREC
      READ
      GATHER MEMVAR
      UNLOCK

   RETURN


   PROCEDURE DISPFORM

* Display record form
      SET COLOR TO BG/N
      @ 1,0 TO 22,79 DOUBLE
      @ 3,1 TO 3,78 DOUBLE
      @ 5,1 TO 5,78
      @  2,29 SAY "MORTGAGE SYSTEM"
      @  4, 4 SAY "Lender ID     "
      @  4,36 SAY "Bank Name     "
      @  7, 6 SAY "Address 1   "
      @  9, 6 SAY "City        "
      @  9,41 SAY "State   "
      @  9,55 SAY "Zip Code   "
      @ 11, 6 SAY "Telephone   "
      @ 11,33 SAY "Extension   "
      @ 13, 6 SAY "Tax ID        "
      @ 15, 6 SAY "Current Rate    "
      @ 16,13 SAY "As of    "
```

```
    @ 15,44 SAY "Variable Rate Mortgages (Y|N) "
    @ 16,40 SAY "Renegotiable Rate Mortgages (Y|N) "
    @ 17,55 SAY "Wraparounds (Y|N) "
    @ 14,47 SAY "Special Financing Offered:"

RETURN

PROCEDURE EDITREC

* Edit current record
    SET COLOR TO BU/N,N/W
    @ 0, 0 SAY "Record: "+SUBSTR(STR(RECNO()+1000000,7),2)
    IF DELETED()
       @ 0,50 SAY "*DELETED*"
    ELSE
       @ 0,50 SAY "           "
    ENDIF
    SET COLOR TO BG+/N,N/W
    @  4,17 GET m->l_id       PICTURE "!!!" ;
            MESSAGE "Enter bank ID"
    @  4,49 GET m->l_name     PICTURE "@X25" ;
            MESSAGE "Enter bank name"
    @  7,17 GET m->l_addr1    PICTURE "@X25" ;
            MESSAGE "Enter bank box address"
    @  8,17 GET m->l_addr2    PICTURE "@X25" ;
            MESSAGE "Enter bank street address"
    @  9,17 GET m->l_city     PICTURE "@X20" ;
            MESSAGE "Enter bank city"
    @  9,48 GET m->l_state    PICTURE "!!" ;
            MESSAGE "Enter bank state"
    @  9,65 GET m->l_zip      PICTURE "99999-####" ;
            MESSAGE "Enter bank Zip Code"
    @ 11,17 GET m->l_phone    PICTURE "(###)999-9999" ;
            MESSAGE "Enter bank telephone number"
    @ 11,44 GET m->l_ext      PICTURE "####" ;
            MESSAGE "Enter bank extension"
    @ 13,17 GET m->l_tax_id   PICTURE "99-9999999" ;
            MESSAGE "Enter bank tax id"
    @ 15,20 GET m->l_currate  PICTURE "#9.9##" RANGE 0.0,20.0 ;
            MESSAGE "Enter current mortgage interest rate"
    @ 16,20 GET m->l_ratedate PICTURE "@D" MESSAGE ;
            "Enter the date the interest rate became effective"
    @ 15,75 GET m->l_vrm      PICTURE "L" MESSAGE ;
            "Does bank offer variable mortgages? (Y|N)"
    @ 16,75 GET m->l_rrm      PICTURE "L" MESSAGE ;
            "Does bank offer renegotiable mortgages? (Y|N)"
    @ 17,75 GET m->l_wrap     PICTURE "L" MESSAGE ;
            "Does bank offer wraparound mortgages? (Y|N)"

RETURN
```

```
PROCEDURE ERRTRAP
PARAMETER errnum
* This procedure is called by ON ERROR. It tries to identify
* the error and, if possible, give the user a chance to
* retry the lock command. Other errors display messages
* before terminating the program.

  PUBLIC exit, retry
  exit  = .F.
  retry = .F.

  ACTIVATE WINDOW errshow
  DO CASE
    CASE errnum = 108
      @ 0,1 SAY 'File in use'
      ACTIVATE SCREEN
      ACTIVATE POPUP rtrycncl
    CASE errnum = 109
      @ 0,1 SAY 'Record in use'
      ACTIVATE SCREEN
      ACTIVATE POPUP rtrycncl
    CASE errnum = 110
      @ 0,1 SAY 'Exclusive open required'
      exit = .T.
    CASE errnum = 111
      @ 0,1 SAY 'Cannot write to a read-only file'
      exit = .T.
    CASE errnum = 124
      @ 0,1 SAY 'Invalid printer redirection'
      exit = .T.
    CASE errnum = 130
      @ 0,1 SAY 'Record is not locked'
      rec_lock = RLOCK()
      IF .NOT. rec_lock
        DO NOLOCK
      ENDIF
    OTHERWISE
      @ 0,1 SAY 'ERROR: ' + STR(errnum,4) + ;
              ' Not network related'
  ENDCASE

  WAIT WINDOW
  DEACTIVATE WINDOW errshow

  IF exit
    CLEAR WINDOWS ALL
    CLEAR
    CANCEL
  ENDIF
  IF retry
    RETRY
  ENDIF

RETURN
```

```
PROCEDURE NOLOCK

* Asks user how to handle a failed lock attempt
  exit  = .F.
  retry = .F.
  ACTIVATE WINDOW errshow
  @ 0,5 SAY 'Cannot set lock'
  @ 1,5 SAY 'Retry or Quit?'
  ACTIVATE SCREEN
  ACTIVATE POPUP rtrycncl

  IF exit
    CLEAR WINDOWS ALL
    CLEAR
    CANCEL
  ENDIF
  IF retry
    RETRY
  ENDIF

RETURN

PROCEDURE GETWHERE

* Gets choice from POPUP rtrycncl
  barr = BAR()
  DO CASE
    CASE barr = 1
      retry = .T.
    CASE barr = 2
      exit = .T.
  ENDCASE

  DEACTIVATE POPUP

RETURN

* End of program
```

Program 14-4. Updating Lender Data Using Record Locks

SET REFRESH TO

If you use the BROWSE, CHANGE, or EDIT command, the SET REFRESH
TO command instructs FoxPro to update the screen regularly. The intervals
range from a second to an hour. Unfortunately, the command does not work
with custom (user formatted) screens.

Setting Multiple Record Locks

A previous section showed how to lock the current record. If we try to lock another one in the same database, FoxPro automatically releases the old lock before setting the new one. However, if we change SET MULTILOCKS from OFF (its default value) to ON, we can lock as many as 8,000 records at one time. No, MULTILOCKS is not the little girl who visited the three bears and tinkered with their network nodes.

With SET MULTILOCKS ON, we have two ways to lock records. First, we can move the record pointer to each one and issue RLOCK() or LOCK(), as in the following program segment that locks all records for the state of Pennsylvania.

```
* Lock all records for Pennsylvania
* before changing interest rate
*
* Allow multiple locks
  SET MULTILOCKS ON
  USE lender INDEX lender
  SET REPROCESS TO 0
* Find all records for Pennsylvania (PA) and lock
* them
  SCAN
  IF state = 'PA'
    rec_lock = RLOCK()
  ENDIF
  ENDSCAN
* Change the interest rate on Pennsylvania records
  REPLACE ALL interest WITH interest + .01 ;
    FOR state = 'PA'
* Remove all locks
  UNLOCK ALL
```

This short sequence locks all Pennsylvania lender records while increasing their interest rates by one percent. (You should have moved to Florida when you had the chance.)

The second way to apply SET MULTILOCKS requires prior knowledge of which record numbers we need to lock. Of course, we rarely have such knowledge. We could even write a program to build a string of record numbers. However, it is generally faster to lock the entire file than to apply a series of record locks.

Determining When to Use Network Commands

What if you want to write an application that runs on both networks and standalone systems? The good news is that FoxPro in the standalone mode ignores most network commands. However, you may want to insure that the program isolates commands related to network functions (such as printer redirection). One approach uses the NETWORK() function. It returns .T. if FoxPro/LAN is running on a network. Therefore, we can use it in a conditional structure to execute network commands. The following code segments illustrate its use.

```
* Test if on a network. If so, open the
* database in exclusive mode to pack it
  IF NETWORK()
     SET EXCLUSIVE ON
  ENDIF
  USE lender INDEX lender
  PACK
  ENDIF

* Test if on a network. If so, reassign
* printer output to a specific device
  IF NETWORK()
     SET PRINTER TO \\server1\laser1=lpt1
  ENDIF
```

Customizing an Application to Specific Network Stations

Most networks identify each station with a number and name. The SYS(0) function returns this information during network operation. Novell uses a 20 character string. The first 15 characters are the station or machine name, the last five are the station number preceded by the # character. We can use the information to limit functions in an application to specific stations. For example, we could allow accounting to edit a client history database, whereas sales can only view data or add new records.

Program 14-5 shows how to limit functions to selected stations. In this example, if SYS(0) returns the first of three listed stations, the program allows editing. Otherwise, it limits the user to viewing the data only.

```
* Program 14-5
*
* Using station names to limit a program's functions

* Set environment
  SET TALK OFF
  SET BELL OFF
  SET STATUS OFF
  SET SCOREBOARD OFF
  IF NETWORK()
     SET EXCLUSIVE OFF
     SET REPROCESS TO 300 SECONDS && 5 minutes
  ENDIF
  ON ERROR DO ERRTRAP WITH ERROR()

* Define three stations
  DIMENSION stns[3]
  stns[1] = 'STATION1       '    &&  Has view and edit rights
  stns[2] = 'STATION2       '    &&  Has view rights only
  stns[3] = 'STATION3       '    &&  Has view rights only

* Define windows/popups
  DEFINE WINDOW getlendr FROM  5, 5 TO  8,30 ;
      TITLE 'LENDER SELECT' SHADOW COLOR SCHEME 5
  DEFINE WINDOW errshow  FROM 10,10 TO 15,60 ;
      TITLE 'ERROR DETECTED' SHADOW COLOR SCHEME 7
  DEFINE POPUP rtrycncl  FROM  5,60 SHADOW COLOR SCHEME 4
  DEFINE BAR 1 OF rtrycncl PROMPT '\<Retry Lock' ;
      MESSAGE 'Re-execute the lock command'
  DEFINE BAR 2 OF rtrycncl PROMPT '\<Cancel Program' ;
      MESSAGE 'Cancel the program. Cannot set the lock'
  ON SELECTION POPUP rtrycncl DO getwhere

* Open database and display first record
  SELECT 1
  USE lender INDEX lender
  DO DISPFORM
  SCATTER MEMVAR
  DO EDITREC
  CLEAR GETS

* Select lender
  DO WHILE .T.
     lenderno = '    '
     ACTIVATE WINDOW getlendr
     @ 0,2 SAY 'Enter a Lender ID'
     @ 1,10 GET m->lenderno PICTURE '!!!!'
     READ
     SEEK m->lenderno
     IF FOUND()
```

```
      IF NETWORK()
        lock_st = RLOCK()
        IF .NOT. lock_st
          DO NOLOCK
        ENDIF
      ENDIF
      DEACTIVATE WINDOW getlendr
      EXIT
    ENDIF
  ENDDO

* Display selected record, edit it, and replace changes
  SCATTER MEMVAR

* Edit mode allowed only for station 1
  IF LEFT(SYS(0),15) = stns[1]
    DO EDITREC
    READ
    GATHER MEMVAR
    IF NETWORK()
      UNLOCK
    ENDIF
  ENDIF

RETURN


PROCEDURE DISPFORM

* Display a record form
  SET COLOR TO BG/N
  @ 1,0 TO 22,79 DOUBLE
  @ 3,1 TO 3,78 DOUBLE
  @ 5,1 TO 5,78
  @  2,29 SAY "MORTGAGE SYSTEM"
  @  4, 4 SAY "Lender ID    "
  @  4,36 SAY "Bank Name    "
  @  7, 6 SAY "Address 1   "
  @  9, 6 SAY "City        "
  @  9,41 SAY "State   "
  @  9,55 SAY "Zip Code   "
  @ 11, 6 SAY "Telephone   "
  @ 11,33 SAY "Extension   "
  @ 13, 6 SAY "Tax ID      "
  @ 15, 6 SAY "Current Rate   "
  @ 16,13 SAY "As of   "
  @ 15,44 SAY "Variable Rate Mortgages (Y|N) "
  @ 16,40 SAY "Renegotiable Rate Mortgages (Y|N) "
  @ 17,55 SAY "Wraparounds (Y|N) "
  @ 14,47 SAY "Special Financing Offered:"

RETURN
```

```
PROCEDURE EDITREC

* Edit current record
  SET COLOR TO BU/N,N/W
  @ 0, 0 SAY "Record: "+SUBSTR(STR(RECNO()+1000000,7),2)
  IF DELETED()
     @ 0,50 SAY "*DELETED*"
  ELSE
     @ 0,50 SAY "          "
  ENDIF
  SET COLOR TO BG+/N,N/W
  @  4,17 GET m->l_id        PICTURE "!!!" ;
          MESSAGE "Enter bank ID"
  @  4,49 GET m->l_name      PICTURE "@X25" ;
          MESSAGE "Enter bank name"
  @  7,17 GET m->l_addr1     PICTURE "@X25" ;
          MESSAGE "Enter bank box address"
  @  8,17 GET m->l_addr2     PICTURE "@X25" ;
          MESSAGE "Enter bank street address"
  @  9,17 GET m->l_city      PICTURE "@X20" ;
          MESSAGE "Enter bank city"
  @  9,48 GET m->l_state     PICTURE "!!" ;
          MESSAGE "Enter bank state"
  @  9,65 GET m->l_zip       PICTURE "99999-####" ;
          MESSAGE "Enter bank Zip Code"
  @ 11,17 GET m->l_phone     PICTURE "(###)999-9999" ;
          MESSAGE "Enter bank telephone number"
  @ 11,44 GET m->l_ext       PICTURE "####" ;
          MESSAGE "Enter bank extension"
  @ 13,17 GET m->l_tax_id    PICTURE "99-9999999" ;
          MESSAGE "Enter bank tax id"
  @ 15,20 GET m->l_currate   PICTURE "#9.9##" RANGE 0.0,20.0;
          MESSAGE "Enter current mortgage interest rate"
  @ 16,20 GET m->l_ratedate PICTURE "@D" MESSAGE;
          "Enter the date the interest rate became effective"
  @ 15,75 GET m->l_vrm       PICTURE "L" MESSAGE ;
          "Does bank offer variable mortgages? (Y|N)"
  @ 16,75 GET m->l_rrm       PICTURE "L" MESSAGE ;
          "Does bank offer renegotiable mortgages? (Y|N)"
  @ 17,75 GET m->l_wrap      PICTURE "L" MESSAGE ;
          "Does bank offer wraparound mortgages? (Y|N)"

RETURN


PROCEDURE NOLOCK

* Asks user how to handle a failed lock attempt
  exit  = .F.
  retry = .F.
  ACTIVATE WINDOW errshow
  @ 0,5 SAY 'Cannot set lock'
  @ 1,5 SAY 'Retry or quit?
```

```
ACTIVATE POPUP rtrycncl

IF exit
  CLEAR WINDOWS
  CLEAR
  CANCEL
ENDIF
IF retry
  RETRY
ENDIF

RETURN


PROCEDURE ERRTRAP
PARAMETER errnum

* This procedure is called by ON ERROR. It tries to identify
* the error and, if possible, give the user a chance to
* retry the lock command. Other errors display messages
* before terminating the program.

  PUBLIC exit, retry
  exit  = .F.
  retry = .F.

  ACTIVATE WINDOW errshow
  DO CASE
    * File is in use
    CASE errnum = 108
      @ 0,1 SAY 'File in use'
      ACTIVATE SCREEN
      ACTIVATE POPUP rtrycncl
    * Record is in use
    CASE errnum = 109
      @ 0,1 SAY 'Record in use'
      ACTIVATE SCREEN
      ACTIVATE POPUP rtrycncl
    * Exclusive open of file is required
    CASE errnum = 110
      @ 0,1 SAY 'Exclusive open required'
      exit = .T.
    * Cannot write to a read-only file
    CASE errnum = 111
      @ 0,1 SAY 'Cannot write to a read-only file'
      exit = .T.
    * Invalid printer redirection
    CASE errnum = 124
      @ 0,1 SAY 'Invalid printer redirection'
      exit = .T.
    * Record is not locked
    CASE errnum = 130
      @ 0,1 SAY 'Record is not locked'
```

```
    * Non-network errors
    OTHERWISE
       @ 0,1 SAY 'ERROR: ' + STR(errnum,4) + ;
                 ' Not network related'
    ENDCASE

    DEACTIVATE WINDOW errshow

    IF exit
       CLEAR WINDOWS
       CLEAR
       CANCEL
    ENDIF
    IF retry
       RETRY
    ENDIF

RETURN


PROCEDURE GETWHERE

* Gets choice from POPUP rtrycncl
    barr = BAR()
    DO CASE
       CASE barr = 1
          retry = .T.
       CASE barr = 2
          exit = .T.
    ENDCASE

    DEACTIVATE POPUP

RETURN

* End of program
```

Program 14-5. Limiting Network Access via Station Names

Checklist for Converting Files from Single User to Multiuser

1. List all files the application uses.
2. List all routines or commands that write data to them or otherwise modify them.

3. Determine if the application must open any files exclusively. For example, a report might need exclusive access to a file. If the data changes while FoxPro is processing the report, the resulting information could be inconsistent.

4. Open all other files as shared using the SET EXCLUSIVE OFF command.

5. Check each command that writes to a file. Has an appropriate lock been set from the first time the program accesses the data?

6. Add a SET REPROCESS TO command to instruct FoxPro how to handle lock setting problems.

7. Add an ON ERROR routine to handle all errors in the program, not just network errors.

8. Remember to manually check the logical values returned by FLOCK(), LOCK(), and RLOCK().

9. If the application must run in network and standalone environments, use the NETWORK() function to determine whether to use network commands. Note that FoxPro ignores some network commands and functions such as FLOCK(), LOCK(), RLOCK(), SET REPROCESS TO, and UNLOCK when running in standalone mode.

10. To limit rights based on which station is running the application, use SYS(0) to retrieve a machine name and ID number.

In any case, test the network version with a few workstations before releasing it for general use.

Summary

In this chapter, we introduced commands that allow FoxPro programs to run on a network. We saw that automatic locks provide considerable protection, especially from several users trying to write to the same file. However, manual locks provide more control and therefore better data protection when users are both reading and writing files concurrently. We examined how to deal with lock failures and provide the user with options using ON ERROR to reference other procedures. We also showed how the NETWORK() function helps us write applications that run in both network and standalone environments.

15

Debugging Your Applications

Debugging is an essential stage of every application. Occasionally, small routines or procedures run perfectly the first time, but even the best programmers find such events unusual. Everyone makes mistakes. FoxPro helps us correct them efficiently and (almost) painlessly. Effective use of debugging tools reduces the time and effort required to test an application.

FoxPro's integrated environment makes debugging much easier than with other database managers. The ability to display an Edit window with the program listing, a Browse window with database values, and the Command window, all while displaying the program output, is just one important feature. Others include the Trace window that displays each program line as it executes and the Debug window that follows selected variable or expression values.

Writing applications requires concentration and the ability to think clearly and logically for extended periods of time. Unfortunately, for most programmers, interruptions are the rule, not the exception. The causes vary. They could be someone with a misbehaving program, a user who cannot find a file, your guru calling from Tibet with the latest stock tip, or the department head who wants still another meeting (mostly to discuss where and when to hold even more meetings). Any interruption that breaks concentration can trigger an error. In practice, few programs work correctly the first time we run them. Obviously, the larger the program, the greater the chance for errors.

Language developers recognize this fact. It is why they include improved tools such as symbolic debuggers and profilers with major compilers to help programmers locate errors. Before looking at the tools FoxPro provides, let us consider what types of errors we generally find.

Types of Errors

There are two major classes of errors, syntax and logical. Syntax errors are violations of a language's structural rules. Usually, they are severe enough to stop compilation. Most compilers try to identify the line containing the error. FoxPro, for example, opens the Edit window and displays the source code, highlighting the offending line. Unfortunately, it finds only one syntax error at a time during compilation. Therefore, you may need several passes to find and correct all your mistakes.

Removing syntax errors does not guarantee that the program will work. During execution, it may encounter other errors. For example, trying to use an undefined variable, applying the wrong index, or dividing a numeric field by zero in the MOD function can only be found during execution. These are logical errors. They are usually something the programmer forgot or set incorrectly but are valid syntactically.

Errors that cause the program to fail are usually easy to find and correct. However, some logical errors are more difficult to uncover. They may not cause the program to fail. Rather, it continues, generating incorrect values. In fact, it may even terminate normally, printing pages of results in the process. Sometimes they are obviously wrong. For example, if your program tries to divide by zero, FoxPro does not flag the error and stop execution. Instead, it sets the result to an overflow value. When displayed or printed, it appears as a string of asterisks.

The real danger occurs when incorrect results are not obvious. Values may look reasonable. Then only careful analysis of selected test cases can show that errors exist. Such mistakes can be difficult to detect and, even after detection, difficult to trace and correct.

Detecting Errors

FoxPro does an exceptional job of trapping syntax errors and pointing to the lines on which they occur. When it reports a syntax error, all you must do is look in the Commands and Functions manual or use F1 for help to find the correct format.

FoxPro also helps locate logical errors that cause the program to fail. For example, if it tries to use an undefined variable in a GET statement, the program stops and displays an alert box. It contains a short description of the error (such as 'Variable not found') along with three options: CANCEL, SUSPEND, and IGNORE. FoxPro also opens the Edit window to display the erroneous line.

> **NOTE**
>
> A complete list of FoxPro errors appears in Appendix B.

Occasionally, we may know exactly how to correct a problem. In such cases, we select CANCEL to exit the program, correct it, and rerun it. But we are seldom so lucky. Let's return to the undefined variable. If it occurs during a GET statement, we know which variable is involved. However, suppose it occurs during the evaluation of a complex expression such as

```
AVGNONDEAL = (TOTALDLRS - SALESDOLRS) / (TOTALUNITS - ;
             SALESUNITS) * 100
```

Any variable could be the undefined one. FoxPro does not identify it. In this case, we SUSPEND the program rather than CANCEL it, then examine the variables. We open the Command window with Ctrl-F2 and print them with the ? command. This simple step quickly determines which variable caused the error.

The IGNORE option tells FoxPro to skip the error and continue executing the program. For minor errors (such as an undefined variable to set screen colors), we might just note them and let the program continue compiling or executing to check for other errors. However, one error may trigger many more, so use the IGNORE option cautiously.

Once we locate the undefined variable, we must determine the cause. The first step in doing this is to identify all lines in which the variable appears. If you have run FoxDoc, you should have a file containing a complete variable cross-reference for the program. If you lack such a listing, use the FIND feature of the Edit window to locate the lines. (You may have to do this for each separately stored program in the application.)

> **HINT**
>
> A current variable cross-reference list is invaluable for large systems, especially when values are used in several modules.

Next examine the variable values at several points in the program. To do this, insert SUSPEND commands to interrupt it without losing anything. SUSPEND opens the Command window, allowing us to use any command to test memory or database values. We can also change them. We can even open the Edit window to view the program logic. However, if we want to continue running the program from the point of suspension with the RESUME command, we cannot change any lines. Nor should we change the active database or move the record pointer.

Trace Window

The problem with SUSPEND is that if we use it often, we do not always know which instance caused an interruption. An alternative is to use the Trace window.

The Trace window echoes each program line as it executes. Actually, it displays a complete listing of the program with the current line highlighted. The lines scroll as the program runs. Although information written to the screen appears behind the trace window, windows opened by the application may cover it. We will discuss ways to solve this problem later.

By itself, tracing can help determine why the program is or is not executing specific lines. It also helps locate errors by line number. Before explaining how to use the Trace window, let's look at its features.

We can open the window in three ways:

- By selecting ECHO or STEP from the Program menu popup. STEP executes just one command and then asks the user whether to cancel or resume the program. Selecting resumption makes it execute another command and ask again. It thus steps through the application. ECHO executes lines continuously, stopping only for user input or when it encounters an error.

- By issuing SET ECHO ON or SET STEP ON from the Command window or from the application. Issuing either from the Command window activates the Trace window immediately to begin tracing program lines. However, in a large program, we usually want to trace only a segment. In this case, issue SET ECHO ON at the beginning of the code you want to trace and SET ECHO OFF at its end. We can mix SET ECHO and SET STEP commands, but only one can be active at a time.

- By selecting the TRACE option in the Window menu popup. If a program was suspended before we opened the Trace window, it appears there. The highlighted line is the one immediately after the SUSPEND or erroneous command. If no program was active, the Trace window is empty.

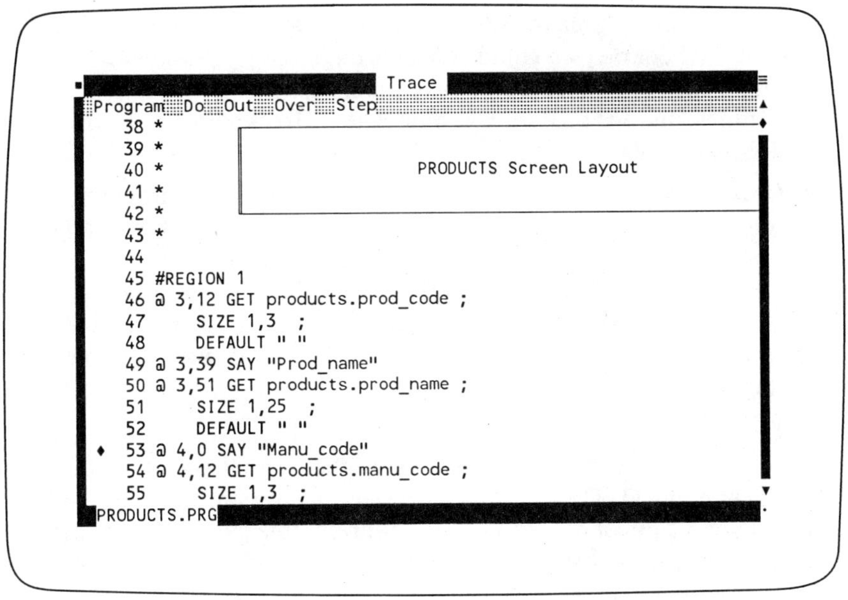

Figure 15-1. Example trace window with a breakpoint marked.

Figure 15-1 shows the Trace window containing an active program. Note that it supports all normal system window controls. Thus if its position interferes with other windows, we can move or resize it.

The Trace window has its own menu of five pads. The first one, Program, contains the following options.

- *Open* displays the Open File dialog. Use it to open any compiled FoxPro program. A common use is to mark breakpoints (they stop execution temporarily). You can then execute the program by selecting DO in the System Program pulldown.

- *Cancel* terminates suspended programs and removes their listings from the Trace window. However, it does not close the window.

- *Line Numbers* adds line numbers to the listing. They help in locating errors.

- *Clear Breakpoints.* Trace retains breakpoint settings until we either exit FoxPro or recompile a module. However, we may have to remove breakpoints following a test without recompiling. Of course, we could scroll through the program and toggle each one. This would take time, especially with large modules, and we could miss some. Clear Breakpoints removes all breakpoints quickly.

- *Trace Between Breakpoints.* Turning trace on slows program execution significantly. If an error occurs near the end of a large program, we do not want to trace all of it. Rather we could place SET ECHO commands inside it to turn trace on and off for the desired segment. But one criterion in debugging is to avoid changing the source code physically. If we mark the line range we want to trace with breakpoints, this option traces only the source code between them.

The definition of the second pad depends on the current status of trace. If no program is running, it is Do. It allows us to select a program and begin executing it. If trace is in the midst of a suspended program, this pad is Resume. Like the RESUME command, it restarts execution at the line where it was suspended.

The Out pad exits the current procedure, stopping at the first command after the one that called it.

We can also skip a procedure by selecting the Over pad. The call must be highlighted (meaning it is the next command to execute). In some tests, we may want to skip long procedures to save time.

Step executes the highlighted command and then stops again at the next executable line. Use it to proceed slowly through the program logic, checking variable values or determining the exact path.

Slowing Down Trace

When using the Trace window, we can control how fast FoxPro executes commands. By pressing Ctrl, Shift, or a mouse button, we limit it to no more than four per second. Of course, ones that take longer, such as indexing, run at normal speed. In addition, if we press and hold any two controls together, we slow execution to no more than two commands per second. The speed reduction applies only as long as we keep pressing the controls. As soon as we release them, execution resumes its normal pace.

Suspending during a Trace

Even if we slow execution of a program during a trace, we still may not understand what is happening. Sometimes, we want to stop the program and check intermediate results or study the display.

Of course, we could just put SUSPEND statements in the source code. Execution stops when it reaches one of them, and the Trace window shows the nearby commands. We can then open the Command window to check intermediate variable values. Afterward, we can resume the program with either the RESUME command from the Command window or Trace's Resume pad.

Note that, when using Trace, we know exactly which SUSPEND interrupted the program.

Of course, if we add SUSPEND commands, we must remember to remove them before distributing the code. If there are many of them, it is easy to forget some. The Trace window provides a better way to interrupt applications during testing. We mark lines with breakpoints. We can activate the window to add them in three ways:

- When the program is already suspended due to a SUSPEND command in the source code or a previous breakpoint in the trace listing

- When program execution is canceled and the Trace window has not been closed

- From the Window pulldown before executing a program

In any case, if the Trace window is visible, we can activate it by pressing Ctrl-F1 to cycle through the windows. Then, by using the arrow keys, highlight the line where you want to add a breakpoint and press the space bar. A small diamond appears at the beginning of the line. Now resume execution or rerun the program from the Command window. When it reaches the breakpoint, it stops just as if we had placed a SUSPEND command there.

When we set breakpoints from the Trace window rather than inserting SUSPEND commands, we need not remove them. They are not saved with the application. Of course, if we leave FoxPro and return later, we must reset them. During a session, we can remove a breakpoint by simply highlighting the line in the Trace window and pressing the space bar. The diamond disappears. FoxPro does not limit the number of breakpoints active in a program. If you have many, you may want to use the Clear Breakpoints option to remove them all.

Closing the Trace Window

The Trace window remains open until we specifically close it with

```
DEACTIVATE WINDOW TRACE
```

or

```
HIDE WINDOW TRACE
```

We can only reactivate it from the Trace option of the Window menu popup. SET ECHO ON or SET STEP ON cannot open it because the DEACTIVATE command removed its definition from memory. Therefore, if you want to use the Trace window in several parts of an application, use HIDE WINDOW TRACE to remove it temporarily and ACTIVATE WINDOW TRACE to restore it.

Reviewing a Program in the Trace Window

When a breakpoint suspends the program, the Trace window displays a few lines around it. The arrow keys scroll through it, highlighting one line at a time. Use this opportunity to set or clear breakpoints.

Stepping through Parts of a Program

One reason for setting breakpoints is to switch between trace modes. Remember, ECHO executes lines continuously, stopping only at breakpoints or for user input. Because it displays each line in the Trace window as it is executed, it slows program execution. Use the Trace Between Breakpoints option to trace only selected segments.

The STEP mode executes just one line at a time. It is like having a breakpoint on each line. With the program suspended, we can review its path and check the values of individual variables.

Debug Window

The second tool FoxPro provides to help locate errors is the Debug window. It displays values during program execution.

Figure 15-2 shows that the Debug window consists of two areas. We put variable names, functions, and expressions in the one on the left. The one on the right displays their current values. Examples of expressions that can appear include:

DBF()	displays the name of the active database
PROMPT()	displays the text of the selected menu prompt
x	displays the value of variable x
x + y	displays the sum of variables x and y
ch = 'B'	displays the logical value of the expression (.T. or .F.)

In fact, we can print the current value of any variable, expression, or function in the Debug window. If a variable is undefined, a blank appears on the right side.

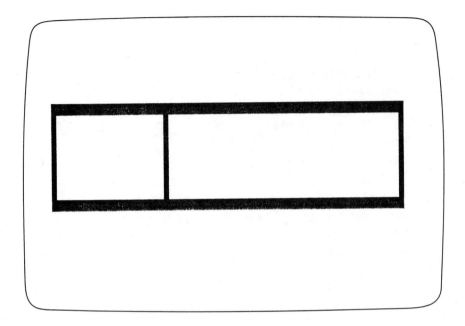

Figure 15-2. Debug window.

Thus the Debug window lets us monitor variables without suspending the program. However, in some cases, values change rapidly or unexpectedly. We can suspend the program from the Debug window each time one changes.

To set a breakpoint on a logical variable or expression, use the arrow keys to highlight it. Then press Tab to put the cursor on the vertical bar separating the two sides of the window. Now use the space bar to toggle the breakpoint indicator, a diamond. This tells FoxPro to interrupt program execution each time its value changes. Note that the value must be logical. The breakpoint does not apply just because a variable changes. The program is interrupted only if the entire expression changes from true to false or vice versa.

Another feature of the Debug window is horizontal scroll bars. The variable name or expression appears on the left side, whereas its value appears on the right. The areas' sizes do not limit the size of the expression or its value since each area scrolls using a scroll bar at the bottom of the window. We can also move the vertical bar separating the two sides to change their relative sizes.

Example of Using the Debug Window

Suppose that we have written a program to read total daily sales information from a database. It uses the data to produce a weekly sales report listing total units, total dollars, and average price. As the task is simple, we create a database with the structure:

FIELD	TYPE	SIZE	DECIMAL PLACES
SALEDATE	D	8	
UNITS	N	4	
SALES	N	6	2

If we index the database by SALEDATE, we can read through it sequentially, accumulating units and sales by week. Whenever a new one starts, we call a procedure to write the previous one's results. Then we begin accumulating data again. Program 15-1 does the job.

```
* Program 15-1
*
* Read daily sales data and produce a weekly summary

* Set environment
SET TALK OFF
CLEAR

* Open database and index
SELECT 1
USE daysales INDEX daysales

SCATTER MEMVAR

* Determine first week of data and initialize accumulators
weekend = m->saledate + 7 - DOW(m->saledate)
weekunits = 0
weeksales = 0
avgprice  = 0

SCAN
* Calculate Saturday ending date
  SCATTER MEMVAR
  IF m->saledate > m->weekend
    DO WEEKLY
    weekunits = 0
    weeksales = 0
  ENDIF
  IF BETWEEN(m->saledate,m->weekend-6,m->weekend)
    weekunits = m->weekunits + m->units
```

```
      weeksales = m->weeksales + m->sales
   ENDIF
ENDSCAN
DO WEEKLY

CLOSE DATABASES
RETURN


PROCEDURE WEEKLY
* Prints weekly results. Formats numeric output
* with the TRANSFORM() function.
   ? "SALES FOR WEEK ENDING: "+DTOC(m->weekend)
   avgprice = m->weeksales / m->weekunits
   ? "  AVERAGE PRICE: $"+TRANSFORM(m->avgprice,'    999.99')
   ?
* Increment week ending date
   weekend = m->weekend + 7
RETURN

* End of program
```

Program 15-1. Accumulating Weekly Sales

Now suppose the program works perfectly for several weeks. Then suddenly it prints:

```
SALES FOR WEEK ENDING: 10/07/90
     AVERAGE PRICE:   ******
```

The asterisks indicate a numeric overflow. Either the number is larger than the formatted area, or it is the result of a division by zero. Let's use the Debug window to help determine what happened.

We must examine other variable values when the error occurs, specifically the date of the record being read, the number of units sold, and the total dollars. We therefore open the Debug window and enter the expressions shown in Figure 15-3.

Note that we display both the week's ending date and the record's sale date. We also display units and sales. We know that an error has occurred when the average price overflows the output field. By comparing its value with the largest printable number, we can skip calculations that do not cause a problem. When an overflow occurs, the comparison becomes true. We add a suspend marker to this line so FoxPro interrupts the program when AVGPRICE > 999.99 changes value. Figure 15-4 shows the Debug window after we run the program again and it suspends.

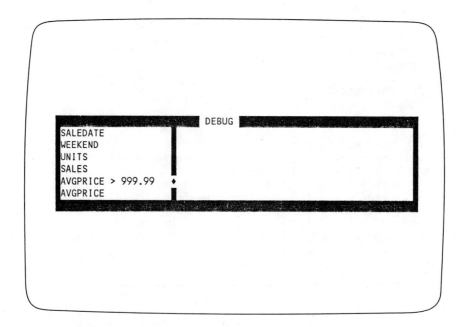

Figure 15-3. Debug window before rerunning Program 15-1.

With the extra information, we quickly see the problem. The average price exceeds 999.99. Either the output field is too small, or the number of units or total sales are wrong.

Now that we know what caused the problem, we either modify the program to handle larger values or correct the input data. Let's assume that the data is correct and the average price field must be enlarged. Let's also test for division by zero. The following lines are the replacements in procedure WEEKLY:

```
? "SALES FOR WEEK ENDING: "+DTOC(m->weekend)
? "  UNITS:          "+TRANSFORM(m->weekunits,' 999,999')
? "  DOLLARS:       $"+TRANSFORM(m->weeksales,'999,999.99')
avgprice = IIF(m->weekunits > 0, m->weeksales/m->weekunits, 0)
? "  AVERAGE PRICE: $"+TRANSFORM(m->avgprice,'  9,999.99')
?
weekend = m->weekend + 7
```

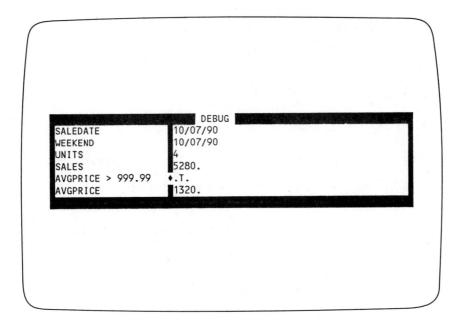

Figure 15-4. Debug window after rerunning Program 15-1.

Combining the Trace and Debug Windows

The combination of Trace and Debug windows provides a powerful debugging environment. We can use Trace to control program execution, set breakpoints, and monitor logic flow. The Debug window can simultaneously monitor the values of memory and database variables as the code executes. Using both windows, we can pinpoint exactly where a value changes and why. While the program is suspended or between steps, we can add variables to the Debug window. The only problem is that the windows occupy space that the program is already using.

Making Room for All the Windows

How do we make room for all these windows on the screen at once? Although FoxPro does not limit the number of open windows, viewing output becomes increasingly difficult with Trace, Debug, and Command windows open. If you have an EGA or VGA monitor, you can increase the number of display lines to alleviate the problem.

FoxPro supports several display modes besides the standard 80 column by 25 row text mode. They include:

CGA	80 columns by 25 rows
COLOR	80 columns by 25 rows
EGA25	80 columns by 25 rows
EGA43	80 columns by 43 rows
MONO43	80 columns by 43 rows
VGA25	80 columns by 25 rows
VGA50	80 columns by 50 rows

To determine what type of graphics adapter your computer has, type

```
? SYS(2006)
```

The EGA43 mode supports 43 text lines on EGA monitors, and VGA50 displays up to 50 lines on VGA monitors. You can tell FoxPro to use a particular mode by issuing SET DISPLAY TO. Typical examples are:

```
SET DISPLAY TO EGA43
SET DISPLAY TO VGA50
```

Of course, using the extra lines in applications is unwise unless you are sure that all potential users have access to them. However, we can put them to work during development. Let the application use the top 25 lines, and move the Trace, Debug, and Command windows below them. Figure 15-5 shows a possible VGA configuration.

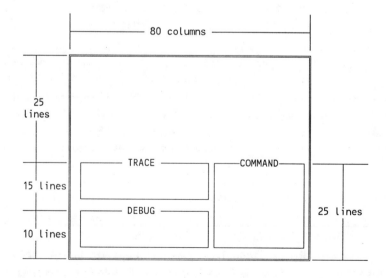

Figure 15-5. Using VGA extended screen modes during debugging.

Operating Errors

Some errors (Table 15-1) are neither syntax nor logic errors. Let's examine a few and see how to correct them.

Table 15-1. Operating Error Messages

Error Message	Error Number
Cannot create file	1102
Cannot open file	1101
Cannot update file	1157
Cannot write to a read-only file	111
File access denied	1705
File write error	1105
Insufficient memory	43
No memory for buffer	1149
No memory for file map	1150
No memory for filename	1151
OS memory error	1012
Out of disk	56
Printer driver is corrupted	1643
Printer driver not found	1644
Printer not ready	125
RUN/! command failed	1405
String memory variable overflow	21
Too many files open	6
Too many memory variables	22
Unable to create temporary work files	401

The inability to create, open, update, or write to a file can be the result of a full disk or directory. Although subdirectories can have unlimited entries, the root directory of a disk has a maximum specified by DOS. An invalid file name can also generate an error. If the application runs on a network, the ability of FoxPro to access, create, or edit files depends on the rights assigned to the directory and the individual user's rights. For example, the message 'File access denied' is a direct consequence of network file security.

Insufficient memory errors can be the result of trying to run FoxPro applications on machines with limited memory or where utilities or device drivers use much of what is available. Possible solutions include:

- Remove memory resident programs
- Add memory
- Provide extended memory
- Use a utility such as 386MAX™ or QEMM™ to relocate DOS and network drivers to high memory (between 640K and 1M)

You can sometimes solve printer errors by as simple an action as turning the printer on (or plugging it in) and putting it in on-line mode. If a driver is required, make sure that it is loaded before executing FoxPro or that FoxPro can find it and load it. Remember, you must have a driver for your specific printer to use styles in reports or labels.

If the error message 'Too many files open' appears, it may refer to the DOS limit. We can raise the limit by increasing the FILES environment variable in the CONFIG.SYS file. The following command sets the maximum number of open files to 50:

```
FILES = 50
```

Files include more than just databases and index files. As far as DOS is concerned, FoxPro itself is a file. In fact, every overlay is a file, as are the keyboard and the printer buffer. To be safe, set the number of files to at least 40. If problems still occur, increase it in increments of 10. Remember to reboot the computer after resetting environment variables. Otherwise, the new values will not apply.

The error message 'String memory variable area overflow' refers to the total amount of space reserved by FoxPro for memory variable strings. The default is 6K. However, we can increase it up to 64K by using the MVARSIZ parameter in CONFIG.FP. Remember to set the environment variable FOXPROCFG to the directory where CONFIG.FP is located. To activate the new value, exit FoxPro and restart it. You do not have to reboot the computer.

The message 'Too many memory variables' refers to a FoxPro limit. Again, the CONFIG.FP file lets us reset the value. By default, FoxPro allows applications to define 256 memory variables. The MVCOUNT parameter can reset the limit as high as 3,600. Ways to reduce the number of required memory variables include:
- Releasing ones no longer needed
- Keeping variables local to their procedures rather than declaring them public

If you change the memory variable limit, you must exit FoxPro and restart it to activate the new value.

Some tricky errors involve sharing and locking files on a network. Carefully review file attributes. Files must be shareable before multiple users can access them simultaneously. Programs can be read only; however, be careful of making database files read only. Even master files require occasional maintenance. It is better to place them in directories where access rights can be assigned by user class. Proper use of record and file locks along with the SET REPROCESS and ON ERROR commands is essential for successful network applications.

ON ERROR Revisited

The previous debugging techniques apply during the development phase. Although one hopes to discover and correct all errors then, the fact is that final releases still contain some. Just think of all the "fixes" and ".01 versions" you see even in major, well-established software packages. In addition, as we saw in the last section, some errors are beyond the programmer's direct control. Therefore, applications should include an ON ERROR procedure.

Chapter 14 introduced the ON ERROR command. We used it to redirect FoxPro to a special procedure that uses the ERROR() function to return an error number. Let's extend that procedure with the aid of the functions in Table 15-2.

Table 15-2. Error-Related Functions

ERROR()	Returns an error number that identifies its cause. Appendix B contains a complete listing of FoxPro error messages and their numbers.
LINENO()	Returns the line number containing the error. To get a source listing with line numbers, use the Print option in the File menu popup or the line number option in the Trace window.
MESSAGE()	Without a parameter, returns the text of the message for the error number.
MESSAGE(1)	Adding the parameter 1 displays the source code line where the error occurred.
PROGRAM()	Returns the name of the program or procedure executing when the error occurred.
SYS(16,n)	This variation of SYS() traces errors through related procedures. It returns the program or procedure name defined by the second parameter. A value of 1 returns the name of the main program, 2 returns the name of the procedure called by it, etc. When we reach the level on which the error occurred, the next value of n returns a null string. The following lines show an algorithm to locate the procedure name where the error occurred.

```
* Find level where error occurred
i = 1
* Continue until SYS(16,i) returns null
DO WHILE LEN(SYS(16,i)) <> 0
  i = i + 1
ENDDO
* Null return is one level below error
  i = i - 1
? 'Error in procedure: ',SYS(16,i)
```

Program 15-2 illustrates the use of a procedure that displays error information. Append it to any application to trap errors. To activate it, insert

```
ON ERROR DO ERRSHOW
```

```
* Program 15-2
*
* Sample driver demonstrates an expanded ON ERROR procedure

SET TALK OFF
SET FULLPATH OFF
ON ERROR DO ERRSHOW WITH ;
    ERROR(),MESSAGE(),LINENO(),MESSAGE(1),PROGRAM()
CLEAR

* Load database files
DO LOADFILE

RETURN

PROCEDURE LOADFILE

* Load sales data
  DO GETSALES
* Load other databases here

RETURN


PROCEDURE GETSALES

* Open sales data file (does not exit, therefore creates
* an error)
  SELECT 1
  USE invtry INDEX invtry

RETURN

******************************************
*                                        *
*    P R O C E D U R E    E R R S H O W   *
*                                        *
* This procedure is activated by the ON  *
* ERROR command. It displays information *
* about the error including:             *
*                                        *
*    - Error number and message          *
*    - Program line number and text      *
*    - Traceback of program/procedures   *
*         called to reach error          *
*                                        *
******************************************
```

```
PROCEDURE ERRSHOW
PARAMETER errnum,errmess,linenum,linecode,prog

* Define two windows for error display
  DEFINE WINDOW err1 FROM 0,0 TO 15,40 ;
         TITLE 'ERROR INFORMATION' SHADOW COLOR SCHEME 5
  DEFINE WINDOW err2 FROM 0,40 TO 20,79 TITLE 'TRACEBACK';
         SHADOW COLOR SCHEME 5
  DEFINE WINDOW err3 FROM 18,2 TO 22,30 ;
         TITLE 'ERROR RESOLUTION' SHADOW COLOR SCHEME 7

* Display basic error information
  ACTIVATE WINDOW err1
  @ 0,1 SAY "An error has occurred in: "+prog
  @ 2,3 SAY "Error: "+STR(errnum,8)
  @ 3,5 SAY errmess
  @ 5,3 SAY "On line: "+STR(linenum,6)
  @ 6,5 SAY linecode

* Find level where error occurred. Look for null return,
* then go back 1, plus two more for the ERRSHOW
* procedure and the ON ERROR call.
  i = 1
  DO WHILE LEN(SYS(16,i)) <> 0
    i = i + 1
  ENDDO
  i = i - 3

* Print traceback
* Trim pathname from procedures and functions
  IF i > 1
    ACTIVATE WINDOW err2
    IF RAT(' ',SYS(16,i)) > 0
      ? LEFT(SYS(16,i),RAT(' ',SYS(16,i)))
    ELSE
      ? SYS(16,i)
    ENDIF
    FOR j = i - 1 TO 1 STEP -1
      ?
      IF RAT(' ',SYS(16,j)) > 0
        ? '   Called by: ' + LEFT(SYS(16,j),;
          RAT(' ',SYS(16,j)))
      ELSE
        ? '   Called by: ' + SYS(16,j)
      ENDIF
    ENDFOR
  ENDIF

* Pause for user to decide what to do next
  ACTIVATE WINDOW err3
  @ 1, 2 PROMPT '\<Cancel' MESSAGE 'Cancel the program'
  @ 1, 9 PROMPT '\<Retry ' ;
         MESSAGE 'Retry the line that caused the error'
```

```
@ 1,16 PROMPT '\<Ignore ' MESSAGE 'Ignore the error'
MENU TO ERRFIX

DO CASE
* Cancel option
  CASE errfix = 1
     DEACTIVATE WINDOWS ALL
     CLEAR
     CANCEL
* Retry option
  CASE errfix = 2
     DEACTIVATE WINDOW err1,err2,err3
     RETRY
 * Ignore option
  CASE errfix = 3
     DEACTIVATE WINDOW err1,err2,err3
     RETURN
ENDCASE

RETURN

* End of program
```

Program 15-2. Expanded ON ERROR Procedure

Figure 15-6 shows sample output from Program 15-2. The error information box tells us that error 1, 'File does not exist', occurred on line 24. It also displays the text of the line.

The traceback box tells us that the error occurred in procedure GETSALES, called by procedure LOADFILE, which is part of program CHAP1502.

The error resolution window provides the standard three choices.

Summary

This chapter examined techniques for locating errors during program development. FoxPro's two most effective tools are the Trace and Debug windows. The Trace window displays each line as it executes. The Debug window lets us monitor selected variables and expressions during program execution.

We recognize that programmers cannot find or control all errors. Therefore, applications must have an error trapping routine. Program 15-2 is a basic procedure that displays information about errors encountered by the user. The user can print the screen, thereby helping the programmer solve the problem.

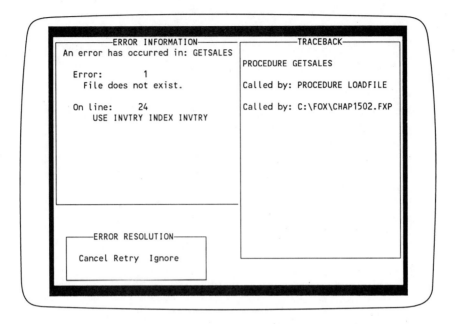

Figure 15-6. Sample output from ERRSHOW.

Appendix A

FoxPro Commands, Functions, and System Memory Variables

This appendix provides a quick reference to FoxPro commands, functions, and system memory variables. It includes descriptions of them and their purposes.

For readers translating applications from FoxBASE, FoxPro Version 1.0, or dBASE IV, special markers designate major enhancements. [F+] indicates ones from FoxBASE+, [F2] ones from FoxPro Version 1.0, and [IV] ones from dBASE IV.

Commands

Command	Description
!	Opens a DOS shell to execute an external command or program. The option FOXSWAP is a memory manager used for large programs [F+,IV]. The option /N specifies how much memory to make available for external programs (see also RUN).
$	Determines if one expression is included in another
?|??	Evaluates expressions and displays results. Includes AT, FUNCTION, and PICTURE clauses [F+].
???	Directs output to the printer without interpreting control codes [F+]
*	Indicates a program comment (see also && and NOTE)

Command	Description
=	Evaluates a list of expressions. It evaluates functions without assigning a returned value to a variable [F+,IV].
&&	Indicates a program comment (see also * and NOTE)
%	Returns integer remainder from a division [F2,IV]
\ I \\	Displays lines of text [F2,IV]
@ BOX	Draws a box with user-defined border and background fill characters [IV]
@ CLEAR TO	Clears an area on the screen or window [F+]
@ EDIT – TEXT	Creates a text editing region [F2,IV]
@ FILL TO	Changes colors in an area or window [F+]
@ GET – CHECK BOX	Creates a check box [F2,IV]
@ GET – INVISIBLE BUTTON	Creates an invisible button [F2,IV]
@ GET – LIST	Creates a list [F2,IV]
@ GET – POPUPS	Creates a popup [F2,IV]
@ GET – PUSH BUTTON	Creates a pushbutton [F2,IV]
@ GET – RADIO BUTTON	Creates a radio button [F2,IV]
@ MENU	Creates a popup menu and adds a shadow option to the menu window [F+,IV]
@ PROMPT	Creates a light-bar menu [IV]
@ SAY/GET	Performs I/O. Includes new options: COLOR [F+] DEFAULT [F+] ERROR [F+] K (PICTURE clause) [F2] MESSAGE [F+,IV] WHEN [F+] WINDOW [F+] The PICTURE clauses for all commands now have a floating dollar sign format [IV].
@ TO	Draws lines and boxes
ACCEPT TO	Reads a character string into a memory variable
ACTIVATE MENU	Displays and activates a bar menu [F+,F2]
ACTIVATE POPUP	Displays and activates a popup menu [F+,F2]
ACTIVATE SCREEN	Redirects I/O to the main screen from a window [F+]

Command	Description
ACTIVATE WINDOW	Displays windows and activates the last one in the list for I/O. The NOSHOW option assigns I/O to a window without making it visible. The options BOTTOM|SAME|TOP change the display order [F+,IV].
APPEND	Adds a blank record to the end of the selected database
APPEND FROM	Adds records to the end of the selected database from a second file. It can specify fields to include, and it defines the delimiter between fields. The ? option displays a list of available files. It can read formats from many popular programs [F+,F2,IV].
APPEND FROM ARRAY	Adds records to the end of a database from a memory variable array [F+]
APPEND MEMO	Adds data to a memo field from a file [F+]
AVERAGE	Calculates the arithmetic mean of a field or numeric expression. It can store the result in an array [F+].
BROWSE	Views and edits the current database. Enhancements include the ability to open a separate window for each work area. It can split windows into linked or independent parts. Options to rearrange and change the width of columns also exist. The KEY clause limits the scope of the records. COLOR and COLOR SCHEME define elements of the window. BROWSE also allows custom field headings. A mouse can control the window size and position [F+,F2,IV].
BUILD APP	Builds an application from a project file [F2,IV]
BUILD EXE	Builds an executable from a project file [F2,IV]
BUILD PROJECT	Builds a project [F2,IV]
CALCULATE	Performs statistical and financial calculations including average, count, maximum, minimum, net present value, standard deviation, sum, and variance [F+]
CALL	Executes a binary (BIN) file previously placed in memory with the LOAD command
CANCEL	Stops executing the current program, closes all open command files, and returns to the dot prompt. The runtime version returns to the operating system.
CHANGE	Activates the browse window in EDIT mode. See BROWSE for changes [F+,IV].
CLEAR	Clears the screen or active window [F+]. Programs must deactivate windows before removing them from the screen.

Command	Description
CLEAR ALL	Closes all database files, indexes, formats, procedure files, and memo files. It releases all memory variables and removes POPUPs and MENUs from memory [F+].
CLEAR FIELDS	Clears the fields specified in the SET FIELDS TO command
CLEAR GETS	Clears all pending GET statements
CLEAR MACROS	Clears from memory all keyboard macros and function key assignments [F+,IV]
CLEAR MEMORY	Clears all memory variables and arrays except system variables. In programs, it releases both public and private variables.
CLEAR MENUS	Clears menus from the screen and memory [F+]
CLEAR POPUPS	Clears popups from the screen and memory [F+]
CLEAR PROGRAM	Clears the compiled program buffer. After recompilation, the old version still executes unless this command is issued [IV].
CLEAR PROMPT	Clears prompts created on the screen or window with the @...PROMPT command [IV]
CLEAR READ	Terminates the current READ [F2,IV]
CLEAR TYPEAHEAD	Clears the typeahead buffer
CLEAR WINDOWS	Removes windows from the screen and memory [F+]
CLOSE ALL	Closes all files
CLOSE ALTERNATE	Closes an open ALTERNATE file
CLOSE DATABASES	Closes all open database, index, memo, and format files
CLOSE FORMAT	Closes open format files in the current work area
CLOSE INDEX	Closes open index files in the current work area
CLOSE MEMO	Closes the window used to edit memo fields [F+,IV]
CLOSE PROCEDURE	Closes open procedure files
COMPILE	Compiles program files (PRG) to object files. It allows wildcards (*,?) in the file specifications [F+].
CONTINUE	Repeats a LOCATE from the current record pointer
COPY FILE	Copies a file
COPY INDEXES	Copies a single key index to a compound index [F2,IV]
COPY MEMO	Copies a memo field's contents to an ASCII file [F+]

Command	Description
COPY STRUCTURE TO	Copies the current database structure to a new database [F2]
COPY TAG	Creates a single key index from a compound index [F2,IV]
COPY TO	Copies selected or all fields from the current database to a new database or an ASCII file. ASCII files can use the tab character as a delimiter [F+,IV]. FoxPro can save database files with memo fields as FoxBASE+ files [F+,IV]. It can produce formats for many popular programs [F2].
COPY TO ARRAY	Copies data from the selected database to a memory variable array. Like SCATTER, it can select fields and specify conditions [F+].
COPY TO STRUCTURE EXTENDED	Copies the structure definition of a database to the fields of a specified database file
COUNT	Counts the number of records in the selected database that meet optional conditions
CREATE	Permits the creation of a new database structure
CREATE COLOR SET	Creates a new color set
CREATE FROM	Creates a new database from the file created by the COPY TO STRUCTURE EXTENDED command
CREATE LABEL	Opens the Label Design screen to create and save a label format. The ? option displays a list of files [F+,IV].
CREATE MENU	Creates a menu using the Menu Builder dialog [F2,IV]
CREATE PROJECT	Creates a project file using the Project Manager [F2,IV]
CREATE QUERY	Creates a query (SQL SELECT command) using the RQBE dialog [F2,IV]
CREATE REPORT	Opens the Report Design screen to create and save a report format. The ? option displays a list of files [F+,IV].
CREATE SCREEN	Creates a screen using the Screen Builder dialog [F2,IV]
CREATE TABLE	Creates a database [F2,IV]
CREATE VIEW	Saves the current environment settings (SET options) in a view definition (VUE) file [F+]
DEACTIVATE MENU	Deactivates a menu bar and erases it from the screen or current window [F+]
DEACTIVATE POPUP	Deactivates a popup window and erases it from the screen or current window [F+]

Command	Description
DEACTIVATE WINDOW	Deactivates windows and erases them from the screen [F+]
DECLARE	Defines a one or two-dimensional memory variable array [F+] (see also DIMENSION)
DEFINE BAR	Defines a single line or item in a popup menu [F+,F2]
DEFINE BOX	Draws a box around text without erasing it. The program must set system memory variable _box to .T. [F+].
DEFINE MENU	Defines the menu bar and name [F+,F2]
DEFINE PAD	Defines a pad on a menu bar [F+,F2]
DEFINE POPUP	Creates a menu popup definition including shadow and color options [F+,F2,IV]
DEFINE WINDOW	Creates a window. The SYSTEM clause adds features to control positioning, size, and other parameters [F+,F2,IV].
DELETE	Marks a record for deletion. The PACK command physically deletes marked records from a file.
DELETE FILE	Erases a file from the disk. The ? option displays a list of files [F+].
DELETE TAG	Removes indexes from a compound index file [F2,IV]
DIMENSION	Creates a memory variable array [F2,IV] (see also DECLARE)
DIR	Lists the files in the specified or default directory. Options can redirect the list to the printer or a file [F+,IV].
DISPLAY	Sends records from the selected database to the screen, printer, or a file [F+]
DISPLAY FILES	Sends file names from the default directory or a specified directory to the screen, printer, or a file. The OFF option suppresses screen output [F+,IV].
DISPLAY MEMORY	Sends the values of all current memory variables, arrays, and system memory variables to the screen, printer, or a file [F+]. A skeleton can display a subset of the variables [F+,IV].
DISPLAY STATUS	Sends all current FoxPro system information to the screen, printer, or a file [F+,F2]
DISPLAY STRUCTURE	Sends the structure of a database file to the screen, printer, or a file [F+]
DO	Executes a command or a procedure file [F2]

Command	Description
DO CASE...ENDCASE	Defines a selection structure that chooses an action from a set of alternatives
DO WHILE...ENDDO	Defines a loop structure that repeats as long as the conditional expression is true
EDIT	Activates the browse window in EDIT mode. See BROWSE for changes [F+,IV] (see also CHANGE).
EJECT	Sends a form feed character or top of form command to the printer
EJECT PAGE	Used with the ON PAGE command to begin a new page in a printed report [F+]
ERASE	Erases a file from the default directory. It displays a list of files to erase [F+] (see also DELETE FILE).
EXIT	Terminates a DO WHILE loop. It also exits SCAN loops and FOR structures [F+,IV].
EXPORT	Copies data from a database to a non-database file format [F2,IV]
EXTERNAL	Identifies undefined files and references for the Project Manager [F2,IV]
FILER	Executes FoxPro's disk file maintenance utility [F+,IV]
FIND	Searches key fields for a literal value
FLUSH	Copies all open buffers to disk [IV]
FOR...ENDFOR	Executes a block of commands a fixed number of times [F+,IV]
FUNCTION	Marks the beginning of a User Defined Function (UDF) [F+]
GATHER	Moves values from an array or set of memory variables into the current database record [F+,IV]
GETEXPR	Executes the FoxPro Expression Builder Dialog [F+,IV]
GO|GOTO	Moves the record pointer to a specific record in the current or specified [F+] database
HELP	Calls the on-line Help facility for any command or function
HIDE MENU	Erases menu bars from the screen or window, but not from memory. The SAVE option puts an image of the menu on the screen or window [F+,IV].
HIDE POPUP	Erases popups from the screen or window, but not from memory. The SAVE option puts an image of the popup on the screen or window [F+,IV].
HIDE WINDOW	Erases a window from the screen or other window, but not from memory [F+,IV]

Command	Description
IF	Selects between two blocks of code, depending on a conditional expression
IMPORT	Creates a new database using data from non-database file formats [F2,IV]
INDEX	Indexes a database in ascending or descending order. It also supports filtered indexes using a FOR condition. FoxPro places blank dates at the beginning of an index. When mixing dates with strings, INDEX supports both DTOC(d,1) and DTOS(d) to translate dates to the format YYYYMMDD. It can also create compact, ascending, descending, and compound indexes [F+,F2,IV].
INPUT	Enters a character string into a memory variable
INSERT	Adds a new record into the database before or after the current record pointer position
INSERT – SQL	Appends a record to the end of the database
JOIN WITH	Merges two databases into a third using related fields
KEYBOARD	Fills the keyboard buffer with characters for later execution. The PLAIN option overrides keyboard macros [IV].
LABEL FORM	Prints labels defined with the CREATE LABEL command. The OFF option suppresses screen output [F+,F2,IV].
LIST	Sends records from the selected database to the screen, printer, or a file [F+]. The OFF option suppresses screen output.
LIST FILES	Sends file names from the default directory or a specified directory to the screen, printer, or a file. The OFF option suppresses screen output [F+,IV].
LIST MEMORY	Sends the values of all memory variables, arrays, and system memory variables to the screen, printer, or a file. A skeleton can display a subset of all memory variables [F+,IV].
LIST STATUS	Sends all FoxPro system information to the screen, printer, or a file [F+]
LIST STRUCTURE	Sends the structure of a database file to the screen, printer, or a file [F+]
LOAD	Reads a binary (BIN) file into memory. A CALL command executes it.
LOCATE	Searches the active database for the next record that matches a given condition

Command	Description
MENU BAR... **MENU** **READ MENU BAR TO**	These three commands together create a pulldown menu system [IV].
MENU TO	Implements a light-bar menu [IV]
MODIFY COMMAND/FILE	Invokes the text editor to edit a command file in the main screen or a window. Options include NOEDIT, NOWAIT, RANGE, and SAVE [F+,IV].
MODIFY LABEL	Opens the Label Design screen to modify a label format. The SAVE option retains the image when you leave the window [F2].
MODIFY MEMO	Opens a window to edit a memo field. Options include NOEDIT, NOWAIT, RANGE, and SAVE [F+,IV].
MODIFY MENU	Modifies a menu using the Menu Builder dialog [F2,IV]
MODIFY PROJECT	Modifies a project file using the Project Manager [F2,IV]
MODIFY QUERY	Modifies a query (SQL SELECT command) using the RQBE dialog [F2,IV]
MODIFY REPORT	Opens the Report Design screen to edit a report format. The SAVE option retains the image when you leave the window [F2].
MODIFY SCREEN	Modifies a screen using the Screen Builder dialog [F2,IV]
MODIFY STRUCTURE	Displays the structure of the current database for editing
MOVE POPUP	Moves a popup [F2,IV]
MOVE WINDOW	Moves a window [F+]
NOTE	Indicates a program comment (see also * and &&)
ON BAR	Activates a popup or menu bar when a popup option is selected [F2,IV]
ON ERROR	Indicates a command to execute when an error occurs during program execution
ON ESCAPE	Indicates a command to execute when the user presses the Esc key during program execution
ON KEY	Indicates a command to execute when the user presses any key during program execution
ON KEY =	Indicates a command to execute when the user presses a specific key during a READ [IV]
ON KEY LABEL	Indicates a command to execute when the user presses specific keys during program execution. It is also available in interactive mode [F+].

Command	Description
ON PAD	Activates the associated popup when the cursor moves to a menu pad [F+,F2]
ON PAGE	Executes a command when a report reaches a specific line number during printing [F+]
ON READERROR	Defines a command to execute when an error occurs during input [F+]
ON SELECTION BAR	Assigns a routine to a popup option [F2,IV]
ON SELECTION MENU	Assigns a routine to a menu bar [F2,IV]
ON SELECTION PAD	Defines a command to execute when the user selects a pad in a bar menu [F+]
ON SELECTION POPUP	Defines a command to execute when the user makes a selection from a popup [F+]
OTHERWISE	Indicates an alternate action in a CASE structure when no specific CASE applies
PACK	Permanently removes records marked for deletion from the selected database. It also packs memo files [F2].
PARAMETERS	Defines memory variable and array names for data passed to a called procedure [F2]
PLAY MACRO	Executes a predefined set of keystrokes. The TIME-OUT option defines the number of seconds between keystrokes [F2,IV].
POP KEY	Restores ON KEY LABEL commands from the stack [F2,IV]
POP MENU	Pulls a menu bar off the stack [F2,IV]
POP POPUP	Pulls a popup off the stack [F2,IV]
PRINTJOB	Identifies part of a program as a report. Initializes the printer and certain system memory variables used during output [F+].
PRIVATE	Defines memory variables for use only in the current procedure
PROCEDURE	Identifies the beginning of a routine in a procedure file
PUBLIC	Defines memory variables as global. It initializes all variables to .F. except FOX and FOXPRO. The ARRAY keyword is optional [F+,IV].
PUSH KEY	Puts current ON KEY LABEL commands onto the stack [F2,IV]
PUSH MENU	Puts a menu bar onto the stack [F2,IV]
PUSH POPUP	Puts a popup onto the stack [F2,IV]

Command	Description
QUIT	Exits FoxPro and returns to DOS
READ	Initiates reading of active @...GET statements. The NOMOUSE clause prohibits the skipping of fields when using a mouse. The TIMEOUT clause terminates the command after a specified number of seconds. Other clauses allow reading GETs stored in multiple windows [F+,F2,IV].
READ MENU TO	Activates a popup menu defined with the @...MENU command [IV]
RECALL	Unmarks records previously marked for deletion
REGIONAL	Creates regional memory variables and arrays
REINDEX	Rebuilds the active index files for the current work area [F2]
RELEASE	Removes memory variables and arrays from memory
RELEASE BAR	Removes options from a popup [F2,IV]
RELEASE MENUS	Removes menus from memory [F+,F2]
RELEASE MODULE	Removes an assembly language (BIN) module from memory
RELEASE PAD	Removes pads from a menu [F2,IV]
RELEASE POPUPS	Removes popups from memory [F+,F2]
RELEASE WINDOWS	Removes windows from memory [F+]
RENAME	Changes the name of a file
REPLACE	Updates fields in a database. It can append character strings to the end of a memo field [F+].
REPORT	Produces a report using the report generator. The OFF option suppresses printing to the screen. The ? option displays a pick list of available reports [F+,F2,IV].
RESTORE FROM	Retrieves memory variables and arrays from a previously saved file. It also restores data saved in a memo field [F+,IV].
RESTORE MACROS	Retrieves keyboard macros previously saved in a file [F+]. It also restores macros from a memo field [F+,IV].
RESTORE SCREEN	Retrieves a screen or window image from a buffer, memory variable, or array element [F+,IV]
RESTORE WINDOW	Retrieves a window definition from a file or memo field [F+,IV]
RESUME	Continues program execution after a SUSPEND

Command	Description
RETRY	Repeats the last command executed just before an error or other interruption
RETURN	Returns control to calling program. It also returns a value when used in a function [F2].
RUN	Opens a DOS shell to execute an external command or program. The option FOXSWAP is a memory manager used for large programs. The /N option specifies the amount of memory to make available for external programs [F+,IV] (see also !).
SAVE MACROS	Saves keyboard macros in a file or memo field [F+]
SAVE SCREEN	Saves the screen or window image in a memory variable, buffer, or array element [F+,IV]
SAVE TO	Saves memory variables and arrays in a file. It also saves data in a memo field [F+,IV].
SAVE WINDOW	Saves a window definition in a file or a memo field [F+,IV]
SCAN...ENDSCAN	Steps through the records of a database file, executing a block of commands for each one [F+]
SCATTER	Moves data from a record into an array or memory variables [F+,IV]
SCROLL	Moves an area of the screen or window up, down, left, or right [F+,F2,IV]
SEEK	Searches the database records by key for a match to an expression. It leaves the record pointer at the first match. If no match is found, it positions the record pointer according to SET NEAR [F+].
SELECT	Activates a work area. Selecting area 0 activates the lowest numbered unused area [IV].
SELECT – SQL	Retrieves data from a database [F2,IV]
SET	Opens the VIEW window [F+,IV]
SET ALTERNATE	Enables or disables output to the ALTERNATE file (see SET ALTERNATE TO)
SET ALTERNATE TO	Directs screen or window output to a file. The ADDITIVE option appends data to a file [F+].
SET ANSI	Determines how SQL string comparisons are made [F2,IV]
SET AUTOSAVE	Enables or disables the flushing of disk buffers after each READ [F+]
SET BELL	Enables or disables the bell after a field entry or at an invalid data entry

Command	Description
SET BELL TO	Defines the bell frequency and duration [F+]
SET BLINK	Selects between extra background colors and blinking for EGA and VGA users [F+,IV]
SET BLOCKSIZE	Defines how FoxPro allocates disk space to memo fields [F2,IV]
SET BORDER TO	Defines the attributes of borders in windows, menus, popups, lines, and boxes [F+]
SET CARRY	The ON option copies some [F+] or all field values from the last record to a new one during data entry.
SET CARRY TO	Defines which fields are carried from last record [F+]
SET CENTURY	The ON option displays dates with 4-digit year formats.
SET CLEAR	The ON option clears the screen when executing the SET FORMAT TO or QUIT commands [IV].
SET CLOCK	Places a clock on the screen [F+]
SET CLOCK TO	Defines row and column position of clock [F+]
SET COLOR OF	Defines colors for BOX, FIELD, HIGHLIGHT, INFORMATION, MESSAGES, NORMAL, and TITLES [F+]
SET COLOR OF SCHEME	Specifies the colors in a color scheme [F+,IV]
SET COLOR SET TO	Loads a previously defined color set [F+,IV]
SET COLOR TO	Specifies the colors of selected screen elements
SET COMPATIBLE	Sets compatible mode to either FOXPLUS or dBASE IV. When set to FOXPLUS or OFF, FoxPro runs FoxBASE programs without changes. When set to DB4 or ON, it runs dBASE IV programs. [F+,IV]
SET CONFIRM	Enables or disables the use of the Enter key to complete a field entry
SET CONSOLE	Enables or disables screen output
SET CURRENCY	Positions the currency symbol to the left or right of the value [F+]
SET CURRENCY TO	Defines the currency symbol [F+]
SET CURSOR	Turns cursor ON and OFF [F2]
SET DATE	Defines the date format as one of the following forms [F+]:

AMERICAN (MDY)	mm/dd/yy
ANSI	yy.mm.dd
BRITISH/FRENCH (DMY)	dd/mm/yy
DMY	dd/mm/yy

Command	Description
	GERMAN dd.mm.yy
	ITALIAN dd-mm-yy
	JAPANESE (YMD) yy/mm/dd
	MDY mm/dd/yy
	USA mm-dd-yy
	YMD yy/mm/dd
SET DEBUG	Enables or disables the Debug and Trace windows [F+,IV]
SET DECIMALS TO	Defines the number of decimal places displayed in numeric results
SET DEFAULT TO	Sets the default drive and directory for I/O
SET DELETED	Enables or disables the use of records marked for deletion
SET DELIMITERS	Enables or disables the display of field delimiters during @...GET statements
SET DELIMITERS TO	Defines the field delimiters for @...GET statements
SET DEVELOPMENT	Compares the dates of source and compiled files to determine if the source must be recompiled before execution [F+]
SET DEVICE TO	Directs the output of @...SAY to the printer, screen, window, or a file
SET DISPLAY TO	Sets the display mode to one of the following: CGA, COLOR, EGA25, EGA43, MONO, MONO43, VGA25, or VGA50 [F+]
SET DOHISTORY	Determines if commands from programs should be placed in the history buffer. FoxPro displays them in the Command window.
SET ECHO	Activates the Trace window for program debugging
SET ESCAPE	Enables or disables the trapping of the Esc key during program execution
SET EXACT	Used in string comparison to force an exact match of not just characters, but length as well. The double equal sign (==) in logical expressions indicates an exact equality test for strings [IV].
SET EXCLUSIVE	Enables or disables use of database files by others on a network
SET FIELDS	Determines if all or only some fields in the database are accessible (see SET FIELDS TO)
SET FIELDS TO	Defines a subset of fields that can be accessed

Command	Description
SET FILTER TO	Defines a condition for selecting records from a database
SET FIXED	Enables or disables the use of the SET DECIMALS TO command
SET FORMAT TO	Opens a custom format file for use with APPEND, BROWSE, CHANGE, EDIT, INSERT, or READ. The ? option displays a list of files. FoxPro supports up to 128 screens in a format file [F+,IV].
SET FULLPATH	Enables or disables the use of full pathnames with file names [F+]
SET FUNCTION	Assigns commands to function keys other than F1. It can assign keyboard macros to them.
SET HEADING	Enables or disables the display of field headings for commands such as AVERAGE, CALCULATE, DISPLAY, LIST, and SUM
SET HELP	Enables or disables FoxPro on-line help [F+,IV]
SET HELPFILTER	Defines a subset of help topics [F2,IV]
SET HELP TO	Identifies a help file for tailoring custom on-line help in an application [F+,IV]
SET HOURS	Selects either a 12 or 24 hour format for time functions [F+]
SET INDEX TO	Opens index files [F2]
SET INTENSITY	Enables or disables highlighting of input fields
SET LIBRARY	Specifies an external library [F2,IV]
SET LOCK	Enables or disables automatic record and file locking
SET LOGERRORS	Routes compilation errors to a file [F+,IV]
SET MACKEY TO	Defines key combination to display Macro dialog window [F2,IV]
SET MARGIN TO	Sets the left margin for printed output
SET MARK OF	Defines the mark character for menus and popups [F2,IV]
SET MARK TO	Defines the date separator character [F+]
SET MEMOWIDTH TO	Specifies the width of memo field output and output for functions ATCLINE, ATLINE, MEMLINE, and MLINE [F+,IV]
SET MESSAGE TO	Displays a message at a specific location on the message line. Keywords LEFT, CENTER, and RIGHT position the message [F+,IV].

Command	Description
SET MOUSE	Enables or disables the mouse [F+,IV]
SET MOUSE TO	Controls mouse sensitivity [F+,IV]
SET MULTILOCKS	Enables or disables multiple record locks
SET NEAR	Determines the position of the record pointer after an unsuccessful database search. When enabled, the record pointer points to the record that is above but most closely matches the search condition [F+].
SET NOTIFY	Enables or disables display of system messages
SET ODOMETER TO	Determines the reporting interval of the progress of database commands such as INDEX and DELETE
SET OPTIMIZE	Turns Rushmore™ query optimization on or off
SET ORDER TO	Defines the master index file [F2]
SET PATH TO	Defines a set of subdirectories to search when a file is not found in the default directory
SET PDSETUP	Loads or clears printer driver setup
SET POINT TO	Defines the character used as the decimal point [F+]
SET PRINTER ON	Enables or disables output to the printer
SET PRINTER TO	Routes output to a printer or a disk file
SET PROCEDURE TO	Opens a file containing additional procedures
SET REFRESH TO	Specifies how often to update BROWSE and memo windows with changes made by other users in a network environment
SET RELATION OFF	Breaks a relation between two database files [F+,IV] (SET RELATION TO also disrupts a previously set relation).
SET RELATION TO	Establishes a relation between two database files. The ADDITIVE option defines multiple relations for a database file [IV].
SET REPROCESS TO	Determines how to handle unsuccessful record and file locks
SET RESOURCE	Saves or ignores changes to the environment resource file [F+,IV]
SET RESOURCE TO	Defines which resource file to use [F+,IV]
SET SAFETY	Enables or disables file overwrite protection
SET SCOREBOARD	Enables or disables a line that shows NumLock, CapsLock, and Insert key status
SET SEPARATOR TO	Defines the numeric place separator character [F+]

Command	Description
SET SHADOWS	Puts shadows behind windows [F+,IV]
SET SKIP	Creates one-to-many relations
SET SKIP OF	Enables or disables menus [F2,IV]
SET SPACE	Determines if a space separates fields and expressions in ? and ?? commands [F+]
SET STATUS	Enables or disables status on line 22
SET STEP	Single steps through a program when ON
SET STICKY	Determines how to display menus when using a mouse in FoxPro. If STICKY is ON, the menu remains open until a selection is made; the user need not hold down the mouse button [F+,IV].
SET SYSMEMU	Determines accessibility of the system menu bar during program execution [F+,F2,IV]
SET TALK	Enables or disables the display of command results [F2]
SET TEXTMERGE	Used to merge text with database or memory variables [F2,IV]
SET TEXTMERGE DELIMITERS	Specifies text merge delimiters
SET TOPIC TO	Determines how HELP topics are selected [F+,IV]
SET TRBETWEEN	Enables or disables trace between breakpoints [F2,IV]
SET TYPEAHEAD TO	Defines the maximum number of characters held in the typeahead buffer. Limited to 128 characters [IV].
SET UDFPARMS	Controls how parameters are passed to procedures and functions [F2,IV]
SET UNIQUE	Determines whether every index key in a database must be unique
SET VIEW	Enables or disables the View window [F+,IV]
SET VIEW TO	Uses the environment saved in a view file
SET WINDOW OF MEMO	Defines the window where memo fields can be edited [F+]
SHOW GET	Redisplays a GET field [F2,IV]
SHOW GETS	Redisplays all GET fields [F2,IV]
SHOW MENU	Displays a menu on the screen or window without activating it. It supports the SAVE and ALL options [F+,IV].
SHOW OBJECT	Redisplays a GET field [F2,IV]

Command	Description
SHOW POPUP	Displays a popup menu on the screen or window without activating it. It supports the SAVE and ALL options [F+,IV].
SHOW WINDOW	Displays a window on the screen or inside another window without activating it [F+,IV]
SIZE POPUP	Changes the size of a popup [F2,IV]
SKIP	Moves the record pointer a fixed number of records in the current database. It can access a record in an unselected database by using the IN option [F+].
SORT TO	Creates a new database sorted by selected fields. It has a DESCENDING option. The FIELDS option can create a sorted file using a subset of the fields from the original file [IV].
SQL – SELECT	Retrieves data from databases
STORE	Places a data item in a memory variable. It can initialize every element of an array [IV].
SUM	Calculates the total of a field in a database. It can place the result in an array [F+].
SUSPEND	Interrupts program execution
TEXT...ENDTEXT	Defines a block of text lines to be sent to the screen or printer. Supports text merge [F2].
TOTAL TO	Computes the total of numeric fields for selected records in one database and places the result in the corresponding fields of another database [F+,IV]
TYPE	Displays an ASCII file on the screen or a printer
UNLOCK	Releases all record or file locks on the active database running on a network. The ALL option releases locks on databases in all work areas.
UPDATE	Replaces fields in the records of the current database with data from another database
USE	Opens a database file and an optional index file in a work area. The ? option displays a list of files. Allows up to 21 open indexes per database [F+,F2,IV].
WAIT	Stops the program until a character is sent from the keyboard or the mouse is clicked [F+,F2,IV]
ZAP	Removes all records from the selected database. It is equivalent to performing a DELETE and a PACK.
ZOOM WINDOW	Changes the size of a system or user window [F2,IV]

Functions

Function	Description or Return Value
&	Macro substitution
ABS()	Absolute value
ACOPY()	Copies arrays [F2,IV]
ACOS()	Arc cosine of a value in radians [F+]
ADEL()	Deletes rows or columns from arrays [F2,IV]
ADIR()	Copies information from current directory into an array [F2,IV]
AELEMENT()	Determines array element number from row and column subscripts [F2,IV]
AFIELDS()	Places database structure information in an array [F2,IV]
AINS()	Inserts a column or row into an database [F2,IV]
ALEN()	Determines the number of elements, rows, or columns in an array [F2,IV]
ALIAS()	Alias of a database
ALLTRIM()	Removes leading and trailing blanks from a string [F+,IV]
ASC()	ASCII version of the first character in a string
ASCAN()	Searches an array for a string [F2,IV]
ASIN()	Arc sine of a value in radians [F+]
ASORT()	Sorts an array into ascending or descending order [F2,IV]
ASUBSCRIPT()	Determines the column or row subscript from the array element number [F2,IV]
AT()	Starting position of the nth occurrence of a case-sensitive substring in a primary string [F+,IV]
ATAN()	Arc tangent of a value in radians [F+]
ATC()	Position of a substring, case insensitive, in a string [F+,IV]
ATCLINE()	Line number of a substring, case insensitive, in a string [F+,IV]
ATLINE()	Line number of a substring, case sensitive, in a string [F+,IV]

Function	Description or Return Value
ATN2()	Arc tangent of a value in radians from sine and cosine values [F+]
BAR()	Number of an option selected from a popup [F+]
BETWEEN()	Determines if an expression's value is between those of two other expressions. Works with numeric values, text strings, and dates [F+,IV].
BOF()	Tests whether the record pointer is at the beginning of the file
CAPSLOCK()	Reports or sets the status of the CapsLock key [F+,IV].
CDOW()	Character string of the day of the week from a date variable
CDX()	Returns the name of an open compound index [F2,IV]
CEILING()	Smallest integer greater than or equal to its argument [F+]
CHR()	Character corresponding to a numeric ASCII value
CHRSAW()	Determines if a character is present in the keyboard buffer [F+,IV]
CHRTRAN()	Translates characters [F+,IV]
CMONTH()	Character string of the month from a date variable
CNTBAR()	Returns the number of bars in a popup [F2,IV]
CNTPAD()	Returns the number of pads in a menu [F2,IV]
COL()	Column position of the cursor
COS()	Cosine of an angle in radians [F+]
CTOD()	Converts a date string to a date variable
CURDIR()	Name of the current DOS directory [F+,IV]
DATE()	Current system date
DAY()	Day of the month from a date variable
DBF()	Name of the selected database file
DELETED()	Determines whether the current record is marked for deletion
DIFFERENCE()	Relative phonetic difference between two character expressions [F+]
DISKSPACE()	Amount of space remaining on the default disk drive
DMY()	Converts a date variable to DAY MONTH YEAR format [F+]

Function	Description or Return Value
DOW()	Number representing the day of the week (1 = Sunday)
DTOC()	Converts a date variable to a string expression. The optional argument <1> converts the date to the format YYYYMMDD for indexing [IV].
DTOR()	Converts a degree value to radians [F+]
DTOS()	Converts a date variable to a character string [F+]
EMPTY()	Determines if an expression is blank or empty [F+,IV]
EOF()	Determines whether the record pointer is at the end of the file. An unselected work area may be checked by supplying an area letter, number, or alias as an optional argument [F+,IV].
ERROR()	Error number if ON ERROR is in effect and an error occurs
EVALUATE()	Evaluates an expression and returns its value [F2,IV]
EXP()	Exponential value
FCHSIZE()	Changes size of file [F2,IV]
FCLOSE()	Flushes and closes a file or communications port [F+,IV]
FCOUNT()	Number of fields in the current database [IV]
FCREATE()	Creates a file [F+,IV]
FEOF()	Determines whether the file pointer is at the end of the file [F+,IV]
FERROR()	Numeric value if an error occurs during a file operation using a low-level function [F+,IV]
FFLUSH()	Flushes a disk file without closing it [F+,IV]
FGETS()	Specified number of bytes from a file or communications port [F+,IV]
FIELD()	Name of a field corresponding to the numeric position in the file
FILE()	Indicates whether a file exists in the default directory
FILTER()	Current filter expression in effect [F+,IV]
FKLABEL()	Function key name corresponding to a numeric value
FKMAX()	Total number of programmable function keys available
FLOCK()	Locks the current database, preventing other users on a network from accessing it. Returns .F. if someone else has a lock on the file or on at least one record in it.

Function	Description or Return Value
FLOOR()	Largest integer less than or equal to its argument [F+]
FOPEN()	Opens a file or communications port [F+,IV]
FOUND()	Returns .T. if the last CONTINUE, FIND, LOCATE, or SEEK did not reach EOF(). Checks an unselected work area if supplied with an area letter, number, or alias as an optional argument [F+,IV].
FPUTS()	Writes characters to a file or communications port. It automatically adds a carriage return and line feed at the end of the string [F+,IV].
FREAD()	Reads a specified number of bytes as a character string from a file or communications port [F+,IV]
FSEEK()	Moves the file pointer [F+,IV]
FSIZE()	File size in bytes [F+,IV]
FULLPATH()	Full DOS pathname of a file [F+,F2,IV]
FV()	Returns the future value of a series of values [F+]
FWRITE()	Writes a character expression to a file or communications port [F+,IV]
GETBAR()	Returns the bar number for the option in a given position of a popup [F2,IV]
GETENV()	Returns a character string containing the specified environment variable
GETFILE()	Displays FoxPro's Open File dialog window. It returns the name of the file selected in the window [F+,IV].
GETPAD()	Returns the pad name for the option in a given position of a menu [F2,IV]
GOMONTH()	Date the specified number of months before or after the one supplied [F+,IV]
HEADER()	Number of bytes in the database header in the selected area [F+,IV]
IIF()	One of two expressions depending on the logical value of a condition
INKEY()	Integer corresponding to the ASCII value of a key pressed. Values of Ctrl-key and Alt-key combinations are system dependent. It can also hide the cursor and check for the press of a mouse button [F+,IV].
INLIST()	Determines if an expression is in a list [F+,IV]
INSMODE()	Toggles the insert/overwrite mode [F+,IV]
INT()	Integer part of a number

Function	Description or Return Value
ISALPHA()	Tests whether a string begins with a letter
ISCOLOR()	Determines whether a color adapter is in use
ISDIGIT()	Tests whether a string begins with a number [F+,IV]
ISLOWER()	Tests whether a string begins with a lowercase letter
ISUPPER()	Tests whether a string begins with an uppercase letter
KEY()	Index expression of the specified index file [F+,F2]
LASTKEY()	ASCII value of the last key pressed [F+]
LEFT()	Specified number of characters beginning at the leftmost character of a string, character field, or memo field [F+]
LEN()	Length of a string, character field, or memo field [F+]
LIKE()	Compares two character expressions [F+]
LINENO()	Relative line number of an executing program [F+]
LOCFILE()	Looks for a file in first the default directory, then the FoxPro path. If not found, it displays the Open File dialog window [F2,IV]
LOCK()	Locks the current record in the current database, preventing other users on a network from accessing it. Returns .F. if someone else has a lock on the record.
LOG()	Natural logarithm
LOG10()	Common (base 10) logarithm [F+]
LOOKUP()	Looks for a record in an unselected database and returns one field from it [F+]
LOWER()	Character expression with letters converted to all lowercase
LTRIM()	Removes leading blanks from a string
LUPDATE()	Date of the last update of a database file. Adding the alias of an unselected database as an argument returns its last update [F+].
MAX()	Largest value from a list of expressions. Expressions can be numeric, character, or date [F+,IV].
MCOL()	Screen or window position of the mouse pointer [F+,IV]
MDOWN()	State of the left mouse button [F+,IV]
MDX()	Returns the name of the open CDX file
MDY()	Converts a date expression to MONTH DAY YEAR format [F+]

Function	Description or Return Value
MEMLINES()	Number of lines in a memo field. The result depends on the MEMOWIDTH setting [F+].
MEMORY()	Remaining memory available in K [F+]
MENU()	Name of currently active menu bar [F+]
MESSAGE()	Prints a message for a current error or the contents of the line that caused the error [IV]
MIN()	Smallest value from a list of expressions. Expressions can be numeric, character, or date [F+,IV].
MLINE()	Specific line from a memo field in the current record [F+,F2]
MOD()	Remainder from integer division
MONTH()	Month number from a date
MRKBAR()	Returns .T. if popup bar is marked [F2,IV]
MRKPAD()	Returns .T. if menu pad is marked [F2,IV]
MROW()	Screen or window row position of the mouse pointer [F+,IV]
NDX()	Name of any index file in the selected area [F2]
NETWORK()	Returns .T. if using FoxPro/LAN
NUMLOCK()	Reports or sets the status of the NumLock key [F+,IV]
OBJNUM()	Returns a GET object's number (used to determine its READ order) [F2,IV]
OCCURS()	Number of times a character expression occurs in the primary string [F+,IV]
ON()	Returns the commands assigned to ON ERROR, ON ESCAPE, ON KEY, ON KEY LABEL, ON PAGE, and ON READERROR
ORDER()	Name of the master index file [F+,F2]
OS()	Name and version number of the current operating system
PAD()	Name of the pad last chosen from a menu bar [F+]
PADC()	Pads or truncates an expression on both sides with a specific character [F+,IV]
PADL()	Pads or truncates an expression on the left side with a specific character [F+,IV]
PADR()	Pads or truncates an expression on the right side with a specific character [F+.IV]

Function	Description or Return Value
PARAMETERS()	Number of parameters passed to the latest procedure called [F+,IV]
PAYMENT()	Amount of each periodic payment on a fixed interest loan [F+]
PCOL()	Column position of the printer. It works even if the output is redirected to a file [IV]
PI()	Numeric value of PI (3.14159265) [F+]
POPUP()	Name of the current popup [F+]
PRINTSTATUS()	Logical indicating whether the printer is ready [F+]
PRMBAR()	Returns the prompt of a popup option [F2,IV]
PRMPAD()	Returns the text of a menu pad [F2,IV]
PROGRAM()	Name of the function, procedure, or program executing when an error occurred [F+]
PROMPT()	Character string containing the option chosen from a menu bar or popup [F+]
PROPER()	Capitalizes letters in a string according to the conventions for proper names. Proper names begin with an uppercase letter, followed by all lowercase letters [F+,IV].
PROW()	Row position of the printer [F+]
PUTFILE()	Displays the FoxPro Save As dialog window to name and save a file [F+,IV]
PV()	Calculates the present value of a future amount [F+]
RAND()	Random number between 0 and 1 [F+]
RAT()	Searches a character string from the right side for the occurrence of another string, returning the position where it is found [F+,IV]
RATLINE()	Searches a memo field for the last occurrence of a character expression, returning the line number where it is found [F+,IV]
RDLEVEL()	Returns the READ level when using nested READs [F2,IV]
READKEY()	Integer corresponding to the key pressed during a READ
RECCOUNT()	Number of records in a database. Checks an unselected work area if supplied with an area letter, number, or alias as an optional argument [F+,IV].

Function	Description or Return Value
RECNO()	Record number pointed at by the record pointer in the current database file. Checks an unselected work area if supplied with an area letter, number, or alias as an optional argument [F+,IV].
RECSIZE()	Record size of the current database file. Checks an unselected work area if supplied with an area letter, number, or alias as an optional argument [F+,IV].
RELATION()	Relation expression for the current area. Checks an unselected work area if supplied with an area letter, number, or alias as an optional argument [F+,IV].
REPLICATE()	Character string formed by repeating a character expression a fixed number of times
RIGHT()	Specified number of characters beginning with the rightmost character of a string
RLOCK()	Locks the current record in the current database, preventing others on a network from accessing it. Returns .F. if someone else has a lock on the record.
ROUND()	Rounds a numeric value to a fixed number of decimal places
ROW()	Row location of the cursor
RTOD()	Converts radians to degrees [F+]
RTRIM()	Removes trailing blanks from a string
SCHEME()	Color pair or pair list from a specified color scheme [F+,IV]
SCOLS()	Number of columns available on the screen [F+,IV]
SECONDS()	System time. Resolution is 1 millisecond [F+,IV].
SEEK()	Performs a seek on a key value as a function. Returns .T. if a SEEK command succeeds [F+].
SELECT()	Number of the current work area if SET COMPATIBLE is OFF. Otherwise, it returns the number of the highest unused work area [F+,IV].
SET()	Status of the SET commands [F+]
SIGN()	-1 (negative), 1 (positive), or 0 (zero), depending on the sign of the numeric expression [F+]
SIN()	Sine of an angle in radians [F+]
SKPBAR()	Enables or disables popup bar
SKPPAD()	Enables or disables menu pad
SOUNDEX()	Phonetic representation of a character expression

Function	Description or Return Value
SPACE()	String containing a fixed number of ASCII space characters
SQRT()	Square root
SROWS()	Number of rows available on the screen [F+,IV]
STR()	Converts a numeric expression to a string
STRTRAN()	Replaces a character substring with a replacement string any number of times in a primary string [F+,IV]
STUFF()	Replaces a fixed number of characters in the primary string with another string
SUBSTR()	Specified number of characters from a primary string or memo field
SYS()	Performs different tasks, depending on its parameters [F+,IV]
SYS(0)	Machine number on a network. Non-networked computers return 1 [IV].
SYS(1)	System date as a Julian day number in a character string. For the date August 4, 1991, it returns the string 2448473 [IV].
SYS(2)	Number of seconds since midnight according to the internal computer clock
SYS(3)	Generates unique file names for temporary files using random characters [IV]
SYS(5)	Current default drive letter (e.g., A, B, C, or D) [IV]
SYS(6)	Current print device. Returns the filename when SET PRINTER TO points to a file [IV].
SYS(7,n)	Displays the latest format file activated by a SET FORMAT TO command [IV]
SYS(9)	FoxPro Serial Number [IV]
SYS(10,d)	Converts a Julian day number to a date string of the form MM/DD/YY [IV]
SYS(11,s)	Calculates Julian day number just as SYS(1) does except that it requires the date as a string rather than using the system date [IV]
SYS(12)	Number of bytes of available memory [IV]
SYS(13)	Printer status: OFFLINE if the printer is not ready, READY if it is
SYS(14,n[,W])	Index expression for index file number <n> in work area <W>. The work area parameter is optional, but the index file number is required [IV].

Function	Description or Return Value
SYS(15,t,s)	Translates characters in string <s> with accents or diacritical marks to ones with the marks defined by table <t>. Fox Software provides the table EUROPEAN.MEM for European users. The translation is necessary to create and maintain indexes correctly [IV].
SYS(16[,n])	Name of the executing procedure. If the numeric expression is included, its value is the number of calling levels to trace the procedure name backward.
SYS(17)	CPU type (e.g., 8088, 80286, 80386, etc.) [IV]
SYS(18)	Name of the field being entered when ON KEY is triggered during a READ [F+,IV]
SYS(21)	Returns number of master index or tag [F2,IV]
SYS(22)	Returns name of master index or tag [F2,IV]
SYS(23)	Amount of EMS memory used by FoxPro [F+,IV]
SYS(24)	EMS limit set in CONFIG.FP [F+,IV]
SYS(100)	Console status as set by the SET CONSOLE ON|OFF command [IV]
SYS(101)	Current default device defined by the latest SET DEFAULT TO command (PRINTER, SCREEN) [IV]
SYS(102)	PRINTER setting (ON or OFF) [IV]
SYS(103)	TALK setting (ON or OFF) [IV]
SYS(1001)	Returns amount of memory available to FoxPro Memory Manager [F2,IV]
SYS(1003)	Full path and filename of the selected database [F+,IV]
SYS(1016)	Returns amount of memory used by controllable objects [F2,IV]
SYS(2000,<expC>[,1])	Name of the first file (or next file when [,1] is used) that matches the skeleton filename <expC>. Each call returns the next match until all matching files in the directory have been returned [IV].
SYS(2001,<expC>[,1])	Current value of the SET option specified by <expC>. For functions with more than one setting (such as SET PRINTER which may be ON or OFF, or set to a filename), the ,1 parameter returns the second one [IV].
SYS(2002,[,1])	Turns the cursor on (if ,1 is present) or off (if ,1 is omitted) [IV]
SYS(2003)	Current default directory on the default drive [IV]
SYS(2004)	Directory FoxPro started from [F2,IV]

Function	Description or Return Value
SYS(2005)	Name of the active resource file [F+,IV]
SYS(2006)	Returns a character string with the type of video graphics card and monitor in use [F+,IV]
SYS(2007,c)	Checksum of the character expression supplied. Can be used to determine if a string has changed [F+,IV]
SYS(2008,n[,c])	Returns and changes the shape of the cursor (switching between insert and overwrite forms) [F+,IV]
SYS(2009)	Switches the cursor between insert and overwrite shapes [F+,IV]
SYS(2010)	Returns FILES setting from CONFIG.SYS [F2,IV]
SYS(2011)	Returns record or file lock status without trying to apply a lock [F2,IV]
SYS(2012)	Returns the memo field block size [F2,IV]
SYS(2013)	Returns system menu names [F2,IV]
SYS(2014)	Returns the minimum path between two files [F2,IV]
SYS(2015)	Returns a unique procedure name [F2,IV]
SYS(2016)	Returns the last SHOW GETS window name [F2,IV]
SYS(2017)	Clears screen and displays FoxPro sign-on screen [F2,IV]
SYS(2018)	Returns the error message parameter [F2,IV]
SYS(2019)	Returns the name and location of CONFIG.SYS [F2,IV]
SYS(2020)	Returns the total size of the default disk [F2,IV]
SYS(2021)	Returns the filter expression of an index [F2,IV]
SYS(2022)	Returns the cluster size of a disk [F2,IV]
SYS(2023)	Returns disk drive used by temporary files [F2,IV]
TAG()	Returns tag names from compound index files [F2,IV]
TAN()	Tangent of an angle in radians [F+]
TARGET()	Alias of the work area that is the target of a relation with the specified work area [F+,IV]
TIME()	Current system time. The parameter 1 returns time in hundredths of a second [IV].
TRANSFORM()	Formats character and numeric variables
TRIM()	Removes trailing blanks from a character string
TYPE()	Determines the type of data in the expression

Function	Description or Return Value
UPDATE()	Determines if data values have changed since the last READ [IV]
UPPER()	Converts character expression to all uppercase
USED()	Determines if the specified database is open in the work area specified [F+,IV]
VAL()	Converts a character expression composed of digits to a numeric value
VARREAD()	Name of the edited field in the current GET or PROMPT during execution of an ON KEY routine during a READ operation [F+]
VERSION()	FoxPro version number
WBORDER()	Returns .T. if window has a border
WCHILD()	Returns number and names of child windows [F2,IV]
WCOLS()	Number of columns in a window [F+,IV]
WEXIST()	Determines if a named window has been defined [F+,IV]
WLAST()	Returns name of window open prior to the current one
WLCOL()	Column of the upper left window corner, relative to the full screen [F+,IV]
WLROW()	Row of the upper left window corner, relative to the full screen [F+,IV]
WMAXIMUM()	Returns .T. if window is maximized
WMINIMUM	Returns .T. if window is minimized
WONTOP()	Name of the topmost window [F+,IV]
WOUTPUT()	Logical indicating whether output is directed to the named window [F+,IV]
WPARENT()	Returns name of parent window [F2,IV]
WREAD()	Returns .T. if window is currently involved in a read
WROWS()	Returns the number of rows in the window [F+,IV]
WTITLE()	Returns the title assigned to a window
WVISIBLE()	Returns .T. if the named window is activated and visible [F+,IV]
YEAR()	Year from a date expression

System Memory Variables

Variable	Description
._ALIGNMENT	Defines output as left, right, or center justified [F+]
_BOX	Determines whether boxes appear around text [F+]
_CALCHEM	Value stored in the calculator's memory [F2,IV]
_CALCVALUE	Value displayed in the calculator [F2,IV]
_CLIPTEXT	Contents of the clipboard [F2,IV]
_CUROBJ	Returns the object number of the current GET field [F2,IV]
_DBLCLICK	Time interval for a double or triple click of the mouse [F2,IV]
_DIARYDATE	Selected date in the diary/calendar [F2,IV]
_GENGRAPH	FoxPro program that takes RQBE results into Fox-Graph [F2,IV]
_GENMENU	FoxPro program used to generate menu code [F2,IV]
_GENPD	Printer driver interface program [F2,IV]
_GENSCRN	FoxPro program used to generate screen code [F2,IV]
_GENXTAB	FoxPro program used to generate cross tabs [F2,IV]
_INDENT	Number of characters to indent the first line of a paragraph [F+]
_LMARGIN	Column position of the left margin [F+]
_MLINE	Returns a memo field offset [F2,IV]
_PADVANCE	Advances output to the top of page using line feeds or a form feed [F+]
_PAGENO	Current page number [F+]
_PBPAGE	Number of first page printed [F+]
_PCOLNO	Current column position [F+]
_PCOPIES	Number of copies to print [F+]
_PDRIVER	Printer driver to use [F+]
_PDSETUP	Specifies a printer driver setup [F2,IV]
_PECODE	Character string that prints at the ENDPRINTJOB command [F+]
_PEJECT	Determines when a page eject is sent [F+]

Variable	Description
_PEPAGE	Last page to be printed [F+]
_PFORM	Name of the print form file used [F+]
_PLENGTH	Number of lines per page [F+]
_PLINENO	Current line position [F+]
_PLOFFSET	Offset of the left side of the paper [F+]
_PPITCH	Printer pitch [F+]
_PQUALITY	Determines whether print should be letter-quality (.T.) or draft-quality (.F.). It depends on the current printer driver [F+].
_PRETEXT	Defines a character expression to preface text merge lines [F2,IV]
_PSCODE	Holds a character string that prints at the PRINTJOB command [F+]
_PSPACING	Determines whether printing should be single, double, or triple spaced [F+]
_PWAIT	Determines whether the printer should wait between pages [F+]
_RMARGIN	Defines the right margin [F+]
_TABS	Location of TAB stops [F+]
_TALLY	Determines number of database records processed by the last database command [F2,IV]
_TALLYTIME	Determines elapsed time for last database command [F2,IV]
_TEXT	Directs text merge output to a file [F2,IV]
_THROTTLE	Specify trace window execution speed
_WRAP	Determines whether automatic word wrap is on [F+]

Appendix B

FoxPro Error Messages

Error #	Error Message
N/A	*Invalid or missing resource file* The file FOXPRO.RSC is either missing or from the wrong version.
1	*File does not exist* Attempt to access a nonexistent file (perhaps because of a misspelling or incorrect disk or directory)
3	*File is in use* Attempt to USE, DELETE, or RENAME a file in use
4	*End of file encountered* Attempt to move record pointer beyond the last record in the file
5	*Record is out of range* Attempt to read a record beyond the number in the database
6	*Too many files open* Attempt to open more files than CONFIG.SYS allows
7	*File already exists* Usually the result of renaming a file to an existing name
9	*Data type mismatch* An expression contains data types that cannot appear together or are of the wrong type.
10	*Syntax error* Syntax error not covered by other error messages
11	*Invalid function argument value, type, or count* Value passed to function is not of expected type or is out of range. May also be caused by passing too many arguments.
12	*Variable not found* The variable used in a FIELD clause is not in the current database.

Error #	Error Message

13   *ALIAS not found*
Either required a work area outside A through J or used an undefined ALIAS

15   *Not a database file.*
Database file lacks a proper header (typically, it is not a DBF file).

16   *Unrecognized command verb*
The word at the beginning of the line is not a valid command.

17   *Invalid database number*
Attempt to use a database number outside the range 1 to 10

18   *Line too long*
The command line exceeds the 1024 character limit, possibly due to macro expansion.

19   *Index file does not match database*
Index uses variables not present in database.

20   *Record is not in index*
Modified the key field without the index being active. REINDEX the database.

21   *String memory variable area overflow*
The combined length of all memory variable strings exceeds the string memory pool size set in CONFIG.FP (default is 6K).

22   *Too many memory variables*
Created too many memory variables. Increase MVCOUNT in CONFIG.FP (default is 256).

23   *Index expression too big*
Index expression exceeds 220 bytes.

24   *ALIAS name already in use*
ALIAS is already associated with another database in use.

26   *Database is not ordered*
Attempt to use an index-related file command without an index or without selecting it

27   *Not a numeric expression*
Attempt to use SUM on non-numeric values

28   *Too many indices*
Attempt to open more than 21 index files

30   *Position is off the screen*
Row or column position is larger than screen or printer allows.

31   *Invalid subscript reference*
Subscript outside range established by the DIMENSION statement

Error #	Error Message
34	**_Illegal operation for MEMO field_** Attempt to use a MEMO field in an INDEX
36	**_Unrecognized phrase/keyword in command_** Command used a phrase beginning with an invalid keyword.
37	**_FILTER requires a logical expression_** Attempt to set a filter without a logical expression
38	**_Beginning of file encountered_** Attempt to move the record pointer ahead of the first record
39	**_Numeric overflow (data was lost)_** A mathematical operation created a number too large to be stored.
41	**_MEMO file is missing/invalid_** Attempt to use a nonexistent MEMO file
42	**_CONTINUE without LOCATE_** Used a CONTINUE command without first executing a LOCATE
43	**_Insufficient memory_** Not enough RAM to complete operation. Try removing TSR programs or unnecessary drivers.
44	**_Cyclic relation_** Attempted a circular arrangement of relations (where, for example, one relation calls a second that calls the first)
45	**_Not a character expression_** Attempt to CALL a module with an expression not of type character
46	**_Illegal value_** An invalid expression in a SET MEMOWIDTH, BROWSE, or @ TO command
47	**_No fields to process_** No fields found, probably because a SET FIELDS TO was in effect
50	**_Report file invalid_** Report description contains an error.
52	**_No database in use_** Executed a database command without having a database active
54	**_Label file invalid_** Attempt to use a label file that lacks the proper format
55	**_Memory variable file is invalid_** Attempt to use a memory file that lacks the proper format
56	**_Not enough disk space_** Operating system reports no room on disk for the last write.

Error #	Error Message
58	*LOG(): Zero or negative* Attempt to take the logarithm of zero or a negative number
61	*SQRT domain error* Attempt to use a negative argument in SQRT
62	*Beyond string* Attempt to read characters beyond the end of the string
67	*Expression evaluator fault* An internal problem possibly caused by damage to an object code file. Recompile the program.
78	*** or ^ domain error* Usually the result of raising a negative number to a power
91	*File was not LOADed* Attempt to CALL or RELEASE a module not LOADed
94	*Wrong number of parameters* Number of parameters in a DO...WITH statement does not match the PARAMETER statement of the called procedure.
95	*Statement not allowed in interactive mode* Attempt to use a command allowed only in programs
96	*Nesting error*
101	*Not suspended* Issued a RESUME without a prior SUSPEND
103	*DO nesting too deep* Exceeded the maximum of 32 levels
104	*Unknown function key* Attempt to define a nonexistent function key
107	*Operator/operand type mismatch* Invalid data type used in an arithmetic, string, or logical operator or function
108	*File is in use by another*
109	*Record is in use by another* Attempt to write to a record locked by another user
110	*Exclusive open of file is required*
111	*Cannot write to a read-only file* Attempt to write to a read-only file
112	*Invalid key length* The index key exceeds 100 bytes.

Error #	Error Message
114	*Index does not match database file. Recreate index.* Index file structure is damaged. Reindex or recreate the index.
115	*Invalid DIF file header*
116	*Invalid DIF vector – DBF field mismatch*
117	*Invalid DIF type indicator*
119	*Invalid SYLK file header*
120	*Invalid SYLK file dimension bounds*
121	*Invalid SYLK file format*
124	*Invalid printer redirection* Either the printer path is not established or the device is not shareable.
125	*Printer not ready* Printer is inaccessible or is timing out.
127	*View file invalid* Attempt to open a view file with invalid data
130	*Record is not locked*
138	*No fields were found to copy* Found no fields during a COPY to a file
152	*Missing expression* Did not find expected expression
164	*PAD has not been defined* Attempt to use a nonexistent PAD. Check the PAD name.
165	*POPUP has not been defined* Attempt to use a nonexistent POPUP. Check the POPUP name.
166	*No menu bars have been defined for this popup* Must define bars for each popup
167	*BAR position must be a positive number* Attempt to define a bar with a negative number
168	*MENU has not been defined* Attempt to activate an undefined menu. Check the MENU name.
169	*ON SELECTION PAD already defined for this prompt pad* Attempt to reissue an ON SELECTION PAD command for a pad
170	*ON PAD already defined for this prompt pad* A PAD with the same name has already been defined.

Error #	Error Message
174	*Cannot redefine menu in use* Attempt to define a menu with the same name as an existing one
175	*Cannot redefine popup in use* Attempt to define a popup with the same name as an existing one
176	*Cannot clear menu in use* Attempt to clear an active menu before deactivating it
177	*Cannot clear popup in use* Attempt to clear an active popup before deactivating it
178	*MENU has not been activated* Attempt to select from a menu before activating it
179	*POPUP has not been activated*
181	*MENU is already in use* Attempt to activate a menu already in use
182	*POPUP is already in use* Attempt to activate a POPUP already in use
202	*Invalid path or filename*
214	*WINDOW has not been defined* Attempt to activate an undefined window
215	*WINDOW has not been activated*
216	*Display mode not available* Attempt to select an unavailable display mode
221	*Label nesting error*
222	*Left margin plus indent must be less than right margin*
223	*Line number must be less than page length*
224	*Column number must be between 0 and 255*
226	*Tab stops must be in ascending order*
230	*Bad array dimensions*
231	*Invalid SET expression* Invalid argument in a SET function
255	*Not a valid RapidFile database*
256	*Not a valid Framework II database/spreadsheet*
277	*Invalid box dimensions*

Error #	Error Message
279	***PROMPTs for this popup have already been defined*** Attempt to use a BAR to define the contents of a POPUP already defined with the PROMPT option
287	***POPUP is too small*** POPUP is too small for selection bars.
291	***ASIN(): Out of Range*** Attempt to take the arc sine of a value outside the range -1.0 to +1.0
292	***LOG10(): Zero or negative*** Attempt to take the logarithm of zero or a negative number
293	***ACOS(): Out of Range*** Attempt to take the arc cosine of a value outside the range -1.0 to +1.0
297	***Invalid Lotus 1-2-3 version 2.0 file format***
332	***WINDOW coordinates are invalid***
337	***Printjobs cannot be nested***
350	***Field must be a Memo field*** Attempt to use APPEND/COPY MEMO with a non-memo field
355	***Macro not defined*** Attempt to use a nonexistent macro
356	***Invalid keyboard macro file format*** Attempt to use a macro file with invalid data
392	***Maximum record length exceeded in import file***
411	***RUN/! command string too long***
412	***Cannot locate COMSPEC environment variable***
507	***Screen code too big for memory***
607	***Maximum allowable menu items (128) exceeded*** A menu is limited to 128 items. If more options are needed, split it into a series of branched menus.
608	***Maximum allowable menu (25) exceeded*** Only 25 menus can be defined at one time. Deactivate unnecessary menus before defining new ones.
611	***Menu item/titles must be type CHARACTER*** Convert all menu items or titles to character type.
612	***No such menu/item is defined*** Value passed to a READ MENU command does not correspond to a defined menu.

Error #	Error Message
689	*Cannot build app/exe without a main program*
691	*Library file is invalid*
693	*Cannot find screen/menu generation program*
694	*Too many extensions specified*
800	*SQL internal error*
802	*SQL could not locate database*
804	*SQL invalid SELECT statement*
805	*SQL invalid HAVING statement*
806	*SQL invalid column reference*
807	*SQL invalid GROUP BY*
808	*SQL invalid ORDER BY*
809	*SQL out of memory*
811	*SQL aggregate on non-numeric field*
812	*SQL statement too long*
818	*SQL no FROM clause*
819	*SQL invalid DISTINCT*
820	*SQL invalid * in SELECT*
821	*SQL invalid temporary file*
822	*SQL invalid aggregate field*
823	*SQL open file failed*
825	*SQL invalid subquery*
826	*SQL invalid select*
828	*SQL illegal GROUP BY in subquery*
830	*SQL index not found*
831	*SQL error building temporary index*
832	*SQL invalid variable*
833	*SQL invalid WHERE clause*
836	*SQL invalid predicate*

Error #	Error Message
839	*SQL canceled operation*
841	*SQL too many columns referenced*
845	*SQL expression too complex*
846	*Cannot GROUP by aggregate field*
851	*SELECTs are not UNION compatible*
860	*SQL multiple row subquery result*
1000	*Internal consistency error* An internal table probably has been corrupted. If reloading the software from the original diskettes does not help, call Fox Software.
1001	*Feature not available* Attempt to use a feature not supported in current version of FoxPro
1012	*OS memory error* Error in DOS free memory chain
1101	*Cannot open file* Cannot open a file because it does not exist, the name is invalid, or you lack access to the directory
1102	*Cannot create file* Cannot create a file because disk is full, the name is invalid, or you lack access to the directory
1103	*Illegal seek offset*
1104	*File read error* Error from operating system during a read
1105	*File write error* Error from operating system during a write, often caused by trying to write to a write-protected disk
1107	*Structural CDX file reference removed*
1108	*Relational expression too long* Relational expression exceeds 60 bytes.
1111	*Invalid file descriptor*
1112	*File close error* Cannot close a file
1113	*File not open* Cannot open a file for either reading or writing
1115	*Database record is trashed* Database header may contain invalid data.

Error #	Error Message
1117	*Wrong length key* Key field length between two files does not match during an UPDATE or SET RELATION.
1124	*Key too big* Compiled version of index expression exceeds 150 bytes.
1126	*Record too long* Attempt to create a database file with a record longer than 4000 bytes
1127	*For/while need logical expressions* FOR or WHILE clause lacks a logical expression.
1130	*'field' phrase not found*
1131	*From file is empty*
1134	*Variable must be in selected database*
1138	*Buffer deadlock*
1140	*FILTER expression too long* Attempt to set a filter exceeding 160 characters
1141	*Invalid index number* Attempt to SET ORDER TO a position in an index list that is unoccupied or outside the range 0-21
1145	*Must be a character, date or numeric key field.* A key field to UPDATE ON must be character, date, or numeric.
1147	*Target is already engaged in relation* There is more than one relationship between currently selected database file and targets.
1148	*Too many relationships* Defined more than 15 relationships between database files
1149	*No memory for buffer* Insufficient memory in system to allocate buffer. Check buffer allocation in CONFIG.SYS.
1150	*No memory for file map* Insufficient memory for a FoxPro internal resource
1151	*No memory for filename* Insufficient memory for a FoxPro internal resource
1152	*Cannot access selected database* Attempt to open a file in an area outside the range 1 to 10 or attempt to reference a field in a database not in use

Error #	Error Message
1153	***Attempt to move file to different device*** Cannot rename files to a different device
1156	***Duplicate field names*** Used the same field name twice in a SORT or COPY command
1157	***Cannot update file*** Usually indicates critical disk problem such as no space or total failure
1160	***Not enough disk space***
1161	***Too many records to BROWSE/EDIT in demo version***
1162	***Procedure not found***
1163	***Browse database closed***
1164	***Browse structure changed***
1190	***Invalid LIB signature***
1191	***Bad LIB file***
1192	***Internal LIB undefined symbol error***
1193	***Missing RTT section***
1194	***Link command failed***
1201	***Attempt to use more than 2048 names*** A single program cannot have more than 2048 active variables.
1202	***Program too large*** Program cannot fit in memory. A program cannot exceed 65,000 bytes.
1206	***Recursive macro definition*** Attempted more than 256 macro substitutions in one statement. Check if the macro references itself.
1208	***Illegal macro substitution***
1211	***IF/ELSE/ENDIF mismatch*** ELSE or ENDIF statement found without IF
1212	***Structure nesting too deep*** Exceeded 64 nested structured programming commands
1213	***Mismatched case structure*** CASE, ENDCASE, or OTHERWISE statement without a corresponding DO CASE statement
1214	***ENDTEXT without TEXT*** ENDTEXT statement lacks a corresponding TEXT.

Error #	Error Message

1217   *Picture error in GET statement*
An invalid PICTURE clause value

1220   *Invalid character in command*
Source line contains an invalid character, probably a control character.

1221   *Required clause not present in command*
Attempt to use a command without a required clause

1223   *Invalid variable reference*
Function used where FoxPro expected a variable, usually caused by using a function name as an array name

1225   *Must be a memory variable*
A file variable appeared where a memory variable or array should appear.

1226   *Must be a file variable*
A memory variable or array appeared where a file variable should appear.

1229   *Too few arguments*
Function call contains fewer than the required number of arguments.

1230   *Too many arguments*
Function call contains more than the permitted number of arguments.

1231   *Missing operand*
The operator used requires two operands, and the second one is missing.

1232   *Must be an array definition*
A DIMENSION statement contains a variable declaration without a subscript argument.

1234   *Subscript out of bounds*
Attempt to reference an array element outside the range defined in DIMENSION statement

1235   *Structure invalid*
Attempt to use a database in CREATE FROM that does not match the STRUCTURE EXTENDED format

1238   *No PARAMETER statement found*
The program called from a DO lacks a PARAMETER statement.

1241   *Improper data type in group expression*
Attempt to use a picture data type (binary) by REPORT in a group expression

Error #	Error Message

1243   *Internal error: Too many characters in report*
The total size of all report headings and expressions is too large for the standard report file. Shorten headings or expressions or write a custom report program.

1244   *Label field type must be character, memo, numeric or date*
Logical data type encountered in a LABEL

1245   *Error in label field definition*
Invalid expression in the LABEL file

1246   *Total label width exceeds maximum allowable size*
Sum of individual label widths and separating spaces exceeds allowable total.

1249   *Too many READs in effect*
Attempted more than 4 nested READS

1250   *Too many PROCEDURES*
Exceeded the number of procedures (1170) allowed in a procedure file

1252   *Compiled code for this line too long*
An internal code buffer problem. Split the line into multiple statements.

1294   *FoxUser file is invalid*
The FOXUSER file is corrupted. Delete it and restart.

1300   *Missing)*
A function is either missing the right parenthesis or has too many arguments.

1304   *Missing (*
A function is missing the left parenthesis.

1306   *Missing ,*
Expected a comma but did not find one, often the result of an improper number of arguments in a function

1307   *Division by 0*
Specified zero as the second argument in MOD()

1308   *Stack overflow – expression too complex*
Nested user-defined functions too deeply

1309   *Not an object file*
Attempt to load a compiled FoxPro program without a proper header

1310   *Too many PICTURE characters specified*
Total number of picture characters for all pending GETs exceeded the 2064 character limit.

1405   *RUN/! command failed*
Insufficient memory to open a DOS shell

Error #	Error Message
1410	*Unable to create temporary work file(s)* A SORT or INDEX file could not create temporary files. Operating system may have detected either a full directory or a permissions problem.
1501	*Record is already in use*
1502	*Record is in use: Cannot write*
1503	*File cannot be locked*
1600	*Not enough memory to USE database* Not enough memory to open database
1604	*No menu bar defined* Attempt to read an undefined menu bar
1605	*No popup menu defined* Attempt to activate an undefined light bar menu
1607	*Maximum allowable menu items (128) exceeded*
1608	*Maximum allowable menus (25) exceeded*
1609	*Maximum menu item length (50) exceeded*
1621	*No pads defined for this menu* Attempt to activate a menu with no pads
1631	*Bad array dimensions* Attempt to declare an array with less than 1 element or more than 3600
1632	*Invalid WINDOW file format* Invalid data encountered in a WIN file during a restore
1637	*File must be opened exclusively to convert memo file*
1640	*No keyboard macros are defined*
1642	*COLORSET resource not found* Attempt to use a COLORSET not defined in the resource file
1643	*Printer driver is corrupted* Attempt to load a corrupted printer driver
1644	*Printer driver not found* Could not find the specified printer driver
1645	*Report nesting error* A function in a report tried to call MODIFY REPORT or REPORT FORM.
1646	*Total field type must be numeric* A report expression includes a non-numeric total expression.

Error #	Error Message
1647	*Improper data type in field expression* REPORT encountered a memo or logical data type.
1649	*No previous PRINTJOB to match this command*
1651	*CANCEL/SUSPEND is not allowed*
1652	*Attempt to use FoxPro function as an array*
1653	*Label nesting error*
1657	*Column number must be between 0 and right margin*
1659	*Cannot convert memo file for a read-only database file*
1661	*Invalid Excel version 2.0 file format*
1662	*Invalid Lotus 1-2-3 version 1.0 file format*
1670	*Invalid Multiplan version 4.0 file format*
1671	*Cannot import from password protected file*
1672	*Cannot append from password protected file*
1673	*Invalid Symphony version 1 file format*
1674	*Invalid Symphony version 1.1 file format*
1677	*User-defined functions must return a value*
1678	*Invalid Lotus 1-2-3 version 3.0 file format*
1679	*Import only Worksheet A for Lotus 1-2-3 version 3.0 files*
1680	*Worksheet A for Lotus 1-2-3 version 3.0 file is hidden*
1681	*PREVIEW clause not allowed with OFF or TO PRINT/FILE*
1682	*Not a user-defined window*
1683	*Index tag not found*
1684	*Index tag or filename must be specified*
1685	*Project file is invalid*
1686	*Screen file invalid*
1687	*Menu file invalid*
1688	*Invalid Paradox version 3.5 file format*
1690	*Database operation invalid while indexing*

Error #	Error Message
1692	*Regional directive must precede first PROCEDURE or FUNCTION*
1695	*COLUMN/FORM allowed only with FROM clause*
1696	*NOWAIT/SAVE/NOENVIRONMENT/IN/WINDOW clause not allowed with FROM*
1698	*COLUMN/ROW/ALIAS/NOOVERWRITE/SIZE/SCREEN allowed only with FROM clause*
1705	*File access denied* Attempt to write to a file protected by the DOS ATTRIB command
1706	*Descending not permitted on IDX files*
1707	*Structural CDX file not found*
1708	*File is open in another work area*
1903	*String too long to fit* Exceeded allowable string length (65,504 characters)
1907	*Bad drive specifier* Invalid drive name used with DIR
1908	*Bad width or decimal place argument* Invalid length or decimal argument in STR()
1999	*Function not implemented* Attempt to use a function not supported by the current version of FoxPro

Appendix C

C Language References

Atkinson, Lee with Mark Atkinson, *Using Borland C++*, Carmel, IN, Que, 1991

Atkinson, Lee with Mark Atkinson, *Using C*, Carmel, IN, Que, 1990

Barkakati, Naba, *The Waite Group's Turbo C++ Bible*, Carmel, IN, Sams, 1990

Dewhurst, Stephen C. with Kathy T. Stark, *Programming in C++*, Englewood Cliffs, NJ, Prentice-Hall, 1989

Flamig, Bryan, *Turbo C++ - A Self Teaching Guide*, New York, Wiley, 1991

Hansen, Augie, *C for Yourself*, Redmond, WA, Microsoft Press, 1988

Kernighan, Brian W. with Dennis M. Ritchie, *The C Programming Language*, 2nd ed., Englewood Cliffs, NJ, Prentice-Hall, 1988

Kochan, Stephen G., *Programming in C*, Carmel, IN, Hayden, 1988

Ladd, Scott R., *Turbo C++ Techniques and Applications*, Redwood City, CA, M&T Publishing, 1990

Lafore, Robert, *C Programming Using Turbo C++*, Carmel, IN, Sams, 1990

Leventhal, Lance A., *Turbo C Quickstart*, San Marcos, CA, Microtrend Books, 1991

Lippman, Stanley B., *C++ Primer*, Reading, MA, Addison-Wesley, 1989

Pappas, Chris H. with William H. Murray, III, *Turbo C++ Professional Handbook*, Berkeley, CA, Osborne/McGraw-Hill, 1990

Schildt, Herbert, *Turbo C/C++: The Complete Reference*, Berkeley, CA, Osborne/McGraw-Hill, 1990

Schildt, Herbert, *Using Turbo C++*, Berkeley, CA, Osborne/McGraw-Hill, 1990

Stevens, Al, *Teach Yourself C,* Portland, OR, MIS Press, 1990

Voss, Greg with Paul Chui, *Turbo C++ DiskTutor,* Berkeley, CA, Osborne/ McGraw-Hill, 1990

Waite, Mitchell with Stephen Prata and Rex Woollard, *Master C,* Mill Valley, CA, Waite Group Press, 1990

Glossary

Abend
Failure, also called a crash, that occurs when a program encounters instructions or data it cannot interpret.

Active window
The window where text is directed.

Address
Identifies a specific memory location, I/O port, or other unit.

Alert
Message warning about an error.

Alert box
Window where an alert appears.

Algorithm
Method for solving a problem in a specific number of steps.

Alphanumeric field
Field that contains letters, numbers, special characters, or any combination.

ANSI
American National Standards Institute. Organization that determines and distributes computer standards related to communications, data, and programming.

Append
Add to the end of an existing structure such as a file.

Application
A program that allows a user to perform work on a computer.

Application development system
Programming language used with associated tools and utilities to create other applications. FoxPro and Turbo C are examples employed in this book.

Application generator
Utility that uses detailed program specifications such as file structures, report and screen layouts, and menus to produce source code. FoxPro includes the application generators Menu Builder and Screen Builder.

Argument
Value used by a function, statement, or procedure to do its work.

Arithmetic operators
+,-,*,/, and (), used to form arithmetic expressions.

Array
Group of related data elements that can be treated as a single variable.

Array element
Single item in an array.

Ascending order sort
A sort in which alphanumeric values are arranged in their normal order (by ASCII value). Numeric values are arranged from lowest to highest, and dates from earliest to latest.

ASCII
American Standard Code for Information Interchange. Originally a 7-bit code allowing 128 characters, including letters, numbers, and special symbols. The 8-bit (Extended) version supports 128 more characters, often used for graphics and symbols from other languages and alphabets.

ASCII file
Data or text file using the ASCII character set.

Assembler
A program that translates assembly language programs into machine code.

Assembly language
Programming language in which each source instruction represents a single machine instruction. Its statements allow symbolic or mnemonic names.

Assignment statement
Statement that places values in variables.

Attribute
Field in a database record.

Auxiliary storage
Secondary storage devices, such as disks and tapes.

Band
Horizontal section of a report. It defines specific elements such as the title, header, groups, details, footer, and summary.

Binary
Number system with base 2; uses only two digits, 0 and 1.

Bit
Binary digit (value is either 0 or 1).

Boot
Procedure used to start up a computer.

Branch
Instruction that transfers control to a point other than the next command in the normal consecutive sequence.

Browse
Display data, often without allowing editing.

Buffer
Memory area that holds data or programs temporarily during a transfer.

Bug
Program error.

Byte
Unit of storage consisting of 8 bits and capable of holding a single character.

C
High-level structured programming language developed at Bell Laboratories. It has most of the power and speed of assembly language, but is easier to use. C++ is an object-oriented extension.

Calculated field
A field derived from an expression involving other fields or variables.

Call by reference
Passes the addresses of parameters. If the subroutine changes their values, it automatically changes the original variables as well.

Call by value
Passes the values of parameters. If the subroutine changes them, it does not affect the original variables.

Case sensitive
Distinguishes between uppercase and lowercase letters.

Catalog
Directory of files.

Character
Any number, letter, or other symbol.

Check box
Option selected or unselected by marking it. Many such options may be selected at one time.

Click
Press and release the mouse button.

Clipboard
Temporary storage area that holds text cut or copied from the screen. Its contents can be placed elsewhere in the same or another document.

Color pair
Combination of a foreground and a background color.

Color scheme
Group of ten color pairs that define the colors of a FoxPro object.

Color set
Group of color schemes that define all objects in FoxPro. Different color sets define colors for CGA, EGA, VGA, and monochrome monitors.

Column
Field in a relational table.

COM file
Machine language program that executes under MS-DOS from a specific memory location.

Command
Action statement in a program.

COMMAND.COM
Command processor for MS-DOS. It prompts the user for commands and then executes them.

Comment
Documentation statement in a program, ignored by translators.

Common fields
Fields that exist in several database files, used to form links or relations.

Compiler
A program that converts statements written in a high-level programming language (such as C) into machine language commands.

Concatenation
Appending one string to another.

Conditional branch
A branch that transfers control only if the tested condition holds (is true).

Configuration
The combination of hardware and software settings that allows a program to run.

CONFIG.FP
Instruction file executed when FoxPro is started.

CONFIG.SYS
Instruction file for MS-DOS that is executed when the computer is booted.

Constant
A value that does not change.

Context sensitive help
Information specifically about the field the user is currently entering.

Control character
Nonprinting characters with ASCII values from 0 to 31 are often used for control purposes.

Coordinate
Pair of numbers that define the row and column position of text or graphics on the screen or printer.

Corruption
Altering of data or programs due to hardware failure, software logic errors, or improper procedures.

CPU
Central Processing Unit, the part of the computer that performs calculations and directs overall operations.

Cursor
Indicator of where the next character will appear on the screen.

Cursor keys
The arrow keys (up, down, left, and right arrow) that move the screen cursor.

Custom software
Software designed for a specific purpose, often for a single user, as opposed to off-the-shelf software that is mass produced for many users.

Cut and paste
Technique used to define and move a block of text in the same or a another file.

Data
The contents of individual fields comprising records in a database.

Database
An organized collection of information.

Data integrity
The state that exists when the data has the correct values and has not been accidentally or maliciously altered or destroyed.

Data name
The name of an individual data element in a record.

Data structure
A set of relationships between data items.

Data type
Characteristics defining a set of data elements.

Database management system (DBMS)
A collection of programs that create, maintain, and report on data stored in a database.

DBF file
Database file in FoxPro and other dBASE-related software.

Deadlock
Condition that occurs when users have conflicting demands and each prevents the others from satisfying them.

Debugging
Process of locating and correcting program errors.

Decimal separator
Symbol used to separate whole digits from fractional parts. It is usually either a period or a comma.

Decimal system
Number system with base 10.

Default
Value assigned or option selected unless the user supplies something else.

Delimiter
Character used to separate items such as fields or arguments.

Descending order sort
A sort in which alphanumeric values are arranged in the reverse of normal sort order (by ASCII value). Numeric values are arranged from highest to lowest, and dates from latest to earliest.

Detail band
Area of a report that displays the contents of the database records.

Device name
Name assigned to a hardware device to reference it in later commands.

Dimension
Axis of an array, defines the number of elements along it.

Directory
File containing information about a set of files, such as their types, locations, and sizes.

Double click
Press and release the mouse button twice in rapid succession. It usually selects an option or performs an action.

Drag
To move a screen object using cursor keys or a mouse.

Dump
An unformatted listing of bytes from memory or a file.

Duplicate key
Two records that contain the same key field information.

Edit (or **edit mode**)
The process of changing field values in database records. It is also used to change programs, label and report definitions, and command-line entries.

Element
One of the values in an array.

Embedded
Contained within, hidden.

Emulate
Operate like something.

Error code
Number or code that identifies the specific cause of an error.

Escape sequence
Series of characters beginning with the Esc character, often used to indicate a nonprinting character or control code.

Exclusive
Reserved for a particular user, preventing others from accessing it.

EXE file
Machine language program that executes under MS-DOS from any memory location.

Expanded memory
Allows IBM PCs to address additional memory by swapping segments with memory below one megabyte.

Export
To transfer information from a database file to an external file.

Expression
Group of names, numbers, and operators used to calculate a value.

Extended ASCII
Characters from 128 through 255, may have different definitions in different computers and printers.

Extended memory
IBM PC memory above one megabyte.

Field
Single element in a record.

Field type
Kind of information the field contains, such as character, numeric, date, logical, or memo.

Field value
Specific data stored in a field.

File
Collection of information stored under a single name.

File format
The physical definition of the fields in a file.

File lock
Object that prevents other users from writing to a file.

File management
Any task related to the organization of files on disks.

File name (or **filename**)
Identifier of a specific file on disk.

File server
A computer in a network that stores programs and data for access by multiple users.

File structure
Organization of the fields in a file.

Filter
A mask or pattern of characters that define a subset of records from a file.

Flag
A binary variable that indicates when a condition or event occurs.

Flat file
A database file unrelated to any other file.

Floating point number
A method of mathematical notation used to represent a wide range of numerical values. The form is a number (*mantissa* or *significand*) to be multiplied by the base raised to a power (*exponent* or *characteristic*).

Font
Character set of a specific design and size.

Footer
Information printed at the bottom of a page or report.

Form feed
Command that tells a printer to advance to the top of the next page.

Format
Arrangement of data on the screen or in a report or label.

Function
A routine that performs a set of instructions and returns a single value to its caller.

Function keys
Keys that can be pressed to implement entire commands or sequences of commands.

Global variable
Variable that is available in every module of an application.

Group band
A horizontal section of a report that defines how to group database records.

Handle
A name or number that identifies a specific object such as a file, typically a pointer.

Header
Printed information that appears at the top of a page or report.

Hexadecimal
Number system with base 16. The digits are:

Decimal	Hexadecimal
0	0
1	1
2	2
3	3

4	4
5	5
6	6
7	7
8	8
9	9
10	A
11	B
12	C
13	D
14	E
15	F

High-level language
Computer language that is task or application-oriented rather than being closely related to the underlying hardware. Each high-level command is typically translated into several machine language instructions.

Hot key
Key that causes a function to execute.

IEEE
Institute of Electrical and Electronic Engineers. The IEEE Computer Society is involved in creating standards for communications, networks, interfaces, and computers.

Import
To read data into a database file from an external source.

Index
A reference table that specifies a read order for database records.

Index key
The database field or fields used to define an index.

Input
Transfer of data from an external source to the computer.

Insert mode
Mode that adds data at the cursor position, moving subsequent text right.

Instruction
Command sent to the computer.

Integer
Whole number (no fractional part).

Interface
A connection between two devices; a program that allows a user to interact with a computer.

Key/key field
Fields used to uniquely identify records in a database.

Kilobyte (K or KB)
1,024 bytes or characters.

LAN
Local Area Network. Group of computers connected electronically over short distances so users can share programs and data.

Library
A collection of programs, procedures, or functions that any application can use.

Lock
Function that prevents others from using a record or file.

Logical field
Field that contains a true or false (yes or no) value.

Logical expression
An expression that is either true or false.

Low-level language
A language that is very close to the machine level (for example, assembly language). It usually has a one-to-one correspondence between source code lines and machine code lines.

Main menu
Top level of options in a program.

Maintenance
The updating of application software to make corrections and extensions and meet changing needs.

Many-to-many relation
A situation in which one or more records in one database are related to one or more records in another.

Many-to-one relation
A situation in which one or more records in one database are related to just one record in another.

Master file
A file that contains reference information on major subjects.

Megabyte (M or MB)
1,048,576 bytes or characters.

Memory resident
A program that remains in memory after it executes.

Menu
A list of available options within a program.

Menu bar
A horizontal line at the top of the screen that contains options (pads).

Menu pad
A word or phrase that identifies an option in the menu bar.

Modular programming
Programming method that divides applications into separate (independent) tasks.

Module
A separate part of an application that can be implemented independently.

Mouse
A handheld device used to move the cursor, point to objects, and select options.

Multiuser
Environment that allows more than one user to work at the same time.

Multitasking
Referring to a computer or an operating system that can perform more than one task at a time.

Nesting
Placement of a structure within a similar structure.

Network
Collection of computers connected to share data, programs, and peripheral devices such as printers or modems.

Null character
Byte with ASCII value zero.

Object
Data structure handled as a unit, perhaps also including variables and procedures (methods).

Object-oriented interface
User interface in which commands and symbols refer to complex objects rather than simple data forms.

Off-line
Not currently connected to the computer.

On-line
Currently connected to the computer.

One-to-many relation
A situation in which a record in one database is related to one or more records in another.

One-to-one relation
A situation in which a record in one database is related to just one record in another.

Operating system
Program that performs the basic procedures for running a computer and on which applications software depends for execution.

Output
Transfer of information from the computer to an external device such as a file, printer, or screen.

Pack
Physically remove deleted records from a database.

Parameters
Items that procedures and functions need to do their tasks.

Parsing
The analysis of a string to divide it into individual units.

Pathname
The full definition of a file's location on the disk. It specifies the drive, directory, and file name.

Peripheral
Any device used to enter data into a computer or display output from it.

Picture
Specification of the type and number of characters that can be accepted into a field or shown.

Pointer
An indicator of where data is stored or operations will be performed. Often an address or offset from a fixed position. Examples are a mouse pointer, a file pointer, and an index pointer.

Popup menu
A menu that appears on the screen as the result of an action.

Procedure
A subroutine.

Prompt
A message to the user asking for input or an action.

Pulldown menu
A menu that appears to drop down from another menu when an option in it is selected.

Radio button
An option shown in a button form that allows only one selection at a time.

RAM
Standard read/write memory, requires power to retain its contents (volatile).

Reboot
Reload the operating system.

Record
A row in a relational table, a unit in a file consisting of *fields*.

Relational database
A database consisting of tables linked via common fields.

Report generator/writer
A program that creates source code for a report from a layout description supplied by the user.

Routine
Part of a program that performs a specific task.

Row
Record in a database.

Runtime module
A module that allows applications to run without providing features needed only during development.

Save
Store on disk or other backup media.

Scroll
Move data vertically or horizontally in a window when there is more than can fit in it.

Scroll bar
Icon beside a window that moves the data vertically or horizontally when selected.

Seek
Find a specific record in a file based on its key value.

Sort
Redefine the order of records in a database based on a key.

Source code
Program written in a form the programmer can understand; it must be translated before it can be run.

String
A sequence of text characters.

Subroutine
A part of a program that performs a specific operation when called from another program. Control returns to the caller when it is finished.

Subscript
Number that identifies an element of an array.

Substring
A string that is part of another string.

Summary band
The last band of a report, usually contains totaling information.

Syntax
The set of rules that govern the structure of expressions.

Syntax error
An error in the format of a program command.

System
Collection of interrelated programs. An accounting system might include a general ledger, accounts receivable, accounts payable, payroll, and inventory.

Table
Database file.

Table lookup
Finding a value in a table rather than computing it directly.

Template
A set of instructions that creates programs that perform specific tasks.

Text editor
Program used to create and edit text files, including programs and data.

Thumb
A diamond that appears in scroll bars, indicating the relative position of the window text in the file.

Typeahead buffer
A storage area that holds keystrokes until the computer is ready to process them.

Unconditional branch
Transfer of control to another program section without any test condition.

Undo
Editing feature that reverses the latest changes.

Unlock
Remove a lock, allowing other users to access the record or file.

Update
Change or edit.

User
The individual who runs an application program.

User friendly
Easy to learn and use.

User interface
The combination of features that let the user control the actions of an application.

Utility
Program that supports the main operations of the computer.

Whole number separator
A character that separates groups of three whole digits to make them easier to read, usually a comma or period.

Wildcard
Special characters used to represent any one character or series of characters.

Window
A separate viewing area on the screen to display data or programs.

Word wrap
Continue text on the next line when the right edge of the screen or window is reached.

Zoom
Enlarge a window to the full size of the screen.

Note: Some of these definitions are derived from E. Thro, *The Database Dictionary* (San Marcos, CA: Microtrend Books, 1990).

Acronyms

ANSI	American National Standards Institute
API	Applications Programming Interface or
	Application Program Interface
ASCII	American Standard Code for Information Interchange
BASIC	Beginners All purpose Symbolic Instruction Code
BIOS	Basic Input Output System
Bit	Binary Digit
BOF	Beginning Of File
CGA	Color Graphics Adapter
CPU	Central Processing Unit
DBMS	Database Management System
DIF	Data Interchange Format
DOS	Disk Operation System
EEMS	Enhanced Expanded Memory Specification
EGA	Enhanced Graphics Adapter
EMM	Expanded Memory Manager
EMS	Expanded Memory Specification
EOF	End Of File
FAT	File Allocation Table
FORTRAN	Formula Translation Language
I/O	Input/Output
ID	Identification
IDMS	Integrated Data Management System
IEEE	Institute of Electrical and Electronic Engineers
KB	Kilobyte (also Kb)
LAN	Local Area Network
LIM EMS	Lotus/Intel/Microsoft Expanded Memory Specification
MB	Megabyte (also Mb)
Modem	Modulator-Demodulator
NETBIOS	Network Basic Input Output System
OCR	Optical Character Recognition
OOPS	Object Oriented Programming System
OS	Operating System

POS	Point Of Sale
QBE	Query By Example
RAM	Random Access Memory
RDBMS	Relational Data Base Management System
ROM	Read-Only Memory
RQBE	Relational Query By Example
SCSI	Small Computer System Interface
SDF	System Data Format
SQL	Structured Query Language
SSN	Social Security Number
SYLK	Symbolic Link File
TSR	Terminate and Stay Resident
UDF	User Defined Function
UPC	Universal Product Code
VGA	Video Graphics Array

Bibliography

Granillo, Robert, *Illustrated FoxPro,* Plano, TX, Wordware, 1991

Jones, Edward, *FoxPro Made Easy,* Berkeley, CA, Osborne/McGraw-Hill, 1990

Olympia, P.L. with Kathy Cea, *Developing FoxPro Applications,* Reading, MA, Addison-Wesley, 1990

Palmer, Scott D., *The ABC's of FoxPro,* Alameda, CA, Sybex, 1990

Rettig, Tom with Ellen Sander and Debby Moody, *Tom Rettig's FoxPro Handbook,* New York, NY, Bantam, 1990

Trademarks

1-2-3	Lotus Development
386MAX	Qualitas
Clipper	Nantucket
dBASE	Ashton-Tate
dBASE III PLUS	Ashton-Tate
dBASE IV	Ashton-Tate
FoxBASE+	Fox Software
FoxDoc	Fox Software
FoxGraph	Fox Software
FoxPro	Fox Software
IBM	IBM
IBM PC	IBM
LaserJet	Hewlett-Packard
Lotus	Lotus Development
Multiplan	Microsoft
NetWare	Novell
Novell	Novell
QEMM	Quarterdeck
Rushmore	Fox Software
Turbo C	Borland International
Watcom C	Watcom Systems
Windows	Microsoft

Other brand and product names are trademarks or registered trademarks of the respective holders.

Index

The Lance A. Leventhal Microtrend® Series
Lance A. Leventhal, Ph.D., Series Director

FoxPro® 2 Developer's Library

by James E. Powell

Experienced software developer James E. Powell provides an extensive "add-on" library of general-purpose user-defined functions (UDFs) and procedures for FoxPro programmers, comparable to libraries costing hundreds of dollars. An inexpensive source of debugged, fully documented programs, the book/disk combination contains over 80 functions that perform array manipulation, database operations, data conversion, data entry and validation, date and time manipulation, development support, file operations, financial calculations, memo handling, and string manipulation. The book includes C functions and a description of the C Application Program Interface. It also has both general and keyword indexes to allow readers to find the functions they need quickly.

Special features:

❏ All routines are selected from working FoxPro applications.

❏ Designed specifically for FoxPro Version 2.

❏ Provides complete source code and a royalty-free distribution license.

❏ Contains detailed instructions for using each function and examples of typical applications.

❏ Stresses modularity, self-documentation, and calling consistency.

❏ Assumes only a minimal knowledge of FoxPro programming.

James E. Powell manages a data processing group for Security Pacific Automation Company Northwest in Seattle, WA. A program designer and developer for over 20 years, he is the author of many mainframe and PC programs, numerous articles and reviews in the computer press, and the book *Designing User Interfaces*.

7 x 9, 400 pages, trade paperback ISBN 0-915391-61-9, $44.95 U.S.
Publication Date: 3/1/92, **Order # MT61**

Available from your favorite book or computer store, or use order form at end of book, or call 1 (800) SLAWSON.

Slawson Communications, Inc. • 165 Vallecitos de Oro • San Marcos, CA 92069-1436

Microtrend® Books
Slawson Communications, Inc.
165 Vallecitos de Oro
San Marcos, CA   92069-1436

$44.95, plus $3.50 for shipping in U.S.
California residents add $3.70 sales tax.

____ Check or money order enclosed
____ Visa ____ MasterCard
Acct. _____
Exp. Date _____
Signature _____

FoxPro 2 Developer's Library (with disk)
by James E. Powell   **MT61**
Publication March, 1992

Name _____

Address _____

City _____ State _____ Zip _____

Country _____

Or order by phone (800) SLAWSON or (619) 744-2299. Visa/MasterCard, check, or money
order accepted.

— —

Microtrend® Books
Slawson Communications, Inc.
165 Vallecitos de Oro
San Marcos, CA   92069-1436

FoxPro 2 MIS Applications
by Bill Chambers   **MT46**
Publication March, 1992

$27.95, plus $3.50 for shipping in U.S.
California residents add $2.31 sales tax.

____ Check or money order enclosed
____ Visa ____ MasterCard
Acct. _____
Exp. Date _____
Signature _____

Name _____

Address _____

City_____ State_____ Zip_____

Country _____

Or order by phone (800) SLAWSON or (619) 744-2299. Visa/MasterCard, check, or money order accepted.

The Lance A. Leventhal Microtrend® Series
Lance A. Leventhal, Ph.D., Series Director

FoxPro® 2 MIS Applications

by Bill Chambers

Shows FoxPro progammers how to develop usable,
powerful, and maintainable MIS systems for finance,
human resources, planning, accounting, sales and
marketing, scheduling, inventory and production
control, and other applications. Covers requirements
analysis, systems design, database design and
normalization, user interfaces, coding, connectivity,
testing and debugging, security, documentation and
support, and system maintenance. Describes user
design documents, data dictionaries, design tools, other CASE aids, testing criteria
and plans, and maintenance logs and reports. Covers networking, multiuser systems,
file transfers, micro/mainframe connections, user documentation, and user training.
Contains many FoxPro programs drawn from actual applications.

Special features:

❑ Written specifically for FoxPro Version 2.

❑ All examples are drawn from real MIS applications.

❑ All programs are well structured, fully tested, and well documented.

❑ Provides an extensive discussion of connectivity, including the role of
networks, multiuser systems, database servers, and SQL.

❑ Shows how to transfer files to and from spreadsheets, word processors, and
other PC applications, as well as minicomputers and mainframes.

❑ Presents standards for design documents, coding, backup, system
documentation, user documentation, user training, and system maintenance.

Bill Chambers is a consultant with over 15 years of computer experience; he has
helped train over 5,000 users on PC-based applications.

7 x 9, 500 pages, trade paperback ISBN 0-915391-46-5, $27.95 U.S.
Publication Date: 3/1/92, **Order # MT46**

Available from your favorite book or computer store, or use order form at end of book,
or call 1 (800) SLAWSON.

Slawson Communications, Inc. • 165 Vallecitos de Oro • San Marcos, CA 92069-1436

The Lance A. Leventhal Microtrend® Series
Lance A. Leventhal, Ph.D., Series Director

A complete, one-stop reference guide to all aspects of IBM PC and PS/2 graphics.

IBM PC and PS/2 Graphics Handbook

Ed Teja and Laura Johnson

This single source will answer all your questions about what the standards are, what works with what, what features languages and operating systems offer, how to upgrade systems, what to buy for specific applications and requirements, and how to make programs run on a variety of computers. The book contains many easily referenced tables and charts for quick access and rapid comparisons of systems, hardware, programs, and standards.

Special features:

- ❏ Covers adapters, monitors, printers, standards, file formats, languages, and applications packages.

- ❏ Includes summaries, a resource list, a glossary, an acronym list, and an annotated bibliography.

- ❏ Focuses on widely used hardware and software for word processing, business graphics, presentation graphics, CAD/CAM/CAE, and desktop publishing.

- ❏ Emphasizes current and emerging standards, such as VGA, 8514/A, Multisync monitors, GKS, IGES, TIFF, Borland Graphics Interface, Microsoft Windows, and Presentation Manager.

- ❏ Describes how to identify the graphics adapter on a system and how to convert between different screen and printer aspect ratios.

Ed Teja and Laura Johnson have been writing professionally about computers and electronics since 1976. A former computer and peripherals editor for *EDN* magazine, Teja has written articles for more than 35 magazines and has published three books.

7 x 9, 480 pages, trade paperback, index ISBN 0-915391-35-X $24.95 U.S.
Available now!   Order # MT35

Available from your favorite book or computer store, or use the order form at end of book, or call 1 (800) SLAWSON.

Slawson Communications, Inc. • 165 Vallecitos de Oro • San Marcos, CA 92069-1436

Order Form

Thank you for purchasing this Microtrend® book. To order additional copies of this book or any of our other titles, please complete the form below, or call **1-800-SLAWSON**.

Name _____

Address _____

City/State/Zip _____

Country _____

Qty	Code #	Title	Price Each		Total
	MD48	Programming Examples Disk for FoxPro 2 Programming Guide	$39	95	
	MT61	FoxPro 2 Developer's Library (with disk) **3/92**	$44	95	
	MT46	FoxPro 2 MIS Applications **3/92**	$27	95	
	MT40	Designing User Interfaces	$27	95	
	MT35	IBM PC and PS/2 Graphics Handbook	$24	95	

U.S. Shipping

Books are shipped UPS except when a post office box is given as delivery address.

Subtotal		
Sales Tax: CA residents add 8.25%		
Shipping Charge: $3.50 per book		
TOTAL		

Form of Payment

☐ Visa ☐ MasterCard ☐ Check

Card#: ⊔⊔⊔⊔⊔⊔⊔⊔⊔⊔⊔⊔⊔⊔⊔⊔

Expiration date: _____

Signature: _____ Date _____

Mail your order to:

Microtrend® Books
Slawson Communications, Inc.
165 Vallecitos de Oro
San Marcos, CA 92069-1436
619/744-2299

Reader Comments
FoxPro® 2 Programming Guide

This book has been edited, the material reviewed, and the programs tested
and checked for accuracy, but bugs find their way into books as well as software.
Please take a few minutes to tell us if you have found any errors, and give us your
general comments regarding the quality of this book. Your time and attention will
help us improve this and future products.

Did you find any mistakes? _____

_____

_____

Is this book complete? (If not, what should be added?) _____

_____

_____

What do you like about this book? _____

_____

_____

What do you not like about this book? _____

_____

_____

What other books would you like to see developed? _____

_____

_____

Other comments: _____

_____

_____

To be notified about new editions of this
and other books of interest, please
include your name and address, and
mail to:

Name _____

Address _____

City/State/Zip _____

Microtrend® Books
Slawson Communications, Inc.
165 Vallecitos de Oro
San Marcos, CA 92069-1436

FoxPro 2 Programming Guide
By Michael Antonovich
Programming Examples

Programming Examples Disk

All programs listed in Michael Antonovich's
FoxPro 2 Programming Guide are available on disk.

Microtrend® Books
Slawson Communications, Inc.
165 Vallecitos de Oro
San Marcos, CA   92069-1436

Programming Examples Disk for
Michael Antonovich's *FoxPro 2*
Programming Guide   **MD48**

$39.95, plus $3.50 for shipping in U.S.
California residents add $3.30 sales tax.
5 ¼" media only

____ Check or money order enclosed
____ Visa ____ MasterCard
Acct. _____
Exp. Date _____
Signature _____

Name _____

Address _____

City _____ State _____ Zip _____

Country _____

Or order by phone (800) SLAWSON or (619) 744-2299. Visa/MasterCard, check, or money
order accepted.